BOUND

FOR THE

PROMISED

LAND

THE

C. ERIC LINCOLN

SERIES ON THE

BLACK

EXPERIENCE

BOUND

FOR THE

PROMISED

LAND

African American Religion and

the Great Migration

Milton C. Sernett

DUKE UNIVERSITY PRESS

Durham & London 1997

© 1997 Duke University Press
All rights reserved
Printed in the United States of America
on acid-free paper ∞
Typeset in Carter and Cone Galliard by
Tseng Information Systems, Inc.
Library of Congress Cataloging-in-Publication Data
appear on the last printed page
of this book.

TO JAN

CONTENTS

ACKNOWLEDGMENTS

This book has been in the works for about a decade, far longer than I wished or anticipated. I am indebted to the authors represented in the bibliography, for all scholarship is collective enterprise. Yet some individuals deserve special mention. Pioneering members of the African American Religious History Group of the American Academy of Religion urged me on with counsel that the project was worth doing. Randall Burkett was especially helpful when I was a research fellow at the W. E. B. Du Bois Institute, Harvard University, in 1987–88, and he gave generously from his impressive treasury of knowledge about sources. David Wills of Amherst College read an early incarnation of the text and provided a number of helpful suggestions. Participants in the Northeast Seminar on Black Religion listened to several chapters in essay form and found enough merit in them to prime the pump. I made several trips to Chicago in the course of research, and each time I returned a bit more energized because of conversations with James Grossman, then of the University of Chicago and now of the Newberry Institute, and others who knew the territory better than I did.

Two geographers at Syracuse University allowed me to sit in on their graduate seminars when I joined the faculty more than two decades ago. A historian by trade with earlier service in a Lutheran seminary teaching American church history, I was eager to expand my horizons. David Sopher, now deceased, taught me something about the geography of religion, and Donald Meinig excelled at the craft of historical geography. I did not stay long enough to earn the geographer's mantle, but Meinig's and Sopher's spatial perspectives raised questions in my mind about how a segment of the story of African American religion might be told with attention to place and region. That *Bound for the Promised Land* did not turn out to be an exercise in the historical geography of African American religion as I had once thought of it as being does not mean that time spent in the geographers' domain at Huntington-Beard-Crouse was lost on me.

Students at Syracuse University and at the Kennedy Institute, Free University, Berlin, patiently heard portions of what is to follow. The Fulbright year in Berlin came at a time when the manuscript was under review at Duke University Press. It was encouraging to receive positive feedback from German students while I awaited final word regarding the potential book's fate. The students' interest in the subject matter was in part a reflection of a too rich diet in American Studies on African American literature. Except through novels such as James Baldwin's *Go Tell It on the Mountain,* few of them had any exposure to African American religion in its historical context. Syracuse University students also deserve credit for keeping me on my toes after teaching African American religious history for more than two decades.

I am pleased that *Bound for the Promised Land* found a home at Duke University Press. The Press published my anthology of primary sources, *African American Religious History: A Documentary Witness,* in 1985 and has continued to keep it in print for wide use in university and seminary classrooms. Now that the "migration book" has been completed, I hope to find time to work on a revised edition of the document anthology that Reynolds Smith, my editor at Duke Press, has asked for.

This book is dedicated to Jan, my wife of more than three decades.

Milton C. Sernett
Cazenovia, New York
February 1997

INTRODUCTION

Migration is a theme of enduring historic significance. The wellspring of the myth of the American national character has been the movement of peoples of European descent across the landscape. Historians in the tradition of Frederick Jackson Turner have explained the United States in terms of the challenge of the western frontier.[1] The historiography of European settlement and migration has so dominated the literature that the internal movement of peoples of African descent is often overlooked. Looking from the perspective of the end of the twentieth century, the movement out of the South of significant numbers of African Americans beginning during World War I is far more important to understanding the peril and promise of contemporary American society than the experiences of, for example, immigrants from Norway making their way to rural North Dakota or of farmers from New England following the Oregon Trail. The Great Migration acted as demographic watershed, the harbinger of economic, political, and social changes that have transformed the United States.

Of about half of black Americans living in 1970 outside what he termed their "old country," historian Bernard A. Weisberger wrote, "for complex reasons, the children of the 'immigrant within,' the northward-moving black still remained unmelted." In contrast, newcomers from outside the

United States, regulated by a series of immigration restriction acts beginning in 1917 and culminating in 1924, were "largely absorbed into the major
currents of American life."[2] The persistent barriers of race, and to a lesser
degree class, that the refugees from the South encountered in the urban
North have their base in the era of the Great Migration. From today's perspective, the story of the internal migration of African Americans is of
greater significance for understanding our contemporary culture than in-
voking the shibboleth of an ethnic "melting pot."

My interest in the voluntary movement of African Americans began in
earnest when I visited the National Museum of American History of the
Smithsonian Institution one Sunday afternoon in the early spring of 1987.
The sun shown brightly over Washington, D.C., and expectations were
that the cherry blossoms would be unusually abundant. Like other visitors, I was there to tour the exhibit "Field to Factory: Afro-American Migration, 1915–1940," which had opened February 5, 1987, and was already
attracting widespread attention.[3] Using visual, aural, and physical artifacts,
"Field to Factory" told the story of hundreds of thousands of African
Americans who sought to start their lives over in the urban North after
new economic opportunities opened during World War I.

I lingered for a long time at many portions of the 7,000 square foot exhibit, looking and listening. Drawn to the objects that Spencer Crew, chief
curator, and his associates had brought together to depict the social history
of ordinary people, I became a silent witness to the power of the material
to evoke the spiritual. Sunday services were over, and African American
churchgoers, dressed in their best, were arriving to spend an afternoon at
the Smithsonian. I overheard several "elders" among the families recount
how familiar many of the artifacts were. It was as if a time machine had
transported them to the rural South, which either they or their parents
once called home. I distinctly recall the comment of a woman who examined the exhibit depicting the interior of a rural church: "We had one like
that in Georgia." The cohort of African Americans who participated in the
Great Migration of the World War I era shrinks with each passing year.
Perhaps that is why the "Field to Factory" exhibit generated such interest,
had its stay at the Smithsonian extended, and toured the country through
the Smithsonian Institution Traveling Exhibition Service. It drew African Americans living in Alaska together in retrospective comradery, and it
stimulated others to dig deeper in archives and call up family memories of
the pilgrimage from South to North.[4]

Few visitors that Sunday afternoon could have been old enough to have participated in the Great Migration of 1916 to 1918, the core experience with which this book deals. The Smithsonian exhibit used the wartime exodus to represent the entire period from 1915 to 1940 when African Americans left the South in waves of varying intensity. One could argue for a Great Migration of 1916 until 1930, since the onset of the Great Depression significantly slowed the black exodus. For metaphorical as well as historical reasons that I hope will become clear, I use the term "Great" primarily in connection with the movement during World War I, but it includes the postwar phases of the 1920s. My chronological boundaries extend into the 1930s and 1940s only for the purpose of examining the impact of the exchange of place epitomized by the Great Migration. I do so in part to make the case that the whole story of the significance of the Great Migration is not in numbers. Its magnitude (including the post-World War I phases) is worthy of note, but many more African Americans remained in the South than left it. By 1930 the majority were still tied to the land. Nevertheless, a new consciousness emerged by the end of the Great Migration era. The city became the critical arena in which the struggle of African Americans to find the "Promised Land" took place.

As we shall see, participants in the Great Migration interpreted their escape from the South as the "Second Emancipation." This term suggests that they had more than material ends in mind when voting with their feet to leave home and seek better lives elsewhere. Though some attention is given in what follows to individuals, my chief concern is with African American churches and denominations. By all accounts, the church was the central institution within which African Americans expressed their corporate self. Surprisingly little attention has been paid to the impact of the Great Migration on churches in the North and in the South. The Second Emancipation's historiography is mostly devoted to socioeconomic considerations, or it is framed by the "race relations" imperative. Scholarly studies that give attention to the Great Migration generally belong to the subfield of urban studies and are concerned with issues of race and class, with ghetto formation, and with labor questions.[5] Cultural considerations are slighted, and a sustained focus on the most important cultural institution in African American communities—the church—is missing.

African American religious studies as a specialty within the American Academy of Religion is nearly a quarter-century old and has yielded a rich and varied harvest. Though we as yet have no comprehensive history, an increasing number of excellent studies contribute to the larger enterprise.[6] When the chronicle of African American religion is written, attention to the impact of the Great Migration must be incorporated. For reasons that will emerge, I view the period when hundreds of thousands of African Americans left the South as critical to our understanding of contemporary African American religion. Before the Great Migration, African American church life developed, with some exceptions, independently in North and South, separated by regional economic, social, and political differences. African American Christians confronted racism in both sections of the country, but the expression of that racism and their ability to cope with it varied from place to place. As a result of the exodus, contrasting expectations of the church's mission came together in the urban North, and a more mixed religious culture emerged. Allan Spear wrote in *Black Chicago* (1967),

> Of all aspects of community life, religious activities were most profoundly influenced by the migration. Before the war, the large, middle-class Baptist and Methodist churches had dominated Negro religious life.... Although they had not completely discarded the emotionalism of the traditional Negro religion, these churches had moved toward a more decorous order of worship and a program of broad social concern. The migration brought to the city thousands of Negroes accustomed to the informal, demonstrative, preacher-orientated churches of the rural south.[7]

Another pivotal outcome of the Great Migration is reflected in the emergence of the first wave of scholarly studies of black churches. The standard by which African American churches were judged was created by those whom I shall call the instrumentalists. These were religious and secular leaders, mostly but not exclusively in the North, who attempted to redirect a greater proportion of denominational resources and the focus of church life from internal to external concerns. The debate between northern Social Gospelers (the instrumentalists) and southern leaders fearful of losing the old-time religion (the traditionalists) reflected in many respects the ideological conflict between W. E. B. Du Bois and Booker T. Washington that lingered long after Washington's death in 1915.

Many discussions of African American churches today assume that their normative mission is to serve the community by being agents of social change. Less interest is given to the internal life of the churches, that is, specifically to churches as arenas in which matters of ultimate meaning and concern are addressed. The Great Migration propelled this preoccupation with black churches as the means to ends other than those of offering members spiritual refreshment and a place to worship. The instrumentalists were influenced by the Social Gospel movement and principally concerned themselves with urban churches. After it became apparent that the Great Migration did not bring about a wholesale redistribution of African Americans, they turned their attention to southern churches, specifically southern rural churches, which were presumed to be retrogressive. One emphasis of this study, then, is on how the instrumentalists came to dominate the discussion of the mission of African American churches, North and South, after World War I.

Debate and discussion of the meaning of African American religion in the last decades of the twentieth century follows channels cut in the aftermath of the Great Migration. The bipolar categories of "protest" and "accommodation" used by contemporary analysts may have replaced the older language of "this-worldly" and "other-worldly," but the tendency to establish mutually exclusive realms constrains our understanding of African American religion.[8] Authors, particularly those who were themselves active in the generational shift toward Black Consciousness or sympathetic to the involvement of churches in the civil rights movement, understandably leaned toward the "protest" model and applauded those denominations that had progressive leadership. In the protest vs. accommodation paradigm certain black denominational traditions fared better than others in the debate over the function and meaning of contemporary African American Christianity. For example, the National Baptist Convention, U.S.A., Inc., received low marks for not being directly involved in the civil rights movement while under the leadership of Joseph H. Jackson.[9] Churches belonging to the "sanctified" tradition, such as black Holiness-Pentecostal groups, also fared poorly in scholarly accounts structured on the paradigm. These varieties of African American religion continue to be labeled "conversionist sects" and are said to exemplify "a desire by many African Americans to return to 'that old-time religion.'"[10] Pentecostalism, particularly under the banner of the Church of God in Christ, is today the fastest-growing religious sector among African Americans, yet it has been the subject of strong criticism for not being in the vanguard of the "protest" movement, and it did not even appear in the U.S. Census of Religious Bodies until 1926.[11]

A historical puzzle exists here that cannot be solved without a deeper understanding of the time crucible when bearers of that old-time religion came into the urban North. Black Baptist and Methodist denominations in the North, having put aside much of the emotional exuberance in their own pasts, looked askance at the newcomers and their exotic spirituality, and the reformers within and without the established churches measured the migrants against the new benchmark of social and political protest. Ironically, the Pentecostalists and their religious kin grew in numbers in urban environments until they outdistanced the older mainstream churches. As we near the end of the twentieth century, debate over the meaning and mission of the black church continues, but signs of convergence have emerged. Black churches are expected to be socially and politically active as well as true to what some have begun to call the "core" African American cultural tradition.[12] This tradition, surprisingly, has its roots in the often-criticized southern and predominantly rural worship practices of the migrants. The emerging canon for the African American church seems to be one that calls for the incorporation of distinctively "black" (variously defined) cultural forms of worship yoked with a prophetic and activist ministry. Once again we must look to the era of the Great Migration for help in understanding the roots of this shift in the paradigm.

To gauge the watershed significance of the Great Migration, I begin in chapter 1 with an overview of conditions in the South before World War I. Chapter 2 discusses the exodus itself within the context of the debate over the future of African Americans. Chapter 3 attempts to probe the deeper meaning of the Great Migration as a salvation event, to see it from the vantage point of the migrants who read providential import into it. In chapter 4 I examine the responses of the principal African American denominations to what many leaders declared was an institutional crisis of unprecedented magnitude. The regional redistribution of large numbers of African Americans not only threatened existing ecclesiastical arrangements but, according to the jeremiad of the day, portended a loss of faith. Chapter 5 considers the challenges set before existing northern African American churches by the influx of thousands of refugees from the South who were considered religious and racial kin. I offer a significantly different assessment of the outreach made by the mainline churches to the migrants than can be gleaned from the older scholarly literature. To present the story of the process by which northern religious communities attempted to change the migrants, and, in turn, the migrant influx altered the urban cultural landscape, chapter 6 discusses one particular northern city—Chicago. "Chicago," Charles S. Johnson wrote in 1923, "is in more than one sense the colored capital and in every sense the top of the world for bruised, crushed, and thwarted manhood of the South."[13] From 1910 until 1920 Chicago's African American population increased 148 percent. The city's religious map was redrawn by the Great Migration, and a more complex and diversified urban religious culture resulted. In chapter 7 the interaction of northern and southern black religious cultures is examined, and an argument is made for the southernization of northern African American religion. Chapter 8 extends this study's emphasis on exploring the long-range impact of the rural-to-urban movements by returning to the South and assessing the point of view employed by pioneering surveys and scholarly studies of African American churches.

This history is not institutional in the narrow sense, certainly not church history by someone who must operate within the constraints of denominational expectations. Yet I consciously highlight the mainline African American denominations because of the inordinate attention that scholarly and popular accounts of the period between the two world wars have given to what is commonly termed "the rise of the cults and sects."[14] By attempting to offset the tilt toward the exotic, I also mean to challenge the assumption that African Americans in urban areas flocked to the so-called cults and sects because the mainline churches failed to make meaningful efforts to meet their spiritual and material needs. My own assessment is more charitable, though the reasons for it can become clear only when we have established how the black church came to be the principal institutional vehicle to which the migrants, and those who sought to assist them, turned when it was realized that the Great Migration was a harbinger of the future.

Finally, readers are forewarned that the perspective occasionally shifts within chapters. These shifts occur because I view the Great Migration as both an event and a process. While the archetypal migrants are those who went from southern fields to northern factories, I recognize, as Carole Marks has argued, that many migrants had earlier experiences as nonagricultural laborers in the urban South.[15] Our lens will focus primarily on the exodus from the South to the urban, industrial North, but we must remember that African Americans also were moving into southern cities during these decades. I also acknowledge that the magnitude of the exodus from the South during the years from 1940 to 1960 was larger than that of the World War I era.

The publication in 1991 of Nicholas Lemann's *The Promised Land: The Great Black Migration and How It Changed America* has stimulated discussion of the migration northward of southern blacks and its effects on contemporary American life. Much of the current debate focuses on the causes of the persistence of black poverty in urban America.[16] Lemann's subject matter, as Tom Bethell pointed out in the *American Spectator,* is essentially about the "unfinished business" that the United States has in overcoming "its original sin of slavery."[17] By the time that Lemann's migrants enter into the Promised Land, the road had been well-traveled by an earlier generation that participated in the first Great Migration. If they came with more optimism, it was because the patterns and formulations of twentieth-century urban African American life were yet to be demarcated and fully revealed. Thus, these earlier migrants may have correctly believed that America's "original sin" could be atoned for by entering into the Promised Land.

In the debate over the nature and mission of the African American church, participants too often set the rural church against the urban church, the other-worldly against the this-worldly, the spiritual against the social. Those partial to activist agendas deemed the rural church retrogressive while hailing urban churches as the vanguard of progress. Those defending theologically conservative, even fundamentalist, definitions of church put the highest priority on "saving souls." The following history of African American churches during and after the Great Migration demonstrates that the traditional framing of the debate in oppositional categories fails to do justice to the diverse ways in which African Americans expressed their religious hope, either institutionally or individually. In my analysis of the Great Migration and African American religion, I do not privilege one side of the debate over another. Instead, I argue that as a result of the Great Migration two differing understandings of the church's function met, and in that conjunction an important transformation and re-creation took place. Perhaps as a result of the following analysis, we shall come to understand that the this-worldly vs. other-worldly paradigm for discussing the African American religious experience should be put to rest. At the very least, I hope to convince readers of the critical importance of the Great Migration. In the words of Hans Baer and Merrill Singer, "As the primary institution available for responding to external threat and challenge, as well as internal aspiration and expression, the African-American church was remade anew in the shadow of the Great Migration."[18]

1

DOWN

IN

EGYPT-

LAND

On the morning of October 21, 1916, Anthony Crawford parked his wagon in front of W. D. Barksdale's mercantile store in Abbeville, South Carolina. The owner of 427 acres of prime cotton land, Crawford raised a family of twelve sons and four daughters and through hard work and persistence had become the wealthiest black farmer in Abbeville County. Exactly why Crawford went in to see the white merchant that fateful day is not known, though Barksdale purchased cotton from area farmers and sold them seed and supplies on credit. Barksdale and Crawford fell into an argument, reportedly over the price of cotton. The merchant accused the farmer of being a liar, and the farmer cursed the merchant. A white mob gathered at the store. Crawford sought refuge in a partially covered pit in the ground at a nearby cotton gin house and armed himself with a sledge hammer. When the mob rushed him, Crawford struck one of his attackers, McKinny Cann, smashing his skull with the hammer. A rock thrown by a member of the mob knocked the black farmer down. Crawford struggled to his feet, someone knifed him in the back, and he lost consciousness.

The Abbeville sheriff arrived and temporarily stayed the bloodthirst of the mob with the promise that Crawford would be kept in jail until it was known whether Cann would live. By midafternoon a second mob gathered at the jail, incensed by talk that the sheriff planned to spirit Crawford away on the four o'clock train. Acting out a scenario that plagued many black communities of the pre-Great Migration South, the mob broke into the jail, took Crawford, tied a rope around his neck, and dragged him through the black sector of town. At the edge of the fairgrounds, the rioters hanged Crawford's lifeless body from a pine tree and fired several hundred bullets into it. The all-white coroner's jury, despite the ritual spectacle enacted in the presence of numerous witnesses, failed to name anyone responsible for the tragedy in Abbeville.

Whites talked of burning the Crawford house but contented themselves with closing down black businesses in Abbeville and passing an ordinance demanding that Crawford's children, nine of whom were married and lived around their father's farm, leave their land within two weeks. Though the resolution was later revoked, the prospects of further antiblack violence precipitated an exodus from the county, as had happened after the Phoenix riot of 1898 when whites attacked blacks who were attempting to vote in Greenwood County, South Carolina. Some migrants from the Abbeville-Greenwood area headed for north Philadelphia, Pennsylvania, where a sizable colony of blacks from the region had already gone. The murder of Anthony Crawford remained for a long time in the collective memory of black Philadelphians.[1]

Crawford's death at the hands of a white mob was not unusual in the pre-World War I decades. The use of rope and faggot to intimidate and punish blacks was common in the South. There were 754 lynchings of blacks in the United States in the first decade of the twentieth century. Between 1900 and 1909, 92 percent of the lynchings took place in the South (including Missouri), as compared to 82 percent in the 1890s. In the nineties 32.2 percent of the victims were white, but between 1900 and 1909 the ratio of white victims decreased to 11.4 percent. As the historian C. Vann Woodward observed, lynching "was becoming an increasingly Southern and racial phenomenon."[2] In 1910 sixty-seven African Americans were lynched. Though the aggregate number of lynchings in the second decade of the twentieth century was not as large as in the 1890s, when lynchings peaked, one person was lynched in the South every five days, and the ratio of black to white lynchings was ten to one, a disparity that held into the 1930s.[3]

Anthony Crawford's murder struck a raw nerve because it took place when many were puzzling over the causes of the black exodus that began as a trickle in the summer of 1916 and rapidly was becoming a major tributary. Contemporary observers pointed to the expanding labor market stimulated by the outbreak of war in Europe as the lure attracting southern blacks from the South. Historians embellish this economic thesis with detailed descriptions of regional disparities in wages, fluctuations in the price of cotton, and the effects of farm mechanization. Wartime and postwar studies emphasized the primacy of economic forces, as did Edward E. Lewis's book, *The Mobility of the Negro,* which helped to canonize the now familiar interpretive paradigm of the "pull" of the industrial demand for labor in the North and the "push" of agricultural disorganization in the Cotton Belt.[4] In *The South Since 1865,* a general survey of changes in the region since the Civil War, John Samuel Ezell flatly stated: "The desire for economic improvement was the Negroes' chief motive for heading north."[5]

Anthony Crawford and his family, however, did not fit the profile of the black tenants or sharecroppers who lived on the razor's edge of economic ruin or of the landless poor who were already drifting to the South's larger towns and cities. By virtue of hard work, thrift, and a good business sense, the patriarch of the Crawfords had become the epitome of success. Following the dictum of Booker T. Washington delivered in 1895 at the Cotton Exposition in Atlanta, Crawford had cast down his bucket where he was. His landholdings amounted to almost 10 percent of all the property owned by African Americans in Abbeville County. His success proved to be his undoing, at least in the eyes of one observer. "Crawford was worth around $20,000 and that is more than most white farmers are worth down here. Property ownership always make the negro more assertive, more independent, and the poor whites can't stand it." They hated to see "a 'nigger' forge ahead of them, and they lay for a chance to jump him."[6] If we are to understand the full significance of the Great Migration as a religious event, then we must come to terms with the deeper meaning of what happened in Abbeville in the fall of 1916.

The murder of Anthony Crawford, who not incidentally had been secretary of the Chappelle African Methodist Episcopal Church for nineteen years and its largest contributor, suggests that the causes of the exodus of nearly a half million African Americans from the South during World War I are not fully exposed by pointing to economic variables. Crawford's mutilated and savaged body, which one witness described as a "mass of bloody pulp," put the lie to the southern myth that by playing according to the rules blacks could coexist with whites with some hope of the good things of life promised by Booker T. Washington's philosophy. In *The Man Farthest Down,* published in 1912, Washington had argued that African Americans were better off in the South than were the depressed classes of Europe in their homelands. He maintained that "more than anywhere else, the colored people seem to have discovered that, in gaining habits of thrift and industry, in getting property, and in making themselves useful, there is a door of hope open for them which the South has no disposition to close."[7] Ironically, Washington's remarks were published during an outbreak of Ku Klux Klan violence in Mississippi that targeted prosperous African Americans of the class to which Anthony Crawford belonged. His murder gave the lie to Washington's proposition that the achievement of material prosperity by African Americans was the solution to "the race problem" in the South.

By briefly surveying conditions of African American life in the South on the eve of the Great Migration before examining the state of health of the black southern church, we can better understand the subsequent exodus as the religious event that it was. African Americans invested the Great Migration with religious meaning precisely because they understood that what happened to Anthony Crawford could happen to them, no matter what their economic status or how carefully they negotiated the dangerous labyrinth of racial politics in the South. The potential for white violence was always present. Without political and civil rights, southern blacks lived a precarious existence. Whatever toehold they had on material prosperity was threatened by their inability to protect themselves against indiscriminate violence.

The *Atlanta Constitution* acknowledged on December 10, 1916, "Lynching was indeed a cause behind the black exodus . . . . The heaviest migration of Negroes has been from those counties in which there have been the worst outbreaks against Negroes."[8] African Americans felt particularly vulnerable to lynch law because the federal authorities had adopted the policy that the "Negro Problem" was something best left to the white South. Following the contested election of 1876, Republicans in order to hold onto the White House gave up on efforts to protect the rights of southern blacks. The Compromise of 1877 gave the election to Rutherford B. Hayes, but it left blacks in the South to the mercy of whites committed to racial supremacy. Conservative southerners used the states' rights argument to deflect any outside criticism of the treatment of African Americans. Frederick Douglass commented on the effects of the doctrine of states' rights, or local white control, in 1889. "This idea of self-government," he said, "destroyed the Freedman's Bureau, drove United States soldiers out of the South, expelled Northern immigrants, excluded Negro citizens from State legislatures, and gave all the power to the Southern slavemasters."[9]

After the approximately 4 million slaves became free by virtue of the Thirteenth Amendment in 1865 and then became citizens of the United States with the ratification of the Fourteenth Amendment in 1868, an air of jubilation prevailed. Many former slaves believed that God had a hand in their deliverance. A black woman in Virginia said of the miraculous end of slavery, "Isn't I a free woman now! De Lord can make Heaven out of Hell any time, I do believe."[10] This atmosphere of hope deteriorated during the Reconstruction period, when it became clear that southern whites and their conservative allies in the federal government would fiercely contest each political or social gain made by the Freedmen. The dismantling of the Reconstruction agencies, coupled with a resurgence of white power in the South and federal complicity with southern white interests, struck hard at the ex-slaves' dreams of freedom, forty acres, and a mule.[11]

In their search for a place free of the domination of whites, some southern blacks experimented with the formation of all-black towns such as Mound Bayou, Mississippi, and Boley, Oklahoma. About sixty such communities were organized between 1865 and 1915, but the total number of inhabitants represented a small proportion of the South's African American population.[12] Lacking federal initiative and support, a massive exchange of place was impossible. In 1879 Senator William Windom of Minnesota, troubled by the failure of the federal government to protect black civil rights, introduced a resolution in Congress to study the practicality of encouraging blacks to leave the South. His proposal drew little support. European immigrants were filling the need for unskilled labor in the North and Midwest, and antiblack sentiment did not confine itself to the South.

Despite the lack of federal relocation assistance, southern blacks needed no persuasion, and some of them sought better lives elsewhere. Shortly after the removal of federal troops from the South and the reintroduction of political control by whites who bemoaned the defeat of the Confederacy, African Americans began to look for a way out of the region. Senator Windom's resolution was blamed for the spread of the Kansas Fever Idea in the rural parishes and counties of Louisiana and Mississippi. However, as historian Nell Painter points out, southern blacks were already anxious to move and were of the belief that the federal government would provide them with free transportation, land, and supplies.[13]

The largest contingent, perhaps four to five thousand, followed Benjamin "Pap" Singleton, a cabinetmaker who claimed "divine inspiration," to Kansas beginning in 1879. Known as the "Exodusters," many of these refugees were from Mississippi, which was one of the first southern states to reintroduce a white supremacist government. Black leaders such as Henry Highland Garnet and Sojourner Truth, veterans of the pre-Civil War abolitionist struggle, endorsed the exodus to "John Brown's" Kansas. But Douglass opposed the Kansas migration on the grounds that it was ill-timed and badly organized. More fundamentally, he believed that by staying in the South blacks could exercise greater political muscle by virtue of their demographic concentration. "The public and noisy advocacy of a general stampede of the colored people from South to the North," Douglass maintained, "is necessarily an abandonment of the great and paramount principle of protection to person and property in every state of the Union."[14] Douglass held the minority position among African American leaders, and he would later temper his optimism that the white South was amenable to change.

Douglass's skepticism of the exodus to Kansas was borne out. It was short-lived and of modest size. Kansas was cold, much of the land was infertile, and nonfarm jobs were scarce. Those who went to Kansas were motivated by a desire for personal liberty and economic opportunity. But they differed from the host of African Americans who fled the South beginning in 1916 in one important aspect. In her detailed study of the Kansas fever, Painter concludes, "The Exodus was a rural-to-rural migration, at least in intent, whereas the later movement was a rural-to-urban. After the turn of the century, the Afro-American quest for land subsided, or turned into a hunt for jobs. In a sense, then the Exodus was atavistic, for the fundamental drift of American population in the late nineteenth and the twentieth century was toward the cities."[15]

In 1880 6,580,793 African Americans lived in the United States, constituting 13.1 percent of the nation's total population. Approximately 90 percent lived in the former Confederate states. In the last decades of the nineteenth century a small percentage of black southerners were leaving the South and settling in northern cities. These migrants were generally individuals whom W. E. B. Du Bois called "The Talented Tenth." They were better educated than most black southerners or had skills with which they hoped to cope in the North.[16] Northern employers showed little interest in importing unskilled black workers from the South, except as strikebreakers or domestic help. For example, when stockyard workers went on strike in Chicago in 1894 and in 1905, management sought black laborers from the South.[17] This outflow to northern industrial centers was the exception that proved the rule. More commonly, African Americans living in the South as the last decades of the nineteenth century got under way expected to re-main there. Their destiny, for good or bad, was intertwined with that of whites, as it had been before and after Emancipation.

In 1886 Henry Grady of the *Atlanta Constitution* began a campaign to attract northern investors. This apostle of the New South was eager to bring his region into the mainstream of American life. To those who asked what was to be done with "the Negro," Grady responded that a "racial in-stinct" would keep blacks and whites separate.[18] Confirmation that African Americans were to be relegated to a separate place in social and political life of the New South came in the watershed decade of the 1890s, when the force of law was added to social custom, notably in the Supreme Court's ruling in *Plessy* v. *Ferguson* in 1896. The decision prescribed segregated seat-ing on trains and served as the legal justification for systematic segregation in many other areas. *Plessy* v. *Ferguson* cast a pall over the lives of black southerners, regardless of education or location, by defining personal lib-erty in spatial terms.[19] Jim Crow laws became more rigid and consistent, and by 1900 signs saying "Whites Only" or "Colored" hung from public facilities all over the South. Whether on the streetcar or at a drinking foun-tain, at school or in a hospital, at work or at play, black Americans, regard-less of their behavior or accomplishments, were reminded on a daily basis that they were still in Egyptland. Ray Stannard Baker, the investigative journalist who wrote for *McClure's* magazine, said after a visit to Atlanta in 1906, "After I had begun to trace the colour line I found evidences of it everywhere—literally in every department of life."[20]

The color line that Baker observed split the southern Populist move-ment in the 1890s. The agrarian radicals attempted to form a third party by appealing to the interests of both white and black farmers. The Popu-list credo and economic doctrines pitted all those who worked the land against corporate greed and monopoly. The South's best-known Populist, Tom Watson, said, "The accident of color can make no difference in the interest of farmers, croppers, and laborers."[21] Efforts to bridge the color line in the Populist crusade came up against deep-seated prejudices and fears of "Negro domination" raised by southern Democrats. The election of Grover Cleveland in 1892 gave southern Democrats additional clout in their contest with the agrarian reformers. To hang onto the votes of white farmers and laborers, Populist leaders ceased to condemn lynching and racial discrimination. Tom Watson's rhetoric became increasingly filled with antiblack sentiment. Once Democratic politicians in the South felt that they had the Populists on the run, they no longer attempted to attract black voters. The defeat of the Populist movement left a legacy of racial bitterness and further isolated African Americans in the South from any significant political participation.[22]

Democratic control of southern politics was now secured. Blacks who attempted to vote were controlled by whites-only primaries, the manipulation of voter registration, literacy tests, the use of unlabeled ballot boxes, and, when all else failed, intimidation and violence.[23] African Americans in the South on the eve of the Great Migration were a subject people without the right of political participation. The political process offered little hope of change from within. The demise of the Populist crusade and the solidification of conservative white power made Booker T. Washington's appeals for loyalty to the region sound all the more hollow. Even in supposedly racially moderate states, such as North Carolina where the African American novelist Charles Chesnutt grew up, conditions worsened. The antiblack outbreak of violence engulfed Wilmington in 1898 and caused Chesnutt to despair all the more. He visited Wilmington in 1901 to study the causes of the riot and incorporated his findings in the novel *The Marrow of Tradition*. Two years later Chesnutt summed up the southern situation: "The rights of the Negroes are at a lower ebb than at any time during the thirty-five years of their freedom, and the race prejudice more intense and uncompromising."[24]

In its initial phase the Great Migration was composed primarily of unskilled young males, but southern black women had left their homes to work as domestics in the North before World War I. Their experiences did not cast a favorable light on the northern city and contributed to the notion that the South was the "Negro's home." With the assistance of Helen Keller, the National League for the Protection of Colored Women was organized to aid those young women who found themselves subject to exploitation and moral risk in the large cities. S. Willie Layten, general secretary of the League based in New York City, wrote in 1910 of the "swarm of

Northern harpies and procuresses whose business is to meet the incoming masses, and under pretense of assisting them to find homes and work, land them in dens of infamy and shame."[25] Ray Stannard Baker addressed the League at its headquarters in January 1910. "One finds something unspeakably pathetic in the spectacle of these untold thousands of Negroes who are coming North," Baker wrote. "To many of them oppressed with the limitations set up in the South, it is indeed the promised land."[26] Layten, whatever her personal views of the North as "the promised land," wanted potential migrants to be better prepared. Pastors of southern churches were sent instructions to be given to women anxious for employment in the North. The women were told not to come until they had learned to do "good housework." Costs were high, the climate severe, employment agents often dishonest, and female migrants were lured into prostitution.

Though a vanguard of southern blacks like these domestic workers came North before World War I, most African Americans remained below the Mason-Dixon Line. At the end of the twentieth century's first decade the U.S. Census Bureau reported that nearly nine of ten African Americans lived in the South (8,749,427 or 89 percent of a total population of 9,827,763). This figure was only slightly less than the 91.1 percent distribution in 1790 when the first federal census was taken. Seven of ten African Americans lived in rural areas or small towns with an essentially agrarian ethos. The census bureau classified places with 2,500 or more inhabitants as urban, hardly significant in light of common definitions of the city, then or now. A town two or three times the size deemed "urban" by the census-takers if set in an agricultural belt was ruled by the ethos of cotton and the accompanying rural culture. Millions of black southerners who were tied to the land, either as tenants or croppers, lived in a state of economic peonage not far removed from the condition of chattel slavery that they, their parents, and their grandparents had known.[27]

Of forty-three cities with African American populations of 10,000 or more in 1910, thirty-three were in the South. Washington, D.C., led with 95,000 African American residents, more than twice the African American population of Chicago and about 3,000 more than its nearest rival, New York City. Birmingham had a black population of 52,305, whereas Chicago had only 44,101, and the comparable counts for Atlanta and Detroit were, respectively, 51,902 and 5,741. In 1910 the statistical center of the nation's black population was 5.4 miles north-northeast of Fort Payne in De Kalb County, Alabama. Since 1880 it had moved progressively farther in a southwesterly direction. More African Americans were classified as rural dwellers than ever before, in spite of the drift toward cities in the South. Black farm owners cultivated nearly 16 million acres, and the number of African American farmers had increased since 1900 in every state except West Virginia and Louisiana. Blacks made up only 6.3 percent of the nation's urban dwellers, 2.8 percent in the South and 2.4 percent in the North.[28]

Rural-to-urban migration accelerated within the South before World War I because of the rise of industrial centers such as Birmingham and the attraction of cities such as Atlanta. Smaller towns like Athens, Georgia, also experienced a growth in black population in the early 1900s. "The constant trend of negroes townwards," Thomas J. Woofter wrote in a 1913 study of Athens, created "a different set of social problems from those presented by the rural negroes."[29] A subsequent examination of Clarke County, in which Athens was located, revealed that both whites and blacks were leaving the land, the white tenant class going to the cotton mills and blacks to towns.[30] In the towns and cities of the South black labor was frequently confined to service and domestic employment. The influx of poorly educated and ill-trained blacks from the countryside to the urban South was seen as a threat by whites, and, beginning with Baltimore in 1911, most southern cities enacted laws to enforce residential segregation.[31]

Though southern cities, magnet like, drew blacks off the land, they were not oases of opportunity. Rural migrants clung to the bottom rungs of the economic and social ladder. Their plight caught the attention of black institutions such as Atlanta University, which held a conference in 1898 focusing on how churches were meeting the needs of the southern urban poor. "Atlanta, with her back alleys and slums," the Rev. Henry Hugh Proctor proclaimed, "is a fine field of work." He urged Atlanta's black churches to "parcel out the field and each take a particular set of alleys for the work of general betterment."[32] Proctor, a graduate of Fisk University who also attended Yale Divinity School, served Atlanta's First Congregational Church from 1894 until 1919. After the Atlanta race riot of 1906, he intensified efforts to reach out to the urban poor, many of whom were recent migrants from the open countryside. First Congregational operated a nonsectarian community center, a home for working girls, an employment bureau, a cooking school, a kindergarten, a gymnasium, and it supported an orphanage and mission work in poorer neighborhoods.[33]

The drift toward southern cities was caused not only by discontent with rural conditions but by the persistent belief that the North was not a viable alternative. James Samuel Stemons wrote in 1898 on "The Industrial Color Line in the North and the Remedy" for the *AME Church Review*. A supporter of the Industrial Rights League, which sought to have employers take a pledge disavowing industrial discrimination on Christian principles, Stemons believed that conditions had actually worsened for black workers in the North since the Civil War. He decried the lack of industrial jobs, racism in the trade union movement, and the failure of the Christian churches to "unlock the doors of manual labor to the colored race."[34] Richard R. Wright, Jr., an African Methodist clergyman with graduate training in sociology, wrote extensively on the economic barriers faced by African Americans in the industrialized North. Of Philadelphia, Wright stated, "Negroes have been largely shut out of mechanical trades, partly because of indifference and occasional active hostility of labor unions, partly because it has been difficult to overcome the traditional notion that a 'Negro's place' is in domestic service, but chiefly because there has been very little and practically no opportunity for Negroes to learn trades."[35] W. E. B. Du Bois accentuated the point, writing in 1903, "In general the Negro in Northern cities has become a problem. The center of that problem is the question of occupations—the problem of work."[36]

Because of discouraging job prospects in the North, those who felt that African Americans should remain in the South had their views confirmed. President William Howard Taft told the graduating class at Hampton Institute in 1914, "After this experience at Hampton today and after studying the North and the South, it seems to me that while the North has apparently been the more fortunate section for a number of decades, it is the South now that has a definite future before it which it can work out; and it is the North which is struggling amid changed and chaotic conditions, the future tendency of which is uncertain."[37] Robert R. Moton, commandant of cadets at Hampton Institute, told the Southern Sociological Congress in May 1914 that the South afforded more opportunity than the North, particularly because the region had been unable to attract foreign immigrants into its labor market. For its own self-interest, Moton asserted, the white South "should offer every possible inducement for the Negroes to remain in the South and on the land where they can rear their children amid physical and moral surroundings conducive to their highest development and greater usefulness to themselves and to the state."[38]

A deep bias against city life conditioned the attitude of some African American leaders. In 1903 Bishop Cornelius T. Shaffer of the African Methodist Episcopal Church answered the question "Shall the Negro leave the South?" with another query, "Are his environments in the South conducive to his working out his highest and noblest destiny?" After arguing that southern blacks experienced humiliation and dehumanization at every turn, Shaffer declared, "I am free to say the Negro should seek another arena upon which to play his part in the great drama of life. . . ."[39] But he advised African Americans to scatter across the country, take up unoccupied lands, and avoid the crowded cities. Cities had a corrupting influence, he believed, a view shared by educators who sought the uplift of southern blacks. "The way of salvation for the Negro," E. C. Branson, professor of rural economics at the State Normal School in Athens, Georgia, opined, "is not along the paved highways of city civilization. In the cities he is waging a losing battle. The ravages of drink and drug evils, the vices and diseases of the slums, make swift and certain inroads upon the race as a whole in the congested centers of our population."[40]

Northern blacks, even those with a vested interest in improving city life, were not enthusiastic about a wholesale flight of African Americans from the rural South to the urban North. The *New York Age,* an African American newspaper generally known for its progressive politics, featured an article "Life Conditions in the City and in the Country" in 1912. The unnamed author felt that conditions for African Americans were worse in northern urban centers than in cities of the South because of the nature of industrial struggle. "The cruel Molock grinds them to powder; only the best of them survive, one in ten perhaps, and that one is not always a strong and useful member of society." The article quoted with approbation the remarks of Booker T. Washington, delivered in 1912 in Carnegie Hall at a meeting of the Men and Religion Forward Movement. Washington had asserted, "In the rural districts, the Negro, all things considered, is at his best in body, mind and soul. In the city he is usually at his worst. Plainly one of the duties of the church is to help keep the Negro where he has the best chance."[41]

The dominant view before World War I was that blacks should not be divorced from the soil. Even George Edmund Haynes, professor of social science at Fisk University and director of the National League on Urban Conditions Among Negroes, bowed to majority opinion. Established in 1911, the Urban League was an outgrowth of two organizations—the Committee for Improving Industrial Conditions of Negroes in New York and the National League for the Protection of Colored Women—

plus research on the social and economic status of African Americans in New York City that Haynes had done.[42] The Urban League concerned itself with helping African Americans secure jobs and adjust to city life. In 1912 Haynes gave an address at the annual Hampton Institute conference. After reviewing statistics on the movement of blacks toward urban centers and noting the agricultural, commercial, and social causes of this demographic trend, Haynes said, "I do not mean to advocate the idea that Negroes *should* migrate from the country to the city . . . ."[43]

Social workers echoed Haynes's concern with urban problems and pointed to the high price black migrants paid on entering the struggle for survival in the northern city. They too expressed reservations about a mass exodus from the South. Lilian Brandt, secretary of the social research committee of the New York Charity Organization Society, wrote in 1905 that African Americans were best suited to agricultural environments. The African American was not, in her estimation, able to cope with urban conditions and would become "a serious problem—a problem which we cannot escape by the reflection that this migration city-ward was no part of our original plan when we brought him to help us develop our new land, and one which is increasing in importance at a rapid rate."[44] Preoccupied with the plight of the urban poor whose ranks had been swelled by European immigrants, northern social workers such as Brandt were content to leave the fate of African Americans in the South to southern whites. They adopted the view implicit in Thomas Nelson Page's 1904 book, *The Negro: The Southerner's Problem*. In it Page asks, rhetorically, " 'Now that the race problem in the South has been laid down and discussed, what solution of it do you offer—what have you to propose to ammeliorate the conditions which have grown out of that problem?' " His answer: "None, but to leave it to work itself out along the lines of economic laws, with such aid as may be rendered by an enlightened public spirit and a broad-minded patriotism."[45]

White conservatives in the South readily accepted the argument that blacks should remain under their tutelage. J. B. Gambrell, editor of the *Baptist Standard* (Dallas), wrote in 1912, "The Negroes we will have with us always." Gambrell believed that the race question was "peculiarly a Southern problem because we are next to it." Echoing the arguments of the antebellum white missionaries who sought access to the slaves, Gambrell pleaded with his readers to assume the task of raising up the "weaker race" to the standards of the white South. Blacks were not going to return to

Africa in "any appreciable number," nor were they going to "die out as a race." They had planted themselves "in the soil to stay," so that white Baptists, for reasons of self-protection if nothing else, should aid in educating them and preparing them for the future. "If the white people of the South," Gambrell maintained, "prove themselves worthy of the Saxon race, which great race that has been the torch bearer of civilization in the ascent of nations through struggling centuries—if the white people will deal kindly and justly by the weaker race, prosperity is assured."[46]

The paternalism of white conservatives was predicated on the assumption that blacks and whites would continue to interact according to the Atlanta Compromise proposed by Tuskegee's Washington. In 1895 at the Atlanta Cotton States Exposition Washington called on both races to cooperate "in all things essential to mutual progress" for the welfare of the South. But he disavowed any interest in "social equality." Du Bois, who was still teaching at Wilberforce University, wrote to Washington in 1895, "Let me heartily congratulate you upon your phenomenal success at Atlanta—it was a word fitly spoken."[47] Du Bois later became Washington's chief ideological rival, waging battle from his new post as professor of sociology at Atlanta University. The Washington-Du Bois debate began in earnest in 1903 when *The Souls of Black Folk* appeared. In it, Du Bois criticized the "industrial" educational philosophy of the Tuskegee Machine and Washington's accommodationist politics. Two years later Du Bois attended the famous Niagara Falls conference that gave birth to the National Association for the Advancement of Colored People (NAACP) in 1909.[48]

Washington's strategy of developing separate black institutions in the South without challenging the dominant power structure became less viable as the nineteenth century gave way to the twentieth. A strain of white racism more virulent than that with which Washington contended in 1895 had become pervasive. Radical white racists displaced temperate advocates of the New South by promulgating the theory of black retrogression. These propagandists of white supremacy asserted that blacks as a "race" could not expect to rise above the mudsill of civilization and were a burden to the South. Historian Joel Williamson argues that the break between Washington and Du Bois needs to be understood against this background. He writes, "In effect, the white people with whom Washington had negotiated a modus vivendi in 1895 were, by 1900, rapidly losing control to people who had radically different ideas about the proper state of relations between the races. In the black belts of the South white attitudes of accommodation rapidly melted into universal rejection, and burning and bloody aggression."[49] The influence of the radical racists became apparent during the Great Migration when some white southerners took perverse pleasure in observing that their northern critics now also confronted "the Negro problem." As one Virginian put it, "We see in the Negroes' dispersal throughout the North not only a relief to our own sorely tried communities, but a distribution of the evils, which their presence creates everywhere you find them in any number."[50]

The plight of blacks in the former Confederate states was compounded by indifference and outright hostility among most white politicians and intellectuals. The southern white perspective dominated academic circles in which the "problem of the Negro" held center stage. John H. Stanfield points out that "empirical inquiries into the conditions of blacks was the province of Southerners or researchers employed in Southern-based institutions."[51] These intellectuals focused primarily on questions of "adjustment" under the assumption that the white South would continue to deal with a large population of blacks in its midst. African Americans were to remain under the tutelage and control of southern whites. Southern missionaries on the topic of race lectured in the North attempting to sell the idea of a "New South" that would prove economically beneficial to northerners at the expense of any interference by liberals on "the race question." The Republican party under the leadership of President William Howard Taft sought alliances with white conservatives in the South at the expense of protecting blacks.

Woodrow Wilson's inauguration in 1913 sealed the fate of the few remaining black Republicans who had survived the retreat of northern Republicans. Democrats who controlled the White House on the eve of the Great Migration put a low priority on improving race relations, supported segregation in federal agencies, and allowed southern white politicians excessive influence in national policy. In 1915 President Wilson permitted the film *Birth of a Nation* to be shown in the White House, and afterward, though the film displayed a blatantly racist attitude at many points,[52] the president said that it was "like writing history with lightning." Given this climate at the federal executive level, it is not surprising to find Williamson telling us that "the southern race problem of the nineteenth century became the national race problem of the twentieth, in part precisely because of the abandonment by the North of the Negro in the South."[53]

African American leaders attempted to mute the shrill voice of racism and to counter theories of race deterioration by pointing to the head-way made in the South since the Civil War. When writing about "Fifty Years of Negro Progress" in 1913 Monroe N. Work focused almost exclu-sively on the economic, educational, and religious strides made by African Americans since Emancipation. After accepting Booker T. Washington's invitation to come to Tuskegee Normal and Industrial Institute in 1908, Work dedicated himself to garnering facts regarding all aspects of African American life. As head of the division of records and research at Tuske-gee, Work, a sociologist trained at the University of Chicago, believed that accurate information concerning the accomplishments and needs of Afri-can Americans "would allow for other things" to improve.[54] Social and political advancement, Work believed, would be enhanced by setting the record straight regarding the progress of the "race" since slavery.

Work accentuated the positive. Since 1863 blacks had accumulated mil-lions of dollars of church property, raised the educational standard of their clergy, and established large denominational bureaucracies, complete with publishing houses. In 1913, Work noted, the South contained fifty col-leges and more than 400 normal and industrial schools for blacks. More than 1.7 million African American children attended public schools. But their schools, especially in the rural areas, were inferior to white schools in equipment and facilities. Work estimated that in 1913 the economic value of black labor to the South was $10 million, and he highlighted the progress African Americans had made in business, trades, and the professions. Using data from the 1910 federal census, Work drew attention to a significant in-crease in black farm ownership since 1863.[55]

Work's effort to counter white racism with empirical evidence of black progress was laudable enough, but statistics in the aggregate could not mask the widespread feeling that many blacks had of being trapped in a region where memories of slavery remained strong. The South was still Egyptland. Whatever the progress made since the Civil War, many blacks in the South thought that their circumstances were becoming more precari-ous. Political disfranchisement, unequal educational facilities, job discrimi-nation, institutional prejudice, and the ever-present threat and reality of physical violence weighed heavily on the minds of those who had been told for far too long that the South was their "natural home." If we confine con-sideration of the Great Migration's causes to the realm of the labor econo-mists, we do so at the expense of understanding what the *AME Church*

Review called the "atmosphere of injustice and oppression" that poisoned the aspirations of southern blacks, regardless of their social status.[56]

Proponents of the Anglo-Saxon philosophy of progress perpetuated an optimistic outlook, even as more and more black southerners were showing their dissatisfaction by going up North or flocking to southern cities. Writers for the *Southern Workman,* the Hampton Institute publication, continued to use words such as "uplift," "progress," "moving ahead," and "forward."[57] Supported by white philanthropy, Hampton Institute, founded in 1868, was a center of the agrarian version of the American Dream for southern blacks. The Hampton and Tuskegee programs held up the goal of becoming self-sufficient farmers to black tenants, sharecroppers, and wage laborers. Despite the movement of blacks off the land, so that eight cities in the South had a black population of more than 40,000 in 1910, the *Southern Workman* and the *Negro Farmer and Messenger,* a Tuskegee Institute publication, held to the vision of a black South that was essentially agrarian. The pedagogical methods and ideological values embodied in the "Hampton-Tuskegee Idea" did not undergo significant change until the late 1920s.[58]

The tenuous nature of the black agrarian gospel became clear in the period just before the Great Migration. When war in Europe broke out in the summer of 1914, cotton exchanges in the South were closed, and farmers, who were sitting on a record crop, saw the price of their product tumble. The extension board of the AME Church reported that many congregations in the South were suffering because their members were unable to dispose of their cotton.[59] The 1915 cotton crop was only 31.4 million acres, the smallest since 1909. Fears that the European conflict would have "calamitous consequences" for the South because of diminishing foreign sales gave way to optimism by 1916, when the price of cotton reached 16 cents a pound. It then seemed as if economic prosperity was within everyone's grasp. Farmers, according to agricultural historian Gilbert C. Fite, were paying off debts, buying clothes, shoes, furniture and automobiles. "Cotton," writes Fite, "was again king across the South."[60]

At least some black farmers were participating in the war-induced prosperity. The *Savannah Press* reported that "Negro farmers are buying automobiles who were content a year ago to ride in an ox-cart, or, at best, in a new red buggy behind a $150 mule."[61] Because of this revitalization of the dream of agricultural prosperity, proprietors of the Hampton and Tuskegee programs clung to the old notion that if black farmers, who had been left in the economic and social backwashes of the South, worked harder, engaged in crop diversification, and became more self-sufficient, they too would enjoy better lives. "The temporal salvation of the Negroes of the South," said one Washington disciple, "is largely in the proper cultivation of the soil."[62]

The perceived improvement of the cotton economy reinforced the prevailing attitude that the African American masses would and should remain in the South. The view that the North was hostile to blacks underscored the idea that whatever trials and tribulations lay ahead, blacks would remain where they were. Fear of the unknown and hostility from whites thwarted earlier attempts to extricate blacks from the South. The Exodusters who went to Kansas in 1879 did not find the Promised Land, and some of the most discouraged of them returned to the South. Interest in the "Back-to-Africa" movement led by Bishop Henry McNeal Turner had drawn a favorable response largely limited to poor blacks in Georgia, Turner's denominational base of power. But Turner's dream died with him. Exodus to the North and West involved only a small percentage of black southerners before World War I. Those whom Du Bois called the Talented Tenth were unable to convince sizable numbers of southern blacks that leaving the South, all things considered, was worth the risk. Northern employers certainly had not expressed much interest in southern blacks, except for young women employed as domestics, strikebreakers of both genders, and some seasonal laborers. The lack of work opportunities for African Americans in the North reinforced a spirit of resignation among southern blacks and the feeling that, whatever the problems of the South, they at least were knowable.

The lack of viable alternatives caused some who were concerned with the plight of southern blacks to conjure up radical solutions. Bishop Lucius H. Holsey of the Colored Methodist Episcopal Church (CME), who like Turner was a Georgian, proposed that the federal government create a separate state that African Americans could call their own and thereby escape "serfdom and slavery."[63] Of Bishop Holsey's plan and of the various schemes put forth by others concerned with "the race problem" in the South, whether segregation, emigration, colonization, expatriation, extermination, or amalgamation, the Reverend C. L. Bonner, pastor of the St. Paul CME Church of Savannah, declared: "My doctrine is, if you let me coin a word, 'stayhereation' and when I say that, I mean stay here as a separate and distinct race, and the God that has brought us thus far can carry us on."[64] Until circumstances changed with the outbreak of the Great War, most southern blacks adopted "stayhereation" because they felt that they had no viable alternative. And, like Bonner, they comforted themselves with religious hope—a hope generations old. Du Bois wrote in his classic *Black Reconstruction:* "to most of the four million black folk emancipated by civil war, God was real. They knew Him. They had met Him personally in many a wild orgy of religious frenzy, or in the black stillness of the night. His plan for them was clear; they were to suffer and be degraded, and then afterwards by Divine edict, raised to manhood and power; and so on January 1, 1863. He made them free."[65]

Since it will be the argument here that the Great Migration era acted as a watershed in African American religious history, it will be useful to illustrate how the religious culture of the black South appeared to commentators before World War I. After a visit to Roanoke Island in 1865, Henry M. Turner wrote of the worship styles he witnessed: "Hell fire, brimstone, damnation, black smoke, hot lead, &c., appeared to be presented by the speaker as man's highest incentive to serve God, while the milder and more powerful message of Jesus was thoughtlessly passed by. Let a person get a little animated, fall down and roll over awhile, kick a few shins, crawl under a dozen benches, spring upon his feet . . . then squeal and kiss (or buss) around for awhile, and the work is all done."[66] To this preacher-politician of the northern-based AME Church, the religious practices of the ex-slaves were not adequate to building up a self-reliant and stalwart people. Bishop Daniel A. Payne, also a native South Carolinian, later appointed Turner as presiding elder of Georgia. Payne, known as the AME's greatest educator, crusaded within his denomination to root out the folk religious practices associated with black religion "way down in Egyptland" and to raise the educational standards of the ministry.[67]

William Wells Brown, the African American writer noted for the novel *Clotel,* toured the South in 1879 and 1880 to assess progress made since Emancipation. In *My Southern Home; or The South and Its People* he sketched a discouraging picture of black religious life. Brown was particularly disturbed by the worship styles of southern blacks and the lack of a trained and progressive ministry. "It will be difficult," Brown wrote, "to erase from the mind of the negro of the South the prevailing idea that outward demonstrations, such as, shouting, the loud 'amen,' and the most boisterous noise in prayer, are not necessary adjuncts to piety."[68] This was an old complaint. The worship style of southern blacks, especially in rural areas, embarrassed the activists who wished to enlist the churches in the battle against white oppression.

About 1890 Lille B. Chase Wyman toured what she termed the "less en- lightened" rural areas of the Black Belt and found that not much in the small, unpainted meetinghouses had changed since the Civil War. This white New Englander possessed a cultural bias against the extravagant worship style favored by many blacks. But she was astute enough to ob- serve that disparaging generalizations about southern black religion might not pertain to regions strongly affected by secular and religious instruc- tion given by northern missionary teachers or to the vicinity of Atlanta, Tuskegee, or Hampton, where black educational institutions functioned.[69] Atlanta University, Tuskegee Institute, and Hampton Institute were islands of progressivism trying to energize southern clergy and churches to do more to transform the lives of those who had the mental, if not the physi- cal, scars of being lashed by the whip of white power for generations.

Atlanta University originated in the post-Civil War educational mission work of northern Congregationalists. President Horace Bumstead began the Atlanta University Conference on Urban Negroes in 1896. In 1903 the university published an important and pioneering study of the black church. It was edited by Du Bois, who had been hired to direct the confer- ences and teach sociology. Du Bois outlined an ambitious plan for empiri- cal research on one topic for each of ten years, and he chose "the religion of Negroes and its influence on their moral habits" as the focus for the 1903 conference. The final report was based on a wide variety of published sources, questionnaires, and information from church officials, clergy, laity, educators, and schoolchildren. Six local studies were conducted, with stu- dents at Atlanta University and Virginia Union University assisting. Both in scale and sophistication *The Negro Church* surpassed any earlier attempt to evaluate the state of health of African American religion.[70]

The Rev. W. H. Holloway, a graduate of Talladega College, conducted a survey of Thomas County, Georgia, for the Atlanta conference. Of the church in extreme southwest Georgia, Holloway wrote, "Here he [the rural African American] learns the price of cotton or the date of the next circus; here is given the latest fashion plates or the announcement for candidates for justice of the peace." Many of the ninety-eight churches were family gatherings presided over by some "venerable patriarch" and the result of congregational splits. "I know of no rural church in Thomas county," Holloway wrote, "whose inception had the careful nursing of an educated, cultured leader." Emotionalism, "the supreme element in the old system," still prevailed, though some preachers wanted to rise above the stereotype of the ignorant country preacher. To compete with popular preachers, however, they too resorted on occasion to "rousements." Holloway felt that some of the fraternal or secret societies, especially the female ones, did a better job than the churches in enforcing moral standards. Lax business methods, heavy debts, and an untrained and often unlicensed ministry plagued congregations. Aware that he was presenting a "gloomy picture," Holloway brightened things somewhat by noting that young people and some of their elders were aspiring to a better-educated ministry and "more intelligent worship."[71]

Students in the senior and junior classes at Atlanta University gathered information on city churches. They found that about half of Atlanta's black population (1900 census: 35,727) was enrolled in a total of fifty-four churches, twenty-nine of which were Baptist and twenty-one Methodist. The other four churches were Congregational, Episcopal, Christian, and Presbyterian. The student researchers discovered a wider range of conditions than Holloway had found in rural southwest Georgia. While pastors of the smaller churches were often poorly educated, those of the larger Baptist and Methodist congregations had been trained at institutions such as Howard University and Gammon Theological Seminary. The Congregational Church, whose 400 active members were said to present "the highest average of intelligence of any colored church in the city," was self-supporting, housed in a well-located, substantial building, and doing charitable work in Atlanta's slums. Most clergy were reputed to be of worthy character, though some with small memberships were said to be progressing neither personally nor professionally. The young investigators were particularly discouraged over illiterate preachers in the small churches doing much to advance the education and moral standards of members.[72]

At the conclusion of its work, the eighth Atlanta conference issued a statement, signed by the black clubwoman Mary Church Terrell, Kelly Miller of Howard University, and Du Bois. It called for a religious rebirth in a "critical period of religious evolution when the low moral and intellectual standard of the past and the curious custom of emotional fervor are no longer attracting the young and ought in justice to repel the intelligent and the good." The statement's sponsors called for "an Age of Faith" in which the "Negro church . . . once purged of its dross . . . will become as it ought to be, and as it *is now*, to some extent, the most powerful agency in the moral development and social reform of 9,000,000 Americans of Negro blood."[73] The participants in the Atlanta conference heard various suggestions for improving the black church, but none was more unanimously endorsed than the need for a better-trained ministry. Lay members in particular stressed that the greatest need was for "an earnest, consecrated, educated, wide-awake, intelligent ministry."[74] In subsequent years Du Bois would continue his campaign for better leadership, arguing in the *Crisis* in 1912 that too few were "men of scholarship and standing" and that "the 30,000 colored ministers fall as a mass far below expectations."[75]

What was the root cause of the retrogressive and often dysfunctional character of far too many churches and clergy? In 1913 Du Bois wrote an editorial in which he castigated the white church for tossing the African American "stones for bread." "Denied higher training for his leaders, denied industrial opportunity to make a living, the self-assertion and self-defense of the ballot, denied even hospitals and common schools."[76] These problems were especially acute in the South, where white church leaders were generally either hostile or indifferent to black churches. "The difficulty of getting valuable expressions on the Negro churches from Southern white people," the Atlanta conference acknowledged in 1903, "is that so few of them know anything about these churches." When whites did venture a visit to a black church, they went "for curiosity or 'fun' and consequently [sought] only certain types."[77]

Carey Breckinridge Wilmer, rector of St. Luke's Protestant Episcopal Church in Atlanta, addressed the conference on May 26, 1903, representing "the Southern white people." He advised black preachers to keep politics out of the pulpit, let white clergy crusade against lynching, and focus on crime instead. "Leave off talking about rights for a while," Wilmer advised, "and direct attention to duties."[78] Earlier in the day the conference heard a speech by Washington Gladden, a northern advocate of the Social Gospel who was then president of the American Missionary Association. Gladden said, "The more strenuously men oppose your participation in political affairs, the more zealously and diligent ought you to be in qualifying yourselves to take part in them."[79] Gladden was cautious not to make what he referred to as "inflammatory suggestions." He spoke against the use of violence as a means of political redress, and he urged southern blacks to use their adversities as the challenge in equipping themselves to assume their rightful place in civic affairs. Du Bois, Miller, and Terrell applauded Glad-

den's remarks, for, restrained as they were, they ran counter to the quietis-
tic counsel of Wilmer and the accommodationist position of Washington.

In 1903, when the conference was held, Washington maintained a position of influence. He had dined with President Theodore Roosevelt in
the White House only two years earlier and used his connections with
the Republican administration to garner support for Tuskegee Institute.
Washington's personal struggle "up from slavery" was epitomized in his
aspirations for all black southerners who came within range of Tuskegee.
Founded in 1881 in Macon County, Alabama, Tuskegee was situated in the
old cotton country where black farmers struggled from year to year to eke
out a subsistence. When Washington first visited the town of Tuskegee, he
noted, "While the colored people were ignorant, they had not, as a rule,
degraded and weakened their bodies by vices such as are common to the
lower class of people in large cities."[80] Once Washington firmly established
himself as the "wizard of Tuskegee," he sought to use the school to transform the daily lives of black sharecroppers and tenant farmers. Beginning
in 1892, Tuskegee held annual conferences to which black farmers from the
surrounding countryside were invited.

By 1914, according to one visitor, the farmers' conference had become
a symbol of the success of Tuskegee's missionary efforts to raise the standards and improve the quality of life of the black farmer. Gone was the
"acre of mules" of earlier years. The modern farmer, "as well dressed and
intelligent as one could wish to see," had replaced the old-time farmer,
"a bent old man with his cob pipe, his dog, his mule, and his wooden
plow." The parade included up-to-date machinery used on the Institute's
thousand-acre farm. The audience cheered as students passed by driving
"a four-horse gang plow, a disc harrow, a roller, a seed drill, a mower,
a binder, a thresher, a corn harvester, a cotton-stalk chopper and trans-
planter." Washington told the throng assembled before him, "Let us make
up our minds that we are each going to do our part to develop the farms,
the gardens, the orchards, the stock, the poultry, the fruit, the vegetables,
and have the best of everything, including houses." At the conclusion of
his remarks, his audience, estimated at 2,500, sang "Give me dat ole-time
religion," but, according to the visitor, "there was no disposition to shout
for the old-time ways of farming."[81]

When he began the farmers' institutes, Washington had not intended to
use Tuskegee Institute as the agent to transform the religious culture of

black southerners. But he soon realized that improving the conditions of black churches, especially those in rural areas, was essential to his larger mission of agricultural education. This emphasis can be seen in issues of the *Negro Farmer,* which was combined with Washington's newspaper, the *Messenger,* in 1915. The editor, Isaac Fisher, a graduate of Tuskegee, acknowledged that "the colored church is still the greatest influence in the life of our people," and he urged churches to do more to improve the social and economic welfare of "the race."[82] The *Negro Farmer* featured progressive farmer-preachers in its "Winners from the Soil" column. In 1914 the paper praised O. J. McPherson, a Baptist preacher in South Carolina and a leader in farm demonstration work, for having grown two 500-pound bales of cotton on one acre. "Such leaders," Fisher wrote, "teaching industry and thrift by example, and preaching the gospel in His name, and walking in the steps of Jesus will help make glad the desert and solitary places of the land."[83] In addition to advising its readership about purchasing feeder cattle and seed corn, the *Negro Farmer* commented on church matters, urging, for example, that the National Baptist Convention present a solid front rather than split as it did in 1915 and cause a "racial calamity."[84]

Booker T. Washington died in 1915, but his disciples kept alive his interest in the country church. The Rev. G. Lake Imes, who was dean of Phelps Hall Bible Training School at Tuskegee in the year of its founder's death, wrote of Washington, "Religion for him meant righteousness and good works, not creeds and councils." Begun in 1892, the Phelps school was specifically devoted to improving the country church and its leadership.[85] A night school for preachers and annual ministers' institutes organized on the model of the farmers' institutes also helped establish the connection between Tuskegee and black churches. Of this aspect of the Tuskegee program Imes wrote, "To Dr. Washington, the ideal country preacher was a man who had his home among the people whom he pastored; who operated a farm of his own, both for support and as an example to his flock; who counted it as much his work to show his people how to buy land and own their homes, to keep a garden all the year round, to save their money and educate their children, as to teach him to read the word of God, to keep the Sabbath Day and to be just and kind and pure, and love their neighbors white and black."[86]

The June 17, 1916, issue of the *Negro Farmer and Messenger* reprinted an article concerning "The Community Church" from *Rural Life,* a publication of the Country Life Movement. It provided a description of the ideal rural church that Washington promoted: "That little church reflects the character of the community. If the meeting house is in good repair, neatly painted, and surrounded with a cleanly cut lawn, with solid well-built steps and evenly graded walk leading down to the roadway, it mirrors a thrifty high-class rural neighborhood, a community of God-fearing, progressive people."[87] Washington's model preacher and model church were pragmatic, not ethereal. Church and preacher were to be agents in improving the quality of life for rural blacks.

Critics, even those friendly to Washington's vision of a better day, argued that the prevailing institutional expression of African American religion on the southern cultural landscape before World War I was far from the ideal portrayed in *Rural Life*. Imes, writing in 1912 on "The Negro Minister and Country Life," noted that in Macon County of seventy-five black preachers, only four or five were not farmers. "But of all those engaged in lifting the Negro," he argued, "the preacher is farthest behind." The black merchant, teacher, and farm demonstrator possessed "special equipment," but the preacher had few practical skills to offer in the battle to improve country life, and, "with the growing usefulness of the school, some have feared that it will replace the church as a social agent."[88]

Speaking at New York's Carnegie Hall in 1912, Washington acknowledged that much improvement needed to be made:

> So long as the Negro in the rural districts is fed upon the old worn-out theological dogmas, instead of getting from the pulpit inspiration and direction in the practical work of community building, connecting religion with every practical and progressive movement for the improvement of the home and community life, so long will he forsake the land and flee to the city. If we would save the Negro, 82 per cent of whom, as I have said, live in the country, he must be taught that when the Bible says, "The earth is full of Thy riches," it means that the earth is full of corn, potatoes, peas, cotton, chickens and cows, and that these riches should be gotten out by the hand of man and turned into beautiful church buildings and a righteous, useful living.[89]

Here was a rural Social Gospel that mirrored the purpose of those in urban areas who attempted to use black churches as instruments of social change by focusing on practical matters.

Washington was a graduate of Hampton Institute, where he received a strong dose of the educational program established by Samuel Chapman

Armstrong, the Union army general who built on the work of the Freed-men's Bureau with assistance from the American Missionary Association. Armstrong, his close associate Robert C. Ogden, a member of Hampton's board of trustees, and Hollis B. Frissell, Armstong's successor, were Christian Social Gospel advocates who believed in "education for service."[90] They used Hampton Institute as a staging ground from which to send converts throughout the South. Hampton had been holding farmer's conferences for a number of years, and in 1903 about sixty Baptist and Methodist clergy were invited to join the farmers to discuss "Co-operation of the Negro Teacher and Minister." The preachers were told that their duty was to help stem migration to the cities by improving the social, mental, and religious life of their people.[91]

S. G. Atkins, secretary of education for the AME Zion Church, reiterated the same theme at the Hampton Negro Conference in 1911. Speaking on "The Place of the Church in Rural Life," Atkins argued that the drift of black youth to the cities resulted from the "decline of parental authority, lack of entertainment in country districts, want of good school facilities, so called 'poor wages,' and ignorance of what to do with the land." The function of the rural church was "to turn the tide back to the country or at least arrest the movement toward the city."[92] In the summer of 1914 twenty-three black ministers met informally at Hampton Institute for an interdenominational discussion of common problems. Like the ministers' conferences held annually at Tuskegee, the Hampton experiment soon became a regular event.

The programs at Hampton and Tuskegee to improve rural life assumed that blacks would remain tied to the land by economic and social constraints. The philosophy of self-improvement offered no significant challenge to the racial status quo and failed to deal with the systemic problems of the rural poor. Programs to use the country church and black farmer-preachers as revitalizing agents were both localized and inadequate. Most religiously active African Americans in the South attended small churches in the open countryside or in towns with a strong rural ethos. The black rural church remained the most significant institution in the lives of the "stationary poor" within the South's caste system. Most reformers expected the rural church to continue as the ideal type—the baseline of African American Christianity. When World War I began and the call for labor went out from the industrial North, the disciples of Washington could do little but watch, repeat tired axioms about improving country life, and call for the cooperation of the sympathetic element among whites. Nevertheless, their attention to the black rural church before the Great Migration was sensible and understandable, for it was still the cultural hearth of the black religious tradition.

Toward the end of 1906 or early in 1907 Du Bois delivered a public address, probably in Atlanta, on the theme "Religion in the South." Having already spoken of the economic history of African Americans in the South as "in effect the economics of slavery and the Negro problem," he now proposed to deal with religion within a similar analytical framework. "The essence of the study of religion in the South," Du Bois asserted, "is a study of the ethics of slavery and emancipation."[93] Because of the Great Migration, historians of African American religion must take into account another variable in order to understand more fully the contemporary state of affairs—the urbanization of African Americans. After the Great War, urbanization joined with slavery and emancipation—Du Bois's historical interpretive keys—to form a trinity. The movement from country to city has been so significant to the lives of millions of African Americans that black religion in the United States no longer can be understood with the interpretative lens of slavery and emancipation focused only on the South. The Great Migration trumpeted a new day, one that Du Bois quickly recognized and championed when the northward flow began.

Whatever their economic situation or prospects, African Americans lived a precarious existence on the eve of the Great Migration. The most virulent forms of white racism could strike out at them without warning, and they, like Anthony Crawford, must pay the ultimate price. Until they had a sign, however, most southern blacks were not willing to leave family and friends, church and home, for Chicago, Detroit, Pittsburgh, or some other northern city where they would be strangers. Until God ordered human events so that a flight from one region of the country to another would not simply be an exchange of Egypts, blacks in the South would "keep on keeping on," trusting in ultimate deliverance. But when the Great Migration got under way, many seized the opportunity to escape, just as did the Children of Israel who had been under Pharaoh's whip and lash. Then it became difficult for the proponents of "stayhereation" to stem the tide with more talk of "uplift" and "progress."

2

"NORTH-

BOUND

THEIR

CRY"

One in ten African Americans lived in the North in 1900, a mere 2 percent of the total population. Northern cities, at least from the vantage point of many black residents and liberal reformers who were heirs to the pre-Civil War abolitionist movement, were not places of golden opportunity. Segregation persisted. African Americans were excluded from public accommodations, trade unions, societies, and churches, and they were forced to concentrate in inferior housing. Northerners who criticized the South for the region's treatment of African Americans found themselves targets of similar barbs. Some of the old abolitionists and their descendants had begun to lose hope, and in their despair they even voiced antiblack sentiments.[1] Neoabolitionists in the NAACP during the organization's first decade operated on the assumption that most African Americans would remain in the South, a point of view shared by defenders of the racial status quo on both sides of the Mason-Dixon Line on the eve of the U.S. entry into World War I. A momentous change was on the horizon.

In the concluding chapter of *A Century of Negro Migration,* published in 1918, Carter G. Woodson wrote, "Within the last two years there has been a steady stream of Negroes into the North in such large numbers as to overshadow in its results all other movements of the kind in the United States."

Woodson, founder of the Association for the Study of Negro Life and History, admitted that his study was not the "last word" on the departure from the South then under way, but he was confident that the entire country would benefit by the intersectional movement of African Americans. It would cause the South to "abandon the policy of treating the Negroes as a problem and construct a program for recognition rather than for repression." As the migrants took their rightful place in the industrial world, Woodson asserted, one could look forward to "the dawn of a new day" in which "the Negro [would] . . . emerge a real man with power to secure his rights as an American citizen."[2]

The migration, which gave Woodson reason to hope and in the midst of which he was writing, has been called the Great Migration because of its numerical size and historic significance. In reviewing *A Century of Negro Migration* for the *Journal of Negro History,* the distinguished African American historian Charles Wesley correctly observed that Woodson's book makes it clear that African Americans had been participating in migrations of various kinds since the end of the eighteenth century. But Wesley, echoing Woodson's argument, regarded the Great Migration as substantially different, not only because of its size, but because African Americans were leaving the South at the invitation of the North with "opportunity waiting."[3]

The Great Migration began in earnest during the spring of 1916, though some observers noticed an increase in the demand for labor in the North as early as 1915. It tapered off with the return of European immigrant workers and the economic slowdown after World War I. At least 400,000 African Americans may have left the South before the signing of the Treaty of Versailles in 1919. In the narrow sense the Great Migration refers to the first great wave of the war years and the secondary phase during the 1920s. From a larger perspective it was the opening chapter in the story of the urbanization of African Americans in the twentieth century. Because the exodus from the South had no definitive terminus, the Great Migration can also serve as a metaphor for the entire period in modern American history when hundreds of thousands of blacks caught "the migration fever" and felt "bound for the Promised Land."[4]

On June 28, 1914, a Serbian nationalist assassinated Archduke Franz Ferdinand of Austria. Austria declared war on Serbia on July 27, and by the following month Germany had invaded Belgium. Though the United States attempted to remain neutral, it was soon assisting France and Great

Britain. After the sinking of the *Lusitania* on May 7, 1915, a declaration
of war seemed inevitable, despite President Woodrow Wilson's early resistance to preparedness demands. On April 2, 1917, Wilson delivered a war
message to Congress, which concluded with a call to make the world "safe
for democracy." Several days later the Senate and House voted in favor of
a declaration of war. The nation's labor force in the fields and the factories
mustered in unprecedented fashion to support the war effort.

Northern industry felt the effects of the European conflict before the
U.S. entry into the war. The supply of immigrant labor rapidly declined
from more than 1 million new arrivals in 1914 to only 110,618 in 1918. Thousands of workers of European origin returned to their native countries.
Northern industrial recruiters were forced to look for a source of labor
previously shunned—southern blacks. Once the United States formally
entered the conflict and the Selective Service Act was passed, the labor
shortage became even more critical.[5] Northern labor agents began recruiting southern blacks to replace immigrant labor in the spring of 1915, but
their activities drew little public attention because of the small numbers
involved. The U.S. Department of Labor received word of "a great migratory stream" flowing out of the South about June 1916, and two black
federal employees, William Jennifer and Charles Hall, were appointed to
make a preliminary assessment of the exodus.

After war was declared, national attention was drawn to the exodus and
its possible effects on the country's ability to muster all of its resources.
Secretary of Labor William B. Wilson asked James H. Dillard, director of
the Slater Fund for Negro Education in the South, to supervise a general
inquiry. Most of the research was done during July and August 1917, with
particular attention being given to Mississippi, Alabama, and Georgia.
The report was issued from the Division of Negro Economics, headed by
George Edmund Haynes, a seasoned analyst of rural-to-urban migration.[6]

In mid-1917 when the Labor Department researchers went into the
South to gather firsthand impressions of the migration's extent, they had
considerable difficulty in estimating its volume. Railroad ticket agents were
of more help than white state and local authorities. These public officials,
according to Tipton Ray Snavely's report of fieldwork in Alabama, had no
reliable data or even much interest in obtaining some.[7] The South's white
press carried alarmist reports of Yankee labor agents luring away black
farmers; there also were predictions of economic disaster if the cotton

crop could not be tended to. A prominent Alabama newspaper featured an article in September 1916 that stated, "All over Alabama landlords show fear in their eyes and anxiety in their voice. 'Our labor is leaving—what is to be Done?' Without the negro workers on the land, the making of cotton is hardly thought possible by many plantation owners."[8] Given this attitude, it is not surprising that white southerners underestimated the size of the Great Migration.

Northerners were just as apt to exaggerate the numbers to discredit propaganda that portrayed blacks as contented and ill-disposed to uproot themselves. The Department of Labor estimated that between 200,000 and 700,000 blacks left the South in an eighteen-month period of 1916–17. The Rev. R. W. Bagnall, an NAACP activist in Detroit, claimed that 500,000 migrants had fled persecution in the South during the six months before November 1916, and he predicted that "fully 5,000,000" would be involved before the Great Migration was over with.[9] Neither Bagnall's claim nor his prophecy were close to reliable figures, but they indicate the tendency of pro-migration activists to exaggerate to make a political point.

The exodus peaked during the summer of 1917, then tapered off when World War I ended; immigrant labor arrived once again, and the country experienced an economic slowdown. A second wave of migration began in 1921 or in the fall of 1922, depending on the definition of critical mass, and it continued with intermittent strength until the beginning of the Great Depression. The second migratory flow followed channels cut by the Great Migration of 1916–18. Statistics on the exodus during the war years are estimates drawn from census data, which is available only in decennial periods. Historians generally assume that the extensive loss of black labor in the South occurred during the last half of the 1910s, when the outbreak of war in Europe sharply restricted immigrant workers.[10] The U.S. Census of 1920 reported that the black population of the North had increased by approximately 450,000 since 1910, while the South's grew by only about 150,000, but the census was widely criticized for undercounting the nation's African American population.[11]

Emmett J. Scott's estimate of 400,000 for the Great Migration may be as usable a figure as any other. Scott's monograph *Negro Migration During the War* was published in 1920 under the sponsorship of the Carnegie Endowment for Peace. Scott had been secretary and assistant to Booker T. Washington and caretaker executive of Tuskegee Institute after Washington's death. He was secretary-treasurer of Howard University at the time of the migration study.[12] James W. Johnson, field secretary of the NAACP, made two trips to the South, one at the beginning of the Great Migration and another at its zenith, and he admitted that obtaining a definite figure on the size of the exodus was difficult. He wrote Charles S. Johnson of the Urban League in January 1918 that estimates of 500,000 and higher were plausible. "I think," he told Johnson, "that most of these people have come from the rural districts of the South rather than from the cities. So far as I know, no means have been found effective in stopping or preventing this migration."[13]

The Great Migration did not begin with one moment in time. Yet for symbolic and narrative purposes, we might as well use Scott's description as any other of the onset of what was later described as a mass hegira. He relates that tobacco growers in Connecticut became alarmed in 1915 over the dearth of common labor resulting from the departure of Poles, Lithuanians, and Czechs for their native countries. These farmers, Scott wrote, "at first rushed to New York and promiscuously gathered up 200 girls of the worst type, who straightway proceeded to demoralize Hartford."[14] In early 1916 the growers sought the assistance of the Urban League in recruiting black students from southern schools for the seasonal work. By summer the Pennsylvania and Erie Railroad was transporting carloads of blacks from Florida and Georgia with promises of free rides for willing workers.[15] The *National Baptist Union Review* informed its readers: "There is a demand north for young colored men and women, occasioned by migration of foreigners to Europe to serve in the Great War. We hope thousands of serious, studious, business-like young folks will at once arrange to take the places of employment now open to them. We advise ambitious young men and maidens of the hightone type to write to their friends north for information and that they at once enter the new field of industry, domestic service and manual labor open to their acceptance."[16]

Railroads, steel mills, and a wide assortment of eastern industries, many of them war-related, soon began recruiting in the South, using black as well as white agents. The Pennsylvania and Erie Railroad sent James H. Duckrey, a black minister from Philadelphia who served as a clerk in the office of William Atterbury, the railroad's vice president of operations, to Florida with an empty passenger train to recruit workers.[17] "Some selection of laborers was attempted," Francis D. Tyson reported to the Department of Labor, "but the procedure of getting workers sometimes amounted simply to backing a train into a Southern city and filling it as quickly as possible."[18]

Most of the early labor recruits were black males, many young and single. Some came as strikebreakers; many were of the "indigent and thriftless" class from the bottom of the South's labor pool. They were grouped in camps along railroad lines and near factories and housed in makeshift dormitories. Subject to vices such as drinking, gambling, and fighting, the men caused alarm among church and civic leaders. Henry Philips, rector of Philadelphia's Crucifixion Episcopal Church, warned that if the churches failed to address the crisis in the camps, they did so at their own peril. "If we do not look after them in the right way," he wrote, "they are sure to look after us in the wrong way."[19] Social Uplift meetings began at the railroad camp at Paoli near Philadelphia in August 1916 at the initiative of the Rev. William A. Creditt, president of Downington Industrial College.

The work of track and roadbed repair was difficult, absenteeism was high, and when migrants learned of higher wages in other places they moved on, seeking better opportunities. By January 1917 the Pennsylvania and Erie Railroad had imported an estimated 12,000 laborers into Pennsylvania, but fewer than 2,000 were said to have remained with the railroad.[20] At a meeting in Philadelphia, newcomers heard W. H. Graham, pastor of a local black Baptist congregation, speak of the difficulties caused by these early recruiting practices. Railroad companies started the movement North by offering free transportation and gathering up station loafers. These individuals had little or no interest in establishing church ties. Graham happily reported that as of March 1917 the practice of indiscriminately importing workers had been discontinued and that new arrivals were "not drones" but eager to work.[21] The Pennsylvania Railroad cooperated in July 1917 by ending its policy of extending free transportation to migrants on its East Coast lines.

The new arrivals struck many Old Philadelphians as a much more uncouth lot than black southerners who had come to their city in earlier decades. The railroad workers were not the Talented Tenth. To use historian Robert Gregg's phrase, they were ill-at-ease with "the same urban culture that black Philadelphians prided themselves on having."[22] In the words of one member of Philadelphia's old guard, Sadie Mossell, "The pessimist groans that [the black community] will never regain [its former position] and points to the previous culture level of Philadelphia Negroes as if it had been permanently drowned by a torrent of migration."[23] The Old Philadelphians looked on the trains bringing black labor up from the South as if they were the carrying folks who would undo everything the Talented Tenth had worked so hard over time to build up.

The nation's extensive railroad network came to symbolize the menace of the Great Migration to some, but to others the iron tracks transported hopes and dreams. Migrants made their sojourn North by automobiles, trucks, buses, and even on ships along the Atlantic coast. Yet railroads symbolized best the passage to the Promised Land. The Illinois Central, which ran from the Deep South to Chicago and beyond, with its various feeder lines reaching into many areas of the rural South, functioned for the upper Middle West's industrial centers as the Pennsylvania and Erie did for the eastern seaboard. Employers sometimes advanced fare money or promised tickets to potential migrants. Many migrants moved along a migratory chain, boarding Chicago-bound trains only after having made incremental steps toward escape from the South. This chain, as historian James R. Grossman points out, might have involved leaving an isolated farm, moving to a plantation center, then to a small southern town, later to a southern railroad center, and finally purchasing a ticket for Chicago, Milwaukee, or another northern city.[24]

Robert Abbott's *Chicago Defender* boosted the exodus by encouraging the formation of migrant clubs and arranging for group discounts and special trains with the Illinois Central. Abbott's paper was widely read in cotton-producing regions of the Deep South. Grossman tells us that Pullman porters dropped copies along the rail lines that tapped into the great reservoir of black labor in the lower Mississippi delta. Preachers sold it to their congregations, and patrons of barbershops devoured it. Copies were passed from hand to hand until worn out, and the illiterate had the *Defender* read to them. A black leader in Louisiana told a U.S. Department of Labor investigator, "My people grab it like a mule grabs a mouthful of fine fodder."[25]

Southern blacks were anxious to know more about "the Great Northern Drive" that Abbott had announced in the *Defender*.[26] A woman wrote Abbott from New Orleans on May 2, 1917:

> Please Sir will you kindly tell me what is meant by the great Northern Drive to take place May the 15th on Tuesday. It is a rumor all over town to be ready for the 15th of May to go in the drive. the Defender first spoke of the drive the 10th of February. My husband is in the

north already preparing for our family but hearing that the excursion will be $6.00 from here north on the 15 and having a large family, I could profit by it if it is really true. Do please write me at once and say is there an excursion to leave the south. Nearly the whole of the south is getting ready for the drive or excursion as it is termed. Please write at once. We are sick to get out of the solid south.[27]

The Great Northern Drive did not materialize, but Abbott continued to promote a mass exodus by touting the advantages of the North over the South and by blowing the trumpet of race solidarity and pride.[28] A correspondent informed Emmett Scott, "White people are paying more attention to the race in order to keep them in the South, but the Chicago *Defender* has emblazoned upon their minds 'Bound for the Promised Land.'"[29]

Southerners tried to discourage blacks from going to Chicago and other northern destinations by harping on the dangers of cold winters, crowded living conditions, and stories about disillusioned migrants who had returned to the "sunny clime" of the South. For example, the *Macon Telegraph* reported on the "unspeakably vile" sanitary conditions migrants found in Detroit and editorialized: "The city is no place for the negro, especially the northern city where no provision is made for housing him and his family. They do best on farms where there is plenty of fresh air and sunshine and little temptation . . . . A negro family can live comfortably and healthily in a two-room cabin on the ground [but] they'll all die of manifold diseases in a three or four-room tenement 'apartment.'"[30] A Georgia newspaper told of migrants returning to their old homes penniless but "glad to have saved enough from their high wages to purchase the pasteboards which mean transportation back to the land of cotton, sweet potatoes, free quarters and free firewood."[31]

Trying to counteract the Promised Land image of the North, Birmingham's *Age-Herald* telegraphed the *Chicago Tribune* in May 1917 for information on the estimated 25,000–30,000 migrants who had flocked to the Midwest's "Mecca for the negro" within the previous year or so. The *Tribune* reported that while Chicago's health department was concerned about the spread of disease from the "overflow of negroes" and white property owners on the Southside were alarmed, many jobs and good wages were still to be had.[32] Had the southern press obtained copies of the *Columbus* (Ohio) *Dispatch,* it could have reprinted accounts of outbreaks of tuberculosis among newcomers and a campaign by the black clergy to preach sermons on health and cleanliness.[33] To compound the plight of the neo-phytes, hucksters preyed upon the fears of migrants struggling to cope with urban life. Some posed as preachers and sold fake insurance and col-lected fees for finding jobs that never materialized.[34]

Despite warnings about conditions in the urban North and dire predic-tions to the effect that African Americans as a "race" would not adapt to city life, the migrant stream continued. In the early phases of the Great Migration, some white southerners contented themselves with the notion that only the worst class of blacks was being lured by the labor agents to seek its salvation in the North. As the exodus assumed proportions of a mass movement, Birmingham's *Age-Herald* acknowledged, "It is not the riff-raff of the race, the worthless Negroes, who are leaving in such large numbers. There are, to be sure, many poor Negroes among them who have little more than the clothes on their backs, but others have property and good positions which they are sacrificing in order to get away at the first opportunity."[35] Many migrants—perhaps most—were refugees from the political and economic repression in the South. Pushed off the land, these desperate people fled farms for the unknown frontier of the city. But others, whom one historian calls "migrant families" as opposed to "refu-gee families," were pulled northward by hopes of better opportunities and generally came from urban areas of the South.[36]

Letters that these migrants wrote asking for information on employ-ment and assistance emphasized their education, skills, and good charac-ter. Witness the following excerpts. "I bore the reputation of a first class laundress in Selma." "I am a skilled machinist and longshoreman." "Being a poor man with a family to care for, I am not coming to live on flowry Beds of ease for I am a man who works and wish to make the best I can out of life." "I finished the course in Blacksmithing and horse-shoeing at Prairie View College this State and took special wood working at Hamp-ton Institute Hampton Va." "I was educated at Alcorn College and have been teaching a few years." "I am employed as agent for the Interstate Life, and acc'd ins. Co. but on account of the race people leaving here so very fast my present job is no longer a profitable one." "I am a Curch member for 38 years I and all of my famely but 3 children so I am not a de Sever." One man wrote from Sauk, Georgia, on behalf of himself and others eager to escape the South, "we are hard working mans no lofers neather crap shooters work is what we want."[37] The editor of the *Southwestern Christian Advocate* attempted to dispel the notion that only the "worthless" element came North by reporting on a visit he made to St. Mark's Methodist Church in Chicago one Sunday in 1919. Twenty-seven migrants joined the church during the service. Each filled out a membership card, showing, he said, "that they had some education. We have seen lawyers, doctors, merchants, mechanics, farmers, that were among the very best families that we have had in the South, who have gone to these cities in the North."[38]

Higher wages in munitions plants, railroad construction, stockyards, and factories were part of the pull of the North. Wages of $3.00, perhaps even $4.00, a day paid in a factory in the North far outweighed the 75 cents that a farmworker earned in the South. Domestic work for females ($2.50 a day) in the urban North proved more attractive than the $1.50 to $3.00 a week paid in the South.[39] George Edmund Haynes discovered that migrants to New York City were earning 50 percent to 100 percent more than they had in the South.[40] Once migrants found employment, they wrote home urging others to leave the South that was their Egypt and join them in a place where, despite the higher cost of living, one could strive for economic improvement as one of the good fruits of the Promised Land.[41]

Interpretations of the Great Migration that pit the economic pull of the North against the political and social push of the South, which migrants subsumed under the general category of racial oppression, miss the point. The lure of better wages in Chicago or some other northern industrial center was merely the obverse of the economic oppression that blacks experienced in the South. In the final analysis, "push" and "pull" factors fold into one category, and migrants, whether from rural or urban parts of the South, came with the expectation that, at the very least, they would not fare worse above the Mason-Dixon Line. R. R. Downs of the AME Church urged northern blacks to welcome the job-seeking migrants without regard to their southern backgrounds. "They are quite far from being beggars, loafers or vagabonds," he wrote. "They may, many of them, come from farms; but we cannot argue from that they are unfit and a menace. Many of them owned farms and are the children of farm owners. Perhaps one might note the crudeness of country manners, but it is not because they are vicious or immoral."[42]

The demand for labor by the North triggered the exodus, but migrants gave a host of additional specific reasons for fleeing the plantations, towns, and cities of the South. On January 1, 1917, several thousand blacks held a mass meeting and march in Atlanta to celebrate Emancipation Day and then adopted the following resolution:

> We recognize the unprecedented situation which confronts us and believe that the hand of providence is pointing the negro to a new sphere of economic, social and political activity, and while we love our native soil and the scenes of our childhood, many things have conspired to cause our people to join others who have gone because their friends and relatives had left, but by far the larger number have gone obedient to the lash of hunger and necessity. Our wives and children are crying for bread. Those who once answered the cry, because of havoc wrought by the boll weevil and by floods, are no longer able to aid us, so when bread is offered the starving negro by the labor agent, it is but natural that he should accept that bread. Better schools are offered our children; and a larger percentage of personal liberty is offered through the more liberal franchise existing in those sections to which our people go. Patrick Henry's craving for liberty finds a hearty response in the breast of the negro. We want more rights accorded us as human beings and better protection for our children.[43]

The labor shortage in the industrial North may have been the immediate stimulus of the Great Migration, but here was evidence of something more fundamental. As Fred Moore, editor of the *New York Age,* told a mass meeting held at the Abyssinian Baptist Church in New York City in 1917: southern blacks wanted a "square deal." "The only people," Moore argued, "who can stop this emigration are the white people in the South, and they can stop it in one way; by putting an end to lynching and injustice to our race."[44]

James Weldon Johnson, acting secretary of the NAACP, investigated conditions in the South in 1917 and concluded that "constant oppression and discrimination" more than low wages caused the migrants to respond to the "economic call northward." He noted, as did other observers, that some families were so eager to flee that they left domestic animals behind unsold and roaming about. In contrast to the first phase of the Great Migration, when the Pennsylvania Railroad sent agents to gather up black labor and "the shiftless, indolent class, eager for a free trip North, responded" with only two day's notice, now "the better class of negro was moving northward, including highly skilled artisans." Johnson felt that nothing since the adoption of the Fourteenth and Fifteenth Amendments rivaled the exodus in importance for African Americans. He appealed to President Woodrow Wilson to utter even "one stray word" on behalf of the victims of violence.[45]

Johnson was to be disappointed, for Wilson studiously avoided any public action to reduce the mounting antiblack hysteria that manifested itself in numerous lynchings during and immediately after the Great Migration. Critics accused the Wilson administration of fostering an atmosphere in which the Dyer Anti-Lynching Bill failed and racial segregation became further entrenched within the federal bureaucracy.[46] Protestant churches, including those of some white denominations in the South, became more vocal in their opposition to lynching and calls for federal action.[47] On March 13, 1918, a delegation from the bishops' council of the AME Church, led by Bishop William D. Chappelle, met President Wilson face-to-face at the White House. Chappelle immediately made known the purpose of their mission—to protest lynchings, mob violence, Jim Crow laws, and discrimination of all kinds directed at African Americans.[48]

The white South was quick to blame the exodus on a variety of pseudo-causes. Blacks were said to have a natural propensity to move about. The ineffectiveness of prohibition laws in the North, one author argued, enticed black lovers of alcohol. The Republican Party was blamed for promoting the exodus in the hope that black voters would increase its political clout. Labor agents frequently were targeted for censure, civil penalties, and bodily injury for being instigators of the migration. Fearing the loss of their labor supply, white planters used threats and intimidation to keep blacks from leaving the land. Labor recruiters from the North were arrested and prosecuted.[49] Realizing that such measures were counterproductive, white progressives called for a reexamination of the white South's treatment of African Americans. Faculty from eleven schools formed the University Commission on Southern Race Questions and issued an open letter in 1917 calling for more equitable treatment as the only way to compete with the economic lure of northern industry.[50]

Because African Americans had a long list of grievances, some leaders boldly and publicly argued that only the most fundamental changes could stem the exodus. In 1917 H. R. Butler, a black clergyman in Atlanta, wrote an open letter to J. J. Brown, Georgia's commissioner of agriculture. Butler was incensed with the commissioner's suggestion that the way to stop the exodus was to pass stiffer laws against labor agents and conscript black

labor to save cotton and corn. Butler introduced Brown to the real labor
agents that were driving African Americans out of Georgia:

> First, mob violence and the lynchers; second, injustice in the courts;
> third, paying first-class railroad fare for fourth-class service; fourth,
> insults to their women and themselves on railroads and street cars;
> fifth, insults in public places, elevators and on the streets; sixth, the
> right to vote and bear arms in defense of their state denied; seventh,
> poor pay for their labor on the farms and public works, while con-
> victs are often used to do the work free labor should be doing; eighth,
> poor schools for their children; ninth, no agricultural schools for their
> children, while they are taxed to pay for such schools for the children
> of their white friends; tenth, taxation without representation in the
> management of the government; eleventh, no representation on the
> juries; twelfth, in some cities and towns, no parks, play grounds or
> swimming pool for their children, yet they are taxed to provide such
> for the children of their white friends; thirteenth, segregation into the
> sickly parts of the cities where the streets are poorly kept and often ne-
> glected; fourteenth, poor encouragement for their efforts to do right;
> fifteenth, the white church and its Christianity in the state, so far as
> I have been able to learn, except in a few cases of a sporadic nature
> in the Southern Methodist, Southern Presbyterian and the Episcopal
> churches, is silent and passive on these wrongs.[51]

Butler felt that his list, while not exhaustive, was sufficient warrant for
the hegira from the South. A similar litany of discontent could be heard
throughout the black South. Viewing the crisis from the North, W. E. B.
Du Bois attributed the exodus to the hegemony of white racism. "No
modern white laborer," Du Bois argued, "would for a moment submit to
the labor conditions under which the mass of Negroes work if he could
escape."[52]

Unsettled conditions in southern agriculture seemed to conspire with
the hostile social environment to increase the lure of the Promised Land.
Though the price of cotton was high in 1916, those without a crop could
not benefit from an improved market. Black tenants were leaving the plantations looking for food because white landlords had commandeered their
potatoes, peanuts, hogs, and chickens in lieu of cash rent. Many black
farmers had been unable to pay their landlords because of the ravages of
the boll weevil and extensive flooding, especially in the Mississippi delta

during the winter of 1916.[53] Also adversely affecting tenant farmers was the decision of some white planters to offset the effects of the cotton boll weevil by diversifying their crops.

A small minority of landlords began to the shift toward mechanized production, thereby displacing more blacks. But the tractor and the mechanical cotton harvester made few inroads into the traditional southern cotton-producing areas. Black labor remained essential to southern agriculture.[54] "We must do something to hold the labor and we must do it quick," the *Montgomery Advertiser* urged in September 1916. The paper prodded landowners to give black tenants the free use of land and seed and supplies to carry them through the season.[55] Littell McClung suggested that planters help "boll weevil tenants" raise what they needed to eat, that farmers in eastern states do their own work "just as the folks do out in Illinois and Iowa," and that Cotton Belt landowners diversify.[56]

These proposals had little effect. White planters resorted to threats and intimidation to keep black labor in place, and they asked for laws to prohibit the activity of labor agents. The African American poet James Weldon Johnson, who moved from Florida to New York, caught the irony of these actions. In 1916 he wrote that the white South had long viewed blacks as "a general nuisance, a handicap, a blot, a curse"—"a burden that it would be only too glad to get rid of at the first opportunity," but "now comes a time when large numbers of colored people propose voluntarily and without expense to their white neighbors to leave, and what is the result? Why, the powers of city, county and state are invoked to prevent them from doing so.[57] The *Georgia Baptist,* an African American church paper, said, "We have been hearing, all of our life, that the Negro was an incubus to the South, a rope around the South's neck, industrially speaking, which the South could not too quickly get rid of, but, no sooner than Negroes, by the thousands, exercising their God-given right of selecting where they shall live and work, make efforts to go to other sections of our country, then—unlawful measures, even, are resorted to, to check their going."[58] The Rev. William De Berry also asked, "Why all this furor of protest, and legislation and pleading with the Negro to remain in the South? Why not let him go and have done with the peril and incubus?"[59] Du Bois mocked those who sought an explanation of the exodus in natural causes and not social injustice: "It seems we have misunderstood Mr. Weevil. We thought him a mere bug, but pshaw! he is the man who put the 'grate' in 'mi-grate', that caused all these hundreds of thousands of Negroes to hurry North in the last few years. We had been mistakenly informed that lynching, poor schools, petty insult, industrial oppression, 'Jim Crow' cars and other little matters of opinion and argument were the cause of our black friends' leaving the South."[60]

The African American educator Jesse O. Thomas distinguished between types of migrants. The "straight migrant" was the individual who went directly from a plantation area or rural community to an urban center outside the South. A "really migrant" was a person who spent some time in one of the larger cities of the South before making the final trip to the Promised Land. Thomas expanded the category of "migrant" to include the many southern blacks who were going from place to place in the South but who never left the region.[61] While our interest is primarily in African Americans who emigrated from the South, Thomas's observations suggest that to be moving and searching for something better, whatever the ultimate destination, was part of the "exodus fever" stimulated by oppressive conditions in the South and strengthened by the call for labor in the North.

Some whites were sufficiently concerned about the economic impact of the Great Migration to entertain proposals for relief. William Jay Schieffelin found this to be the case when he investigated conditions in North Carolina and Virginia in June 1917. The white press contained articles pleading for better treatment of blacks and emphasizing "how really dependent the white people are upon the negro in almost every way." The "race question," Schieffelin reported, had become a matter of wide discussion, and white students in southern universities and colleges were studying ways to improve the education, sanitation, and health of African Americans. Progressive white southerners and educators, such as Willis D. Weatherford, were being heard with renewed interest when they argued that the South's greatest economic need was "an intelligent and able-bodied laboring class." Schieffelin thought that public opinion was favorable to the proposition that while most southern blacks should be taught agriculture and trade pursuits, the training of black ministers, doctors, and teachers was also necessary. "Schools such as Fisk and Atlanta University," he reported, "are now receiving the approval of Southern white men which hitherto was accorded only to Tuskegee and Hampton." Schieffelin predicted that the exodus would prove beneficial to those blacks who remained in the South by fostering interracial understanding, better treatment, and the improvement of schools and living conditions.[62]

Black educators of the Tuskegee and Hampton traditions echoed a similar theme in an attempt to slow down the exodus. Participants in the twenty-sixth annual Tuskegee Negro Conference in January 1917 urged blacks to stay on the farm, diversify, combat the boll weevil, and seek the assistance of sympathetic whites in dealing with the unrest caused by inadequate legal protection. "Right here in the South," the conference declared, "are great and permanent opportunities for the masses of our people. This section, we feel, is just entering upon its greatest era of development. Here your labor in the future is going to be in still greater demand."[63] Nearly 2,500 farmers gathered for a conference at Utica, Mississippi, in January 1918 and heard speeches from a variety of Washington's supporters, including George Washington Carver, director of agricultural research at Tuskegee. The conference adopted a statement that urged blacks to buy land, pay for it, and build houses in order to "gradually intrench themselves in the respect and homage of the people of their community."[64]

In the summer of 1918 the Rev. Richard D. Stinson, principal of the Atlanta Normal and Industrial Institute, traveled for seven weeks in the industrial North to investigate how black migrants there were faring. He returned more convinced than ever "that the South is fitted for the present and future home of my people" and called on the white South to open its public and private coffers to revitalize industrial education. He admitted, however, that "many of the ministers and leaders of the race are preparing to go to other sections of the country where large numbers of our people are going weekly."[65] At a camp meeting in Arlington, Georgia, in September 1917 Stinson expressed dismay that migrants had sold their farms, horses, buggies, livestock, and household furniture "for a trifle" to start over again in an alien region, and he called for whites to support industrial education for the masses as the solution. "Let the two races treat each other right," Stinson argued, "and there is plenty of room, wealth, and happiness for the white man and the negro in this section."[66]

E. W. Cooke, superintendent of the Snow Hill Normal and Industrial Institute in Alabama, echoed Stinson's sentiments. While admitting that there were "dark spots about in the Southland," he was against a wholesale exodus. Cooke avowed: "Some of us know about the mule and forty acres of land, we did not get. As for my part, I am willing to say as one of old: Where the white Southern people go I will go; where they lodge, I will lodge; their people are our people and their God our God. This is the day for us to choose whom we will serve. As for me and my house, we will serve the South. Not that I love the North less, but I love the South more." Cooke ridiculed Du Bois "and others of his type, who have such an abundance of hot air"[67] for advising blacks to flee the South. Of those who wrote or came to him asking for advice, Cooke said at another point, "We have in nearly every case made them see that they should 'Cast down their buckets where they are.'"[68] Cooke's use of Booker T. Washington's well-known imperative is further evidence that antimigration sentiment was especially strong among those black educators whom critics called cogs in the Tuskegee Machine.[69]

The *Crisis*, of which Du Bois was editor, was not lax in countering Washington's disciples. "It has long been the custom of colored leaders," the October 1916 issue stated, "to advise the colored people to stay in the South. This has been supplemented by the startling information on the part of Southern whites that they are the 'best friends of the colored people', etc." The *Crisis* argued that the exodus was "the only effective protest that the Negroes *en masse* can make against lynching and disfranchisement."[70] In March 1917 the journal took issue with the intent of the Tuskegee resolutions that were recently issued. "With the subject matter of the various resolutions we have no quarrel. In few cases do we dissent from the statements, taken by themselves; but we do solemnly believe that any system of Negro leadership that today devotes ten times as much space to the advantages of living in the South as it gives to lynching and lawlessness is inexcusably blind."[71] G. Douglas Johnson published a poem in the magazine that aptly described the debate between advocates of remaining in the South and proponents of the Great Migration who saw it as fundamentally a flight from persecution. To the query, "OH, black man, why do you northward roam and leave all the farmlands bare?," Johnson responded, "I have toiled in your cornfields and parched in the sun. I have bowed beneath your load of care."[72]

When Robert R. Moton, Washington's successor as principal of Tuskegee Institute, visited African American troops stationed in France during the war, he urged them to return to the South when peace came, buy land, and resume farming.[73] Moton's efforts to dampen the exodus fever did not sit well with the pro-migration camp. According to an editorial in the *Amsterdam News,* Moton betrayed African Americans by advising migrants to return to the South. "Have Major Moton's Southern backers in the crazy claim of race leadership so few black peons about that the worthy Major would have us all return across the Red Sea of the Dixon-Mason line into the land of Egypt to help fill the Jim-crow cars and work the convict farms?," asked the *News* incredulously. Moton had spoken of conditions in New York City where migrants were said to be huddled together in quarters like pigs, subject to colds, consumption, and death. "Is not the Major a bit muddled in his geography?," the *News* asked. "Is it really of New York City or of the ill-paved, poorly-lighted, badly-ventilated, segregated districts of the Southern cities, where even sewage connection is sometimes denied, that he speaks?" "Personally, we WOULD like to return to the South—at the head of an army."[74]

Thus the debate raged along lines delineated before World War I, though intensified by the exodus of so many in so short a time. In January 1923 the Urban League held a National Conference on Negro Migration at the Russell Sage Foundation in New York City. The *AME Church Review* thought the meeting especially timely because of reports from bishops of the three major black Methodist connections as well as from leaders of other churches that large numbers of their constituents were once again leaving the rural districts of the South and heading northward.[75] Having been caught off guard by the wartime migration, church officials hoped to obtain consensus on how best to cope with another outflow from the South. White and black leaders as well as representatives of northern employers who used migrant labor attended the conference.

The program included Frederic Howe, U.S. commissioner of immigration at Ellis Island; Oswald Garrison Villard, publisher of the *New York Evening Post* and grandson of the abolitionist William Lloyd Garrison; Hollis B. Frissell, principal of Hampton Institute and ardent champion of a practical, industrial education for blacks; Eugene Kinckle Jones, executive secretary of the Urban League; George Edmund Haynes, professor of social science at Fisk University, the League's executive secretary; E. J. Triary, Jr., employment manager of the Erie Railroad; and Richard R. Wright, Jr., editor of the AME's *Christian Recorder*. The conference concluded with a set of resolutions directed at the North as well as the South. Participants acknowledged that the unprecedented exodus of blacks since the spring of 1916 was caused by unusual industrial opportunities in the North and the fear of personal violence in the South. Conference resolutions called for improving the health, education, and economic conditions of southern blacks and for the orderly administration of justice. Northerners were urged to assist black migrants by providing them with information on the many services offered by both public and private agencies as well as counseling them on how to dress and act in the northern urban environment.[76]

The Urban League resolutions did not go far enough for Butler R. Wilson of the Boston branch of the NAACP. He wished to have the following amendment incorporated: "That Negroes be encouraged to leave the South until the South shall accord them their political rights; shall enforce the law; protect them against mob violence; open to them school advantages and protect their women and children against intolerable persecution."[77] Conservatives managed to defeat the amendment 46 to 34. The original set of resolutions, proposed by Jones and moved by Kelly Miller of Howard University, then passed.[78] Nevertheless, pro-migration activists in the North continued to call for a mass exodus from the South.

The Southern Sociological Congress met in Blue Ridge and Asheville, North Carolina, from July 30 to August 3, 1917. Like the earlier Urban League meeting, the congress was composed of a wide variety of black and white leaders. Program participants included Bishop G. W. Clinton of the AME Zion Church; Willis D. Weatherford, international student secretary of the YMCA; George Edmund Haynes; Worth M. Tippy, secretary of the Commission on the Church and Social Service of the Federal Council of Churches of Christ in America; the Rev. Richard Carroll, a black clergyman from Columbia, South Carolina; and the Rev. Henry Hugh Proctor of Atlanta. Judge Gilbert Stephenson of Winston-Salem, North Carolina, attempted to minimize the significance of the migration by attributing it to "unskilled, unmarried, unreliable young fellows." "Many of these young bucks," Stephenson claimed, "already have criminal records and, going North, add to their bad reputations. They are the ones who cause riots." Haynes and Proctor rose in response. Haynes noted that the exodus was greatest in areas where poor economic conditions were combined with the greatest amount of race friction. Proctor stated that blacks were "restless" because of the "double standard not only of conduct and character, one code for white and one for black, but also of wages; while unfortunately, expenses have increased on a single standard, that of the white man." Proctor drove home his message to the conference with the following statement: "This is the most unique movement in history. The colored race, known as the race which is led, has broken away from its leaders."[79]

Du Bois understood perhaps more clearly than most of his contemporaries that the Great Migration, while a domestic American event, had implications for the historic struggle of people of African descent wherever the diaspora had carried them. Of the U.S. entry into World War I and the demographic and social changes that followed, Du Bois wrote, "This war is an End, and, also, a Beginning. Never again will darker people of the world occupy just the place they have before."[80] African Americans by leaving the South validated the fight against colonial oppression wherever it existed. The Great Migration was a revolutionary event, a harbinger of the demise of colonialism that would gain momentum as the twentieth century progressed.

The first serious study of the causes and consequences of the Great Migration appeared in 1919. Published by the U.S. Department of Labor under its Division of Negro Economics, *Negro Migration in 1916–17* set the tone for most of the studies of the exodus that followed.[81] James H. Dillard supervised the government study. After reviewing the various causes said to be stimulating the Great Migration, such as poor treatment in the South and threats to the region's cotton crop, Dillard summed up the push-pull model: "However the influence came, and whatever concurrent causes may have operated all will agree . . . that 'better wages offered by the North have been the immediate occasion for the exodus'."[82] A close reading of *Negro Migration in 1916–17,* however, suggests a theme in need of more elaboration. W. T. B. Williams, the only black member of the government-sponsored research team and a graduate of Hampton Institute and Harvard University, was sent to Florida to investigate causes of the exodus in its early stages. Migrants did cite better wages as an important reason for leaving their native region. But Williams heard something else. A woman in Florida told him, "Negroes are not so greatly disturbed about wages. They are tired of being treated as children; they want to be men."[83] This woman's insight suggests that the Great Migration was more than a response to the pull of industrial opportunity in the North. It was most fundamentally a mass movement in rebellion against conditions in the South, a revolution against oppression, which many participants and observers saw as a divinely inspired "Second Emancipation."

The transformation of African American life that began after the Civil War and the end of slavery has been the subject of many historical studies, each of which concludes that the promises made to the newly emancipated turned sour as Reconstruction ended and the South descended into a maelstrom of economic and racial oppression. The Great Migration signaled a dawn of new opportunity. From the perspective of the urban crisis of the closing decade of the twentieth century it is difficult to appreciate the enthusiasm that African Americans expressed for the North once the Great Migration began. Though discouraged by the collapse of the postwar boom of 1920–21, black southerners continued "Going to the Promised Land" in significant numbers until the Great Depression. It was a time of hope, of new beginnings, of greater opportunity. By giving the northward migration this cultural dynamic, African Americans framed it as more than a response to work opportunities.

The post-World War II migration exceeded the core Great Migration in number of participants, but it had a different dynamic. "Framed by persisting racial oppression and lagging Southern economic development," historian Peter Gottlieb writes, "the 1945–70 period of black migration was hardly a buoyant redistribution of population around new frontiers of economic opportunity. . . . Black out-migration from the region became a recourse, rather than a strategy, for individual and group betterment — almost a movement of resignation and despair."[84] By way of contrast, the exodus from the South during the Great Migration years was tantamount to a religious pilgrimage out of the Wilderness into the Promised Land.

3

THE

SECOND

EXODUS

In early 1917 the Rev. C. M. Tanner of Allen Temple AME Church in Atlanta was busy gathering evidence for a book he proposed calling "The Second Exodus." During a tour of the farming sections of southwest Georgia, Tanner found large plantations, formerly using from fifty to seventy-five plows, without a single black hand. "In some instances our people," Tanner reported, "have simply locked the doors of their homes and gone to the train, leaving household furniture, cooking utensils and their other possessions." Though he disclaimed the prophetic mantle because he thought "the facts in the case are so patent that the hazy vision of the prophet need not be attempted," Tanner predicted that by midsummer a million more African Americans would join the more than 400,000 that he estimated had left the South since the autumn of 1916. "I, for one," Tanner asserted, "cannot believe that it is other than one of God's ways to solve the vexed problem of race adjustment."

Like many of his contemporaries, Tanner saw the hand of God in the unfolding drama. He wrote, "The scripture is being fulfilled every day in our very sight, and it is certainly the intention of divine providence to make our people in this movement profit by it. . . ." Alternative interpretations were freighted with despair. Unless ultimate meaning could be found in the Great Migration, Tanner feared that his people would become "the sport of the gods and the pawn of fate."[1]

Tanner's attempt to invest the Great Migration with transhistorical meaning points to the religious dimension of the exodus. Participants framed it as more than a temporal response to economic and social forces; it was viewed as a religious event—another chapter in the ongoing salvation history of African Americans, rich in symbolic and metaphorical content. Tanner was not alone in seeking to probe the deeper meaning of the hegira from the South. In a declaration issued to "colored ministers North, South and West" the AME Ministers' Alliance of Birmingham stated: "We feel and believe that this great exodus is God's plan and hand. The great door of industrial, financial, political, educational, moral and religious hope has been thrown wide, and in a mysterious way, God is moving upon the hearts of our people to go where He has prepared for them."[2] On what it called "the all-absorbing question," the *Georgia Baptist* commented in December 1916, "We repeat what we said before—we believe that God's hand is in all of this."[3] The paper urged blacks to leave sections where they were badly treated and join the march to the Promised Land. The northern press reinforced the impression that something momentous and mysterious was under way. Announcing the formation of the citywide Negro Migration Committee, the *Philadelphia Record* stated, "The whole populations of many colored Southern towns and villages, men, women and children, with their pastors, barbers and storekeepers, are pouring into the city . . . ."[4]

Southerners saw the migrant flood at its source, getting the impression that everything was in motion. But whites read the exodus differently from blacks. Given the prevailing ideology of white supremacy and black servitude, this difference is no surprise. White southern Methodists, Hunter Dickinson Farish writes, believed that African Americans were in the South "by the providence of God" for "some wise and gracious purpose" and that the exodus of blacks ran counter to God's plan.[5] Some whites active in missionary and educational work among blacks in the South were surprised but not altogether mystified by the migrants' sudden departure. They heard the voice of black discontent cry out in sources such as the *Southwestern Christian Advocate,* which was published in New Orleans on behalf of black Methodism. The *Advocate* found that the treatment which blacks endured was sufficient warrant for the exodus. An editorial, published on September 7, 1916, read: "We are disfranchised, we are hedged about and we are lynched without redress. Even a worm sometimes will recoil and a half dead hound will resent constant mistreatment . . . . If our Southern friends are anxious to prevent this immigration to the North, they have the remedy in their own hands. It will not be by coercion or threats, or arrests, it will be because the South recognizes the Negro as a human being with all the rights and privileges of a human being."[6]

Alarmed by the loss of the mainstay of their economic well-being and fearing that the northward migration would become a mass exodus, some whites in the South awoke to the economic importance of African Americans to the region, and, like Pharaoh of old, they sought to hold on to their labor. The *Macon Telegraph* bleated, "He [the black Southerner] has been with us so long that our whole industrial, commercial and agricultural structure has been built on a black foundation. It is the only labor we have; it is the best we possibly could have—if we lose it, we bankrupt!"[7] Whites, complaining of the loss of hands that picked cotton, did what they could to counteract the migration fever. The *Atlanta Constitution* attempted to slow the exodus by featuring accounts of the penalties of migration, notably the high incidence of death and disease caused by the supposedly rigorous climate of places like Newark, New Jersey.[8] Such accounts did not discourage black southerners who believed that their sojourn out of the land of oppression was divinely ordained. Trains running from the Mississippi delta to Chicago carried the chalked message, "Bound for the Promised Land," and thousands were caught up in flight from persecution.

Strong appeals were made to potential migrants by pro-exodus forces in the North. Northern black churches touted the milk and honey of the Promised Land and helped in the recruitment of southern workers. For example, Mother Bethel AME Church of Philadelphia sent flyers below the Mason-Dixon Line to help combat pessimists who were harping on the cold weather and other problems in northern cities encountered by migrants. The flyer told of higher wages, better schools, the right to vote, and justice administered according to the law as advantages of the North. True, Philadelphia had tents of wickedness; Satan's forces, the flyer acknowledged, were well-organized, but the migrants would have a "haven of safety" if they made Mother Bethel their church.[9]

Exodus enthusiasts like those in Mother Bethel capitalized on the long tradition among blacks in the South of viewing the North as the Land of Hope. In his study of the Great Migration Emmett J. Scott observed that the oppressed dreamed of the North as the Promised Land, the Ark of Safety, the House of Refuge.[10] Frederick Douglass said of the spiritual

"O Canaan" that it carried a double meaning: Canaan was Heaven where the children of God would finally be at peace, but it was also the North where the sound of the slave driver's whip was not heard. Harriet Tubman was called the Moses of her people because she led them out of slavery into the Promised Land. Drawing on this collective memory forged in the struggle against slavery, migrants placed an interpretation on the exodus that went far beyond economic explanations.

The search for a deeper meaning to the outflow of thousands from the South touched everyone. Some interpretations drew on earlier flights to freedom when the South's "peculiar institution" still had the force of law. Noting that Detroit's black population had increased from 5,500 in 1914 to more than 30,000 in 1918, W. J. Black observed, "No longer fugitives from slavery, coming north over the 'underground railroad' on which Detroit was a station, these new workers for the industrial north are eagerly imported by those who deal in labor as a commodity."[11] Black was correct in stressing the importance of work, but his words also point to the more fundamental hope of liberation felt so deeply by the migrants. By joining in the march to the Promised Land, the migrants were participating in the latest, perhaps the final, scene in the divinely inspired drama of black salvation.

In this context it is easy to understand why contemporary authors looked back to the Civil War and Emancipation as the new migration's primary historical parallel. Richard Wright, Jr., told the readership of the *Christian Recorder,* "If his [the migrant's] movement brings the South to appreciate the Negro as a labor asset, it will be quite as much an emancipation as that proclaimed by Abraham Lincoln January 1, 1863."[12] The *Negro Year Book* for 1918–19, compiled by Monroe N. Work, echoed this sentiment: "No event since Emancipation of the Negroes from slavery so profoundly influenced the economic and social life of the Negro. It may be said that whereas the Thirteenth Amendment granted physical emancipation, the conditions brought about by World War I made for the economic emancipation of the Negro, in that he found for the first time, opportunity to go practically anywhere in the United States and find employment along a great many lines, many of which had hitherto [been] closed entirely to him."[13]

The widespread view of the Great Migration as a providential event put additional pressure on potential participants. Who dared show fear or hang back if God's hand was directing the course of history? The transition from oppression to greater freedom was understandably dramatic. An informant for the *Chicago Whip* compared the crossing of the Ohio River to the entry of the Israelites into the biblical Land of Canaan. He told of the elderly man who got as far as Cincinnati and then took a train but became confused about which car he should ride in. A redcap went to great lengths to convince the old man that north of the Ohio River he was in the Promised Land; there were no Jim Crow cars.[14] One of the most symbolically powerful examples of investing the Great Migration with religious significance also took place along the Ohio. When a group of 147 migrants reached the river that once marked the threshold of freedom for fugitive slaves, they knelt and prayed. The men stopped their watches, and old spirituals were sung. "I done come out of the Land of Egypt with the good news" brought tears of joy. On reaching "Beulah Land," one woman was so overcome with emotion that she felt a physical lightness to the air, a quality unknown in the land of bondage.[15] This "lightness" of spirit was replicated in the rhetoric of northern cheerleaders for the exodus.

Northern black leaders also showed symptoms of having "exodus fever." Struck by the ultimate significance of it all, Richard Wright, Jr., believed that the liberation from oppression in the South promised much for black residents in the North as well. "If a million Negroes come here," he wrote in 1917, "we will have more Negro business, better churches, more professional men and real political power, and the Negro in the North will begin to get a social position not based upon mere charity."[16] High hopes. Compounded by the desperation of those who wanted to come to the Promised Land, expectations of a new day rose to unprecedented levels.

The Great Migration was particularly subject to providential interpretation because of its suddenness and size. It possessed a mysterious quality. Many wondered, "Why should such vast numbers of Southern blacks decide to leave at the same time?" Having no accurate counting of the magnitude of the exodus, and hearing stories from many southern places of people precipitously departing, people had a natural tendency to view the movement as part of a divine plan, a window of opportunity never to be opened again. The *Chicago Defender* shouted:

THE BARS ARE BEING LET DOWN in the industrial world as never before in the history of this country. The fact that the white man is not seeking our services because of his interest in us matters little at this particular juncture. What most concerns the thinking people among

us is will the great mass of toilers take advantage of this golden opportunity? Will they appreciate the fact that they are on trial, and give
the very best service possible that they may make good, so good that
when the war is over and foreigners again invade our country they
will find little for them to do?[17]

Black southerners were told by exodus enthusiasts in the North that this
was no time to wait. Freedom's train was on the roll.

The temptation to join others who were participating in the divine
drama was strong. Since this movement was God's doing, so the argument
went, all should climb aboard freedom's train. Migrants were said to be
leaving in "droves" and "by the thousands." One poem, published in the
Chicago Defender, captured the urgency of the exodus:

THEY'RE LEAVING MEMPHIS IN DROVES
Some are coming on the passenger,
Some are coming on the freight,
Others will be found walking,
For none have time to wait.[18]

This poem was widely distributed in the South, much to the consternation of white authorities. Several black youths were arrested and sent to a
prison farm in Georgia for possessing a copy.[19]

Investigators from the North, including researchers sent down by the
federal government, observed the exodus fever in many parts of the South.
Reports distributed in the North contributed to the notion that something
momentous and mysterious was happening. One researcher went to a railroad station to see a friend who was leaving and found a chaotic scene.
People were milling about "like bees in a hive," and officers were going up
and down the tracks trying to keep them back. The investigator reported:
"One old lady and man had gotten on the train. They were patting their
feet and singing and a man standing nearby asked, 'Uncle, where are you
going?' The old man replied, 'Well, son, I'm gwine to the promised land.'[20]
Others when asked where they were bound simply replied, "Going north."
Monroe Work and Charles S. Johnson said that the migrants they interviewed did not question "the whys or wherefores." They simply went, "led
as if, by some mysterious unseen hand which was compelling them on."[21]
A correspondent for the *New York Evening Post* was told by a Georgia informant that the exodus from those districts of the South where the plague

of lynching was the worst was " 'like nothing known on the earth since the Children of Israel came out of Egypt.' " [22] W. T. B. Williams, an investigator for the U. S. Department of Labor, discovered that great crowds were leaving Alabama without any security for the future except the confidence that God had opened a way for them. "Moving out is an expression of their faith," he concluded.[23]

Songs and poems current in the years of the Great Migration drew on biblical imagery and employed religious metaphors. W. E. Dancer, a graduate of Tuskegee Institute, wrote the poem "Farewell! We're Good An' Gone" in which he said of those whom he called Hagar's chaps: "It's true we love de South all right, But, yes we love God too; An' when he comes ter help us out, What's left fer us ter do?" [24] The belief in a haven in the North was so strong that reservations about what migrants might find there were overcome by anticipation of deliverance from the South's oppression. One poem, "Northboun'," celebrating the exodus, captures the spirit of the migrants:

> Huh! de wurl' ain't flat
> An' de wurl' ain't roun'
> Jes' one long strip
> Hangin' up an' down
> Since Norf is up,
> An' Souf is down,
> An' Hebben is up,
> I'm upward boun'.[25]

George Edmund Haynes told those attending the National Conference on Social Work in 1917, "We are sometimes told that this migration is due to some racial tendency; to a roving disposition; to instability of race character. But as one of our folk songs expresses it, the Negro is inching along like the poor inch worm, hoping that Jesus will come with freedom and opportunity bye and by somehow, somewhere." [26]

Just as Pharaoh's army pursued the escaping Israelites, southern authorities attempted to stop the Second Exodus. Police arrested potential migrants as they attempted to board trains, and at several places in the South wholesale roundups were made.[27] According to one pastor who was afraid to have his name published, many of the desperate had to steal away at night when their plans of going North became known.[28] A minister of the Methodist Episcopal Church in Newborn, Alabama, wrote that more than a thousand men and women had left his area for the North and West because of oppressive economic conditions. He professed to be on the verge of starvation himself but admitted, "As leaders we are powerless for we dare not to resent such or even show disapproval."[29] Subject to harassment and arrest, perhaps even physical violence, many ministers kept their pro-migration views to themselves or gave advice to those thinking of leaving in ways not subject to scrutiny by the authorities.

Bolder voices demanded that southern whites recognize the signs of the times and take immediate steps to rectify the conditions that motivated the migrants to flee oppression. W. H. Randolph of Lynchburg, Virginia, wrote a lengthy letter to the editor of the *Richmond Planet* in which he argued that the South would, like ancient Rome, become one of "the depraved and fallen nations of the earth" unless whites changed their ways. He forewarned, "Mankind may plan, but God directs the issue." Randolph predicted "awful, inevitable consequences" because "God will not let His justice sleep forever" and would deliver the oppressed, just as the ancient Jews were freed from Egyptian bondage.[30] In search of a deeper meaning to the movement of thousands out of the South, participants and commentators turned time and again to the biblical precedent of the Jews escaping from bondage.

The appearance of the boll weevil on the eve of the Great Migration caused much comment and also received theological interpretation. Like the plagues sent to soften the heart of the Egyptian pharaoh, the boll weevil infestations were seen as supernatural visitations. Preachers, Thomas T. Woofter wrote, "warned their congregations not to fight the pest because it was sent by God and therefore had some sort of divine status."[31] God was punishing the white South and liberating the oppressed. Rumors spread that a great calamity was soon to befall the South. Boll weevil infestations and widespread flooding were only harbingers of worse to come.[32] These natural disasters were likened to the plagues that befell the biblical land of Egypt when Pharaoh Ramses refused to let the Israelites leave. During the height of the boll weevil infestation in the early 1920s, a black worker on a southern road project was overheard singing, "Boll weevil here, boll weevil there, boll weevil everywhere; Oh, Lordy, ain't I glad!" The white auditor reported "a note of genuine gladness, almost of exultation in the voice singing it, like the note one hears between lines in the Old Testament songs of Jews triumphing over the downfall of their enemies. It seemed a song of emancipation."[33]

In this climate of uncertainty and feverous expectation, community meetings were organized on the premise that the "best class" of white and black citizens should get together to "settle" the question. This view was held by the Rev. H. D. Canaday, presiding elder of the Atlanta district of the AME Church, who spoke at Bethel church in Atlanta in November 1916 and called for a new spirit of cooperation between blacks and whites. B. R. Holmes, of the Holmes Institute in Atlanta, whom the *Atlanta Constitution* hailed as "one of the leading negro educators of the south," believed that the exodus was "endangering the prosperity of the south."[34] He too urged emergency meetings to discuss cooperative action.

One such meeting was held at the courthouse in Thomasville, Georgia, on June 10, 1917. The audience heard speeches by white leaders (the mayor, a judge, and a local clergyman) and from several black clergy and teachers. According to the *Macon Telegraph*, "The whole sentiment of the meeting was amicable, the negroes [many of whom had come in from the surrounding rural areas] applauding enthusiastically the speeches of the white men and the advice given by them. Resolutions were drawn by a committee expressing the desire that the people of the two races continue to live together as they have done in the past and that steps be taken to adjust any differences between them, etc."[35] Schools associated with the philosophy of Booker T. Washington were frequently used as sites for meetings to devise ways in which the "best class" of southern blacks and whites could stop the exodus. These meetings raised questions about the wisdom of going North and muted the Macedonian call of those who saw the exodus as divinely inspired. The more skeptical raised questions.

What if the Promised Land turned out to be a chimera? This question concerned the Scotland County Farmers' Tri-Annual Conference, which convened at Laurinburg, North Carolina, on February 2, 1917. Farmers, preachers, and teachers heard A. L. Mebane of the Agricultural and Technical College at Greensboro speak on the migration question. Mebane argued that many of those who had left were of the "floating class," while those of his people who had remained were "of the higher type." This contrast would give northern employers a false impression "of the real worth and high standing of our people." Mebane predicted that when the war ended, European paupers would again flood the country, driving African Americans out of work. "If this should be the case," he warned, "their seeming prosperity would be like Jonah's gourd vine which grew up in one night, only to be cut down by a worm before the morning sun had risen."[36] After Mebane's speech, conferees discussed ways to keep the more efficient black farmers from following their weaker brethren. The crop lien evil received special censure as one of the contributing causes of black dissatisfaction. The Rev. Richard H. Bowling of the First Baptist Church, Norfolk, argued that whatever problems migrants might encounter in the North, the exchange of place would be far better than "constant reminders of 'race, color, or previous condition of servitude'—the jim-crow car, the jim-crow seat, and all the rest of the jim-crow legal code" were in the South. "The foreign Jew," Bowling maintained, "finds here [in the United States, especially in New York] an Eastside and a Ghetto, but he finds in addition freedom from fear of the ever recurring pogrom and a lesser degree of religious intolerance and racial prejudice. It is exactly the same with the South-leaving Negro. He finds a colder climate and a slightly different civilization, but he finds in addition a larger freedom in every way."[37]

Efforts to stop the exodus did not always go as planned. In early 1916 a circular letter was sent to white businessmen in Jacksonville, Florida, inviting them to a meeting at Mt. Zion AME Church to discuss the migration crisis. Organizers hoped to enlist the support of prominent African Americans in their efforts to stop the loss of black labor. They were disappointed in the case of John B. Hurst from Florida, AME bishop of the eleventh episcopal district. According to the *Chicago Defender,* when he was asked "to open a discussion that would pave the way to an amicable getting together of the Race which would tend to put a quietus on the evacuation of the south by our people," Hurst threw down the gauntlet. He condemned discrimination, lynching, and murder, and he predicted that unless the South made tangible improvements at once, its economy "would feel the full force of the result of the long mistreatment of the Race by the Southern white man." The *Defender* praised Bishop Hurst for "not [being] deceived into victimizing himself."[38]

Though Hurst did not succumb to what the *Defender* called the "propaganda of the South," other black clergy were used to cool the migration fever. Press reports of their sermons, letters, and speeches usually introduced them as "important" and "well-known" race leaders. One such naysayer was J. H. Eason, pastor of a Baptist church in Woodlawn, Alabama, and president of the Baptist state association. Eason complained that the exodus was tantamount to a stampede and that it "was the result of a destruction of the influence of the negro leaders among our race." A Birmingham paper gave a précis of one of Eason's sermons in which the preacher reportedly said, "There are many signs of hope and promise in the skies for better things in the South for us as Negroes. Be manly and patient. Don't move too fast and in such large numbers. Several things must come up to us as a race before we can enjoy many rights and blessings that we desire. It matters not where you go. Look well before you jump."[39] The *Atlanta Constitution* featured a letter in August 1917 from I. N. Fitzpatrick, who identified himself as "an old colored Georgian, pastor of St. Peter AME church and president of the Law and Order league." Fitzpatrick had earlier delivered a sermon at the annual session of the Atlanta district conference in which he counseled against deserting the South. He was challenged by another clergyman and took to the columns of the *Atlanta Constitution* to defend himself. Fitzpatrick echoed a theme familiar in the psychology of white supremacy and black docility. The South was the "negro's best home," because "Southern white people know the idiosyncrasies of the uncultured negro and, with such, sympathy will make allowances for his shortcomings and defects." In other sections "no patience, sympathy or credit" would be extended him, and "spot cash decides his fate." Fitzpatrick acknowledged that some civic and political rights were denied southern blacks, but he contended that when the race qualified itself "as a unit" it would be accorded every right. He counseled "time, patience, endurance, prayer and faith in God" and predicted that when the "glorious epoch" of interracial harmony was achieved, blacks would flock back to the South.[40]

Fitzpatrick and Eason might be dismissed as solitary and servile voices, given bogus leadership status by whites. D. D. Crawford, however, was corresponding secretary of the General Missionary Baptist Convention of Georgia, an association of African American churches. He wrote in the *Atlanta Constitution* in January 1917 that he was opposed to a wholesale exodus "unless it is absolutely necessary for race preservation." He argued that whites had started the exodus and only they could stop it. Mob violence against blacks was the primary culprit. Crawford claimed that he had "flattering offers to go north," but he had decided to stay in order to help the masses of his people. His executive post with his denomination entailed the responsibility of placing clergy. Because he felt that "our preachers are our real leaders," he was trying to assign strong pastors to every community to stabilize things. He appealed to the state's spiritual leaders "to exert every honorable effort to bring about peace and prosperity, brotherly love and forbearance in our great state." Then he added a sharp note: "To the white man I would say that we have his religion and civilization. We believe we are right. Do not make infidels of us."[41]

As the Great Migration grew, concerned observers in the South intensified the call for interracial consultations on how to deal with the crisis. "Forces from within must co-operate with those from without," D. D. Crawford wrote, adding, "I believe the state chamber of commerce should take up this question with the leaders, real leaders—not demagogues—of my people, and earnestly and honestly seek a solution."[42] Crawford represented the segment of southern black clergy who were against any precipitous exchange of place. Some argued that the demand for black labor in the North was only temporary because European immigrants would return and displace blacks after the war. Others feared migrants would succumb to the social degradation of urban life. A minority felt that the South, with its predominantly rural culture, was the natural habitat for African Americans. Conservatives asserted that the fate of the race would have to be worked out in harmony with progressive whites of the region. Even critics of the southern condition, such as Elias Cottrel, of Holly Springs, Mississippi, a bishop of the CME Church, cautioned against indiscriminate migration. Cottrel warned potential migrants against precipitous departure to an unknown land where they would have to live among strangers and thereby cut the bonds of familiarity with place and people.[43]

When preachers tried to dampen the migration fever, they encountered skepticism and hostility from those yearning for something better than life in the South. Signed only as "From an unknown party, but a member of the Race," a letter appeared in the *Chicago Defender* in 1916 from a disgruntled subscriber in Pensacola, Florida. The letter writer resented talk among "some male members of the Race" who said that "the Defender is all bull" in urging the exodus. "For my sake and for the sake of others," the letter read, "please put it in the paper explaining to the nuts that the train that's taking members of the race from the South is not carrying them away to starve and freeze." "THE PREACHER OF THE BIG ZION CHURCH is in the pulpit preaching to the members of the Race telling them not to come North. . . . He is telling them when the train puts you off in the North you all have got no place to put us and nothing for us to eat till we can get something, [and] are part of them that are gone there have frozen to death for want of fire."[44] When Bishop Benjamin F. Lee attempted to persuade black southerners not to abandon their homes so precipitously in the early stages of the Great Migration, W. A. McCloud of Wadley, Georgia, sent a letter to the *Chicago Defender* that Robert Abbot happily published: "I wander did the Bishop read of Lynching of that good Citizens of Abbeville, s.c., who was worth $20.00 and hundard of outher good men who has been hung up by thes Midnight Mobes. and yeat the bishop Adise them to stay in a cuntry like that. it seems to me that all the bishop wants is for his church to Live and the rest may die."[45]

Several letters written by Richard Carroll of Charleston, South Carolina, illustrate how difficult it was for black clergy to speak against a movement thought by many to be the work of God and a second Emancipation. Carroll was an ardent proponent of the philosophy that the South was the best place for blacks to work out their salvation—"financially, spiritually, morally and intellectually." He preached this message in the North and the South, amplifying it with appeals to blacks to avoid retaliation for the suffering they had endured and pleading with whites to give blacks good wages, protection of the law, justice in the courts, and better schools. He admitted that it had not all been in his words "smooth sailing" among his own people, but he vowed to continue his efforts regardless of personal consequences.

Carroll was troubled, however, by a visit he had in October 1916 from a friend of his, the Rev. Bolivar Davis of Savannah. Davis reported that more than 10,000 laborers and mechanics had left his city, including 500 members of his church. Davis was preparing to follow them. Carroll confessed that the visit left him sad and deeply concerned. In December, Carroll received a letter from Davis, whom he had sent to preach among blacks in Alabama. Davis reported that everyone there too was restless, that he could not assemble a meeting, and that he was leaving for Pennsylvania. "I will pass through Columbia," Davis wrote, "and will stop if you have anything to offer. The Northern fever is raging down here."[46]

Carroll decided to do some investigating. He went to Greenwood, South Carolina, to check out a rumor that a large company of migrants was about to leave. He arrived to find a crowd estimated at more than 2,000 milling around the railroad depot, anticipating a Saturday night departure. Informants said the scene was common to Greenwood. Seventy-five members of Greenwood's black Baptist church had already left, and more were thinking of following them. H. C. Tillman, son of Senator Benjamin R. ("Pitchfork Ben") Tillman, informed Carroll that among the prospective migrants were farmhands who had already signed contracts for the next year. Carroll was surprised that planters were offering little resistance, as he had heard that whites in Georgia were using various forms of intimidation to keep black labor.

Carroll thought of climbing onto a boxcar and warning the crowd about the folly of leaving so precipitously. He refrained because, as he readily acknowledged, "some of the colored population have the idea that I am paid by white people to speak against the migration movement." He claimed that this charge was false because he already had offers to move to Ohio and Pennsylvania where he believed he could make more money in one year than he earned in five years in South Carolina. Carroll was motivated instead by the conviction that southern blacks and whites had to work out their problems together. He remained convinced some whites held a similar view. He had heard B. D. Gray, secretary of the Southern Baptist Home Mission Board, speak at an African American church in Newberry. Carroll reported that Gray "wept much" as he told the congregation, "Stay among your friends. We have not treated you right; we are going to do better. Let us, white and colored, unite to solve the race problem on Southern soil. We are in debt to you colored people. First of all, we owe you the Gospel; then we owe you protection before the law. There will be no more outrages when we take up the problem and solve it by the Gospel."

Carroll acknowledged that many blacks felt that "God is in this movement," but he believed that had governments in the South remained "in the hands of the Gen. Wade Hampton type," conditions would not have reached such a low ebb. The "best element" in both races could "handle their bad folks." He asked, "Is it too late for us to begin the great work?" The continuing exodus of southern blacks answered his question. "The trouble about the thing," he acknowledged, "is that some of the best negroes are leaving."[47] African American clergy who shared Carroll's point of view tried to use the exodus as a means of calling the white South to repentance.

Some of the most progressive black religious leaders in the South also had reservations about the exodus. The Rev. Henry Hugh Proctor of Atlanta was widely known for his attempts to meet the problems of the city by innovative programs at First Congregational. Proctor weighed carefully the advantages and disadvantages of going North. During an evening sermon in early January 1917 he counseled all those that were truly dissatisfied to go, as it would "be better for all concerned." But he advised potential migrants, "Look, however, before you leap. Know where you are going and for whom you will work. Understand how much you will get and how much you will have to pay out. Pay your own fare and carry along enough to pay your way back. Do not expect to find Paradise in the North, but go to meet any hardship before you in a manly way."[48]

In pleading with their members to remain in the South, black ministers risked being labeled sycophants of the white power structure, perhaps even paid agents. But if they justified the exodus by criticism of the existing order, they risked much more. Emmett Scott described their dilemma:

> For the pastors of churches it was a most trying ordeal. They must watch their congregations melt away and could say nothing. If they spoke in favor of the movement, they were in danger of a clash with the authorities. If they discouraged it, they were accused of being bought up to hold negroes in bondage. If a pastor attempted to persuade negroes to stay, his congregation and his collection would be cut down and in some cases his resignation demanded. In some smaller communities the pastors settled this difficulty by following their flock, as was the case of three who left Hattiesburg, Mississippi, following their congregations.[49]

Church losses reached critical proportions in many places in the South causing denominational officials to take unusual action. The bishops of the AME Church warned pastors who had lost their congregations not to come North because they would have "no places" until new churches could be organized.[50] As evidence began to mount that the first wave of migrants encountered less than desirable conditions in the North, doubts increased. AME Bishop William D. Chappelle, a native of South Carolina, openly condemned the Ku Klux Klan and the harsh treatment black tenant farmers received at the hands of white landlords, yet he appealed to AME clergy to discourage the exodus. His apprehension about the Great Migration derived from evidence of its detrimental effect on congregational life. Chappelle estimated that 5,000 to 8,000 members of the South Carolina conferences had been lost in 1922.[51] A representative of black Baptists in Georgia thought that 69,000 members were lost in the same year. The losses, coming as they did after the first wave of 1916 to 1918 during the war underscored that the exodus was not a transitory phenomenon.[52]

Ministers who first opposed the migration, debating its merits with their elders or deacons, found it difficult to remain behind while leaders of their congregations packed up, often in great haste, to begin new lives in

Chicago or some other northern industrial center. It was very difficult for preachers to voice reservations about the Great Migration over the opposition of laity who were staking everything on pursuing new lives elsewhere. Members slipped away on the Saturday midnight train, leaving their pastor with vacant pews the next morning.[53] Several enterprising northern employers, banking on the stature of black clergy among potential migrants, sought to stimulate the flow of labor out of the South by offering ministers free passes on the railroads.

The self-generating character of the movement was captured by the African American educator W. T. B. Williams, himself a southerner. He was one of the contributors to the U.S. Department of Labor study published in 1919. After noting that the Great Migration started without organization or leadership, Williams reported, "The Negroes just quietly move away without taking their recognized leaders into their confidence any more than they do the white people about them. A Negro minister may have all his deacons with him at the mid-week meeting, but by Sunday every church officer is likely to be in the North. They write the minister that they forgot to tell him they were going away. They rarely consult the white people, and never those who may exercise some control over their actions. They will not allow their own leaders to advise them against going North."[54] Williams knew of a "Reverend Carter" of Tampa, who spoke against the migration from his pulpit and was stabbed the next day for doing so.

The Rev. L. G. Duncan, pastor of Cherry Street AME Church in Dothan, Alabama, experienced some of the frustrations inherent in being a religious leader in the Black Belt during the height of the exodus fever. At first he thought the exodus was merely a local affair, but as it intensified he discouraged it by urging his people to stop quitting their jobs and selling their homes. His pleas, contained in open letters published in the *Dothan Daily Dispatch*, had little effect. Neither did reports concerning the harsh climate, sickness, and death among migrants in the North. In March 1917 Duncan informed the *Montgomery Advertiser* that more than a hundred of his members had left and more were going. Duncan felt that he had no recourse but to urge the Christian white people of Alabama to use their influence with lawmakers, judges, sheriffs, mayors, councilmen, railroad officials, and others in authority to find a remedy that would end the exodus. To those whites who read the same Bible he did, Duncan said, "I appeal to you because there are thousands of us who have no intention of leaving the South, where our mothers and fathers have labored to make this Southland 'blossom like a rose,' where our church edifices and school houses stand as a monument to our sacrifices, to say nothing of our homes and personal property. Yes, there are thousands of us who want to continue to live, die and be buried in the South."[55]

Duncan may have been present in Montgomery at the statewide meeting held in February 1917 of AME clergy and laity. With Bishop Benjamin F. Lee of Wilberforce, Ohio, presiding, the assembly adopted a series of resolutions, one of which went considerably further than Duncan's appeal. It read: "Let us all together like one man ask for our suffrage, fairer treatment in the courts, and protection at the hands of those in authority. Let us ask the best white people to stop the angry, brutish mob which makes it a practice to mob members of our race in many cases for nothing. Let us ask for better pay for our work, remembering that the high cost of living demands it. Let us ask for encouragement when we do well and take care of ourselves."[56] Emboldened by the realization that the white South might be more receptive to reform when the economic welfare of the region was at risk, these African Methodists took their case directly to those who held power.

Freedom to voice dissent varied according to the circumstances of individual clergy. Those in the larger cities of the South were more at liberty than ministers in small towns and rural areas to critically comment on the exodus. Henry H. Proctor of Atlanta, pastor of the first black institutional church in the South, gave a series of lectures in which he argued that the antidote to migration fever was not all that mysterious; whites must give blacks "a square deal, based on the golden rule."[57] Northern ministers came to offer advice to their southern counterparts. For example, J. H. Duckry of Philadelphia spoke to the Baptist Ministers' Union in Montgomery in January 1917. He declared that his family loved the South and would not have left it except for the lack of honest treatment and fair wages. His mother and sister, both of whom had recently died up North, requested that their remains be placed with those of kin in southern soil. Duckry had recently visited several plantations and found many people starving. He urged the Baptist ministers to place the grievances of their people before the white power structure, even if that meant going to Montgomery and confronting Alabama's governor, Charles Henderson.[58]

Black Baptists in western Tennessee also discussed the exodus and offered the by now perfunctory statement that the "good white people" of the South deplored the maltreatment motivating many migrants. The fundamental issue, however, was the failure of progressive whites to remedy the situation. The Baptist ministers admitted that their people felt that they had no alternative but to join the exodus. So the clergy organized a committee to call on the white mayor, newspapers, civic organizations, and business leaders.[59]

African American clergy were struck by the irony that their people were being displaced from the farms and were without work in the cities when white officials were urging blacks to support the war effort. In Charlotte, North Carolina, an interdenominational committee presented a memorial to the chamber of commerce decrying the lack of economic opportunity for blacks. More than 50 percent of the available African American workers in the city were unemployed.[60] In 1918 350 ministers assembled at Strait University in New Orleans to hear representatives of the National Committee on Churches and the Moral Aims of the War. They were told that 120,000 black soldiers, many of them fighting in France, were engaged in a crusade to make the world safe for democracy. Henry A. Atkinson of New York City, the committee's secretary, said, "A democracy that is good for the world must be a democracy that will acknowledge justice for every man in America and for every individual an opportunity to develop according to his ability to the highest point possible."[61] In the minds of many in his audience, patriotism and justice were intrinsically linked.

Thirty thousand African American men served overseas during the "Great War for Democracy" as combat troops. After facing German guns, many of these soldiers returned home expecting to be accorded fair treatment and better economic opportunities. Secretary of War Newton D. Baker appointed Emmett J. Scott a special assistant in October 1917 because federal authorities recognized that the participation in the European theater by African Americans was bound to affect the home front. The *Crisis* gave voice to the sentiment of many black returnees in May 1919: "*We return. We return from fighting. We return fighting.* Make way for Democracy! We saved it in France, and by the Great Jehovah, we will save it in the U.S.A., or know the reason why."[62]

The patriotism issue surfaced during the Great Migration because of the rumor that German agents had stimulated the exodus. This aspersion on the loyalty of African Americans did not escape the notice of the Lott Carey Baptist Foreign Mission Convention, which met in Richmond in 1917. Delegates felt compelled to urge African Americans to uphold the flag and support President Wilson. The *Charlotte Observer* argued that such advice was unnecessary: "There is not a negro preacher or a negro editor in the South who is known to have in any way encouraged slacking, nor has there been among them anti-draft talk."[63] William Anthony Aery of Hampton Institute wrote in the *New York Tribune*, "Those who really know negroes —rank and file as well as leaders—scout the sporadic rumors that German agents have or have had any appreciable influence among American negroes." The real cause of the flight from the South was the desire for "the common everyday justice accorded to American citizens."[64] Monroe Work urged northern social agencies to redirect their resources now that black Americans were demonstrating their patriotism in the war effort. "Some of the agencies which have heretofore been used for the uplift of foreign immigrants," he wrote in 1917, "could now be used for the uplift of Negro migrants, among whom are no hyphens, whose loyalty is not doubted."[65]

If the finger of blame was to be pointed at all, some felt it ought to be directed at the forces in the South that were driving blacks off the land. The Rev. Henry Hugh Proctor wrote a letter to the *Atlanta Constitution* that turned the loyalty question back on the white South.

> Germany's new acquisition of immense agricultural resources in the conquest of Russia makes it increasingly evident that the winning of the war will not be at the point of the sword, but at the edge of the hoe. And it is more and more up to our country to provide food for the armies of the allies, our own south being the granary of the nation, it becomes correspondingly clear that the great battle for world freedom must be beaten out in the fields of the Southland. Whatever, therefore, tends to depopulate the south of its laborers or breaks their morale is hostile to the interests of the armies of the allies. Those who commit or condone violence upon the weak and defenseless are unwittingly giving aid and comfort to Germany and Austria. A campaign from pulpit and press at this season of planting and when many laborers are tempted northward would be a strong stroke for the freedom of the world.[66]

J. Q. Johnson, pastor of St. Paul AME Church in Montgomery, made a similar argument in the spring of 1917: "This is no time to cramp labor by low wages, when the President of our beloved country is calling to men to fight the war to a finish by remaining in the furrows to feed a starving world."[67]

The disruption of church life during the war years was a far more important problem for the clergy than rumors of German infiltrators. The magnitude of the problem varied from region to region. The *Southern Standard* reported in October 1916: "The entire lower country is so stirred up that many of the churches cannot have meeting where there have been the largest attendance, and some of the preachers say that they cannot get congregation enough to have service, for the reason that those who have not left are saving up money to go with."[68] At a meeting of the Birmingham Ministerial Alliance, held in April 1917, J. B. Carter, pastor of Bethel AME Church in Ensley, Alabama, reported that a church in Avondale had gone from 300 to 60 members. Many of his own members had gone or were thinking of leaving, including some who were earning good wages in Birmingham's steel plants.[69] Since the typical small town or rural congregation numbered fewer than 100 members, the loss of key individuals or several families was a serious matter. Members of urban churches also were leaving and were not being replaced by those who were moving into southern cities as temporary way stations on the trip North. Church losses continued during the revival of the exodus in the early 1920s. A clergyman of the Methodist Episcopal Church wrote in 1923,

> As district superintendent for seven years, touching twenty-five counties in Mississippi, the State which had, according to the census of 1910, almost one-tenth of the Negro population of the United States of America, my observation and experience lead me to state that the exodus is still on and will no doubt continue gradually toward the North and West for some years. In many places hundreds have gone within the last few months. Many churches have depleted memberships because of the exodus. Seventy-five were counted that left one community within twenty-four hours.[70]

Confronted with the prospect of dwindling congregations, some ministers joined in the exodus and attempted to reconstitute churches in the urban North. A. L. James of Ocala, Florida, found his flock so depleted that he went to New York City. Within two days he came across twelve families in Harlem who were former church members. He was soon busy reestablishing his church in the new environment. At a mass meeting at Abyssinian Baptist Church at which this story was recounted, Adam Clayton Powell, Sr., also reported, "In a parish in Georgia another negro preacher found that thirty families had moved away in one week without his knowing it."[71] In some instances ministers arrived in the North with enough members of their old congregations to immediately organize a church. The

Rev. R. H. Harmon brought twenty-eight members of his congregation from Mississippi to Chicago. He told a *Defender* reporter, "I am working at my trade. I have saved enough to bring my wife and four children and some of my congregation. We are here for keeps."[72]

Leaving the church community in which they had prayed and sung for many years was difficult for many migrants. Once established in the Promised Land, they sought to reconnect with their Christian brothers and sisters in the South. They wrote back as soon as possible to their pastors, informing them of their whereabouts and how they were faring in their new homes. A migrant who had found work in Pittsburgh wrote to his pastor, "I hope you & sis Hayes are well & no you think I have forgotten you all but I never will how is ever body & how is the church getting along. . . ." He described how other migrants were coming to the "smoky city" by the carload, begging for some place to stay. His wages were good at $75 a month. He was fortunate enough to find lodging with an African American clergyman and his wife who owned a four-story home with a piano in the parlor and an organ in the sewing room. Pittsburgh had churches of all kinds, including, he reported, "some real colored churches." He was especially struck by the fact that in Pittsburgh he did not have to "mister every little white boy" whom he encountered. He had not heard the epithet "nigger" since he had been in Pennsylvania. Nevertheless, he professed to love "the good old south" and prayed that God might yet redeem his native region so that everyone could be respected regardless of color.[73] A migrant to Dayton, Ohio, who worked for $70 a month in a hotel, promised to send a portion of his salary back home and extended his love to church members who had remained.[74] Another migrant living in Chicago also vowed to send in his church dues and asked his pastor in Union Springs, Alabama, "Let me know how is our church I am so anxious to no. My wife always talking about her seat in the church want to know who accupying it."[75]

One woman who came to Chicago wrote to her church sisters describing with great joy her newfound home. The letter, something of a classic, appears in the study done of the Great Migration by Arna Bontemps and Jack Conroy in 1945. It deserves special attention because it captures the mixture of religious hope and concern for a better life that many migrants brought with them on the journey to the Promised Land.[76]

My dear Sisters: I was agreeably surprised to hear from you and to hear from home. I am well and thankful to be in a city with no lynching and no beating. The weather was a great surprise to me. I got here just in time for one of the greatest revivals in the history of my life—over 500 joined the church. We had a holy-ghost shower. You know I like to run wild at the services—it snows here and even the churches are crowded and we had to stand up last night. The people are rushing here by the thousands, and I know that if you come here and rent a big house you can get all the roomers you want. I am not keeping a house yet, I am living with my brother. I can get you a nice place to live until you get your own house. The houses are so pretty, we has a nice place. I am very busy I work in the Swift Packing Co., in the sausage department. My daughter and I work at the same place. We get $1.50 a day, and the hours are not so long, before you know it, it is time to go home. I am so thankful the Lord has been so good to me. Work is plenty here, and we don't loaf we are glad to work. Remember me to Mrs. C. and T. and tell all the children I am praying for them. Hurry up and come to Chicago it is wonderful. I hope I see your face before I die.

Pray for me I am heaven bound. Let know if you are coming soon as I will meet you at the railroad and bring you to my house, and what a good time we will have thanking God and going to church.

In a note enclosed with her letter the writer gave greetings to another friend and all her hometown and asked that "five gallons of country syrup" be sent her.[77]

The longings for church friends and country syrup represented the emotional hold that the South still had on this Chicago sister. Many migrants also found it difficult to break ties with the communities of faith into which they had been born in the South. Some retained their membership long after removing to the North. Kinship ties were strong, and it was difficult to make that final break. No doubt they felt the need to get established in their new communities before formally severing ties with the congregations of which they had been so integral a part, which they thought of as family, and to which they expected to return on visits.[78] When the day came to make the break, the exceptionally faithful migrants asked their old pastors for letters of dismissal that would allow them to become full members of churches in the North. One migrant wrote from Dayton in 1917, "Dear Pastor: I have join the church up here and I authorize the church to write my letter of dismission but they say they have not heard enything from the church at all. Sister ———— ———— wrote to you she ask for my letter so I can join here in full and if the church hold me for enything on why say to them I will know what to do."[79]

After finding new religious fellowships to join in the North, migrants continued to express care and concern for the Christian brothers and sisters they left behind. A migrant to Akron, Ohio, told of a Baptist church she joined that was overcrowded with migrants from Alabama and Georgia and adding ten to twelve new members every Sunday. The pastor was planning to build a new brick church and was a "wel to do preacher," taking in $50 and $60 each Sunday. Nevertheless, her thoughts turned toward the South. "I never liked a place like I do here except home. Their is no place like home How is the church getting along. . . . Write me."[80]

Participants in the Great Migration thought of themselves as recapitulating the exodus of the children of Israel out of Egypt. But observers noted a significant difference between the saga of the Israelites and that of the hundreds of thousands who fled the South where, as one unidentified black pastor put it, "whipping has become a pastime."[81] W. E. B. Du Bois attempted to assess both the scope and the causes of the Great Migration in the spring of 1917. He estimated that about 250,000 black laborers had left the South and rehearsed the familiar litany of immediate causes—the cessation of immigration from Europe and consequent need for common labor in the North; the push of the boll weevil and widespread flooding, especially in middle Alabama and Mississippi; outbreaks of violence against blacks, notably in northern and southwestern Georgia and in western South Carolina; and back of these immediate causes, the general dissatisfaction with conditions in the South. Du Bois saw something unique in the Great Migration: "It is interesting to note that this migration is apparently a mass movement and not a movement of the leaders. The wave of economic distress and social unrest has pushed past the conservative advice of the Negro preacher, teacher and professional man, and the colored laborers and artisans have determined to find a way for themselves."[82] Du Bois quoted an unnamed black preacher from Mississippi in support of his contention that thousands were leaving without a Moses: "The leaders of the race are powerless to prevent his going. They had nothing to do with it, and, indeed, all of them, for obvious reasons, are opposed to the exodus. The movement started without any head from the masses, and such movements are always significant."[83]

Other prominent African Americans agreed with Du Bois's interpretation of the Great Migration as essentially an unstructured movement of the masses. Adam Clayton Powell, Sr., touted as the "most influential clergyman" in New York City, investigated conditions in the South and concluded: "This migration differs from all others in that it has no visible leader. The colored people have become disgusted with the leadership of 'corn-stalk' preachers, weak kneed professors and spineless politicians. . . . The masses have done more to solve the negro problem in fifty weeks without a leader than in fifty years with a certain type of leader."[84] "The Movement North is unorganized," Richard R. Wright, Jr., wrote in the *Christian Recorder*, "100, 000 Negroes have moved without any leader, without any organization, and with nothing but an individual motive and longing."[85]

Astute observers in the South likewise commented on the absence of a Moses. Monroe Work wrote, "Unlike the Kansas exodus, and the back to Africa movement, the migration of 1916–1917 was leaderless. The name of no individual, nationally or even locally, stands out anywhere as a leader in this movement. In the Southland, there was not a single meeting held in the interest of the movement; but, as was said, 'Just simultaneously, all over the South, about a year ago, the Negroes began to cross the 'Mason and Dixon Line.'"[86] The *Cleveland Advocate* said, "There is no mistaking what is going on; it is a REGULAR EXODUS. It is without head, tail, or leadership. Its greatest factor is MOMENTUM, and this is increasing, despite amazing efforts on the part of white Southerners to stop it. People are leaving their homes and everything about them, under cover of night, as though they were going on a day's journey—leaving forever."[87] Charles R. Graggs wrote in the *Dallas Express*, "The strangest thing, the real mystery about the exodus is that in all the Southland there has not been a single meeting or promoter to start the migration. Just simultaneously all over the South about a year ago, the Negro began to cross the Mason and Dixon line . . . . Who knows, then, what the providence of God is in this exodus."[88] The Rev. C. M. Tanner summed up the feelings of many in the North and the South: "Strangely enough, this exodus is thus far without a Moses. No one man alone seems to have stirred these people to unrest and activity."[89]

That no single "earth-born soul to look to as leader" emerged did not surprise an editorialist for the *Southern Standard*. The writer noted that black preachers were "running the risk of their lives" in parts of the South where the exodus fever was high. Those who complained of the ill-treatment of their members or who spoke against the illegal sale of whisky about the meeting houses were prevented from returning to their churches.

"Any Negro will be playing with his life to attempt to advise the right [to fair treatment] among his race." Yet there was "one safe leader whom men cannot harm, who has declared in His word that 'Vengeance is mine. I will pay.' He is leading the people." The editorialist extended the biblical analogy one step further: "The prayers of the righteous prevaileth much and like the Israelites in the land of Egypt prayed, the Negro has prayed, and his groans and cries have been heard. But like Moses risked his life back in the land of Egypt because God had found him worthy, there must be some Negro or Negroes to take God on their side and lead the race to the promised land. We do not need the cloud and fire, but those humble souls looked after."[90]

The editorialist's plea for a Moses to emerge did not happen. No "Pap" Singleton was at the head of the column of migrants as had happened during the exodus to Kansas in 1879. Nor was there the equivalent of Bishop Henry M. Turner, whose powerful voice in AME circles had been heard from the sixth district of Georgia and Alabama from 1896 until 1908. Both Turner and Booker T. Washington died in 1915, leaving a vacuum in black leadership in the South.

The absence of a Moses at the head of the refugee column during the Great Migration is frequently cited as the reason why migrants gravitated toward new messiahs in the North. In her study of black Judaism in Harlem, Ruth Landes argued that ordinary Harlemites were country folk who had been "uprooted from their centuries-old rural adjustments by the demands of industry, a process facilitated by the drastic decline of the plantation economy, and packed into urban centres where alterations in their traditional values disorient them thoroughly." Bewildered and frightened migrants stampeded, Landes maintains. "One flight leads repeatedly into Black Judaism; another impulse led to Garveyism; the most recent has led into pastures of Father Divine. The people flock to the most understanding spokesman of their panic."[91] But Marcus Mosiah Garvey did not accompany the refugees from the South as Moses did the Jews in the Old Testament. The Jamaican-born Garvey arrived in New York City on March 23, 1916, unknown to anyone. He did not capture much public attention until two years later when he began publishing *Negro World* and promoting his vision of black pride and unity. Garvey and his Universal Negro Improvement Association, only set fully in motion after the end of the wartime influx of migrants, capitalized on the migrants' urban-produced frustrations.

With the luster of the Promised Land worn off by brutal realities of the struggle for survival in the city, many migrants looked for a Black Moses, someone to lead them to a more tangible heaven.

The renowned African American sociologist E. Franklin Frazier recalled that as a child he often heard "Negroes express the hope that some Moses would appear among them and lead them to a promised land of freedom and equality." Booker T. Washington had been Moses to some, but "this was," Frazier knew, "chiefly an echo of the white man's appraisal and soon died down when the Negro heard a message of patient industry, unsweetened by any prospect of a glorious future." Garvey with rhetorical flourishes of a new Promised Land—the African "motherland"—offered new hope and caught the imagination of many who had come out of the South. Garvey's detractors, Frazier noted, attempted to portray his movement as limited to West Indians. African American preachers who were influential among migrants from the South were said to talk against Garvey. Nevertheless, Frazier wrote in 1926, "foreign Negroes [meaning Jamaicans] have successfully converted hard-shelled Baptists to the Movement in spite of the opposition of their ministers."[92] We should not make the mistake of conflating the Garvey story with that of the Great Migration. When the exodus began, Garvey's charismatic appeal was an unknown quantity.

Questions arose concerning the fate of those who went along with the tide. Who would care for the migrants in the North? What would become of their own traditions and culture amid strangers in the Canaan that lay before the hopeful, yet anxious souls heading to the Chicagos, Detroits, and Pittsburghs of the Promised Land? The possibility of cultural assimilation in the North worried southern black leaders like R. T. Pollard, president of Selma University in Selma, Alabama. For those whose personal fortunes were tied to black institutions in the South, going North entailed as much peril as promise. Pollard queried those who passionately advocated removing to some northern city: "Can the Negro maintain his institutions,—schools and churches especially—in the North as he has done in the South? There may be, as are now, mixed churches and schools in the North, but who will be the pastors, the deacons or stewards, the presidents, the teachers? The separation of white people and Negroes in the South has been a blessing in disguise to the Negro. It provided pastors, deacons and stewards, bishops, presidents and teachers and more than all these, a training in leadership in those things that he never could have gotten otherwise."[93]

Pollard's concerns point to one of the historical ironies of the pre-Great

Migration South and, more generally, to the nature of black-white relations after the Civil War. Enforced segregation fostered separate cultural institutions among blacks. In the South, black churches were as alien to whites as white churches were to blacks. In religious affairs blacks operated independently. Social distance was fostered by cultural differences and maintained by fear and intimidation. Black religious leaders, especially in small towns and rural areas, were expected to refrain from criticism of racial apartheid and shun political activism. Blacks were denied access to the political, educational, economic, and social circles of whites, where the real power lay. Thus African Americans in the South turned within—to their churches, and secondarily, to such organizations as the lodge. On the eve of the Great Migration, the church was the paramount focus of community life. It was, in Carter G. Woodson's phrase, an "all comprehending institution."[94]

How would such an institution fare when transplanted into a northern city? What purposes would it serve? Who would be its leaders? These were reasonable concerns for African American leaders in the South during the Great Migration. But in considering the fate of southern black institutions in the North, Pollard missed an important consideration. The exodus analogy fails to capture the complexities of the Great Migration in several important ways, chief of which is that the North was not altogether an alien land. The Israelites were led into the land of Canaan and instructed to take possession of their Promised Land by driving the inhabitants out, for the Canaanites were strangers to the God of Israel. African Americans who made their way North into the cities during the war found them inhabited by professors of a similar faith, black and white Christians, and by people who could also claim historical ties to Africa and the African American sojourn in the South. African American Christians in the North had worked out arrangements to suit their particular situations and understandably expected to control the assimilation of the southerners. For example, Chicago had a Colored Baptist Union, consisting in 1915 of fourteen churches. The organization had the power to regulate the location of any new Baptist churches organized in the city.[95]

In the spring of 1917 the Interdenominational Ministers' Alliance of Philadelphia held a reception for the recently arrived. The Rev. W. G. Parks of Union Baptist Church delivered a welcoming address which illustrates that the exodus from the South was not strictly analogous to the flight of the Jews from Egypt. Parks told the migrants,

You my friends are our brothers and sisters and as members of the race, though we came before you, we are not able to say in bidding you welcome that this is your land of Goshen, and that you may be located here in the best part of the city, for none of us are governors; neither can we say that this is your land of Canaan, that the inhabitants are be to be driven out and the land divided among you, for there are those here in charge of the land and the government who are of another race, by whose sides we have labored and into whose council many of us have been called for the purpose of discussing ways and means of giving you employment and housing you in quarters suitable to your health and general welfare.[96]

Since they shared religious and racial heritages with northern black Christians, the migrants fully expected a warm reception and a helping hand, despite Parks's reservations.

The established black churches of the North took on the task of assisting and assimilating the migrants with the assumption that their position as the dominant cultural anchors in the community would be preserved. Nannie H. Burroughs, in her capacity as corresponding secretary of the Woman's Convention Auxiliary, told Baptist women that the churches and social agencies of the North ought to embrace the mission to the migrants as "leaven that will leaven the whole lump." She argued that the migrants were coming into freedom as a person "shut up in a dark room or fettered for a long time" and that they had to learn "how to walk, how to work, how to spend, how save, how to live." "The masses of our people are intoxicated now," Burroughs told the auxiliary, "but when they sober up they will rebuke and repudiate the leaders of their day if they fail them in this hour when they should be eyes for the blind, feet for the lame, ears for the deaf, and a tower of strength for the weak."[97] In framing the task of the northern churches as one of rescue and uplift, Burroughs and others who campaigned on behalf of the migrants assumed that existing black churches would retain their dominant position in the expanding ghettoes. This was especially true of cities like Philadelphia where the AME Church leaders, as Robert Gregg observes, were especially prominent and often interacted with whites on behalf of all sectors of the black community. Their leadership role came into question as a result of the diverse nature of those who arrived in Philadelphia after World War I in search of a portion of the Promised Land. "With the Great Migration and the ghettoization of the black community," says Gregg, "African Methodist theology and ideology could no longer unite people who arrived in the city from such different backgrounds and who, once there, were increasingly cut off from the white community."[98]

Northern whites, fearing destabilization of existing racial arrangements, were all too eager to turn the welfare of the migrants over to northern black churches. This was particularly true in Albany, New York, because of the size and distribution of the city's black population. African Americans were scattered throughout the city's nineteen wards until waves of migrants arrived during and after the war. A housing crisis arose; whites became anxious about migrants moving into their neighborhoods; and the Albany Inter-racial Committee asked real estate agents to recommend remedial measures. The solution suggested by the real estate lobby reveals that a segment of the northern white community was ready to accept the white southern solution to "the Negro question." The agents argued that "the colored people should be grouped by themselves in a section laid out and developed for that purpose" because their dispersion throughout Albany was embarrassing to whites. Had opponents of the migration who feared that relocation in the North left no room for "race" leaders and "race" institutions known of the Albany plan, they could have rested easy. In order to sell the concept of residential segregation, the realtors advised, "Call a meeting of the Negro preachers—for the progress of the city. A Negro zone should be diplomatically established with the cooperation of the Negro clergy, who in turn would be able to increase many times the size of their congregations."[99] The Albany plan was never formally adopted, but in that city and across the urban industrial North, African American migrants from the South discovered that life in the Promised Land was but one more chapter in the odyssey of a pilgrim people.

In 1930 Harold M. Kingsley, pastor of Chicago's Church of the Good Shepherd, cast a retrospective eye on the time fifteen years earlier when so many entered the Promised Land buoyed by high spirits. Conscious of the despair that the depression had brought, Kingsley invoked the spiritual dimension of the Great Migration and said of the African American migrant, "In his sermons, editorials and songs, he saw a parallel between his coming out of the South and the Hebrew children coming up out of the land of Egypt, out of the house of bondage. Crowded trains, piled high with baggage of all descriptions and of no description, echoed with his songs, 'Go Down, Moses, Tell Ole Pharaoh to Let My People Go,' 'Let Us Cheer the

Weary Traveler,' 'I'm So Glad, Trouble Don't Last Always,' 'Pharaoh and His Army God Drowned,' and 'I Wonder If the Light Will Ever Shine on Me.' "[100]

Kingsley believed that no "finer spiritual venture" existed in modern American history than the deliverance of the migrants from the South. He compared their odyssey to that of the Pilgrims on the *Mayflower* in 1620. When the seventeenth-century English separatists established their new Zion in New England's wilderness, they did so as ecclesiastical orphans. The Church of England washed its hands of the Puritan settlers who formed the Massachusetts Bay Colony. In contrast, leaders of the black denominations understood that they had both a moral and a racial obligation to provide material and spiritual care for the thousands who were marching toward the Promised Land.

As we prepare to examine the response of the principal black Protestant denominations to the intersectional migration of thousands of their members, the religious character of the exodus needs to be reemphasized. While government officials worried about the impact of the Great Migration on the labor supply and the war effort, whites in northern cities looked on the migrants as alien invaders and feared for their neighborhoods; at the same time, "race" leaders among African Americans in the North viewed the exodus as an opportunity to increase their political clout. Southern black conservatives tried to stem the exodus. But for many participants the Great Migration was the handiwork of God and the fulfillment of an oppressed people's hopes. They left their homes and churches fully expecting to be welcomed by Christian sisters and brothers in their New Zion. As one potential migrant, a chauffeur in Georgia, said in a letter he signed "ONE OF THE NEGRO RACE, "I think peple as a race ought to look out for one another as Christian friends . . . the peple is getting so bad with us black peple down south hear. Now if you ever help your race now is the time to help me to get my family away."[101]

4

"OUR

WANDERING

ZION"

Late in the summer of 1917 the episcopal council of the African Methodist Episcopal Church met at Wilberforce University, the denomination's
mother school. The bishops were deeply troubled. Only a year earlier the
AME denomination had celebrated a century of self-professed "forward
movement." In 1903 W. E. B. Du Bois applauded the oldest of the three
major black Methodist denominations as "probably . . . the greatest voluntary organization of Negroes in the world."[1] This accolade was justified
in light of the progress made by the African Methodists since they had
organized as an independent body in 1816 under the leadership of Richard
Allen. Now, believing the fate of Christian civilization was at stake in
the Great War and cognizant of the momentous social changes occurring
across the nation, the bishops confronted an institutional crisis. They drew
attention to the unsettled conditions among their people with specific reference to the "sudden and simultaneous departure of multitudes" from the
South. This exodus, they believed, necessitated concerted action and an
immediate response because thousands of black Christians had left or were
leaving "to seek a new home under new and untried conditions."[2]

Church leaders did not anticipate the Great Migration and were not
prepared to deal with the impact it was having on existing organizational

structures and members everywhere. The growth of black urban and industrial America and consequent loss to denominational structures of members in the South posed problems not seen since the post-Civil War competition to attract and hold the newly freed slaves.

African American denominational priorities before World War I grew out of premises derived from the nineteenth century when the field of expansion had been in the South, and, to a lesser extent, in the newly settled regions of the West. Then it was assumed that allocations of personnel and money ought to be expended on preserving institutional structures in those places where each church body had its greatest strength. Since the majority of African Americans lived in the South and were thought likely to remain on the land, their religious needs were to be met by enhancing services to them where they were. Southern whites claimed this to be the special responsibility of the black denominations and of schools such as Hampton and Tuskegee. The essentially white northern denominations that built churches and schools for southern blacks in the pre-World War I era did so on the assumption that the South was the African American's "natural home."[3]

The rush of African American migrants to northern cities presented fundamental problems to the black denominations with membership rolls weighted toward the South. In 1890 W. S. Scarbourgh observed in a preface to Wesley J. Gaines's *African Methodism in the South* that his denomination's "greatest field" had been in the South "both as to churches and as to membership."[4] The AME Council of Bishops acknowledged that the Great Migration, no matter what positions had been taken by individual bishops on the question of whether or not African Americans should leave the South, entailed enormous corporate risks. "Our church work," the bishops said, "is situated in the very heart and centers of the portions deserted, and those to which many thousands come."[5] Since the Civil War, southern black Methodists had increased their numbers disproportionately to northern constituents in the national bodies. Yet they lacked parity in the inner circles of power. Intersectional struggles resulted. The election and addition of bishops to episcopal councils frequently became battles over regional influence. Southerners wanted a greater voice in church affairs, which had been dominated by northern-based bishops whose influence derived from pre-Civil War ecclesiastical arrangements. The claims of the southern wings of the various denominations became more difficult to ignore in light of what the membership rolls were showing.

The federal religious census of 1906 reported that the three principal black Methodist denominations had a combined membership of 852,315. The AME Church was 85.9 percent southern, the AME Zion Church 88.6 percent, and the CME Church 98.6 percent. The AME and the AME Zion denominations originated in the urban North in the post-Revolutionary era and achieved independence, respectively, in 1816 and 1822. The CME Church was a product of the post-Civil War desire of black Methodists in the South to establish a religious body that perpetuated the distinctive southern folk religious ethos rooted in the "invisible institution" of slave culture before Emancipation. In 1906 the Colored Methodists, organized in 1870 at Jackson, Tennessee, had about one-forth as many members as the total of its two northern rivals. With 172,996 congregants, the CME Church nearly matched the AME Zion Church with its 184,542 members, but it was decidedly smaller than the AME Church with 494,777. The CME was strongest in Georgia, Mississippi, Tennessee, and Alabama.

The northern-based black Methodists lacked ready access to a southern constituency until the Civil War. At that time they moved quickly to gather a harvest among the newly freed slaves. In 1906 South Carolina, Georgia, and Alabama were the leading AME states, while North Carolina, Alabama, and South Carolina prevailed in the membership totals for the AME Zion Church. The influx of members in the South created sectional tensions and struggles for power within each denomination, chiefly over the election of bishops and the apportioning of monies solicited from congregations. In the campaign for territorial expansion and membership during Reconstruction the black Methodists in the northern states competed not only with the Colored Methodists but among themselves. Historic differences over the episcopacy and lay participation thwarted unification efforts by representatives of the AME Church and the Zion connection in the second half of the nineteenth century. The Colored Methodists were not party to the negotiations because of residual resentment over being ostracized by the northerners as "rebels" and "democrats" during Reconstruction struggles.

By 1908 the Tri-Council of Colored Methodist Bishops had been formed. Prospects for a united front by all three bodies brightened. At its meeting in 1911 in Mobile, Alabama, the Tri-Council adopted a resolution endorsing organic union. Twenty-nine bishops issued a joint address in which they stated: "This federation of bishops is of small influence compared with that of the confederation of churches, but to our churches it means much in advancing the thought and hope of making Methodism among Negroes one co-operative body, capable of great resistance to evil in our special communities as well as of great corrective powers in recalling and saving, training and cultivating our fellow man in general."[6] Before the Mobile meeting Solomon Porter, an AME clergyman, voiced another goal of organic union, one that went beyond narrow denominational concerns: "Think of it from the standpoint of race unity. . . . The very object lesson of unity would stimulate the whole race."[7]

The hoped-for lesson failed to materialize, even though the challenges brought about by the Great Migration were recognized by all concerned. Representatives of the three black Methodist denominations met at Louisville in February 1918 to deliberate on what to do. Their collective judgment was that they were facing unprecedented "duties, responsibilities and opportunities." And they resolved:

> We realize the dangers and evils incident to the migration on the part of a race in its constructive period or its transition from a state of bondage, ignorance and poverty to a state of freedom, industry and education. But, we realize also the benefits of such a movement and that the danger consists not so much in the disposition to migrate as it does in the lack of disposition to make a careful study of the industrial and economic conditions of the section to which they go and to adequately prepare themselves to meet the demands of their new environment. We recognize the right of our people to migrate from one section to another with a view of bettering their conditions.[8]

When the Tri-Council finally authorized the drafting of a plan for the proposed "United Methodist Episcopal Church" it met heavy fire. The articles of agreement known as the Birmingham Plan were ultimately rejected by the CME, which was afraid of being swallowed up by the much larger AME Church.

Thus, the Tri-Council preserved only the appearance of fraternal relations among black Methodists during the critical first phase of the departure of hundreds of thousands from the South. It provided a forum for the bishops of the three bodies to discuss mutual concerns, but it did not have the power to organize resources across connectional lines or to overcome the spirit of rivalry endemic among black Methodists.[9] This competition had resulted in a number of schisms so that the Tri-Council, even if it had been successful in forming a new and united body, could not have brought all black Methodists under one jurisdiction.

Lewis V. Baldwin, historian of the Spencerite tradition, reminds us that there have always been "invisible strands" in the tapestry of black Methodism in the United States. These smaller traditions emerged as a result of nineteenth-century splits from the AME Church, or, as is the case with the African Union Methodist Protestant and the Union American Methodist Episcopal Churches, they lay claim to the movement toward independence led by Peter Spencer in Wilmington, Delaware. The African Union Church, or Union Church of Africans, founded in 1813, preceded Richard Allen's separately organized African Methodists. But unlike the AME Church, the Spencerites, already two factions by the 1850s, remained a small and territorially limited connection. The UAME had an estimated 5,000 members in 1900 and only about 28,000 nearly seventy years later. The African Union Methodist Episcopal Church, about 4,000 strong in 1900, had only doubled its ranks by the 1970s. Baldwin attributes the slow growth to institutional chaos and declension born of bickering among African Union leaders, the lack of a strong connectional authority, loss of pastors and congregations to the AME Church, and an inability to marshal meager institutional resources to benefit from the arrival of migrants during the critical decades of the twentieth century when everything was in flux.[10] The Reformed Methodist Union Episcopal Church, credited with 4,000 members in 1900, had only eighteen congregations and about 3,800 members in the early 1980s. Born of a dispute within the AME Church in Charleston, South Carolina, in 1885 over the leadership of the charismatic William E. Johnson, the Reformed Church suffered a double threat. It was subject to losses generated by the outflow of black Methodists from the South, and it was not in a position to glean a harvest from among them in the North. The same fate plagued the Reformed Zion Union Apostolic Church, organized in 1869 by James R. Howell among the freed slaves in southeastern Virginia.[11] A critical mass was necessary to be able to compete in the membership wars that took place in the large cities of the North once black denominations awoke to the urgency of the institutional crisis confronting them. Connections too small or too fragile simply did not have the means to cope with the manifold challenges entailed by the transition to an urban, industrial order.

Of the three connections in the Tri-Council, the AME Church was the largest and oldest. The 1906 religious census credited the AME with 6,647 churches in forty-three states and territories. Membership increased from 494,777 in 1906 to 548,355 in 1916, and the number of clergy mounted from an estimated 6,200 in 1906 to 8,175 in 1916. Fifteen episcopal districts, two of which were in Africa, constituted the denomination's territorial structure.[12]

The AME Zion denomination was the Tri-Council's second-oldest and largest connection. With 184,542 communicants and 2,204 churches in 1906, it grew to 257,169 communicants and 2,716 churches in 1916. Nearly 4,000 clergy were on its rolls in 1916. The Zion Church, like its AME counterpart, conducted its official business in quarterly, annual, and general conferences. In 1906, 63 percent of its membership was female.

The CME Church was the smallest of the three major black denominations that were discussing possible merger. With 172,996 members and 2,381 churches in 1906, it had grown to 245,749 members and 2,621 churches by the end of 1916. Fewer than 2,000 members lived outside the South in 1906, and the CME was the most rural in membership of the three black Methodist bodies. It originated in the tumultuous Civil War years when thousands of black Methodists were leaving the white Methodist Episcopal Church, South. By 1866 only 78,742 "colored members" of the 207,000 claimed in 1860 remained, and steps were taken to stem the exodus. Separate "colored conferences" were set up, and in 1870 the first General Conference of the Colored Methodist Episcopal Church was organized at Jackson, Tennessee.[13]

With a membership composed almost entirely of former slaves and with leaders who were both southern and, until the beginning of the twentieth century, born in slavery, the CME was often at odds with the AME and AME Zion Churches because they emphasized a trained ministry and styles of worship developed in the urban North. Northern black leaders, having honed their political skills in the abolitionist struggle, derided the Colored Methodists because of their willingness to accept economic support and counsel from white southern Methodists. Far less political than the AME and the AME Zion Churches, the CME also exhibited a religious style that reflected the folk ethos of slave religion, much to the consternation of educated black missionaries working among the freed slaves.[14]

Despite opposition from their denominational and racial kin the CME grew from nine charter conferences in 1870 to thirty-four by 1916. Most Colored Methodists resided in rural areas and small towns, with heavy concentrations in Mississippi and Georgia. The denomination's polity and doctrine followed traditional Methodist lines. The CME functioned with an itinerancy system, published the *Christian Index,* and operated schools and colleges, such as Lane College in Jackson, Tennessee, and Paine College in Augusta, Georgia. As the most southern and most rural of the three major black denominations, the CME Church stood the greatest chance of being undercut by any regional shift in the country's African American population.[15]

The black membership of the predominantly white, northern-based Methodist Episcopal Church was greater on the eve of the Great Migration than either the AME Zion or CME connections. Largely as a result of aggressive missionary activity among former slaves after the Civil War, the white Methodists could count 174,000 black members in 1870. These members were organized into all-black conferences with white bishops. Sentiment grew strong for black bishops, but an effort to amend church law in 1904 to allow for the election of "race" bishops failed. Some black and white leaders in the Methodist Episcopal Church began to look favorably on the possibility of having the black membership join the proposed union of the three major black denominations. I. Garland Penn, one of the corresponding secretaries of the Freedmen's Aid Society and a prominent black in the Methodist Episcopal Church, was instrumental in arranging for a meeting of the Committee on Federation of Colored Methodists in Cincinnati during June 1915. Here, representatives of the three black Methodist denominations plus white and black leaders of the Methodist Episcopal Church discussed practical measures for cooperation, federation, and the possibility of eventual union of black Methodists. They drew up an agreement, which stated in part, "Whatever may be the reasons or the expediency of separate organization of our common stock, today, thank God and the spirit of Him, His Son, the Brother of us all, we see eye to eye on the great fundamentals of our common denominational life."[16]

The joint commission was particularly concerned over the "waste of money, men, opportunity and influence" in the divided affairs of black Methodism. The proposal made little headway. As a correspondent to the *New York Age* put it, "While here and there among high officials of the church there is a voice calling for the peaceable withdrawal of the colored members, it is the opinion of both white and colored leaders in the church that a vote on the proposition would result in a landslide for the 'standpatters.'" S. H. Norwood, a leading clergyman of the all-black Washington

annual conference, argued that leaving the Methodist Episcopal Church
would raise the charge of "'jim-crowism, race segregation' in high places,
in spiritual things."[17]

The presence in the South of 3,189 black churches and 315,000 members
of the Methodist Episcopal Church in 1918 proved to be the stumbling
block in reunion negotiations.[18] White southerners wanted to set the black
annual conferences off as a separate unit, while white northerners were reluctant to do so, despite the fact that the Methodist Episcopal Church had
maintained a de facto form of Jim Crowism in the all-black churches and
conferences. H. H. White, a southern representative in the negotiations,
voiced the sentiments of the racial conservatives: "The commission will
continue to be divided on the Negro question until such time as the Northern Church sees fit to, and is able to put its negro membership in a separate
church. When the Methodist Episcopal Church recognizes the fact that the
whole question is one of race rather than class, the prospects of union will
be brighter."[19] Penn argued that the issue was "not a social question but
one of racial opportunity."[20] Penn's plea was lost on the white negotiators.
Talks of church union broke down. When the Methodist Episcopal Church
and the Methodist Episcopal Church, South, finally merged in 1939, black
Methodists were put in a Jim Crow nongeographical conference known as
the Central Jurisdiction.[21]

Apart from the Methodist Episcopal Church, the Roman Catholic
Church was the only other predominantly white church body to have more
than 50,000 African American members before U.S. entry into the great
European conflict in 1917. The special religious census of 1906 counted
44,982 black Catholics, and the census ten years later tabulated 51,688. Except for Louisiana and Maryland, the black Roman Catholic presence in
the southern states was marginal. Catholicism failed to make significant
gains in a region dominated by Baptists and Methodists both before and
after the Civil War.[22] Many migrants were exposed to Catholicism for the
first time when they crowded into urban areas of the North and competed
for jobs and living space with the Irish and other traditionally Catholic
ethnic groups.

Several other predominantly white denominations had small black memberships of note. The Presbyterian Church in the U.S.A., like the Methodist Episcopal Church, had gone into the South after the Civil War to
do educational and missionary work among the freedmen. It had approximately 5,000 black members in the South in 1870 and 30,000 in 1915.

Historians have attributed the Presbyterians' slow growth among southern blacks to the denomination's emphasis on a trained ministry and its middle-class orientation.[23] The Protestant Episcopal Church had about 20,000 black members in 1906 and several thousand more in 1916.[24] Perceived as even more elitist than the Presbyterians, Episcopalians resisted elevating blacks to the episcopacy. One black had been appointed to Haiti in 1874, another to Liberia in 1885. Edward Thomas Denby became suffragan bishop of Arkansas in 1916, but this position was not sufficient to satisfy the aspirations of black Episcopalians such as George Alexander McGuire. Inspired by the "racial vision" of Marcus Garvey, who came to the United States to start his mass movement in 1916, McGuire organized an independent Episcopal congregation in New York City.[25]

The religious censuses of 1906 and 1916 failed to specifically attend to the emergence of black Pentecostal and Holiness churches. The absence of data on them is significant. Holiness and Pentecostal groups existed, of course, but they were too few to fall within the statistical net of the census-takers. It is important, however, to introduce them here, for hindsight shows that these churches grew exponentially as a result of the swelling black populations of northern cities.

Charles Harrison Mason, a Baptist clergyman in Arkansas, accepted the holiness teaching of entire sanctification in 1893. He and Charles Price Jones founded what became known as the Church of God in Christ in an old cotton-gin house in Lexington, Mississippi, about 1894. After attending William J. Seymour's Azuza Street Pentecostal Mission in Los Angeles in 1907, Mason split with Jones over the necessity of receiving the gift of tongue-speaking. The Holiness faction, led by Jones, became the Church of Christ (Holiness), U.S.A., which today has about 10,000 members and at one time almost merged with the predominantly white Church of the Nazarene. Mason's Pentecostal group kept the name Church of God in Christ (COGIC). The COGIC, with a membership today approaching 6 million, has had its headquarters in Memphis since 1907. Though strongly represented in rural areas of the Mississippi Valley, the COGIC branched out during the Great Migration era to such northern cities as Chicago, Detroit, Pittsburgh, and Philadelphia, and the New York borough of Brooklyn.[26]

As a result of the Great Migration the Pentecostal and the Holiness movements, which spawned scores of groups other than the COGIC and the Church of Christ (Holiness), U.S.A., became important alternatives to the near hegemony of the Baptist and Methodist denominations. Joseph

Washington, Jr., writes, "Holiness and Pentecostal churches were . . . the creations of experienced urban life, stemming directly from the new mobility of blacks. Its was only in the urban milieu that one could put together Holiness dogma, Pentecostal answers, black music, and the deepest depression into a whole shape and sound limited neither by tradition nor fears of being put-down by wise fools or foolish wisemen."[27] A fuller account of the reasons why recently transplanted southern blacks found a spiritual home in Pentecostal and Holiness fellowships is long overdue.

But on the eve of the Great Migration no other religious label was more firmly identified in the public mind with African Americans than that of Baptist. Black Baptists outnumbered black Methodists before the Civil War and maintained their numerical advantage at the time of the first federal religious census in 1890. This plurality held true for four successive national counts, the last in 1936. The 1906 census reported 2,141,998 members for the National Baptist Convention in the South (fifteen states plus the District of Columbia). Only about 120,000 members resided in the North. At the close of 1906 the National Baptist Convention was the largest black denomination in the country, with churches in thirty-three states, the territory of New Mexico, and the District of Columbia. Georgia, Mississippi, Alabama, and Texas led the Convention in number of organizations and members. With more than 17,000 clergy plus many licentiates and more than 18,000 churches, the National Baptist Convention was an institution of immense influence. This influence was felt especially among African Americans in the South where the denomination had its greatest strength. Its exact membership before the Great Migration is difficult to determine. Victor I. Masters, after diligent efforts to sort out conflicting claims, estimated that black Baptists in the South approximated 2.7 million in 1915.[28]

Unlike the two major northern African Methodist denominations that achieved connectional independence before the Civil War, black Baptist consolidation at the national level did not materialize until the late nineteenth century. The jealously guarded principle of congregational autonomy, ideological debates concerning cooperation with white Baptists in missionary and educational endeavors, and uncertainty over the functions and powers of national conventions impeded the road to unity. Only local, state, and regional associations emerged before the Civil War. With the rise of black Baptist nationalism in the post-Reconstruction era, sentiment grew for a unified denomination that could symbolize racial and religious independence. The Baptist Foreign Mission Convention was founded in Montgomery in 1880, followed in 1886 by the American National Baptist Convention. In 1893 the National Baptist Educational Convention organized to further the cause of an educated ministry. A preliminary but ultimately inadequate move to surmount localism and regionalism resulted in the Tripartite Union of 1893. Two years later, the National Baptist Convention was constituted, bringing together the Foreign Mission Convention, the American National Baptist Convention, and the National Baptist Educational Convention. Elias Camp Morris, born of slave parents and pastor of the Centennial Baptist Church of Helena, Arkansas, became the united organization's first president. He served twenty-seven years. During Morris's tenure, the National Baptist Convention underwent periods of great internal discord while simultaneously having to confront challenges in a rapidly changing external world.[29]

The strongest challenge to Convention unity and Morris's leadership came to a head just before the Great Migration over control of the National Baptist Publishing Board. Established in 1896 and headquartered in Nashville, the board was a highly successful business enterprise with the principal mission of producing church and Sunday School literature. Richard Henry Boyd, a veteran organizer of Baptists in Texas, moved to Nashville in 1896 and incorporated the NBPB as a legal entity separate from the Convention. An astute and aggressive businessman, Boyd copyrighted board materials in his name, used the profits to build a new publishing house on property he owned in Nashville, and ventured into the manufacture of church and school furniture. By 1911 the NBPB employed 150 clerks, stenographers, and skilled workers.[30] Boyd's success raised concerns about Convention control, and President Morris established a committee to oversee the growing dispute. In his address to the annual session of 1914 Morris attempted to rein in the independent Boyd, but the Philadelphia meeting adjourned without any resolution of the controversy.[31]

In September 1915 the National Baptist Convention reconvened in Chicago for its thirty-fifth annual session. An estimated 15,000 to 20,000 delegates assembled in the Chicago Armory where[32] they witnessed an acrimonious legal and personal battle between the Morris and Boyd factions. The Morris majority drew up a new charter to embody what was termed the "Popular Policy of Convention Control of Boards" and asked Boyd to give an accounting of the financial records of the NBPB. The dispute moved from the armory to the courts. After a judge determined that the anti-Morris faction was a rump convention, Boyd and his supporters withdrew to establish the National Baptist Convention, Unincorporated.

The unincorporated body met in Kansas City, Missouri, in September 1916 under the leadership of E. P. Jones. Jones denounced the Chicago session as a "flagrant usurpation of power" and spiritedly defended Boyd and the publishing board, which he described as "the greatest of its kind owned and operated by black men throughout the breadth of the universe."[33] The National Baptist Convention met in Savannah that same month. President Morris applauded his supporters for having successfully fought off the Boyd camp's efforts to establish "oligarchy in Baptist Institutions."[34] Morris kept control of the incorporated body until 1922, the year of his death, but he devoted much of his time and energy in the years after the schism to defending the majority's actions at the Chicago meeting.

Most delegates who withdrew under the banner of the National Baptist Convention, Unincorporated, were from Texas and Arkansas. The rival national bodies fought over the state conventions and regional associations, and uncertainty prevailed regarding the number of members and churches allied with Boyd and his camp. As the federal Bureau of the Census was about to publish its report on religious bodies for 1916, it received the erroneous information that reunification had been accomplished; the census thus listed only the National Baptist Convention, crediting it with 2,938,579 members, a 29.9 per cent increase from 1906.[35] When the 1926 census was compiled, the unincorporated body received no separate tabulation, though it was credited with 243 churches that were reported in 1916 with the National Baptist Convention. Boyd and G. B. Hancock, statistical secretary of the unincorporated body, claimed 750,000 members in 1915.[36] Since some congregations were affiliated with both conventions, and membership statistics were subject to dispute in the wake of the Chicago division, the exact strength of the rival black Baptist conventions remains uncertain. When the Morris-led National Baptist Convention met in Savannah in 1916, it was said to have in excess of 2.5 million members.[37] The National Baptist Convention, U.S.A., contained approximately 90 percent of the black Baptist congregations in 1926.[38]

In the years after the schism at Chicago, during which thousands of black Baptists were participating in the Great Migration, emotions ran high and the resources of both church bodies were devoted to the battle. Law suits flew back and forth, and pulpits were denied preachers who represented the contending parties. Boyd told the *Nashville Globe* in March 1918 that the whole affair had been "a regular cat and parrot wrangle."[39] The Chicago break had long-lasting consequences, chief of them the inability of the two conventions to forge any kind of a common strategy to deal with the institutional impact of the Great Migration.

Given the fratricidal warfare among Baptists and the failure of the three largest Methodist bodies to form an alliance, the chances for cooperation across denominational lines looked bleak. Nevertheless, Richard R. Wright, Jr., urged black religious leaders to convene in summitlike fashion. "If we had the authority," Wright declared, "we would call an ECUMENICAL COUNCIL OF DARK SKINNED CHRISTIANS . . . . With a problem of migration making such changes in Negro life as have not been made since Emancipation, is not the combined counsel of the race needed?"[40] Wright's appeal for such a council of race leaders went unanswered. No ecumenical structures existed for Baptist and Methodist cooperation beyond scattered interdenominational alliances that focused on local matters. The Fraternal Council of Negro Churches, whose founder and first president was Bishop Reverdy C. Ransom of the AME Church, would not be organized until 1934.[41]

The three largest black Methodist churches and the National Baptist Convention did belong to the Federal Council of Churches. Organized in 1908, the council was controlled by white Protestants, and little attention was paid to the needs of African Americans during its formative period. The council's assimilationist philosophy was echoed by key black representatives. In 1912 W. A. Blackwell, pastor of an AME Zion congregation in Chicago, delivered an address to the council on the theme, "The Uplifting of a Race." His message illustrates how little thought these interdenominational representatives were giving to the plight of African Americans. "The reports from our large cities, made by experts in this line of Christian activity, and carefully giving to us the line of battle to save our foreign population, leave out any reference to the Negro as a distinct social order from that of the white native American."[42] Blackwell believed that this was "a sign of a better reign of Christ's Spirit" because the council's reports had not treated African Americans as a separate concern. A more plausible interpretation is that the council was preoccupied with the plight of immigrants from Europe who had settled in the large northern cities and had not yet perceived African American urban dwellers as a significant social "problem."

The Federal Council of Churches' executive committee did not authorize the formation of an interracial Committee on Negro Churches until 1914. In 1916 the committee declared itself in favor of enhancing the work of black churches located in towns and rural areas, and it stated its opposition to lynching. During the war years the committee barely functioned; eventually, it was combined with the Committee on Negro Troops and Communities, which had the purpose of assisting black denominations in their ministry to African American soldiers.[43] When the migration question came before the Federal Council of Churches in December 1916, it did so in striking fashion. Bishop Wilbur P. Thirkield, a white Methodist from Louisiana, had just presented the report of the Committee on Negro Churches in which he called attention to the increasing number of blacks leaving the South but gave scant attention to the root causes. J. R. Hawkins, financial secretary of the AME Church, tried to set the record straight: "Conditions have become intolerable. The whole problem rests with white men who have control of the government and the railroads, and municipalities. If you want to settle it right, go back to your homes, and confer with a few Negroes, who will tell you the truth, if it be guaranteed that they won't be run away from their homes. They love their homes, but life is not worth living there."[44] Reverdy C. Ransom echoed Hawkins's sentiments by chiding the white representatives: "Here you gentlemen are telling us that the European war is the chief challenge to American Christianity, when 250,000 Negroes are fleeing northward, some of them for their very lives. Is not this the chief challenge of Christianity?"[45]

The Federal Council of Churches, though it included black denominations with a membership of nearly 4 million, did not fully recognize the importance of the black exodus from the South until 1919 when interracial violence erupted in several northern cities. Then the Committee on Negro Churches warned, "We must face frankly the fact that a most dangerous inter-racial situation threatens our country. The problems growing out of the presence of two races in America are clearly seen to be nation-wide and the adjustment must necessarily be made on the basis of national responsibility. The migration of thousands of Negroes to the North emphasizes this fact. The outbreaks in several cities and the persistence of the anarchy and treason of lynch-law imperil our democracy."[46]

Motivated by fear of a national crisis, the council engaged George Edmund Haynes to conduct studies of the migration question in which he was to focus on problems resulting from urban congestion and the adjustment of rural blacks to industrial life. Born in 1880, Haynes had earned a Ph.D. in sociology from Columbia University in 1910. His tenure as director of Negro economics for the U. S. Department of Labor during World War I had already given him an opportunity to examine the problems of black migrants.[47]

Richard R. Wright, Jr., served on the Committee on Negro Churches of the Federal Council of Churches, but like other representatives of the black denominations he felt that assisting the migrants was the special obligation of the black churches. In the aftermath of the Civil War black northern church leaders had claimed that because blood is thicker than water they had the inside track in the race of northern denominations, white and black, to capture the allegiance of the ex-slaves and take possession of church properties formerly used as slave missions by southern whites. Now as their racial kin were coming North, African American church leaders echoed the themes of duty to the race and race unity. In August 1916 Wright asked rhetorically in the *Christian Recorder*, "Should Negroes Come North?," and gave a resounding "Yes." "We stand for Negro immigration, and throw out our arms of welcome to every Negro who desires to come," he declared.[48]

Wright recognized that a regional shift in the distribution of the country's African American population had the potential of disrupting existing patterns of race adjustment in the North. The infusion of "new blood," he argued, portended more black businesses, larger black churches, and greater black political clout, perhaps even the election of blacks to Congress. Wright believed that the exodus of as many as 2 million blacks from the South also would prove beneficial to those left behind. The white South's fear of "Negro domination" might lessen, he asserted, if the region had to divorce its labor problem from the race question by seeking to attract European immigrants.

Given Wright's belief that the Great Migration offered the prospect of a better day for African Americans as a race, it is no surprise that he sounded the exodus trumpet loud and long. He urged southern blacks to come North and swell the ranks of African American institutions. To African American Christians in northern cities such as Philadelphia, where Wright lived, he said: "Get these Negroes in your churches; make them welcome; don't turn up your nose and let the saloon man and the gambler do all the welcoming. Help them buy homes, encourage them to send for their families and to put their children in school. Welcome them, welcome them; yes bid them thrice welcome. They are ours, as good as our fathers were, and no worse than we are."[49]

Wright challenged fellow African Methodists to cooperate in meeting the migrants' needs. Wright's own study of urban social and economic conditions in the industrial United States had convinced him that churches needed to adopt new methods of ministry and service in the city. In 1917 he went to the Federal Council of Churches to ask it to assist his denomination in organizing a commission on social service. A decade earlier he said of the larger urban black churches that they were doing "an immense amount of unsystematized charity and social work, but it is largely done to secure money to pay Church debts and not for the social uplift. These churches are run chiefly on the small town church plan, with everything proportionately greater than in the small town."[50] Wright's sociological studies of urban life made him keenly aware that a large geographical shift of southern blacks would place unprecedented demands on black churches and necessitate a bolder and more socially active kind of ministry.

Though African American denominational leaders sympathized with the plight of southern blacks, they were more hesitant than Wright about calling for a mass exodus. The Great Migration did not have the moral clarity of the nineteenth-century abolitionist and temperance crusades in which an absolute evil could be identified and fought against. In the abstract, of course, the liberation of the oppressed was the work of Divine Providence, but practical considerations had to be weighed in the balance. The AME bishops who met at Hot Springs, Arkansas, in early 1917 told southern blacks not to sacrifice their homes and belongings in precipitous fashion. Potential migrants were urged to have a definite destination in mind and to investigate conditions in the North before leaving. AME pastors in the South were told to provide certificates of character to their members who were bound for the Promised Land because of reports that the bulk of the migrant population was shiftless or even criminal.[51] Most AME bishops were far from endorsing a wholesale migration, such as that called for by Robert Abbot, the flamboyant publisher of the *Chicago Defender*. Many did not share Wright's view that northern black communities could absorb a great mass of southerners who had no experience in coping with the harsh realities of American life.

Some AME leaders openly opposed the migration, or they expressed such strong reservations about being overwhelmed by a southern army in need of uplift that they cautioned against the exodus. Anti-migration bishops with large southern memberships attempted to protect their episcopal districts. Bishop Levi J. Coppin of Philadelphia, who was familiar with the social and environmental conditions in the North and a champion of the "uplift" campaign, warned against the "tempting lure" of the big city.[52] Bishop Benjamin F. Lee attended a meeting of the South Alabama Conference in December 1916 and gave strong counsel: "We beg to advise you who are still in the South to remain on the farms, and buy small or large tracts of land while you can, and practice honesty, industry, and frugality. Practice the habit of saving; purchase lots and build houses; cultivate a friendly relationship with all races."[53] Lee believed that the chief cause of the "restlessness" of southern blacks was inferior education. He held out the hope that white farmers and businessmen would soon awake to the need of improving school facilities to keep black labor in the South. In the meantime, southern blacks were to rally around "the church as the Ark of Safety on this troubled sea." Lee echoed Booker T. Washington's belief that the black church would be the agent for improvement. The church, Lee argued, "is the magnet in every group of negroes, the great soul from whose center go the investigations for better homes, and higher degrees of honesty, intellectual development and moral character."[54] Elevated to the episcopacy in 1892, Lee served as senior bishop from 1916 to 1924. He thus had a vested interest in seeing that African Methodism did not suffer institutional losses because of the Great Migration.

Lee's attitude toward the Great Migration did not represent the entire AME episcopate, though many local clergy in the South echoed his sentiments. Bishop William H. Heard of Mississippi spoke favorably of the superior economic, educational, and social advantages of the North at a mass meeting held in 1917 at Mother Bethel in Philadelphia.[55] Bishop John B. Hurst of Baltimore also endorsed the exodus.[56] In some cases, what bishops and preachers said made little difference to those eager to escape. L. G. Duncan, pastor of the Cherry Street AME Church in Dothan, Alabama, in a letter published in the local press urged his people to stay where they were. He later admitted, "It had but little effect upon them. They continued to go." More than a hundred of Duncan's members had left and more were about to, though he tried to discourage them with warnings about cold winters, disease, and death in the big cities of the North. Like Hurst, Duncan felt that the "real remedy" was in the hands of southern whites. He had interviewed blacks who were packing to leave, and they had told him,

" 'I am going where I can get more for my labor,' 'where I can educate my children,' 'where I can vote,' 'where I can get justice at law,' 'where I can get better treatment on the railroad trains and street cars,' 'where I won't be lynched.' " [57]

Bishops deliberated, church officials met, and pronouncements of one kind of another were issued, but southern blacks were deciding for themselves what to do. Local clergy became alarmed. It was becoming increasingly clear that the Great Migration was drawing away the core membership of theretofore relatively stable congregations. J. B. Carter, a preacher in the AME South Alabama Conference, saw firsthand how strongly the lure of economic opportunity in the North weakened church ties. Some of the most prosperous African Methodists in his part of the state had left. One man, whom Carter knew to be making "a big salary" in Detroit, encouraged others to come, thereby setting off a chain reaction. "Even in my own church," Carter acknowledged, "there is the greatest unrest among some of my congregation who are employed in the steel plant, and what make good wages." [58] T. M. Coffee, presiding elder of the Bessemer conference, also called attention to the loss of that segment of the South's black population that formerly provided local African Methodist churches with dependable support. Coffee reported that "many of the very best" were leaving, not just "the alley negroes, the shiftless class that are discontented." [59] Even the clergy were going. One minister went to visit his bishop after losing fifty-two of his ninety-six members in only six months. "Bishop," he confessed, "I just come up here to notify you that I'm getting ready to follow my flock." [60]

Bishops and local clergy within the AME Church were not the only religious leaders caught up in the debate over the Great Migration. Bishop J. J. Clinton of the AME Zion Church was based in North Carolina, a state that was his denomination's principal source of members. Clinton endeavored to discourage migration, telling those seeking to leave that they would be "surrounded by an entirely foreign atmosphere" in a strange land. [61] Bishop Wilbur P. Thirkield of the Methodist Episcopal Church expressed particular concern over the dwindling membership of the "colored conferences" in the South. He reported that from 40 percent to 90 percent of the membership of some Louisiana Methodist churches had enlisted in the pilgrimage to the Land of Hope. The Rev. G. E. Queen, a denominational colleague of Thirkield, appears to have acknowledged the inevitable. He advised white Methodists to conduct more missionary work in northern cities to prevent transplanted members from being lured into competing denominations.[62] Others, too, were forced to reckon with the fact that urban America was to be the next missionary frontier. Several preachers of the CME Church, finding their congregations depleted, requested reassignment to those cities in the North to which their members had gone.[63]

As the magnitude of the Great Migration became clearer, AME leaders came to realize that the exodus posed a critical challenge to existing ecclesiastical arrangements. The regional distribution of power was one of a number of patterns likely to be disturbed. R. R. Downs of the AME Church discussed the matter candidly in *Voice of Missions.* Southern delegates formed the majority of representatives to the General Conference, the highest lawmaking body of the church. Voting blocs of any significance were always to be taken seriously in the hotly contested election of bishops. Downs warned against standing on "selfish provincialism of geographical lines or political division" in dealing with the migration question. He worried that partisans might be tempted to encourage the exodus so as to "shift from south to north, the seat of legislative authority." Downs called on leaders in both northern and southern sections to assume a national perspective. The AME, he argued, should know no Mason-Dixon Line. To those northern members who had reservations about the migrants, Downs said, "Upon their own merits they must stand or fall; our fears are the products of our own diseased imagination and our doubts of them evidence our lack of faith in the Negro and our own moral weakness." Downs then urged northerners to give their brothers and sisters in the faith a ready reception and a helping hand, for they were expected to be "institutional propagators."[64]

The Great Migration posed a special challenge to the most southern of black Methodist bodies. Approximately nine out of ten members of the CME Church lived in the South, according to the religious census of 1906. The CME had little success in breaking beyond its regional boundaries before World War I, and northern industrial centers were yet to be explored by the denomination. In 1917 Bishop Randall Albert Carter made several investigations of northern conditions for the CME and then appealed to the readership of the *Christian Index:* "THERE MUST BE MORE CHURCHES ESTABLISHED IN ALL OF THE LARGE CITIES OF THE NORTH AND EAST AND NORTHWEST FOR OUR PEOPLE OR SERIOUS RESULTS WILL OBTAIN IN THE FUTURE. The opportunity and duty of the C.M.E. Church are great and urgent. WE MUST BUY SOME OF THE VACANT CHURCHES OFFERED FOR SALE AT ONCE AND PLACE SOME OF OUR

BEST PASTORS IN THEM TO GATHER THE PEOPLE LEST THEY PERISH."[65] Carter set his sights on Detroit and other industrial centers. Elected at the General Conference in St. Louis to the office of bishop with more votes than any candidate in the history of the denomination, Carter was the right man to spearhead the move of the CME into the North. Credited with setting up more than 250 churches during his career, he was called by his admirers the "Little Giant" and the "Great Expansionist."[66]

The CME had long been perceived by its denominational rivals as an exclusively southern body and an inferior one at that. But Carter saw a chance to alter those perceptions because of the unsettled conditions created by the Great Migration. He believed that the rigid denominational lines that African Americans clung to would be cast off in the North. Once settled, migrants would visit the congregation nearest to them that displayed the most zeal in attracting new members. It was therefore important that representatives of the CME move aggressively before members fell by the wayside or were lured into other church bodies.

Carter toured the North, going from Chicago to Detroit, in July 1917. J. Arthur Hamlett, editor of the *Christian Index,* accompanied him and reported in detail on how the bishop was received by CME members who had already migrated to Detroit. Carter spoke in AME churches that CME members were attending because their connection's flag had not yet been planted in the city. When word reached them that Carter had arrived, they responded, "He is our Bishop and from home." Hamlett tells us that in order to shake their bishop's hand migrants waited in the aisles and around the doors of the churches where Carter preached. The displaced CME folks told their bishop, "We want our own church; we want to hear our own preachers; there are hundreds of members here of our church." Before Hamlett and Carter left Detroit, they expected to have a hundred members organized into a CME congregation.[67]

The bishops of the CME held a number of meetings to discuss strategies for grouping, organizing, and retaining members who were relocating. The stakes, at least as perceived by these institutional propagators, were high. At a meeting held in Cleveland in October 1918 the bishops sounded a call to arms. There were to be no slackers. "Dereliction upon the part of the leadership of our Church," the bishops warned, "may result in the loss of a number of our members, sufficiently large as to indicate that we are retrograding which would so seriously reflect upon us." The bishops discussed ways to prevent institutional regression and decided on a singular course of action. "We further agreed," they informed the CME membership, "that we should have a building in some noted city as a Mecca for our wandering Zion." They chose Cleveland and asked all CME members to help raise $50,000 for the purchase of a structure from the Christian Scientists.[68] Western Pennsylvania was another center of CME activity. Because large numbers of migrants were employed in the steel industry, an opportunity arose and Carter seized it. The CME created a new Pittsburgh district in 1916, and Carter obtained $2,000 to buy property for the first CME church in that city.[69] In 1919 he made his home in Chicago, and from that strategic point he supervised the expansion of his beloved connection in the North.

The AME Zion Church also recognized the need to position itself to take advantage of the changing conditions of African American religious life. Leaders met in Chicago in the fall of 1917 and discussed how best to marshal the denomination's resources in order to expand its base in the North. Only a few percentage points less southern than the CME Church, the Zion connection also had to readjust itself in light of the Great Migration. The Rev. James Mason played on connectional pride when relaying the plan of the AME Zion bishops to the readers of the *Star of Zion:* "Are we to safeguard and save Zion Methodists from aggressions without, and self-satisfaction, indifference, and in-efficiency within?"[70] J. H. Ellison, presiding elder of the Western New York District Conference, added another dimension to the discussion. Older northern churches that welcomed migrants could expect to experience spiritual renewal and financial bolstering; southern migrants were eager to become willing church workers.[71]

In 1920 Bishop G. L. Blackwell of the Fifth Episcopal District reported that Zion Methodists had advanced in the North because of the Great Migration, particularly in the Michigan Conference, which included Detroit and Chicago. The denomination had five churches in Chicago and three in Detroit by 1920. "We must refrain from naming others," Blackwell wrote, "suffice it so say that the most remarkable progress has been in the Michigan Conference, where we have sought to meet the growing needs of the large influx of our members from the South. The membership has grown from 1105 in 1916 to 3709 in 1920."[72]

Because of the episcopal structures under which black Methodists operated, they theoretically had greater capabilities than black Baptists to garner and redistribute resources, thus capitalizing on the opportunities for church expansion in the North. In the nineteenth century African Methodists advanced quickly from their cultural hearth in the eastern cities of the North to the interior of the country by sending out missionaries who organized congregations. Then, after the Civil War they expanded many times over by moving into the South and claiming the ecclesiastical contraband of the ex-slaves as their own, often taking in entire congregations at a time.[73]

The story that unfolded during and after the Great Migration reads differently. African Methodists had to face the possibility of net losses unless they found a way to reach, regain, and hold the southern members who were at risk of becoming a scattered people throughout the North. Unlike earlier seasons of denominational growth, that of the Great Migration era took place in urban settings where many religious options existed within the black community, and already established black churches, some of them founded by free blacks before the Civil War, claimed the territory. In ways that patterned events after the Civil War and during Reconstruction, representatives of the black Methodist denominations also had to contend with the presence of Methodists "of color" under the episcopal control of white Methodists.

During the Great Migration era, the Methodist Episcopal Church also expressed concern about maintaining its African American constituency. In some sections of the South from 40 percent to 90 percent of the membership of congregations had left, and churches in the Washington and Delaware conferences, through which main rail lines from the South ran, did not have the resources to accommodate the migrants. The Rev. G. E. Queen acknowledged that local pastors were overwhelmed and called for the appointment of special missionaries so that the Washington and Delaware conferences could increase in size and offset the drain on the southern conferences.[74]

Denominational loyalty, structure, and leadership were all critical to success in the competition to maintain organizational prestige. But everything depended on having adequate financial means to push forward domestic missions on the front lines of battle in the urban centers to which migrants flocked. J. R. Rankin, secretary of the AME Church extension board, discovered how difficult the task was. He reported that by 1918 the church's southern districts had lost a large portion of their membership "because of the conditions of the times which threatened the very life of our Church."[75] Assessments for the work of the church-at-large by means of financial assessment—called the Dollar Money plan—were not being met. Rankin pleaded with the southern wing of his church to set aside intersectional rivalry and respond to the emergency needs created by the exodus. The missionary department, Rankin avowed, was unable to provide much assistance. Its budget was devoted to the foreign mission field, especially to Africa. Not a few bishops had risen to high seats in the councils of the church by promoting the importance of saving souls there.[76] Could the church now put as much emphasis on domestic needs in the North as it had on foreign missions? This question was critical.

Domestic missions had to make ends meet out of the 4 percent of the Dollar Money that was controlled by bishops of individual districts. Annual conferences customarily kept back monies earmarked for domestic missions to support projects within the districts' geographical borders. This option prevented effective redistribution of funds to northern cities where the need for new churches was most critical. Rankin estimated that any northern city to which at least 5,000 migrants came would have 600 to 700 AME members new to the city and in need of spiritual care. He acknowledged that two-thirds of the migrants who had been church-affiliated in the South were Baptists, while only one-third were Methodists. Rankin worried that in many places the AME Church was unknown and thus no denominational representatives were there to greet "our people emigrating." He warned colleagues that "the other denominations [were] receiving into church relations the people from our Zion, if they are received at all."[77] In 1917 the membership of the AME Church extension board turned over. The new board took a more aggressive posture by proposing a fund of $25,000 to provide church homes in the North for those leaving the South.[78] Need far outstripped resources. In 1918 the board had to report that it could not furnish the special appropriations requested by those who were concerned with providing missions for migrants.[79]

Other black denominations shared the AME's dilemma of not having an effective means of raising financial resources for allocation and distribution at the national level. Bishops had to cajole and plead for monies sufficient to support the varied enterprises of their respective districts in ordinary times, and they had no contingency funds adequate for national emergencies. Black Methodists were generally poor; church contributions often came at great sacrifice. The perennial struggle for funds sufficient for denominational operations was compounded during the Great Migration years by the disruption of congregational life in those parts of the South caught up in the exodus. The loss of church elders and deacons to the North proved an additional burden to congregations already struggling to stay financially solvent. An air of uncertainty about the future prevailed. As secretary of the Department of Church Extension and Home Missions for the AMEZ Church, John C. Dancy watched developments with a sense of alarm. He reported that because of the "general exodus from the South," a critical need existed to house members who had gone North. The large northern churches were debt-ridden, and southern congregations, to whom Dancy appealed, were weakened by the loss of many of their strongest supporters. Dancy told the AMEZ leadership that the problem was not about to resolve itself through inaction. The exodus fever was "constantly spreading."[80]

The frenzy to go North prevailed in Baptist as well as Methodist circles. Because Baptists prided themselves on the lack of denominational super-structures, their institutional reaction to the Great Migration is more difficult to reconstruct. The National Baptist Convention gave little attention to organized mission work and social service in northern cities before World War I. When Elias C. Morris addressed the ill-fated Chicago meeting of the National Baptist Convention in 1915, he urged a united effort to open mission fields in India, Africa, "and on all the isles of the seas" after the war. He spoke of the joint ventures in theological education and evangelism aimed at southern blacks between the National Baptist Convention and the Home Mission Board of the Northern Baptist Convention (white). Similar efforts, directed toward northern blacks, awaited future discussions with the American Baptist Home Mission Society.[81]

Black Baptist efforts to advance home mission work had long been snared in the thicket of racial and denominational politics. In 1895 the Southern Baptist Convention agreed to match dollar-for-dollar the monies raised by the Convention for domestic missions. Use of the funds was restricted to the southern states. After the National Baptist Convention schism in 1915, representatives of the Southern Baptist Convention attempted to act as intermediaries in peace talks. While the warring factions fought for control of the various boards, the white southern Baptists tried to continue support of the Home Mission Board without siding with either the incorporated or unincorporated bodies. Reunion talks eventually broke off, and the Southern Baptist Convention threw its support toward the National Baptist Convention, Inc., which prevailed in the court battle over control of the Home Mission Board.

But the battle had been costly. Contributions from state associations fell off. President Morris of the incorporated body was worried. With so many members on the move, he implored his constituency, "Let each Baptist act, and act quickly that our denomination may take its proper place among the churches of the country."[82] By 1918 the Home Mission Board was nearly $2,000 in debt, and many state boards either did not exist or were inactive.[83] The Rev. Joseph A. Booker, secretary of the Home Mission Board, acknowledged in 1919 that a five-year effort to use the last Sunday in May as Home Mission Rally Day had been "a dismal failure." Though the cooperative plan with the white board still existed, not all state associations had active home mission boards, and many of them lagged in contributions. Booker's national board was forced to design a program of state apportionments and issue a call for greater cooperation between the various state and district organizations. Fully aware of the traditional Baptist predilection for congregational autonomy, Booker stressed that this plan did not "smack of centralization of government."[84]

When the National Baptist Convention, Inc., met in annual session at Indianapolis in 1920 the delegates heard that the home missions picture had not improved. "The only money your Board has had for general missionary work," Secretary Booker acknowledged, "was the money given it by the Home Mission Board of the Southern Baptist Convention, and the few dollars we could pick up through mail through the state members of the Board, and through the sale of literature of its own making." Booker believed that the Great Migration intensified his denomination's lack of ability to conduct effective domestic missions. With so many congregations in the South having lost members and others in the North having "just set up housekeeping," the need for support was unprecedented. Many clergy with scattered or weakened congregations no longer had regular salaries. The southern state associations, the principal source of mission contributions, were themselves in financial crisis. Booker defended the Home Mission Board against charges that it had for far too long been interested primarily in work in the South by pointing out that the Home Mission Board of the Southern Baptist Convention had restricted its matching funds (about $5,000 or $6,000 a year) to the southern field.

The Boyd-led Baptists were also handicapped in their ability to address the institutional crisis precipitated by the Great Migration. They blamed their troubles in part on favoritism shown their rivals by the white Southern Baptist Convention. The *Atlanta Independent* reported that the Morris faction held control of the home missions money when the National Baptist Convention, Unincorporated, met in Atlanta in 1917. Partial to Boyd and the National Baptist Convention, Inc., the *Independent* castigated preachers loyal to Morris for "creating dissension, preaching strife, fighting in the streets, telling lies, publishing slander," and, in general, making their living "by intriguing and keeping up a disturbance in the denomination for salaried positions most largely financed by our white brethren."[85] In 1918 the Southern Baptist Convention sought to resolve the debate by declaring that it would send mission support "in due proportion and equity" to each of the black conventions but that it would finance no individual who engaged in furthering strife within Baptist circles.[86]

Charity alone was insufficient to meet the needs of either Baptist convention. Morris's presidential address in 1920 drew attention to the effects that the Great Migration had on his denomination's ability to provide for the religious care of a "wandering Zion." "The tremendous migration of our people from the South to the North and West," Morris reported, "has transferred much of the problem of missionary activity to those sections. The going of our people into sections which are perhaps more highly cultivated, and where the environments are different from those which they left, does not reduce the problem but rather increases it; for most of the people who leave the South go into the cities of the North and West, and in their new surroundings at once need the help of missionary effort."[87] Attempts failed to forge a cooperative plan between the Board of Missions of the National Baptist Convention, Inc., and the American Baptist Home Mission Society, the domestic missions agency of northern white Baptists. In addition, a plan to link several black state associations in the North in domestic mission activities proved unworkable because funds from the southern associations came in so scantily.[88] By 1924 the Home Mission Board of the National Baptist Convention had to admit that it was stymied. Despite pleas from many quarters that some funds given by the Southern Baptist Convention be diverted to the North because of the great need there, the board was unable to do so. Ironically, northern white Baptists had given some funds for mission work in the West, which S. S. Odum, chairman of the Home Mission Board, thought was important. "Unless we take hold and go to the rescue of our brethren in the field," Odum argued, "then the Mormons and other denominations will take the field that rightly is ours."[89]

But the greater challenge was dereliction of duty in northern cities, not losses to the Mormons of Utah. The Home Mission Board struggled to dispel the notion that it was politically a southern board. Only in 1921 was its corresponding secretary able to report, "The brotherhood of the Negro

Baptists of this Convention has been so well cemented by the trowel of love and denominational loyalty that the Mason and Dixon line has been blotted from our map."[90] Despite the emergence of this national perspective, conditions in the field were far from ideal. The secretary acknowledged that because of the exodus from the South of "thousands and thousands of our people," there was a critical need for missionaries "to gather our people into proper folds" in the North. The Home Mission Board was also being called on to assist congregations in the South that had been so weakened by the Great Migration that they needed financial aid. In summing up the task at hand, the secretary said, "We have quite a number of destitute fields both North and South where there are no churches at all and no regular preachers and in many cases no opportunity for religious worship."[91]

The male leadership of the National Baptist Convention did not have the entire responsibility of conducting mission work and aiding churches. Nannie H. Burroughs led the fight of Baptist women to obtain a greater voice in denominational affairs. An experienced teacher who had organized the Woman's Industrial Club in Louisville, where she was secretary for the Foreign Mission Board of the National Baptist Convention, Inc., Burroughs had a gift for organization and motivation. Her speech, "How the Sisters Are Hindered from Helping," at the annual meeting of Baptists in Richmond in 1900 led to the establishment of the Woman's Convention Auxiliary to the National Baptist Convention.[92] The Woman's Convention before World War I expressed concern about urban conditions in the North and supported a number of social workers and missionaries. In 1914 Burroughs, then the auxiliary's corresponding secretary, reported that hundreds of small Baptist churches were springing up in cities like Pittsburgh, Chicago, New York, Washington, D.C., and Philadelphia and were in need of better spiritual leadership. Burroughs characterized a type of urban preacher as "always an unlettered, lazy, green coat, self-appointed, sliding elder, who is too slippery to be caught by the collector and too crooked to be straightened out by any court." These preachers and their churches, "often a front room of a shacky residence," Burroughs warned, "are going to lead to the spiritual, moral and financial undoing of that mass of credulous, emotional people, who will follow any man who can turn on the 'rousements' and make them shout and scream like hornets are stinging them."[93]

To counter this trend, Baptists were asked to establish institutional churches to serve as beacons of religious enlightenment and social service. The stakes were high, for as S. Willie Layten, president of the Woman's Convention Auxiliary, told her coworkers in 1916, the country was entering into a time of great peril and, paradoxically, of great promise. Human institutions were being put to their final test, Layten declared. "During the very near future human history will behold its mightiest revolutions, its most dreadful retributions and judgments, preparing the way for Christ to take to Him His great power and reign." She challenged the Baptist women: "The opportunity for giving the gospel-education to Negroes is larger today than ever before; and now is the time to lift up the banner of the gospel in our denominational work with fresh courage and unwearying effort."[94]

The women hoped to expand their activities but were drawn into the battle that absorbed so much of the time and energy of the male leadership after the 1915 split. Both sides laid claim to the Woman's Convention training school for girls in Washington, D.C. Established by Burroughs in 1909 on six acres with a farmhouse, the school became famous for Burroughs's program of "the 3 Bs—the Bible, bath and broom: clean life, clean body, clean home." The training school offered classes in cooking, sewing, childcare, typing, shorthand, and bookkeeping, among other things. It was the pride of the women's auxiliary.

The women sought to restore peace between the male-dominated national bodies while retaining control of the school under the Woman's Convention. To critics who accused her of seeking personal gain by attempting to maintain the training school's independence, Burroughs responded, "The legal owner of this property is the Woman's Convention. That organization will never have to spend one cent in court nor one hour in a fight to get what is theirs. I am not a rogue. I am a trustee."[95] It took all of Burroughs's political skills to negotiate the labyrinth of black Baptist politics and still keep legal and fiduciary control of her school under the Woman's Convention. Burroughs and her board of trustees eventually won the struggle to remain independent of the male-dominated parent body. Most of the school's support derived from Burroughs's lecturing and fund-raising.[96]

The Woman's Convention Auxiliary sponsored social workers and missionaries who labored in northern cities during the Great Migration era, but the dissension among the men made its work all the more difficult. Historian Evelyn Brooks Higginbotham maintains that the Woman's Convention "embraced the sociological emphasis of the Social Gospel Movement and secular progressivism" as early as 1912. This understanding of the mission of the church was accompanied by sharp criticism of male clergy who "preached 'too much Heaven and too little practical Christian living.'" The gender conflict within the National Baptist Convention, this assessment suggests, involved a redefinition of the church's mission as well as the issue of male domination.[97]

In the black church tradition much of the burden for assisting the poor and needy and of building up new missions fell to women. W. E. B. Du Bois observed in 1909 that women did "the larger part of the benevolent work" in African American churches.[98] The resources of the Baptist Women's Missionary Convention and the Woman's Parent Mite Missionary Society of the AME Church, to use but two examples of important female voluntary organizations, were directed primarily toward missionary work in Africa. Women in local congregations did a great deal of charity work, as much as their means allowed. Higginbotham has observed that before the Great Migration the missionary and service programs conducted by Baptist women reflected a "moralistic emphasis and concern for 'respectable behavior' [that] translated into a belief in the primacy of spiritual over material progress."[99] The adequacy of this emphasis came into question, especially as other organizations, like the National Association of Colored Women, expanded their efforts for civic and social betterment, and local organizations such as the Ida Wells Club in Chicago challenged the hegemony of denominationally based women's groups.[100] Recognizing the urgency for cooperation with nonchurch-based groups, Layten spoke of the special needs of black women migrants at the tenth biennial meeting of the National Association of Colored Women in 1916. In 1918 she urged members of the Woman's Convention to work with the NACW in its efforts to document the patriotism and contributions of black women during World War I. Not too sharp a distinction, however, should be drawn between the church and civic organizations of black women during these years; their leadership and membership rosters often overlapped.[101]

The black clubwomen and church women who led in the campaign to improve urban conditions were in the vanguard of a new understanding of religion and the city. Church historian Robert T. Handy notes that American Protestantism in the nineteenth century had a close affinity with rural culture. "Agrarian leanings and the values of the Protestant world," he argues, "tended to reinforce" each other. This affinity remained, even after social indicators revealed that the United States was becoming a more urban culture. Evangelical Protestants viewed the large cities as modern Babylons in which tens of thousands went astray on the path of unrighteousness. Hostility to the city surfaced among Protestants fearful of the influx of immigrants from Central and Southern Europe who swelled the ranks of Roman Catholicism. The Prohibition movement and passage of the Eighteenth Amendment in 1919 had widespread support among Evangelical Protestants, who associated liquor with urban life. Handy concludes, "The city as a menace to be resisted and redirected into familiar Protestant patterns—this was the predominant understanding among Protestants at the turn of the century."[102]

White liberal Protestant denominations were the first to come to terms with the unique challenges of church life in the urban United States. Black denominations, for a variety of reasons theological and social, were wary of the propagators of the Social Gospel movement. Theological fundamentalism ran deep in many black church circles, and many black clergy in the South were themselves fearful of large cities and their sinful ways. The Great Migration forced the encounter of the black church and the city more intensely than ever before. When denominational leaders spoke of the Second Exodus as a time of great testing, with institutional survival at stake, they were not over-reacting.

The major African American denominations, with the exception of the CME, had their historical origins in northern cities. But they experienced their greatest increase in the rural areas and small towns of the South after the Civil War. Like many of their white counterparts, black denominational leaders made their way to the higher ranks of the clergy by pastoring churches in small towns and rural areas. When promoted to larger churches in urban centers, they tended to perpetuate styles of leadership and church methods with which they were accustomed. The few black institutional churches that did exist in northern cities before the Great Migration tended to have ties to predominantly white denominations. St. Phillip's Episcopal Church in New York City and Philadelphia's Episcopal Church of the Crucifixion and Berean Presbyterian Church were the most prominent examples of churches with social service programs.[103]

When a handful of ministers in black denominations experimented with new methods in an effort to redefine the urban church's mission, they encountered suspicion and resistance. This reaction was experienced by two African Methodist ministers in Chicago. Reverdy Ransom founded Institutional Church and Social Settlement in 1900 at 3827 Dearborn Avenue in a structure formerly used by the First Presbyterian Church as a railroad mission. Then thirty-nine years old and a convert to the Social Gospel, Ransom had studied at Oberlin College and Wilberforce University. Described by historian Ralph Luker as "the foremost black spokesman for the social gospel of his generation,"[104] Ransom was first assigned to Chicago's Bethel AME Church. Concerned that Chicago's black churches were not effectively serving newcomers to the city, he left Bethel and set up Institutional Church with programs that included kindergarten, cooking and sewing classes, nursery, social club, employment agency, and manual training classes. Richard R. Wright, Jr., and Monroe N. Work, students at the University of Chicago Divinity School, assisted Ransom with the boys' club. Chicago's *Inter-Ocean* compared Ransom's church to Jane Addams's Hull House and Graham Taylor's Chicago Commons, institutions already noted for urban social service.

Ransom's attempts to expand the scope of church work as well as his increasing involvement in electoral politics and racial protest organizations did not sit well with some of his clerical colleagues. Bishop Abraham Grant prohibited him from preaching on Sundays, and conservatives warned their congregations against participating in Institutional Church programs. Hearing in 1904 that he was about to be transferred to Indiana by Bishop C. T. Shaffer, Ransom resigned his post and left Chicago for Boston. His replacement, J. W. Townsend, took over with the self-declared purpose of remaking Institutional into "a regular AME Church, to cut out the social foolishness, and bring religion back."[105] Many years later Ransom reflected on the failure of his colleagues to meet the challenges of urban social ministry. "Most of the preachers of Negro churches of the day strenuously opposed it [ICSS]. It was entirely beyond their conception of what a church should be. Their only appeal was preaching, praying, singing, shouting, baptizing and Holy Communion, but going out into the streets and highways, bearing a message of social, moral, economic and civic salvation they did not believe to be a function of the church."[106]

If it is fair to generalize from the fate of the ICSS, then many African Methodist preachers before the Great Migration functioned with a definition of the church's mission derived from rural and small-town models. They had not yet come to terms with the unique demands of an urban ministry in the twentieth century. Wright wrote in 1905 that organized church work by African American churches only encompassed education, missions, and personal charity.[107] Historian Robert Gregg examined the African Methodist understanding of the church's mission in the pre-Great Migration period from 1890 to 1915. His analysis of the thought of Levi J. Coppin, an important AME clergyman and bishop from Philadelphia, confirms Wright's observation. Coppin, editor of the AME *Church Review* between 1888 and 1896 and bishop between 1900 and 1920, viewed the mission to black sharecroppers in traditional terms of charity and uplift.[108]

After Ransom left Chicago, Richard R. Wright, Jr., established his own pioneering urban mission in 1905, known as Trinity Mission and Culture Center. Introduced to the Social Gospel by Shailer Mathews and other faculty at the University of Chicago Divinity School, Wright wrote his thesis on "The Industrial Condition of Negroes in Chicago." With little to go on except his own idealism and conviction that the Christian church ought to offer the poor more than praying and preaching, Wright opened Trinity Mission at 155 West 18th Street. He admitted that he had outgrown the fundamentalist theology of the black church, which he said "took but little account of social conditions and concerned itself chiefly with 'getting to heaven.' "[109] Wright's mission was located among an estimated 7,500 blacks who lived north of 22nd Street and between Michigan and Clark and who were, according to the *Chicago Inter-Ocean,* "practically shut off from all the benefits" of the established black churches, many of which had already relocated farther south among the more well-to-do. Wright had to confront every imaginable social need. He worked as a porter, messenger, and unskilled laborer to support himself while preaching, teaching, and offering a variety of social services.

Overwhelmed by the task, Wright left Chicago in 1907 to begin graduate work at the University of Pennsylvania. While a special fellow in sociology he continued to promote more effective social work on the part of African American denominations and local churches.[110] In 1909 Wright became editor of the *Christian Recorder,* the AME Church's periodical with the largest circulation. In 1912 he assumed similar responsibilities with the *AME Church Review.* These posts gave him a platform from which to prod his denomination to a greater recognition of the special needs of the urban poor. For example, just as the Great Migration was beginning in earnest, Wright chided denominational leaders, especially those in charge of large city churches, for putting too little emphasis on people and too much on obtaining fine buildings that encumbered the faithful with debt. He urged churches to employ social workers, nurses, school and home visitors, and probation officers as well as supplying better recreational opportunities for youth.[111]

Wright and Ransom belonged to a small but vocal group of black clergy who tried to expand the traditional understanding of "church" on the eve of the Great Migration.[112] Another pioneering Social Gospel advocate was William De Berry. Educated at Fisk and Oberlin, he came to Springfield, Massachusetts, in 1899 and gradually transformed a small Congregational church into a large, multiservice institutional church that employed social workers and had a housing department and an employment bureau. By the mid-1920s St. John's operated a boarding home for girls, a social center for boys that included vocational training, a farm and summer camp, and an apartment house. De Berry had the advantage of belonging to a liberal, predominantly white, and northern church body with a reformist record in attempting to meet social as well as spiritual needs.[113]

Black Baptists had the reputation of being strongly against departing from the sin/salvation model of ministry. Yet a few pioneering clergy in the urban North cut across the grain of social conservatism and theological fundamentalism in their own denomination. Hardly a liberal by the standards of the day, Elijah John Fisher did recognize need when he saw it. After coming to Chicago from Georgia in 1902 he expanded the membership of Olivet Baptist from 600 to nearly 4,000 and positioned the church so that his successor, Lacey Kirk Williams, who assumed Olivet's pulpit in 1916, had the resources to expand social services once the migrants started to pour into the Windy City.[114]

S. Mattie Fisher, Elijah Fisher's daughter, was one of the first trained black social workers in the United States. In 1918 she and a Mrs. Jessie Mapp conducted 5,082 interviews to find out how Olivet could best assist the migrants. In their report to the Women's American Baptist Home Mission Society, Fisher admitted, "at first we did not know how to begin, and it would have been amusing to have seen how timidly we did approach those in the homes."[115] Their earnestness and persistence paid off, for, based on the survey, Olivet organized a variety of programs at its community center and attracted many migrants who joined the church. Williams recalled that during this period of "upheaval and adjustment in the Negro community, no membership drives or 'go to church' movement was needed to bring about the great enrollment; those who found the church helpful in weekday affairs gladly made it their place of worship on Sundays."[116]

Nevertheless, African American institutional churches were the exception rather than the rule on the eve of World War I.[117] The special demands of ministry in an urban industrial environment were not yet fully met or understood by most black clergy. The social problems that arose in black communities in the wake of the Great Migration outstripped the resources of the African American denominations and demonstrated the inadequacy of traditional methods of dealing with social problems, such as the mutual aid societies popular in the nineteenth century and church-based charities. The established churches in the North had not developed institutional mechanisms to address the multiple social and economic needs of blacks whose church ties were weak or nonexistent, nor were they prepared for the strains the Great Migration placed on preexisting church structures.

Critics of the churches, including voices from inside, believed that the most important institution of black life and culture needed a revolution in thinking as much as a cornucopia of material resources if the crisis was to be met. Miles Mark Fisher, himself a Baptist preacher, characterized the state of African American religion in the pre-Great Migration era: "Prior to the world-war the negro preacher was expounding otherworldly topics in addition to an occasional sensational or practical sermon." Fisher, then on the faculty of Virginia Union University, cited as confirmation the summary of the black religious situation given by Bishop John Hurst of the AME Church in the *Christian Recorder* in 1914: "The Negro church has remained disinterested and almost dormant in regard to problems that especially affect it."[118] Others echoed Hurst's critique of the black church. Preachers typically invoked the Bible as the solution to social problems. Biblical literalism and theological fundamentalism proved the order of the day. As was true of salvation-centered white Protestantism, sermons heard in many black churches focused on deliverance from the wages of sin and the redemption of individuals. Not much was said about the fundamental economic and political structures of American society. Individual misbehavior, not corporate evil, drew the preachers' wrath.

When ministers did engage in direct attacks on social evils in their communities, their campaigns tended to concentrate on the sins that were targeted by their nineteenth-century counterparts. Some became involved in campaigns to rid their neighborhoods of houses of ill-repute, as Adam Clayton Powell, Sr., did when he became pastor of Abyssinian Baptist Church in New York City in 1908. Others promoted the virtue of temperance in the use of alcohol. The Rev. William W. Brown of Metropolitan

Baptist preached in Harlem against what he described as "Sabbath desecration, neglect of church duties, Sunday games, gambling, immoral plays
with improper dancing, and open pool halls."[119] The Great Migration
posed a problem far more complex and far less amenable to moralistic jeremiads than the personal sins with which churches traditionally dealt. The
exodus, like all social movements of great consequence, was beyond anyone's ability to confidently predict its outcome or its consequences.

In summary, black religious leaders saw the exodus from the South as
full of great peril. Their people were being scattered across the land like
a "wandering Zion." Differences of opinion existed as to whether or not
great numbers of black southerners ought to be part of it. The existing
structures of the established denominations reflected a nineteenth-century
ecclesiology and were weighted toward the pre-World War I demographic
majorities in the South. Sectional tensions emerged in the debate over the
redistribution of resources that some leaders felt was necessary in order to
respond to the institutional crisis precipitated by the Great Migration.

Because of their ecclesiastical polity, black Methodists theoretically stood
in a better position to capitalize on the new opportunities for church expansion opening up in northern industrial centers. But rivalry among them,
reminiscent of the post-Civil War period, prevented a unified effort. The
Federal Council of Churches offered little support. Black Baptists suffered
the lingering effects of the acrimonious split of 1915 and found it very difficult to gather the necessary resources for an effective and efficient domestic
missions program at the national level. An air of uncertainty prevailed.

Many black religious leaders believed that the Great Migration posed
a threat to the institutional vitality of their denominations unless a way
could be found to stem the diaspora of their members and their loss to
others. The Great Migration could prove to be a blessing in disguise, but
only if the black churches aided the hand of providence by regathering
their scattered Zion and rebuilding anew in the Promised Land. A small
number of northern ministers attempted to institutionalize the principles
of the Social Gospel movement. Given the experiences of Wright and Ransom with the bureaucracies then in place, it was not altogether clear that
the African American denominations had the will to redefine their mission
to adequately respond to the needs of the migrant host. The time of testing was at hand.

5

"INTO THE PROMISED LAND"

In 1920 Ralph Borsodi and his family fled New York, bought seven acres of land near the city, and in the summer began an experiment in subsistence farming by canning tomatoes. The derelict farm near Suffern was without plumbing, running water, gas, electricity, or steam heat, but life in the country promised deliverance from the uncertainties and perils of city life. Borsodi and his family had lost their rented home during the 1920 housing shortage engendered by the Great War. Unwilling to join the army of New Yorkers of all races in the struggle to find decent urban housing, Borsodi looked to the country as his family's New Canaan in which security, health, leisure, and beauty could be found. While his wife canned garden produce, Borsodi mused on what he called the "thralldom of our factory-dominated civilization" and discovered, so he claimed, "an entirely new theory of living" in the art of domestic production.[1]

African American migrants from the South could have told this back-to-the-land enthusiast about the bitter fruit of hardscrabble lives in the open country. It is no small irony that African Americans by the hundreds of thousands were entering the factory-dominated civilization of the North in search of the Promised Land as middle-class European American city dwellers were escaping to the developing suburbs or the countryside.[2]

Black migrants came to the city with their own hopes and dreams, which were not that much different from those of Ralph Borsodi, his wife, and two children. They also wanted a host of tangibles and intangibles under the catch-all of "a better way of life." Some migrants were tired of the vagaries of sharecropping and hoped that in this exchange of place they might obtain a surer hold on economic security. Others were refugees from persecution to whom the North, whatever the hardships, offered the promise of something better. As one migrant put it, "To die from the bite of frost is far more glorious than that of the mob."[3] Escape from the South, declared Chicago's *Record Herald,* was tantamount to a "Second Emancipation."[4]

"By 1910," Charles N. Glaab and A. Theodore Brown write in *A History of Urban America,* "American culture can be said, in a number of senses, to have become urbanized, and this marked a significant change in the character of American society."[5] Glaab and Brown emphasize that the decade 1900–1910 was the last one in which immigrants from Europe accounted significantly for the growth of northern cities. Once the Great War began, northern urban populations swelled primarily because of the influx of African Americans from the South. The encounter of southern blacks with the northern city exacted a high emotional toll. Farah Jasmine Griffin's study of migration narratives, epitomized by Richard Wright's autobiography *American Hunger,* highlights the literary form in which "the arrival of Southern blacks is marked by an immediate confrontation with a foreign place and time, with technology and urban capitalism, with the crowd and the stranger."[6] Civic leaders did not anticipate the magnitude of the migrant flood and were understandably unprepared to deal with the multiple needs of newcomers—emotional, spiritual, and material. They did not envision the transformation of urban America when, in the words of historian Richard Sherman, "the black ghetto . . . replaced the black belt as the symbol of the American dilemma."[7]

The influx of European immigrants strained the social fabric of the urban United States before the arrival of southern blacks. Disillusioned reformers were already questioning liberalism's assumptions about the possibilities of social uplift and the transforming influence of America's melting pot. The racial composition of the Great Migration sent a tremor throughout the ranks of urban progressives who subscribed to the notion of the meltable ethnic.[8] W. E. B. Du Bois emphasized this fact in an address before the Up-to-Date Club of Youngstown, Ohio, in 1917: "Every year 1,000,000 immigrants land at Ellis Island and dissolve themselves into the population of our country. This does not worry you. But this sudden colored movement to the North fills you with apprehension. Unconsciously you have made a caste settlement in your minds and this immigration has changed the well-ordered thoughts of your social problems."[9]

Much was at stake in the unfolding of the exodus drama. The refugees from the South, including those able to articulate their motivation only in the notion that they wanted a square deal, were participants in the historic struggle for African American liberation. Because the exodus was thought of as a second Emancipation with repercussions for all African Americans, giving the migrants a helping hand became a moral and racial obligation. A black minister in New Britain, Connecticut, believed that God had "put it into the hearts of some of the large establishments to solicit the help of the negro race" and that the exodus was God's answer to his prayers to "send men of my race from the Southlands."[10] Hamilton Travis, president of the Federation of Colored Organizations of New Jersey, invited the cooperation of "our white neighbors with whom we have lived on terms that have given to the progress of both races," but he acknowledged that those of "common blood" would "perhaps more than any . . . be the gainers or losers" in the campaign to "assimilate our brothers who have come to us from the Southland."[11] Black residents of Boston were urged to organize committees to teach newcomers proper methods of living to prevent deterioration of their own standing in the community.[12] The AME Council of Bishops described problems stemming from the exodus as "varied and serious" and urged "ceaseless vigilance and untiring activity" in making sure that life in the Promised Land did not become "a new form of bondage."[13]

Some northern African American leaders worried that the Great Migration would undercut the arrangements whereby a black minority had secured a small, though inequitable, share in the material benefits of urban life. Doubts about assimilating southern migrants came from many quarters, even from some who had initially been cheerleaders for the Great Migration. "The level of intelligence and efficiency in these newcomers," Du Bois asserted in 1923, "is almost inevitably below that of the Negro already established in the North." White public opinion lumped the new with the old, and racial prejudice and segregation increased. Of the black northerner's "peculiar dilemma," Du Bois wrote, "He knows that his southern brother will and must migrate just as he himself migrated either in this generation or the last. He feels more or less acutely his own duty to help the newcomer, and the Negro churches and charities of great cities like

Chicago and New York have done a marvelous work in this direction even though it has fallen far below the need."[14]

Was the dilemma of the northern black all that unusual? Other established ethnic groups assisted their own in coping with urban life in the United States. Kelly Miller, dean of the College of Arts and Sciences at Howard University, argued that migrant laborers from the South did not have the advantage of a helping hand such as the Catholic Church gave European immigrants. Unless African American churches and other northern agencies rose to the challenge, he warned, "the last state of the race would be worse than the first."[15] Du Bois also thought that the stakes were higher for African Americans than for other groups: "the black Northerner knows what this migration costs."[16] "It means," Du Bois editorialized in the *Crisis,* "undoubtedly, increased hardships for them; it will bring proscription and temporary difficulties, but anything that means freedom to black slaves should be welcomed by their free northern brothers."[17] At the tenth anniversary meeting of the NAACP in 1919 Eugene Kinckle Jones urged the celebrants to action on behalf of the migrants because "when they come into our communities they are confronted with a new environment. The North is just as new to them as Europe is to an American. Much more so."[18]

Welcoming the migrants proved difficult in part because of preexisting character stereotypes. In 1911 Richard R. Wright, Jr., already was observing a general impression among northerners that crime increased when southern blacks settled in northern cities. For example, the *Toledo Times* called on "the respectable colored population" in the city to assist local authorities in dealing with a growth in crime that the newspaper claimed was caused by "the influx of so many of their people from the south, and the general character of the newcomers."[19] Wright attributed what he termed "serious pathological conditions" in many American cities, not to defects in the personal character of migrants, but to the essential nature of urban life. In an essay, "The Economic Conditions of Negroes in the North: Tendencies Downward," Wright wrote: "The rapid concentration into small areas of hundreds of thousands of people, of different antecedents and training, dependent upon certain large industries, has caused the multiplication of social problems practically unknown in this country a century ago." Wright urged his readers to understand that in the transition "from a simple country environment to a complex city one, we must necessarily expect an excess of pathological situations."[20]

The Rev. A. L. Scott, whose church was located in Boston's South End, was also careful not to attribute a rise in criminal behavior to the character of the migrants. He, as Wright intimated, felt that the urban environment was hostile to good moral deportment. Four liquor stores were located near his church, the average weekly wage of breadwinners was only $12.00, and migrant families lived in shacks "below the laws of sanitation."[21] E. E. Swanston, an AME Zion clergyman, attributed many of the problems of African American migrants to the influence of the poorer classes of European immigrants. "Illiteracy, vices, crimes and oriental peculiarities," he wrote in the *Star of Zion,* "are alike imbibed as far as Negroes come under the direct influence of the immigrants."[22]

Pittsburgh authorities rounded up a group of seventy-one migrants in the winter of 1916 and threw them into the workhouse, although none had committed a crime. The Rev. J. C. Austin led a committee of supporters who met the migrants at the door of the courthouse after a judge ruled that their incarceration was illegal. The migrants were escorted to Austin's Ebenezer Baptist Church for a banquet, speeches, and special services. The committee phoned local employment agencies and found jobs for most of those who had run afoul of white Pittsburgh's fears of being overwhelmed by black vagrants. Housing was located, and the men received winter clothing. About fifty of them joined Austin's church. Austin then went to Augusta, Georgia, to conduct a campaign to better prepare those who wished to come to Pittsburgh.[23]

In other cities as well, hostile northern whites aggravated the plight of the migrants and made the task of those who sought to assist them more difficult. Antiblack outbreaks of violence in the urban United States preceded the arrival of the migrants during World War I, but ingredients were present for intensified racial conflict during the Great Migration. Competition for jobs and housing created strains between African Americans and European immigrants. To protect their precarious economic foothold, African Americans supported restrictions on immigration from Southern and Eastern Europe.[24] Whites reacted with panic as they witnessed newcomers from the South swell the existing black areas and then break out of those boundaries into traditionally white neighborhoods. With the renewal of immigration during the economic depression after the conflict in Europe ended, many industrial centers witnessed labor strife and became racial tinderboxes. Racial violence, sparked by a single incident, could and did erupt without warning.

Such was the case in East St. Louis and Chicago. The tragedy in East St. Louis began on July 2, 1917, after white workers, many of them employed in the stockyards and packing plants, became convinced that blacks were being imported to take their jobs. A rumor spread that a black man had killed a white man in a robbery attempt. Whites attacked blacks indiscriminately.[25] The Chicago race riot began on July 27, 1919, when whites began throwing rocks at black teenagers swimming near the 29th Street bathing beach. The ensuing chaos exacted a far greater toll in deaths, injuries, and property damage than the East St. Louis conflict and led to a major investigation of the causes of interracial urban violence.[26] Walter F. White of the NAACP drew a direct connection between the migratory movements from the South and the increase of racial hostility and violence in Chicago, arguing that southern white migrants helped spread "the virus of race hatred" that was directed at black migrants having difficulty in adapting to their new environment and who were, he admitted, "at times irresponsible and sometimes even boisterous."[27] Sociologist Allen Grinshaw has counted eighteen major interracial disturbances in the country from 1915 until 1919.[28]

Both the potential and the reality of heightened racial discord weighed heavily on the minds of northerners who felt responsible for the migrants. Thousands paraded in silent protest up Fifth Avenue in New York City on July 28, 1917, in the wake of the race riots in East St. Louis and elsewhere. The African American press noted that virtually every black church was represented and that denominational differences were set aside in this display of unity.[29] At a mass meeting held at Mother Bethel AME Church in Philadelphia various speakers condemned the antiblack violence and urged the migrants not to lose heart. "We deplore the few uncivilized happenings which have occurred, such as the East St. Louis riots," declared the Rev. H. Y. Arnett of Wilmington, Delaware. "These are the rare exceptions, and, be assured from me, they will not be repeated. In the North riots may come in hot haste, but the law is here and brings the offenders to a just punishment."[30]

The guardians of community order in the North turned to black church officials for advice as the thermostat of interracial conflict rose. In July 1917 W. S. Scarborough, president of the AME Church's Wilberforce University and other African American leaders met with the chamber of commerce of Columbus, Ohio. These white businessmen expressed alarm over the advent of the "colored legion" from the South and hoped that Scarborough would offer sage counsel. "I would rather that our brethren from the South come more gradually than in such numbers," Scarborough told chamber representatives, "but now that they are here, let us help put them on their feet."[31] Noting the violent outbreaks in many cities and warning that "the persistence of the anarchy and treason of lynch-law imperil our democracy," the Federal Council of Churches issued a statement in 1919 calling on religious organizations to meet the crisis "or leadership will pass not only to secular agencies, economic or socialistic, but to forces that are destructive of civilization."[32]

In this crisis-filled atmosphere many voices argued that the task of assisting migrants to be self-sustaining was not only the sacred duty but the special provenance of local black churches and clergy. The old notion of the historic centrality of religious organizations to African American communities again came into play, and the burden fell accordingly. "The most powerful agency in the community," Richard R. Wright, Jr., argued in his study of black Philadelphia in 1907, "is the Negro church, which in many cases is the only agency which reaches the thousands who come to the city."[33] Du Bois ranked churches ahead of any other institution as the "real units of race life" on which "the bulk of organized efforts of Negroes in any direction should center."[34] Even Robert Abbott's *Chicago Defender,* which was frequently critical of the clergy, acknowledged, "The minister occupies the position of moral, spiritual and, in a sense, the social leadership of the Race. They [*sic*] have the ear of the people even more than a newspaper, for they reach a multitude of people who neither read [n]or think."[35]

Prominent voices within the black denominations agreed that the church was to be the primary agency in addressing the migration question. When the Bush Terminal Warehouse Corporation in New York City began to experience difficulties with migrant labor, it sought assistance from the New York League on Urban Conditions in 1918. The Urban League chapter found that 75 percent of the men employed at Bush Terminal had been in the North less than two years, and it placed a welfare worker in the company to assist them. The *Voice of Missions* of the AME Church applauded the Urban League's action but countered that "these new situations illustrate most effectively how necessary it is for the church to have a new home missionary program for the new age."[36]

The African American press in the South helped popularize the expectation that when the migrants entered a northern city, their religious kin would be there to welcome them. The *Charleston Messenger* editorialized in 1919:

> The Christian Church is the greatest institution that exists among the colored people to-day. The Negro church represents a larger number of the members of the race than any other organization. It has the masses of our people in its membership. It has their confidence and they give it a support that is remarkable when we consider their small means. The churches have for a long time been the community centers for our people. The leaders of the church have very largely been the leaders of the community. It is also true the church has molded the public sentiment of our race in a very large measure. They have been taught by the living voice of the pulpit. He has been to them a source of information and inspiration. Through these critical times through which we are passing we trust that the Negro church may still have the leadership of the Negro race.[37]

While saluting the importance of the church, this editorial contains a note of concern regarding the future. Norfolk's *Journal and Guide* echoed this concern in 1919: "There has been no period in the history of Afro-Americans when our great church organizations needed more than now the services of strong and capable men. These are perilous times, and unless signs fail, there are critical times ahead, and we need as bishops, as preachers, and as leaders in every department of our racial activities the strongest men that we can summon to these places of leadership."[38] Such expressions suggest that many were watching African American churches with a critical eye during the Great Migration years.

When we add black southerners' expectations to the widespread belief that churches were to be the bulwark among institutions in ameliorating problems attendant to the Great Migration, the burden becomes even heavier. Historians of post-Civil War African American life and culture agree that no institution in the South was more critical to those who became migrants than the church. "For the great mass of black people" Joel Williamson writes, "probably the local church—the Mount Zions, the Bethels, and Ebenezers—began to support a life that included satisfying styles of politics, social structure, and entertainment as well as religion."[39] The church was important in urban as well as rural settings. After studying southern cities from 1865 to 1890, Howard N. Rabinowitz concluded,

"The churches were the single most important institutions in the lives of urban Negroes."[40] The combination of southern tradition and northern expectations provided many people concerned with the effects of the Great Migration with reason enough to target the black church as the institution most responsible for handling what Mary McCleod Bethune termed "the social challenge of our generation." Writing for *Opportunity* in 1925 when it was clear that the city and not the country was to be the battleground for millions of African Americans seeking a more "abundant life," Bethune put the church ahead of all other agents, even trained social workers, as the means by which the challenge was to be met.[41]

Most migrants came as refugees with little material capital to reconstruct their lives in northern cities. How well-prepared and willing were African Americans in the North to assist them, or as the *Pittsburgh Courier* expressed it, to engage in "a remarkable opportunity for racial civic activity"?[42] In 1901 Du Bois wrote "that the history of the Negro in northern cities is the history of the rise of a small group growing by accretions from without, but at the same time periodically overwhelmed by them and compelled to start again when once the new material has been assimilated."[43] Du Bois was specifically referring to the post-Civil War influx of "the freed immigrants from the South," but his words were prophetic of the Great Migration.

Philadelphia was felt by Du Bois to best illustrate how African Americans native to the North periodically confronted the challenge of assimilating newcomers from the South. In an extensive study of the city published in 1899 he gave special attention to the institutional structure of the African American community. He reiterated the axiom that the church was central to communal life, but when he enumerated the functions of Philadelphia's black churches "in order of present emphasis," raising the annual budget was in first place while efforts at social betterment placed sixth and last.[44] Nevertheless, Du Bois emphasized, "all movements for social betterment are apt to centre in the church."[45] In a later study, done at Atlanta University with assistance from the John F. Slater Fund, Du Bois used data from the special federal religious census of 1906 and returned to the theme of "efforts at social betterment." He concluded that most benevolent work in African American churches was done by churchwomen, was locally rather than nationally organized, and could be subsumed under the category of Christian benevolence or charity.[46]

Before the Great Migration few African American churches in the North had social programs as extensive as those in white institutional churches that grew out of the Social Gospel movement. "Institutional churchwork among the colored people," social worker Maude K. Griffin wrote in 1905, "is yet in its infancy compared to that maintained by many of the churches of the white race."[47] It has been noted that Reverdy Ransom's Institutional Church and Social Settlement pioneered in urban social ministry and offered a variety of services that went beyond traditional expressions of Christian benevolence. Du Bois hailed Ransom's experiment as the "most advanced step in the direction of making the church exist for the people rather than the people for the church."[48] But others questioned whether or not Institutional, or for that matter, Richard Wright, Jr.'s, Trinity Mission, were truly churches.

With constituencies rather than memberships, Institutional and Trinity were probably closer to the settlement-house model than to the traditional church. Had settlement houses for blacks existed in Chicago, some of the burden might have been lifted from the churches. But historian Thomas Lee Philpott notes that "the settlements founded by blacks themselves were the poorest-equipped, the most severely underfinanced, and the shortest-lived."[49] Of the nine settlements established for black Chicagoans between 1900 and 1916, only one still operated at the time of the race riot of 1919. Other institutions in northern black communities, however, engaged in social service activities. "The field wholly occupied in the South by the church is shared in the North by the labor union, the social club, lectures, and political and other organizations," the Chicago Commission on Race Relations concluded after investigating the riot of 1919. "Some of the northern churches, realizing this," the commission observed, "have established employment agencies and other activities of a more social nature in response to this new demand."[50] Chicago aside (to be dealt with more intensively in chapter 6) it is worth sampling church-based relief efforts in other cities of the North to which migrants came. The strength of church-based social services to migrants varied from city to city, and generalizations drawn about work done in one urban center do not necessarily apply elsewhere. Each city has its own story to tell.

In New York the evolution of community outreach programs was tied to the demographic changes in Harlem and the movement uptown of the older black churches. In 1909 the *New York Age* urged churches to establish rescue missions and other agencies to assist those who would otherwise be abandoned "to the pity and more often the oversight of white charity workers."[51] Because of an influx of migrants from the West Indies and the South, a housing shortage existed in Tenderloin (27th to 42nd Streets) and San Juan Hill (57th to 64th Streets). The move up to Harlem, a process almost complete by 1920, was under way as the Great Migration began. Historic congregations in Manhattan, such as St. Philip's Protestant Episcopal Church, Bethel AME Church, and Mother Zion AME, were torn between going to Harlem and seeing their memberships dwindle at downtown locations. The National League for the Protection of Colored Women surveyed Harlem in 1917 and found 20,000 African American residents; nineteen black churches representing eight denominations; fifty-six saloons; and seven street gangs with such names as the "Harlem Rats" and the "Fifth Avenue Bottle Gang."[52]

The move to Harlem was not without risk. Congregations sometimes split over the prospects of relocating and rebuilding. This happened at Mother Zion AME after J. H. McMullen announced in 1908 that he wished to leave to become pastor of a mission church in Harlem.[53] Members of Abyssinian Baptist opposed Adam Clayton Powell, Sr.'s attempt to move to Harlem from the church's West 40th Street site. The Rev. R. D. Wynn, one of Powell's predecessors, dreamed that God had instructed him to lead his flock to Harlem, but the congregation refused, and after a pastorate of sixteen years Wynn resigned.[54] Before the onset of the Great Migration, Abyssinian put up tents on vacant lots in Harlem for mass worship and organized a group called the Highways and Hedges Society to encourage people from the streets to attend. By 1910 Abyssinian was holding branch services in Harlem.

Powell waged a movement "on to Harlem," but his members were unwilling to abandon their valuable midtown property. Powell was already living in Harlem when he began his campaign to convince Abyssinian Baptist members to relocate. In 1917 Abyssinian still had only a mission outpost.[55] In 1918 the church at the midtown Manhattan location had 3,487 members and was the largest Baptist congregation in the East and the second-largest black Baptist congregation in the country; only Olivet Baptist in Chicago outranked it. In 1919 the congregation did agree to hold one of its regular services each month at Harlem's Young's Casino. Powell pressed for more. In 1920 the *New York Age* announced that Abyssinian had purchased six lots at West 138th Street for $15,000.[56] By 1920 Harlem had an African American population of 73,953, about 70 percent of the black population in all of Manhattan.

The number of members opposed to the move to Harlem increased when plans were filed in May 1921 proposing a structure that cost almost $300,000. Sensing the need for dramatic action, Powell read his resignation on the second Sunday in December 1921: "I am leaving your church to devote myself to evangelistic campaigns, the delivering of lectures and the publishing of sermons because you do not believe in progressive and aggressive leadership."[57] The tactic worked. Within weeks contributions to the building program were flowing in. Fifteen days after Powell announced his resignation, Abyssinian sold its midtown Manhattan property for $190,000, and on April 9, 1922, the church broke ground in Harlem and construction began, financed largely by members who pledged one-tenth of their weekly earnings. The final service was held at the old site on the third Sunday in January 1923. Once established in Harlem, Abyssinian opened a soup kitchen for hungry migrants and made a concerted effort to recruit new members. Powell's church grew to become one of the most important institutions in Harlem, in part because of its multidimensional social ministry that included a community house.[58] Powell was convinced that a more effective and enlarged ministry was possible in Harlem because it was rapidly becoming the lodestar for black migrants.

The debate over the cost of rebuilding anew in Harlem initially caused Abyssinian to lose ground in the competition for new members and made relocating more expensive.[59] The same was true for Mt. Olivet Baptist Church, which did not move to Harlem until 1925. By that time, construction costs and property values in Harlem had skyrocketed and its West 43rd Street edifice had become less valuable. In 1902 Mt. Olivet had been the largest black church in New York City; by 1929 it ranked only tenth. In contrast, Metropolitan Baptist, which had its own building in Harlem as early as 1907 and was originally known as Mercy Street Baptist, benefited from the influx of migrants. Under the leadership of William W. Brown, Metropolitan grew from 300 members in 1914 to 3,500 in 1920. Brown was successful in part because he addressed more than the spiritual needs of his members. By 1918 Metropolitan was already operating a butcher shop, a grocery, and a hardware store for its members. Brown encouraged real estate investment, purchased houses in Harlem to rent to members, and encouraged cooperative business enterprises.[60]

St. Mark's Methodist Episcopal Church remained on West 53rd Street in Manhattan until the 1920s, but it established the Salem Memorial Mission in a Harlem storefront on West 124th Street about 1902. Three women attended the first service. The congregation eventually purchased property on West 133rd Street in 1910. By 1916 it had nearly a thousand members in Harlem. Frederick Asbury Cullen, Salem's pastor, pioneered in social ministry. He was successful in attracting migrants with a combination of evangelistic preaching, emphasis on personal salvation, and a progressive social philosophy. On occasion, Cullen, the foster father of Harlem Renaissance poet Countee Cullen, invited the controversial revivalist G. Wilson Becton to aid him in enlarging Salem's appeal to the masses. Through an extensive athletic program Cullen worked with youth gangs, and he was one of the organizers of the 1917 Silent Protest Parade.[61]

St. Phillip's Protestant Episcopal Church also conducted a variety of community service projects, such as offering apartments at reasonable rents. Innovative as these measures were, they did not wholly satisfy critics who hoped to broaden the traditional understanding of "church" among African Americans. Many of the auxiliary activities of churches like St. Phillip's failed to reach beyond the core membership and those who already were linked in some way to the Christian community. But such programs did attract more members and solidify the power base of black churches in Harlem. After 1926, of the important black churches, only St. Cyprian's was located outside Harlem.[62]

Professionally trained African American social workers were few during the Great Migration years. George Edmund Haynes was certainly the most prominent. Educated at Fisk, Yale, Columbia, and the New York School of Philanthropy (later the New York School of Social Work), he kept constant vigil on the progress being made by northerners in the crusade to help migrants adjust to city life. In 1924 Haynes, then secretary of the Commission on the Church and Race Relations of the Federal Council of Churches, told a conference of professional social workers that they faced "great obstacles" in persuading black churches to adopt scientific methods of community service. Nevertheless, he believed that the struggle was necessary. "Trying to look at the matter without bias," Haynes said, "it seems to me that many of our efforts have not carried over to the masses of the Negro churches which have already a hold upon the thousands who have developed the churches for more than a hundred years and now find them their social agency. If we get our plans accepted in the programs of those churches, much of our effort would not need to go into building social service programs and trying to force Negroes into them."[63] Eugene Kinckle Jones of the Urban League thought that some progress was being made in the post-World War I years. He wrote in 1923, "Many Negro churches have caught the vision and are building community churches and are adding social service features to their religious programs."[64] Jones's was a far different assessment than that made by James Weldon Johnson in 1915. Johnson then complained of the many storefront churches springing up in Harlem: "These superfluous churches create such a financial drain that the race does not build and maintain hospitals, old folks' homes, or orphan asylums."[65]

In some cases relocation to Harlem by historic black churches in Manhattan undercut their ability to meet the social needs of the thousands of southerners who flocked to New York City. Historian William Welty concluded that the move to Harlem preoccupied ministers and prevented them from addressing structural inequities in urban African American life. He writes,

> Increasingly after 1910, the time, energy and money of Manhattan's black churches and black ministers were spent in establishing locations in Harlem. The growth of the more successful of these churches was phenomenal as the number of black New Yorkers rapidly increased. As time spent on matters of moving, buying property, erecting new buildings and refurbishing old ones increased, the time spent on other social concerns declined. Most noticeably lacking were projects designed to help newcomers adjust to the city. The prevailing spirit seemed to be that of hoping to make the churches attractive enough so that all newcomers would be drawn to membership.[66]

Welty's observation, specific as it is to New York, does not necessarily reflect the state of affairs in other cities, especially in light of the stimulation to greater diligence provided by the Great Migration. But it does bring into focus the tension between two views of the church that existed almost everywhere that migrants settled. The traditionalists understood the church to be primarily an oasis for spiritual refreshment in a desert of urban affliction. The progressives—termed here, instrumentalists—desired to use the church as an agency of social regeneration, marshaling the forces of the spirit on behalf of tangible ends such as decent work and decent housing.

W. E. B. Du Bois and Richard R. Wright, Jr., epitomize the instrumentalist understanding of "church." They called for a radical reorientation of the mission of African American Christianity in order to meet the crisis. Du Bois advocated a "new Negro Church" with more systematized business activities, less frenetic revivals as a tool for recruitment, and greater concern for education and employment.[67] In 1907 Wright, while a research fellow at the University of Pennsylvania, surveyed the social work efforts of African American churches. Perhaps more than any other critic he attempted to obtain a realistic picture of what churches were doing rather than be content with the commonplace that the church was the central institution of African American life, and therefore all was well. Wright concluded that only a few congregations had "attacked the problems of real city Negroes" and that large churches in urban areas had grown "not because of social work, but almost invariably because of the personality of the pastors and their peculiar method of preaching." Wright termed the charity and social work being done "unsystematized," and he argued that pastors who boasted of growing congregations ignored large turnovers in membership. He noted that in Chicago one church had grown from 1,300 members to 1,500 in six years, but it had taken in and lost some 1,600 in the same period. Wright acknowledged that newly arrived migrants did seek out the church because it represented "part of their old environment transplanted to the new place," but once they were accustomed to city life, many migrants fell away.

Wright was astute enough to recognize that churches no longer had the monopoly that they enjoyed in the small towns and rural areas of the South. They had to compete with "theaters, skating rinks, baseball games, saloons, pool rooms, race tracks and amusement gardens, as well as with Sunday labor and Sunday picnics and society functions." Wright acknowledged that city churches "give alms, help bury the dead, care for the sick, take part in politics, have numerous concerts and entertainments," and that many had "social clubs; some have libraries, and all are to some degree employment bureaus." But he complained that "these churches are run chiefly on the small town church plan, with everything proportionately greater than in the small town." What social work was done was for the purpose of securing "money to pay Church debts and not for the social uplift."[68]

These were harsh criticisms, but Wright tempered his conclusions by pointing to some of the obstacles faced by urban African American churches. He noted that because churches were being "easily filled" with the arrival of newcomers from the South, a blindness to real progress prevailed. Many churches were in debt, and the poverty of members made "the cost of active, systematic city social missionary work . . . practically prohibitive." Wright also believed that denominational competition detracted from concerted action. Then, too, the itinerant system practiced by African

American Methodists reassigned clergy before extended social work could be conducted. "Another difficulty," he wrote, "is the religious ideals of the mass of Negroes, which are chiefly emotional and connected so much more with heaven and hell than with earth and daily life." Progressive clergy, he contended, found it difficult to address earthly affairs when many judged success by the degree of emotional enthusiasm fostered by a minister.[69]

Wright wrote in his divinity school thesis of "a fierce struggle for survival in the lowest ranks of labor" in the cities, and he called for a "practical religion" to meet the crisis of the industrial condition.[70] When Wright became editor of the *Christian Recorder* he finally had a vehicle through which he could address the AME denomination as a whole on questions close to his heart. He campaigned for a social service commission at the connectional level. In 1918 the AME Church adopted Wright's plans for a commission designed to bring the denomination closer to social problems of the day "such as organized labor, prohibition, women and industry, home life, industrial life, education, morality, housing, sanitation and public comfort."[71]

Wright focused on the material needs of the migrants, but other helpers in the North worried most about the task of assimilating the migrants into existing African American communities. Fearing that the flood of refugees from the South would overwhelm them, overtax their churches and societies, and jeopardize the hard-won gains made by northern blacks, they set themselves to the task of baptizing, so to speak, the unwashed. George A. Myers gave voice to the widespread belief that the welfare of the old guard in northern cities was at risk. He spoke for Cleveland's African American elite when he declared: "The law abiding citizens should feel it incumbent upon them to go among these people and labor to enlighten their understanding relative to the laws. Now is the time for our race organizations to get busy and do something. Otherwise, riot and ruin will run amuck. Jim Crowism and segregation will follow and Cleveland, where we have always enjoyed our rights, will be as rampant with race prejudice and discrimination as is the south today."[72] William N. De Berry, the pioneer in institutional church work at St. John's Congregational Church in Springfield, Massachusetts, echoed this emphasis on the need for socialization. He urged that the exodus be "regulated by a process of selection which would eliminate the riff-raff and secure the better class of Negro laborers."[73]

No such sorting mechanism existed, and all classes came, from the back-alley poor to the professional. Skilled and unskilled workers, single men and those with families, the churched and the unchurched, young and old, all represent but a few of the variations among the migrant flood. Alarmed by the fear that migrants would mistake liberty for license, thereby upsetting existing racial accommodations, and genuinely concerned to alleviate the hardships faced by migrants in their new environments, northerners called for quick action. They looked to the churches first. But were other viable agencies able to lend a helping hand?

One obvious place to turn was the National League on Urban Conditions among Negroes, which was organized in 1910 and incorporated in 1913. Yet delegates attending the annual meeting of the Urban League in December 1917 heard that the League's efforts during the year consisted mainly of advocating that local communities conduct social work among the migrants.[74] The development of local branches was uneven across the industrial North. Not until 1919 when the National Urban League had thirty local branches did it more closely approximate a national organization.[75] Where branches did exist, they served the function of coordinating and stimulating efforts by other groups to assist the migrants. Pittsburgh's Urban League, established in 1918, worked cooperatively with other civic organizations, including Associated Charities, the Society for the Improvement of the Condition of the Poor, the Public Health Nursing Association, the Travelers' Aid Society, and local businesses and schools. When the room registry of the YWCA failed to assist African Americans, the League began its own listing of available housing.[76]

Often those most eager to see extraecclesiastical civic agencies prosper had southern backgrounds. These individuals sought to exercise leadership on behalf of the migrants as they had done within black communities of the South. For example, the campaign to establish a black YMCA in Buffalo was spearheaded by southern-born residents such as the YMCA director, William Jackson, who was influenced by Booker T. Washington's educational philosophy. The Rev. J. Edward Nash of Michigan Avenue Baptist, who was born in the South and was dealing daily with the challenges of assisting migrants, was instrumental in efforts to establish an Urban League branch in Buffalo.[77] That city's experience serves as a cautionary reminder that the secular and sacred organizational spheres often overlapped, particularly so when ministers participated in civic groups or offered church space and support to secular organizations. Despite the emergence of secular agencies such as the Urban League and the cooperation of such groups as the Travelers' Aid Society, African American churches remained at the center of the northern institutional response.

African American clergy and churches faced a long list of problems in this campaign. At a meeting of the Cleveland branch of the Ohio Federation for Uplift Among Colored People a Methodist minister gave voice to the principal obstacle confronting those who sought to assist the migrants. "The race question is always uppermost in the minds of whites," said the Rev. Pazavia O'Connell, "and our people must adjust themselves to prejudices against them."[78] Discriminatory practices in housing compounded the difficulties that migrants faced. Cleveland's Ministers' Alliance, composed of nine African American clergy who were said to speak on behalf of two-thirds of the city's black population, was greatly concerned that migrants were being forced into Ward 11, where prostitution and other criminal activities were protected from police raids.[79] Newark's Hamilton Travis, worried that his southern kin would become spiritually corrupted by city life, urged united action so that the migrants might "maintain the religious standards that are always a part of the lives of our people." Fearing that thousands seeking their El Dorado in the North would arrive blind to the realities of discrimination, Travis warned that "the Land of Promise does not accept the black man in all times and in all places."[80] In Philadelphia, black clergy cooperated with the NAACP in combating the influence of saloons, gambling dens, and other places of vice.[81]

Black opponents of the exodus from the South, such as Kelly Miller, pronounced the effort to enable the migrants to adjust to urban life a high-risk enterprise. Though an original board member of the NAACP and a crusader for racial justice, Miller was pessimistic about "safeguarding the moral and social life of these people suddenly thrust into a new environment." He predicted that "without proper restriction and control" the migrants would mistake "liberty for license," thereby prejudicing public opinion. This would "reproduce Southern prescription in the Northern states, and the last state of the race would be worse than the first." In order that the "centre of gravity of the race problem" not be shifted to the North, Miller urged that African American churches emulate the Catholic Church, which helped European immigrants assimilate into the American city. "The negro churches where these laborers are at work," he argued, "should be encouraged to reach out and lay hold upon every workman who comes to the Northern communities."[82]

Opponents and advocates of the exodus placed so heavy a responsibility on the black churches of the North that whatever measures were taken inevitably failed to satisfy expectations. Any indication of reluctance on the part of northern blacks to embrace the migrants without equivocation was promptly attacked as evidence of racial disloyalty. As late as 1923 the *Freeman* of Detroit was chastising its readership, "Too many of us are asking why these people do not stay South and thereby stop the prejudice. Too many of us are trying to belittle these good people. If we would do our duty by getting them started rightly in accordance with their desires, they would be rapidly and properly assimilated to our and to the community's credit."[83] The hostile white press in the South was quick to trumpet these calls for united action as evidence of the folly of the black exodus. The *Atlanta Constitution* called the problems faced by migrants the "penalties of migration."[84] Du Bois countered, arguing, "The North is no paradise — as East St. Louis, Washington, Chicago, and Omaha prove; but the South is at best a system of caste and insult and at worst a Hell."[85]

Mary McCleod Bethune, the Methodist educator and head of the National Association of Colored Women from 1924 until 1928, believed the exodus ought to continue despite the hardships encountered by migrants and the melancholia of skeptics. In 1925 Bethune wrote that the social challenge of her generation was to assist newcomers to the city "to make the adjustments necessary to a full possession and enjoyment of the manifold blessings and privileges of urban life." She appealed to the churches and all agencies of organized philanthropy and charity to join with social workers in meeting the challenge.[86]

Bethune, a woman whose leadership skills benefited many groups, looked to cooperative efforts by a variety of church and civic agencies to drive the engine of social reform. But she could not fail to acknowledge that much unsystematic aid went on. The more seasoned migrants helped recent arrivals, and an intricate but often hidden network of voluntary assistance developed. The African American artist Jacob Lawrence was the son of former migrant parents and grew up in Harlem when it was being transformed into a mecca of African American culture. "I didn't know the term 'migration,'" Lawrence recalls, "but I remember people used to tell us when a new family would arrive. The people in the neighborhood would collect clothes for the newcomers and pick out coals that hadn't completely burned in the furnace to get them started."[87]

At the same time, northern black church leaders attempted to provide spiritual care for the refugees from the South almost as soon as the Great Migration began. The size and diversity of the migrant flood compounded the problem of assimilating newcomers into existing religious structures.

Single men recruited in the first phase of the Great Migration were not inclined to settle down and join established churches. These workers went from job to job, and they reputedly demonstrated few of the moral values and behaviors expected of regular church members. The migrants housed in camps by the railroads proved to be a special challenge.

One Thursday evening in November 1916 AME Bishop Levi J. Coppin decided to reach such migrants by going directly to the Pennsylvania Railroad Camp at Point Breeze in south Philadelphia. One of his companions, W. Spencer Carpenter, sent the following report to the *Christian Recorder:*

> We arrived at the camp shortly before eight o'clock, and promptly on the hour the service began. After the singing of a few hymns by the men, which was followed by prayer and Scripture reading, Bishop Coppin announced his text, Matthew XXV, 14, 15, and with the same fervor and power the bishop displays when he addresses large assemblies or preachers before great congregations, he preached a wonderful sermon to about 50 men, basing his thoughts upon the parables of 'The ten virgins,' and 'The pounds and talents.' Gripping his hearers from the moment he began to preach, he held their attention constantly and, rising to the heights of his sermon where he pleaded with his hearers to live clean, decent, honest lives, using always the talents God had given them to the glory of God, the men broke out in fervent 'amens' and applause.[88]

The New York, New Haven and Hartford Railroad imported hundreds of migrants to work in the tobacco fields of Connecticut. According to the *Crisis,* the men "were collected without discrimination and they represented all kinds and conditions . . . especially the worst."[89] The Rev. Edward Goin, an African American clergyman, outfitted a boxcar as a social center and enlisted the aid of black students from Yale in a campaign of social uplift. In Pittsburgh thousands of men lived in barracks constructed by the large steel companies. Fighting and drunkenness were common. Steel company owners gave permission for local African American clergy to circulate among the workers, and they funded the erection of several churches in expectation that religious influence would contribute to a more stable work force.[90]

At one end of the spectrum, then, was the transient migrant with few associational ties, moving north and from city to city with little likelihood, or even interest, of becoming connected with a church. On the other end, evidence indicates that black southerners were able to forge direct links with preexisting institutions in the North because of the network of previous ties with family or community. The largest clientele for the relief and service efforts of the northern black churches probably fell somewhere in mid-spectrum. Individuals and families who hoped to start their lives again in the urban North did so in incremental stages. Finding food and shelter, getting a job, and learning to find one's way around the city could take priority over joining a church.

Before additional church-based efforts to assist refugees from the South are examined, it should be mentioned that migrants themselves displayed considerable resourcefulness in coping with many practical difficulties. Some pooled their resources in migration clubs, thereby obtaining discounts from the railroads, and came North in the company of others who could cushion the cultural shock of the city and provide solace, if not material aid, in the struggle to find work and housing. Migrants who established themselves wrote home to encourage others to follow. The phenomenon of chain migration provided a degree of rationality to an otherwise chaotic experience of striking out for the unknown.[91] Certain urban neighborhoods, perhaps only a few blocks along one side of a street, magnetlike drew folk from the South who had been friends and neighbors down home. Such was the case with newcomers from Hattiesburg, Mississippi, who formed a migration club with Chicago as their destination. Club members soon had a barbershop and other small businesses operating much as they did down South. Eventually, they convinced their former preacher to join them in this miniature Hattiesburg on the South Side.[92]

The northern cities, which received a small number of migrants relative to their populations, were able to cope fairly successfully with the newcomers, especially if the local black clergy took hold of the problem. This successful coping holds true for Springfield, Massachusetts, and Toledo, Ohio. By March 1918 about 2,000 migrants had settled in Springfield. William N. De Berry claimed that these former southerners were making the adjustment "without excessive difficulty." He praised Springfield's leaders for helping to find suitable housing. The chief of police was quoted as saying that the migrants gave him very little trouble.[93] De Berry played an important role in facilitating what appears to have been a relatively smooth reception for the migrants. An early advocate of the institutional church model, he supervised a multidimensional ministry at St. John's that included instruction in hygiene and sanitation and the management of modern apartments.[94] When Everett Johnson surveyed Toledo on the eve of the Great Depression, he found an African American population of about 14,000, approximately 4 percent of Toledo's total. Some 84 percent of the city's African American migrants had been in Toledo an average of nine years. While the city's black residents were not without their problems, the churches had been particularly active as social and welfare agencies.[95] In Columbus, Ohio, African American clergy also took the lead in finding jobs for migrants and in assisting their adjustment to urban life.[96]

Northern black communities with sizable African American populations before the Great Migration were theoretically better-equipped to handle the crisis precipitated by the migrant flood than those with small and unorganized black populations. Black Chicago, with a population of almost 35,000 on the South Side by 1910, had a highly active and diverse institutional life. Historian James Grossman argues that between 1900 and 1915 the creation of the physical ghetto in conjunction with increasing racial discrimination led to the emergence of a new class of leaders with an economic and political base in the African American community. "Adapting Booker T. Washington's doctrines of racial solidarity and self-help to the Northern city," Grossman writes, "these business leaders and politicians de-emphasized the fight for integration and dealt with discrimination by creating black institutions." The South Side boasted "a bank, a hospital, a YMCA, an infantry regiment, effective political organizations, lodges, clubs, professional baseball teams, social service institutions, newspapers, and a variety of small businesses" by 1915.[97] But the existence of these race institutions did not relieve churches of the task of extending a helping hand to newcomers, and success in doing so depended on the leadership of individual clergy.

The Rev. Lacey Kirk Williams of Olivet Baptist Church exemplifies an urban pastor who was quick to recognize the urgency of the mission to the migrants in a city that was a major receiving point of the influx from the South. He sent members of his church to the Chicago terminal to meet incoming trains, and they also directed migrants to places where they could receive assistance. Williams arrived in Chicago from Texas on the eve of the Great Migration. He soon transformed Olivet into a social service center along the lines of Jane Addams's Hull House. Olivet took migrants in, fed them, clothed them, and assisted in finding them housing and employment. The church hosted a wide variety of social, educational, and recreational activities, including a health and baby clinic.[98] Olivet's reputation as an oasis of mercy in the urban desert spread rapidly throughout the South, and migrants were soon writing letters directly to Olivet asking for a helping hand. W. M. Agnew wrote from Aberdeen, Mississippi, in 1917 asking for assistance in obtaining employment in Chicago's packinghouses. He stressed that he was a Baptist and that his mother had been the most important woman in the Baptist church he belonged to for thirty years.[99]

In contrast to black Chicago, black Cleveland, according to historian Kenneth Kusmer, "had almost no functioning structure of secular institutions that could be used in a crisis" before the Great Migration.[100] Cleveland's African American population was neither as large nor as geographically concentrated as that of Chicago; integrated schools and neighborhoods in Cleveland offset tendencies toward ghettoization. Aggressive black leadership did not emerge before World War I. The local ministers' alliance that came into existence before the Great Migration was judged "ineffectual."[101] The arrival of thousands of black southerners was accompanied by an increase in residential segregation and discrimination in public facilities, with the result that by the end of the 1920s Cleveland began to resemble Chicago. Along with the new group of leaders who stressed race pride and race solidarity, separate black institutions of a secular nature emerged in Cleveland in the wake of the Great Migration. Older black residents found the transition difficult to accept and tended to romanticize the premigration era. "Time was," one resident declared in 1928, "that Cleveland was the freest from race prejudice and the fairest city in the United States not excepting Freedom's birthplace Boston. Today we have only two unrestricted privileges left, the Ballot and the Public Schools."[102]

As a result of a threefold increase in African American population during the Great Migration, the accommodations made by Cleveland's black middle-class leadership to the racial status quo came under duress; calls were issued for the churches to meet the crisis. Cleveland's Baptist churches, which were more likely to be involved in welfare work among migrants than the elite churches, were rewarded by gains in membership. Antioch Missionary Baptist Church, under the leadership of Horace C. Bailey, for example, expanded to become Cleveland's largest black congregation. As part of its social service program, Antioch organized youth clubs and converted two nearby houses into recreation centers for neighborhood use.[103]

Before the explosion in its southern migrant population, black Detroit, like black Cleveland, lacked a well-developed institutional infrastructure.

With only 5,741 blacks in 1910, dominated by an old guard of professionals, businessmen, and public servants who functioned within existing political and racial arrangements, Detroit did not foster "race men" as Chicago had. Most African Americans were clustered on the east side of the city, but, just as the Great Migration was beginning, political opportunities to build "race" organizations were undercut by a new charter that replaced the old apparatus of ward and precinct. The African American elite, known as the "Cultured Colored '40'," functioned in an integrated world. Historian David Allen Levine writes that the old guard was fearful because the influx of southern blacks threatened its fragile relationships. When Eugene Kinckle Jones came in 1916 with the intent of starting a branch of the Urban League, the old guard ran him out of town.[104]

In July 1916 Forrester B. Washington, an alumnus of Tufts College with a year of graduate study in sociology and social service at Columbia University, conducted a survey of Detroit's efforts to assist migrants. According to the *Detroit Tribune,* there was concern that "no efforts were being made here to care for the newcomers, except by the forces of vice and crime."[105] Washington became the first director of Detroit's branch of the Urban League, and he enlisted the aid of African American clergy, who read lists of job openings from their pulpits.

Detroit's Bethel AME Church pioneered in community outreach. The church opened a department of social service in 1911 and added a labor and housing bureau in 1916 "with the coming of our people in large numbers."[106] Bethel's labor exchange distributed work cards and published a notice in the *Voice of Missions* to the attention of "honest, industrious men and women of our race" for "good paying positions" in steel mills, cement works, and railroad shops, and on farms, on wharves, and in domestic service.[107] The Rev. J. M. Evans reported that during March 1917 Bethel's social service bureau found employment for 197 men and 189 women, and openings still remained. "We have an agreement with a cigar manufacturing company in this city," Evans informed the *Christian Recorder,* "to furnish them 100 girls of our race variety, if we can find them."[108]

Referrals from churches apparently made a difference to potential employers. Washington said of the efforts of the Detroit Urban League, "I wish all of the 10,000 who have been placed by us could have been secured through the churches because, from our experience, I believe they would have been diligent, regular and zealous in their work."[109] George E. Haynes asserted that this testimony underscored "in a superlative degree the industrial value of the church to the new-comers and to the community which benefits by their labor."[110] Nevertheless, in his own survey of conditions in Detroit, Haynes called on the city's African American churches to do more to meet the needs of the migrants in the areas of housing and leisure and to sponsor a community house in the "Negro district." Detroit's African American population grew dramatically from 7,000 in 1915, to 40,000 in 1920, and to 80,000 in 1925.[111] In response to the crisis, most black churches established social service programs of one kind or another, although many of them were modest.[112]

Philadelphia attempted to meet the multiple needs of the migrants through cooperative action among agencies such as the Travelers' Aid Society and the Armstrong Association. Led by John T. Emlen, a Philadelphia banker who had taught a year at Hampton Institute, the Armstrong Association in 1908 began to concern itself with employment opportunities for the city's blacks. Richard Wright, Jr., served as the association's first field secretary, and William A. Creditt, pastor of First African Baptist Church, and Charles A. Tindley of Bainbridge Methodist Episcopal Church, served on the board of directors. After Wright became editor of the *Christian Recorder* in 1909, the association's work languished until A. L. Manly became the new industrial secretary in 1913. Manly, a Hampton graduate, transformed the Armstrong Association into an effective employment agency for black workers. Though not formally affiliated with the Urban League, the Armstrong Association functioned much like a local branch of the national organization and became, according to historian Charles Hardy III, "the center of black labor affairs after the onset of the Great Migration."[113]

The Philadelphia campaign to aid southern refugees involved more than finding them employment. In 1917 black and white social workers organized the Central Committee on Negro Migration with subcommittees on receiving immigrants, education, housing, sanitation, employment, recreation, courts, relief, and churches. Wesley "Pops" Graham, pastor of the First Baptist Church, chaired the subcommittee on churches and sought to stimulate concern for the religious needs of the migrants among existing black congregations. New Sunday schools and services in the railroad camps were the most visible results of this effort.[114] During the war years efforts to meet the religious needs of the migrants were overshadowed by the demand for social services, and until the crisis passed few opportunities occurred by which to assess the effectiveness of Philadelphia's outreach. A survey, conducted in the spring of 1924 under the auspices of the Philadelphia Housing Association, revealed that almost six of ten household heads reported that, although they had been church members in the South, they did not belong to any church in the city. This status was particularly true of migrants from places in the South with populations between 2,500 and 10,000.

Frederick Miller argues in his analysis of the 1924 survey that these statistics "contradict the notion that migrants easily continued church activity after moving north."[115] Miller's assessment suggests that a significant portion of the migrants, even some who were beneficiaries of the social assistance rendered by black churches, were not readily or intimately involved in congregational life. This failure of the churches to become the key agent may have stemmed from the fact that a variety of secular and charitable agencies shared with black churches an interest in helping migrants adjust to city life. For example, the Philadelphia Academy of Medicine, composed of eighty African American physicians in the city, as well as dentists and pharmacists, conducted medical inspections and gave lectures on housing, sanitation, and health care. Stereopticon talks were presented in black churches on how to avoid pneumonia and tuberculosis, which were said to be the two most common diseases among migrants.[116]

In Philadelphia, as elsewhere in the North, the rush of southern blacks to the city created fears that congestion and poor sanitation would lead to an outbreak of contagious diseases in Black Belt districts. Chicago's health commissioner, on receiving a dispatch from Philadelphia reporting that 2,000 migrants were ill and 700 dying in hospitals from tuberculosis, stated: "We have the same problem here that they have in Philadelphia, but I think prompt measures will prevent an outbreak of disease. We will cooperate with the police department."[117] In a statement prepared by Richard R. Wright, Jr., and adopted at the Interdenominational Ministerial Reception to the Incoming Colored People from the South, Philadelphia's African American clergy took issue with the notion that the migrants were a health menace. Increases in the rate of sickness and death resulted from residential overcrowding caused by enforced racial segregation. "We call upon all land lords and agents," the clergy declared, "merely to treat us as human beings, and the great housing problem will disappear."[118]

Adequate housing was important, but without a job, entry into the Promised Land meant little. Lacking employment, some migrants fell prey to urban vices such as drinking and prostitution, so much so in Pittsburgh that volunteers from each existing Baptist church were sought to assist caseworkers from the morals court, especially where the proceedings involved migrants who were Baptists.[119] Both formally and informally, churches assisted in obtaining jobs for migrants in many cities. In Detroit the Urban League sent lists of openings to the black clergy for dissemination on Sunday mornings.[120] Migrants could go to the labor exchanges operated by the churches and receive a signed work card which assured potential employers that they were healthy and honest. African American clergy elsewhere set up mechanisms by which migrants could obtain in formation and advice about jobs. Churches in Newark organized a Negro Welfare Day during which local clergy strategized about solutions to the employment needs of African Americans from the South and sponsored mass meetings to enlist the aid of the general population. The Rev. J. W. L. Rountree of Trenton made a special effort to convince migrants to take farm jobs because of the critical shortage of farm help during the war years. He had few takers and complained that the lure of the mill and factory was difficult to overcome.[121]

Since migrants needed jobs, the minister who could deliver them enhanced his chances of recruiting newcomers as church members. Large companies fostered special links with black churches to obtain reliable labor. The Ford Motor Company cultivated ties with selected ministers in Detroit. John Marshall Ragland, employment secretary of the Detroit Urban League, wrote in 1923, "To be employed by the Ford Motor Car Company seems to be the crowning achievement of all comers to Detroit."[122] African American ministers were eager to bring relatives of their members from the South to the Motor City. In 1919 Robert L. Bradby, pastor of Second Baptist Church, Detroit's largest African American congregation, lunched with Henry Ford. The industrial baron was seeking to lessen interracial conflicts at the Highland Park and Rouge plants and to increase worker efficiency. Bradby promised to recommend "very high type fellows" to the company. When these migrants came to Detroit, they understandably joined Second Baptist, located on Macomb Street. Bradby's church became the largest African American congregation in the city, displacing Bethel AME Church. The *Detroit Tribune* reported in 1917 that Second Baptist had an average attendance of nearly 2,000 and was so popular that potential worshipers lined up each Sunday morning outside its doors. Some had to be turned away.[123]

Father Everard W. Daniel of St. Matthew's Episcopal Church was also in Ford's good graces. The auto magnate donated a parish house to the congregation, and it was useful that Ford's "Negro-relations executive" was a member of the congregation. Historian David Levine observes that these arrangements between selected black clergy and big business were mutually beneficial. "Ford Motor Company got tractable workers, and the ministers got prosperous congregations, which insured prosperity for the churches."[124] So well-established did links of this kind become that historians August Meier and Elliott Rudwick were able to conclude, "It became virtually impossible to obtain a job at Ford without the recommendation of a minister or other influential member of the black community."[125] "The fact is," Ralph Bunche claimed, "that the possibility of getting a job at the Ford Motor Company has been the incentive in many instances for Negroes joining church."[126]

In Chicago and Pittsburgh similar relationships between black ministers and potential employers were established. The Rev. Archibald J. Carey could get jobs for his members in the meat packing plants of the Swifts and Armours because of connections with the white elite. In turn, he voiced little sympathy for the labor movement and endorsed capitalism as the salvation of the black worker.[127] Some black clergy in Pittsburgh got sizable donations for their churches and were allowed to hold services on company property for assisting with the assimilation of migrants into the steel mills. "Since they and their churches benefited from industrial philanthropy," historian Dennis C. Dickerson concluded, "few among the black clergy protested against racial discrimination in hiring, promotion, and job assignments."[128]

The labor question did not receive sustained attention in official church circles until the episcopal address of the General Conference of the AME Church at St. Louis in 1920. The delegates were then told,

> The Twentieth Century industrial plant cannot be manned by men not yet advanced from the Eighteenth Century method of industry, therefore we believe it is the duty of the General Conference of the African Methodist Episcopal Church, because it has, in almost every instance, taken the initiative in the cause of the Negro Race, to appoint a Labor Commission, consisting of three bishops, three elders and three prominent labor leaders, whose duty shall be to collect data and facts as to labor conditions in general, and that of Negro labor in particular, also a list of industrial plants, employing Negro labor and

those who do not, and seek through every and all honorable means, a wider door of opportunity for Negro laborers, and such an adjustment and relation as will give them equal wages for equal work.[129]

To enhance opportunities for black labor, northerners conducted a campaign to help migrants understand the nature of "work" in U.S. factories. The Rev. W. A. C. Hughes, director of the colored work board of Home Missions and Church Extension of the Methodist Episcopal Church, visited many industrial centers where migrants lived and worked. He reported that employers were generally satisfied with migrants' work— "with but one criticism, i.e., 'he is slow.' A chemist in the Westinghouse plant put it thus: 'They do their work measured by long-metre hymns.' " [130] The campaign for worker efficiency was carried into the churches. In Chicago the Urban League called on clergy to spread the message that regularity and efficiency on the job were essential to industrial advancement.[131]

Migrants were told how to seek work, how to handle themselves before white bosses, and how to adjust to the demands of industrial rather than agricultural work. Northern black leaders played a role similar to that of the missionaries and teachers who went South after the Civil War to assist the freed slaves in adjusting to their new circumstances. Civic leaders preached the Gospel of Efficiency. They believed that the urban industrial order, for good or ill, functioned differently from that of the rural South. Acutely aware of complaints by many white employers that migrants brought with them work habits not conducive to profits, black clergy, often in cooperation with the Urban League, sought to reeducate newcomers. Assuming that the seasonal rhythms of farmwork in the South were ingrained in the migrants, northerners chastised newcomers who worked until payday, then laid off or went elsewhere in search of another temporary El Dorado. But not everyone giving advice could be trusted. The *Chicago Defender* warned the unemployed about "scheming preachers" who for 50 cents offered information on jobs that turned out to be bogus.[132] The campaign to reeducate migrants about the nature of northern labor competition intensified when European immigrants returned after the war.

Now the cry went out that unless black workers could be converted to the Gospel of Efficiency, they faced losing out in the struggle for survival in every northern city.[133] Morris Lewis urged black workers in the North to watch their step: "Lest we be crowded out of our new-found employment, we must make ourselves indispensable; make ourselves agreeable—

physically as well as mentally, and stand as a real, loyal American against the inroads of unsound immigrants who might invade our shores."[134] When the economy began to recover, Emmett J. Scott thought it unnecessary to look to foreign shores when a large labor supply was close at hand. "These colored Americans are not aliens," he argued. "They have never sought to disrupt the Government nor do they harbor bolshevistic or anarchistic ideals."[135] After the implementation of federal restrictions on immigration, industries again looked to the ranks of southern labor. *Opportunity* editorialized in January 1923: "The weary struggle of the Negro population for status thru self-improvement and recognition, aided by their friends, goes on. . . ."[136]

In addition to assisting with employment, local churches helped migrants with much-needed emergency aid for basic needs. Charles S. Cooper of the Kingsley House in Pittsburgh reported that when the regular social agencies became overtaxed, black churches threw open their doors and fed and housed migrants. One church converted its entire building to temporary migrant housing.[137] The Rev. S. L. Carrothers allowed Roosevelt Temple in Newark, New Jersey, to be used as a temporary stopping place for migrants. They could store their belongings, cook meals, and sleep in the temple until rooms and work were found for them.[138] Philadelphia's black clergy encouraged their members to rent out rooms to migrants, which resulted in some members having a lucrative income during the war years and going on to purchase row houses for themselves.[139]

Many more examples could be given of the practical ways in which African American churches and individual African American Christians in the North assisted the migrants. But how are we to judge the effectiveness of these efforts? One young African American investigator attempted to measure the progress being made in Philadelphia. Sadie Tanner Mossell's 1921 study, "The Standard of Living Among One Hundred Negro Migrant Families in Philadelphia," collected information on migrants from the South who had come to the city during the war years. Mossell's research emphasizes that housing and employment concerns brought together a variety of organizations, civic and religious, in cooperative ventures. Social workers, church officials, and representatives of industries such as the Pennsylvania Railroad and the Franklin Sugar Refining Company had been called together by Bishop Philip M. Rhinelander of the Protestant Episcopal Church in a joint effort. The Interdenominational Ministerial Union, which Mossell claimed embraced "all Negro ministers of the city," developed a detailed plan to aid migrants and try to enroll them in Philadelphia churches. She cited Calvary M.E. Church as being particularly active. It reportedly had 4,200 children in its Sunday school and distributed fifty "buckets of soup daily during the winter of 1918, and coal to all who needed it."[140]

Mossell surveyed a hundred families in Philadelphia's 29th ward, six and one-half city blocks that from 1916 until 1919 went from almost entirely white to black. She gathered information on migrant families' standard of living by examining their income and expenditures on the assumption that those amounts would reveal something of how migrants had adapted to the city. However, she was not entirely sure that standard-of-living criteria were sufficient to address the larger question of the assimilation of migrants into Philadelphia's already established African American community. "Quantities of goods," she admitted, "can be purchased by the man who will work for them. But culture and education are bred after years, sometimes generations of toil."[141]

Mossell's conclusion underscores what has been intimated elsewhere. The mission to the migrants was not one but two. The task of providing material assistance—housing, employment, emergency aid—was paired with efforts to acculturate and assimilate the migrants into the African American communities of the North, a mission thought all the more urgent because of fears that newcomers with their southern ways jeopardized the gains that northerners had made. Mossell herself endorsed the mission and predicted benefits for all: "By adopting such means to train the migrant and to remove racial handicaps, it is believed that generations hence will pronounce the migration of 1917–18 to Philadelphia, not the cause of the fall of the culture of the talented tenth, but the beginning of the spread of that culture to the Negro masses."[142]

This goal was certainly the consensus of the African American churchmen who attended a conference on migration problems held under the auspices of the Commission on the Church and Race Relations of the Federal Council of Churches in February 1923. The conference report acknowledged the postwar renewal of the exodus from the South and called on the council's constituent bodies to unite in an effort to promote the welfare of migrants. As many organizations had done in the summer of 1916 when the magnitude of migration was becoming apparent, the Federal Council looked to religious institutions as so central to African American communities that little progress could be made without enlisting them in the cause. The African American was, in the council's language, "a tremendous religious asset; he is a church-goer; he seeks the church environment; he is amendable to the church appeal."[143]

The Great Migration stimulated a redefinition of "church appeal" by fostering a greater emphasis on the instrumental use of religious organizations. African American churches underwent a significant redirection of institutional energies and focus as a result of the crisis precipitated by the exodus from the South. Programs of social service multiplied, and ministers began to give more attention in their sermons to the practical needs of their constituents, such as housing and employment. Before World War I Miles Mark Fisher judged that African American preachers expounded primarily on "otherworldly topics" and were "disinterested and almost dormant" on social, political, and economic questions. Then came war, the call for labor, and the flight from field to factory. In this context, confronted by new problems in the cities, "the church had a real program before it." "Many religious groups," Fisher wrote, "began definitely to care for the needs of the communicants."[144]

Though their capacity to meet the multiple needs of the migrants was overtaxed, and though they expressed ambivalence regarding the impact that a massive exodus would have on existing urban race relations, African American Christians in the North did recognize a special obligation to offer a helping hand to their racial kin. Churches bore an especially heavy burden because they were singled out as the institution most central to the African American experience. Churches in some cities assumed the role of principal care-givers by default. No other institution, black or white, existed with as much grassroots support in the black community and as much potential for doing good. The historic black denominations lacked a coordinated strategy, a national program, and the means to put much money at the disposal of the local church. But African American congregations in the North did respond as well as they were able.[145] Some were sidetracked into emphasizing church growth over social service; others were handicapped by the lack of a theology of social activism. But many broke free of the limitations of traditional forms of Christian charity and the pessimism about changing the world found in the old-time religion. They developed effective ministries to the migrants that established a benchmark for urban churches in the African American religious tradition still useful today.

6

WHEN

CHICAGO

WAS

CANAAN

Refugees from the South often dreamed of a specific place in the Promised Land. For many of them this was the mecca of the Midwest—Chicago—and by focusing our lens on it we can better understand the Great Migration's impact on the religious culture of the North.

Chicago was well-known to many potential migrants before their departure from the South. "The lure of no Northern city was as irresistible for the black hordes from the South," Charles S. Johnson observed, "as Chicago in the West, known far and wide for its colossal abattoirs, whose placarded warehouses, set close by the railroad, dotted every sizable town of the south, calling for men; Chicago remembered for the fairyland wonders of the World's Fair; home of the fearless taunting 'race paper,' and above all things, of the mills clamoring for men."[1] "You could not rest in your bed at night for *Chicago*," said a man from Hattiesburg, Mississippi, who had heard of the city's vast meat packinghouses.[2] Chicago's "black Joshua," Robert Abbott, publisher of the *Chicago Defender*, advised potential migrants to stay where they were until the summer of 1916. But when unskilled industrial jobs became available in large quantity, the *Defender* helped transform the migration into a crusade and once set a date, May 15,

1917, for the Great Northern Drive. Abbott touted the advantages of urban life and Chicago's attractions, such as the excitement of "the Stroll" on State Street from 26th to 39th Streets with its saloons, dance halls, and movie theaters.[3] Abbott and agents of Chicago's industrial sector did their job well. Chicago took in an estimated 50,000 to 70,000 African American migrants from the South from 1916 through 1919, the peak years of the Great Migration.

Newcomers were directed to the city's South Side, where a Black Belt was already identifiable by 1900. Then Chicago's 30,150 African Americans resided in a narrow, nineteen-block strip, running from 12th to 31st Streets, and four blocks wide, from Wentworth to Wabash Avenues. As residential segregation increased in the years before the Great Migration, the Black Belt pressed southward. It was hemmed in by the Rock Island Railroad and the working-class immigrant communities to the west and by the South Side Elevated Railroad and wealthier white neighborhoods, including Hyde Park, to the east. During the next decade the Black Belt expanded down to 55th Street despite the relatively small growth of the entire African American population. In 1910 77 percent (34,335) of Chicago's blacks lived on the South Side. By 1920 the Black Belt would include 92,501 African Americans, or 84 percent of the city's total African American population. Between 1910 and 1920 the black population of Chicago increased by 148 percent, largely as a result of the Great Migration. In 1910 less than one-third of the city's blacks lived in census tracts that were more than 50 percent black. By 1920, caused in large part by the use of restrictive covenants by white property holders and white flight, one-half of all African Americans resided in tracts that were at least half-black.[4]

The massive influx, chiefly from the Deep South, during the years of the Great Migration reinforced the residential concentration and cultural impact of the Black Belt. New arrivals were both directed to the ghetto by already established patterns of racial and residential segregation and drawn there by a desire to participate in the social and cultural life of the "city within a city." The church was thought to be the most important black-controlled institution on the South Side. In her description of social bonds in the Black Belt in 1905 Fannie Barrier Williams wrote of the twenty-five "regularly organized" black churches: "Aside from the ordinary functions of preaching, prayer, class meetings and Sunday-school, the church is regarded by the masses as a sort of tribune of all of their civic and social affairs."[5] Assuming this assertion to be the case, it is all the more important to examine how the Great Migration altered the religious map of Chicago's African American community.

Anchored by historic congregations such as Quinn African Methodist (1847), Olivet Baptist (1850), and Bethel African Methodist (1862), religious life in the Black Belt was highly structured before the U.S. entry into World War I. Olivet served as the mother church of at least twelve Baptist congregations by 1900. Numerous other black Baptist churches came into existence by means of the time-honored Baptist principle of self-authentication. At least forty-seven black Baptist churches existed in the Chicago area by 1902, not all of which were recognized as "regularly organized." Most of these churches were located in the Black Belt. In 1916 the AME Church claimed eight congregations on the South Side. The rival AME Zion denomination established a presence in Chicago as early as 1875 with the organization of a congregation later known as Walters Memorial located at 3800 South Dearborn Avenue. In 1907 the CME Church planted its flag in Chicago when St. Paul's CME Church was established in a storefront at 4008 South State Street by J. H. T. Wells and fourteen members.[6]

Chicago's importance as a religious mecca for African Americans was well-established before World War I. In 1911 two hundred missionaries of the AME Church, representing every state in the union, held a convention at Quinn.[7] The annual conference of the CME Church was hosted by St. Paul's in 1910 and presided over by Bishop Isaac Lane.[8] In 1915 the National Baptist Convention gathered in Chicago's armory, with an estimated 15,000 to 20,000 delegates.[9] They doubtless carried home news of the wonders of Chicago as well as reports of the bitter falling out of the Boyd and Morris factions, which led to denominational division. Unlike the biblical Children of Israel who entered Canaan with a mandate to occupy the Promised Land, the migrants arriving in Chicago found their Canaan already in the hands of coreligionists.

The Black Belt's churches were burdened with the responsibility of welcoming their spiritual kinsmen from the South. The Great Migration afforded them a challenge and an opportunity. "Of all aspects of community life," historian Allan Spear wrote in *Black Chicago*, "religious activities were most profoundly changed by the migration."[10] These changes took place on the religious landscape of the South Side largely as a result of the arrival of African Americans whose very presence added a new dynamic to the existing religious and racial arrangements. By the end of the Great Migration era, the religious life of the South Side had been transformed in an enduring fashion.

Thousands of new arrivals to the Black Belt offered dramatic opportunities for expanding the influence and prestige of existing congregations and the birth of new ones. In 1938 the historian of Chicago's Bethlehem Baptist Association recalled,

> Along came the World War. The migrating Negro from the South came to fill vacancies of the white foreigner who went home to fight. Many things started; among them the storefront churches. We put an ad in the paper to help the needy. Oh! was I sorry. I went down to the Union Station to meet them and there was a twenty-car train full, young men, old men, women and children. Olivet and every other church was overrun. The people joined so rapidly. The people would say "Let's join the church folks." When the large churches filled up, the storefronts began getting up. The storefronts became congested. Chicago became so congested with the population increasing that the people sought tenement places and any other available place to hold services. From these storefronts, some great churches have gone far. Among these are: Pilgrim Baptist Church, St. Luke Baptist Church, Little Rock Baptist Church, and Liberty Baptist Church. Many made good. God was working out our problems.[11]

The established black churches first attempted to accommodate the newcomers by adding additional services. Olivet held three separate worship services at 10:30 A.M., using overflow space in addition to the main auditorium. Nevertheless, hundreds were turned away on Sunday mornings. Olivet's membership grew from 3,900 in 1915 to 8,430 in 1919, and the need for larger facilities became apparent.[12] As white congregations and synagogues abandoned the South Side and relocated to escape the expanding Black Belt, Olivet's leadership saw an opportunity to obtain more adequate facilities. First Baptist, the oldest white Baptist church in Chicago, saw its membership decline to 403 by 1918. White families sold their homes for whatever they could get. "No eloquent preaching, no social service," a report stated in 1918, "could save a church in a community that was nearly 100 per cent Negro" or long survive when "Negroes are steadily pushing down the alleys southward with their carts of furniture."[13]

Olivet moved from its old location at 27th and Dearborn into First Baptist's building on the southeast corner of South Parkway and 31st Street.[14]

The edifice with its imposing Gothic spires of Alabama stone was described by the *Chicago Defender* as "one of the handsomest and up-to-date churches on the South side."[15] Olivet's estimated 7,000 to 8,000 members obtained the property for $85,000, of which $10,000 was donated by First Baptist. The *Christian Century* editorialized, "This is the second building to be transferred from whites to blacks among Chicago Baptists during the past six months and it will be followed by some similar action on the part of other denominations without doubt." The editorial added that Olivet's work had been enhanced "by the advent of thousands of negroes from the southland, recently attracted to Chicago by the favorable industrial situation."[16]

White Methodists also contributed by default to the transformation of the South Side's religious map. In 1917 South Park Avenue Methodist, described as "one of the most valuable pieces of property owned by the denomination in Chicago,"[17] was turned over to African Americans. Methodists had only 200 black members in Chicago in 1903. By 1918 they claimed 5,000 in four churches—South Park, Fulton Street, North Side, and St. Mark's—and were touted as successfully dealing with the "problems of assimilation."[18] The *Southwestern Christian Advocate* editorialized, "In no other city in America are the Methodist people facing their responsibility in the influx of a large Negro population as the Methodists in Chicago are doing."[19] The *Advocate* was hailing the transfer of Trinity Methodist Episcopal Church to the denomination's black members. It was said to be "the largest and best equipped plant in all Methodism for Negroes." It had "two auditoriums, well furnished, two pipe organs, one costing eighteen thousand dollars, three great pianos, kitchen, dining room, many Sunday School rooms, pastor's study, spacious and well furnished gymnasium, shower baths, hot and cold water, and a four-story community house."[20] This was hardly an act of voluntary charity, forced as it was by patterns of racial segregation intensified by the Great Migration. White Methodists first experimented with exclusively black congregations in the Middle West in 1895, when St. Mark's was begun in a storefront with about twenty-five members. In 1916 this church, pastored by the Rev. John W. Robinson, had more than a thousand members and was in the midst of a campaign to build larger facilities at South Wabash and East 50th.[21]

Roman Catholicism in Chicago was also struggling to adapt to the racial transformation of the South Side. In 1917 St. Monica's, which had been founded by Father Augustine Tolton, the first black Catholic priest ordained in the United States, and located at 36th and South Dearborn, was made an all-black parish by decree of the George W. Mundelein, archbishop of Chicago. Mundelein refused to say anything regarding the morality of the "distinction of color," which he admitted "enters very often into the daily happenings in our city." He reasoned, "Because of circumstances that do exist here in this city, I am convinced that our colored Catholics will feel themselves much more comfortable, far less inconvenienced, and never at all embarrassed if, in a church that is credited to them, they have their own sodalities and societies, their own church and choir, in which they alone will constitute the membership, and for even stronger reasons the first place in the church should be theirs just as much as the seats in the rear benches are."[22] The *Chicago Defender* viewed this pronouncement as a "big step backward" and countered: that "Chicago is not below the Mason and Dixon line. We want no separate institutions of any kind, especially if they be forced upon us as was St. Monica's school and now the church."[23]

In addition to the flight of white Protestants and the adoption of race-based parishes by Chicago's Roman Catholic leaders, premigration African American churches contributed to altering the religious landscape. There was constant church movement from northern to southern sectors of Chicago's Black Belt and from poorer to better facilities. Although often sold below market value as estimated before the Great Migration, the new facilities burdened black congregations with debts over many years.[24] Church growth was essential in part to pay for the larger and better-equipped buildings. When congregations defaulted on mortgages, they were forced to move into less prestigious quarters. As the larger and wealthier black churches improved their status by purchasing edifices in the better neighborhoods farther south in the Black Belt, smaller and poorer churches took over their former quarters. For example, Liberty Baptist, which began in April 1918 as a prayer band in the home of Mrs. Birtie Bone, bought the old Olivet site at 27th and Dearborn.[25] A few congregations, such as Quinn and Walters AME Zion, held their ground as members moved into formerly all-white neighborhoods and away from the deteriorating older black districts. Others, such as the founders of Bethesda Baptist, who withdrew from Olivet in 1900, bought property farther south than the Black Belt extended. In the wake of the Great Migration, congregations like Bethesda that were financially able to escape the pressures of population density, poverty, crime, and vice moved down the corridor of the Black Belt. Soon Bethesda at Michigan and 53rd was said to be "in the very heart of the better strata of the Negro residential district."[26]

Since existing congregations could not accommodate all the newcomers, Chicago became the birthplace of many new churches during the Great Migration era. Monumental Baptist is an illustrative example. In 1918 a prayer band met in the home of Mrs. Ida Windsor. As their number grew, members obtained the services of the Rev. J. H. Smith, formerly of Alabama, who opened up a storefront at 3029 Cottage Grove. But when the Woodfork Bank collapsed, the congregation lost its financial capital and its ability to support a full-time pastor. In 1919 it merged with the Come and See Baptist Church. Some members withdrew, and in 1921 they called a minister from Alabama. He soon had a church of about a hundred members, many of them Alabamians. In 1921 Monumental purchased an old theater at 3128 Cottage Grove.[27]

Baptists used the prayer group as one of the most effective means for church growth. Because of overcrowding in existing churches, recent migrants frequently met in homes. They treasured the intimacy of these gatherings, composed of people from their own state, perhaps even from their old communities and a common religious culture. One of the first prayer bands formed in Chicago during the migration era met in 1915 at the home of Mr. and Mrs. J. A. Fink at 242 West 45th Street. Calling themselves the Union Grow Prayer Club, this circle began with only five members. But by September 1916 these believers had organized a church that met in different homes—thus the name "Pilgrim." In the next few years Pilgrim was indeed peripatetic, moving from a storefront at 4910 South Wentworth, to Wright's Hall at 44th and State, then to 20 East 45th, and by 1918 to 37th and Indiana.[28]

Though storefront churches predate the Great Migration, numbers increased dramatically as the Black Belt's population swelled, the established churches became overcrowded, and new arrivals set up churches for themselves.[29] More popular with Baptists than with Methodists, whose clergy viewed appointments to such facilities with little enthusiasm, storefronts served as temporary quarters until congregations could afford more traditional houses of worship. However, some congregations went from storefront to storefront over many years. Storefronts were frequently sites for the renewed formation of congregations that had left the South. Members migrated to Chicago and then invited their minister to join them to reorganize a church depleted by the exodus. For example, Robert Horton, a Baptist deacon from Hattiesburg, Mississippi, joined a migration club that went to Chicago; there, he opened the Hattiesburg Barber Shop in 1917. He and the other deacons of Hattiesburg's First Baptist Church encouraged their pastor, who initially opposed leaving the South, to join them.[30]

When the University of Chicago researcher Robert Sutherland conducted his walking tour of the Black Belt in October 1928, he still found more Baptists than any other denomination in storefront and house churches. Eighty-seven, or 65.9 percent, of the Baptist churches were so situated, while only twelve, or 34 percent, of the Methodist congregations occupied commercial space or houses. Approximately 86 percent of the Holiness groups met in storefront quarters.[31] Most storefront and house churches were located in the more economically depressed parts of the Black Belt, chiefly north of 39th Street. These storefront churches became a permanent feature of the religious landscape on the South Side. In 1938 Chicago had 266 storefront congregations in areas that were at least 50 percent African American. Congregations averaged about thirty members.[32]

African Americans who preferred Pentecostal and Holiness religious beliefs and practices further enriched the religious pluralism that emerged when Chicago was perceived as Canaan. Details regarding the earliest history of Sanctified and Holiness churches in Chicago are sketchy.[33] By 1919 twenty congregations were active in the city. This number grew to fifty-six in 1928 and reportedly contained 19 percent of all African American church members.[34] This growth in large part resulted from the Great Migration because southern blacks transplanted to the urban environment sought to capture both the intimacy and the religious style of down-home churches. They found new spiritual havens in the many neighborhood Holiness and Pentecostal fellowships.

Chicago offered migrants a far greater choice in religious affiliation than did the South where most churchgoing African Americans were either Baptists or Methodists. After settling in on the South Side, newcomers could shop around for a church in which they felt comfortable. Historian James Grossman depicts the richness of the market:

> A migrant could choose from among large churches like South Park Methodist Episcopal which had been organized by fifty Mississippians before the exodus and had grown to twenty-five hundred by 1919; any of the "old-line" churches dominated by middle-class Old Settlers

and featuring intellectual sermons on topics of social and political relevance; small churches such as St. John AME, which promised "old Time religion" revival tents; "rescue missions" offering services every night; and eclectic sects like the Church of the New Jerusalem, where the pastor "preached from a deck of cards." [35]

The diversification of religious institutions among African Americans was a significant feature of the northern urbanization process. This fact alone suggests that African American religious history must be read differently because of the Great Migration. No implication is suggested that established denominations were displaced by so-called cults and sects that appeared in northern cities between the two world wars, though scholarly fascination with the religiously exotic might make it appear so. [36] The essential story in Chicago is not the multiplication of religious groups on the margins of Christian orthodoxy, but the growth and transformation of the mainline Protestant traditions.

This transformation was in large part brought about by the religious preferences of migrants from the South and by attempts of the mainline churches to reach out to them. Many migrants found it difficult to adjust from the southern religious ethos to that of the large city churches. One woman left Olivet Baptist for a smaller church because the pastor used words she could not understand and, as she recalled, "I couldn't sing their way. The songs was proud-like." [37] A migrant who felt uncomfortable at Pilgrim Baptist complained that "nobody said nothing aloud but there were whispers all over the place." [38] A woman left one church because it was "too large—it don't see the small people. . . . The preacher wouldn't know me, might could call my name in the book but he wouldn't know me otherwise. Why, at home whenever I didn't come to Sunday School they would always come and see what was the matter." [39] While we should not exaggerate the cultural differences between migrants and Chicago's established black churches, they are important for understanding why some newcomers sought to organize their own congregations or felt like spectators rather than family in the established churches.

In 1938 Robert H. Mays interviewed Joseph Borgere, a native of Alabama, regarding such cultural differences. Borgere, who arrived in Chicago about 1925 and was head janitor at the Tivoli Theater, commented, "I am a Baptist. I go to Pilgrim Baptist Church [Junius Caesar Austin, pastor] when the weather permits. . . . When I first went there I told them, 'I don't understand your churches in Chicago, you don't open your doors and take in members. Where is your mercy seat'? I asked them whose church was it, *Austin's or God's?* I told them if it was God's church *I am heir to it,* because God is my father. They didn't like this kind of talk; it was not good for Austin."[40] Austin assumed Pilgrim's pulpit in 1926 after eleven years in Pittsburgh where he was active in assisting migrants. A noted preacher, he built Pilgrim into the third-largest church in the National Baptist Convention by 1930. To attract and hold migrants like Borgere who wanted more of a small church's intimacy, Pilgrim offered participation in more than a hundred auxiliary organizations.[41]

C. O. Murphy, pastor of St. Luke's African Methodist Zion Church in Grand Rapids, Michigan, argued, as did many northern black clergy, that the southern migrants should join the mainline African American churches.[42] But tension between the Old Settlers and newcomers developed over differences in worship styles. Newcomers who went from church to church looking for one in which they would not feel ill at ease became known as "church-tramps." The *Chicago Defender* frequently lectured migrants regarding their behavior in Robert Abbott's adopted city. Abbott warned them to avoid "scheming preachers and labor agents."[43] He also worried about the impact that migrants were having on the culture of the South Side. The September 10, 1921, edition of the *Chicago Defender* contained a spirited defense of the religious establishment:

> In view of the large number of churches there is positively no excuse for church members converting their private homes into places of public worship. Prayer meetings are very proper when held in churches. These religious enthusiasts do not seem to realize that residential neighborhoods are liable to have people living there who do not share with them in their demonstrative manifestations of religious devotion. Loud and noisy declamations and moans and groans from sisters and brothers until a late hour in the night are not only annoying but an unmistakable nuisance, which should not only be discontinued, but if necessary, prohibited.
>
> We hope our ministers will take up this subject in their respective pulpits with a view of discouraging this nuisance and insist upon religious meetings being held only in churches that are dedicated and provided for the purpose. Another religious evil is the large number of so-called missions presided over by self-appointed missionaries, who

prey upon the public in the guise of religious piety instead of earning their living by honest labor. In addition to these we have a large number of street corner preachers whose religious enthusiasm is measured by the number of dollars they can fleece out of a confiding public. Our regularly ordained clergy should for their own sake, as well as for the good of the community, take the lead in a movement to crush out these questionable practices.[44]

The *Defender*'s jeremiad demonstrates that Chicago's mainline churches were facing competition from religious entrepreneurs who operated outside traditional denominational conventions and appealed to the religious preferences of the newly arrived migrants.

Despite the multiplication and diversification of religious options in Chicago, many migrants joined a church bearing a readily identifiable label. The established denominations found it possible to start new congregations during the migration era, as the AME did with Coppin AME Church at 47th and State in 1919, because of the abundance of potential recruits.[45] The Dearborn Street AME Zion Church, whose growth had been nearly stagnant since its founding, tripled in membership in three years as a result of the Great Migration, taking in 351 new members in 1919. This growth no doubt was related to the service rendered to newcomers by the congregation. The Dearborn Street church arranged with the Chicago Urban League to send recent arrivals directly from the railroad station to the church, which stayed open day and night.[46] One migrant, attending an unnamed Baptist church, wrote back to Georgia regarding the Chicago experience. "The colored people are making good. They are the best workers. I have made a great many white friends. The church is crowded with Baptists from Alabama and Georgia. Ten and twelve join every Sunday. He [the pastor] is planning to build a fine brick church. He takes up 50 and 60 dollars each Sunday."[47]

Individual congregations profited from the influx of potential new members, but it was a buyer's market. Established churches competed with one another and with new churches set up by migrants themselves. Freedom of religious affiliation could not be curtailed by Chicago's cultural gatekeepers, white or black. The migrants acted on the American principle of the freedom of religious affiliation to such a high degree that preachers were forced to sell their wares alongside the many new businesses being formed in the expanding black ghetto.

The religious map of Chicago's South Side became even more diverse with the formation of nondenominational or "community" churches. The People's Community Church of Christ, Metropolitan Community Center, was organized in September 1920. Its founder, W. D. Cook, had been pastor of Bethel AME but was not in harmony with other AME clergy in Chicago who had formed a coalition "with the view to dictating and shaping the religious and political policy of the AME Churches of Chicago and vicinity."[48] Though popular among Bethel's constituents, Cook was transferred out of Chicago by Bishop Levi J. Coppin at the annual conference in Des Moines in 1920. Lay leaders from Bethel had an audience with the bishop before the reading of appointments and were given to believe no change in Cook's status would be made. Cook's removal precipitated a revolt in the congregation. About 2,700 members (out of about 5,000) withdrew to Unity Hall at 31st and Indiana and formed what was commonly known as Metropolitan Community Church. A church pamphlet describing the origins of Metropolitan attributes Cook's failure to be reappointed to the animosity he faced when he refused to open his pulpit to politicians for "renumeration."[49] One suspects conflict between Cook and Archibald J. Carey, the most prominent AME clergyman active on the political scene of whom Harold Kingsley wrote in 1929, "The recent upheavals among the A.M.E. churches [have] been rather disastrous to the morale and these church quarrels have possibly lowered the church in general in the estimation of Chicago Negroes. Criticism is usually leveled at Bishop Archibald Carey for holding a political as well as an ecclesiastical position. There is no doubt that Bishop Carey has built a most powerful machine which functions like a rock crusher."[50]

Cook, known as "the man who just missed being Bishop," established a community center in conjunction with his church so that they would have a greater impact on the Black Belt's civic and social life. In 1921 Metropolitan, which had grown to 3,000 members, purchased the Masonic Temple homes on Forest Avenue to house community center activities. Religious services were held at Wendell Phillips High School.[51] Other community churches also emerged in the wake of the Great Migration. In 1923 about 600 members of St. Mary's AME withdrew under the Rev. J. Harvey to form Cosmopolitan Community Church. The Rev. J. G. Garrison also spurned AME authorities and joined Harvey. In 1922 the Rev. J. A. Winters, pastor of St. Paul's, left the CME denomination, took about 500 members with him, and founded the People's Church of Christ and Progressive Community

Center. Cook attempted to bring these community churches into a miniature association and sought an advisory relationship with the Chicago Missionary and Extension Society of the Congregational Church. The association was never particularly viable, but the community churches offered migrants another alternative on Chicago's already crowded religious map.[52]

When Cook severed his connections with the AME Conference, the *Defender* declared, "The purpose of the new movement is for the improvement of the religious, moral, industrial and civic conditions of the Race."[53] This may have been but formalistic piety, for Robert Abbott customarily applauded anyone he deemed a "Race" man or a "Race" institution. But if we keep in mind Lacey Kirk Williams's judgment in 1929 that Chicago's black churches were "suitable only for paying, prayer and preaching,"[54] then the question of whether or not the Great Migration stimulated African American clergy to become more involved in the public arena, specifically in electoral politics, deserves attention. Olivet's leading minister faulted the churches of the Black Belt for being "more interested in preaching, worship, ceremonies, the things of the sanctuary than they are in the urgent, vital needs of a struggling humanity."[55] The most direct way to help the community necessitated participation in the struggle for political power in a city where politics was highly ethnicized.

Carl Sandburg wrote in 1919, "The Black Belt of Chicago is probably the strongest effective unit of political power, good or bad, in America."[56] Sandburg's remark, whether accurate or not, does underscore the historical significance of African American politics in Chicago. Even before the Great Migration, African Americans looked to Chicago with high expectations. Ida B. Wells wrote in the *Alpha Suffrage Record* in 1914, "Chicago, as we have said many a time before, points the way to political salvation of the race. Her colored men are colored men first — Republicans, Progressives and Democrats afterwards. In the last twenty years, on but one spot in this entire broad United States has the black man received anything like adequate political recognition and that one spot is Chicago."[57] I do not propose here to review the complex history of African American politics in Chicago, a subject treated extensively in a number of excellent studies.[58] My primary concern is to examine how the Great Migration influenced the involvement of African American churches, specifically the clergy, in urban politics.

Any discussion of pre-World War I politics in the Black Belt must take into account the role of the African Methodist clergyman Archibald J.

Carey, who arrived from Georgia in 1898. Carey was pastor of Quinn until 1904, of Bethel from 1904 until 1909, and of Institutional from 1909 until 1920, when he was elevated to the episcopacy. Carey emerged as the "ambassador from the 'Black Belt' " by virtue of his connections with Chicago's white-controlled political machine. Given the volatile nature of ethnic and party politics in which the African American vote in the Second Ward could prove crucial in close elections, courting individuals such as Carey became a top priority for the contending factions of the Republican Party. Blacks were still understandably hostile to the Democrats, but their loyalty to the Republicans could not be taken for granted when the party of Lincoln was itself divided between machine or professional politicians and reform or progressive factions. The vote in wards with concentrations of African Americans took on added significance in a political system that John D. Buenker has described as "a non-ideological competition among interest groups."[59]

Those who came to Chicago during the Great Migration entered into a political labyrinth that was the result of decades of racial and ethnic interaction. Lacking an independent political vehicle as envisioned by Edward Wright, an Illinois legislator and attorney, Chicago black leaders continued the protest tradition of John Jones, who was the spokesman for the city's African American community from the 1850s until his death in 1879. They sought to gain what they could from the white machine interests. Historian Charles Branham wrote of the pre-migration period:

> The transformation from the civic-protest tradition to organizational politics, the emergence of a small cadre of full-time black professional politicians, and the conflict between race politics and the patron-client relationships contracted between black and white politicians characterized black politics in Chicago before the Great Migration. The emerging Negro elite attempted, through politics, to translate intraracial status into political influence and to manipulate its personal and occupational prestige within the black community to serve as a buffer between white leadership and the black masses. The institutional and social circumscription peculiar to the black urban experience, plus the pre-existing tradition of ethnic representation and group politics, combined to aid this new elite in translating credibility with black voters and contacts with white politicians into limited political influence.[60]

The activities of the black clergy in Chicago politics before 1915, given the limited evidence at hand, seem to conform to this interpretation.

The Rev. E. J. Fisher dominated affairs at Olivet Baptist from 1903 until 1915. Though described as averse to "office-seeking" and the taking of "filthy lucre" in exchange for his endorsement, Fisher did accept appointments for his political support of Republicans in both city and state elections.[61] Fisher also received financial aid from prominent white politicians to complete the construction of Olivet in time for the twenty-fifth annual session of the National Baptist Convention at his church in 1905. Fisher's son and biographer, Miles Mark Fisher, attributes the animosity his father received from other black Baptist clergy to the close relationship that he maintained with white Baptists: "This 'Union' tried to eliminate him and Olivet as factors of power with white Baptists," the son writes, adding, "However, the white brethren considered Olivet stronger than the combined churches of the 'Union' and would follow no policy that did not include Olivet."[62]

Lacey Kirk Williams assumed Fisher's mantle as principal pastor at Olivet in 1915. He apparently attempted to maintain his independence amid the growing political factionalism within the Black Belt. His biographer states that when the Great Migration "sprang into full flower less than a year after his arrival," Williams decided that the newcomers must be kept from becoming "the political pawn of scheming politicians."[63] Miles Mark Fisher's claim in 1922 that Williams "never attended a political meeting and it is not certain that he is a party to any faction"[64] is suspect. Unlike Fisher's father, who supported Oscar De Priest and William Hale Thompson, Williams was known to be sympathetic to the reform forces led by ex-governor Frank O. Lowden. Lowden named Williams to the commission to investigate the race riot of 1919. Williams also allowed his name to be linked to national Republican operatives. Olivet's pastor did not, however, become one of the key players in Chicago politics at the ward level in the transition from the civic protest tradition of the Jones era to the interest-group politics of the postmigration decades.

Given Williams's prominence among Baptists in Chicago, one wonders why he did not take a more active part in electoral politics. Perhaps out of principle he decided to stay above the factional fray. More likely he was too involved with the political machinations of the National Baptists and the management of Olivet's immense program to have time and energy for Chicago city and ward politics. Williams arrived in the city when the stage was already dominated by Archibald J. Carey, who was not reluctant to engage in machine politics as practiced according to the city's unique rules. Carey did not let party affiliation dictate his loyalties at the local level. In 1911 he supported Carter Harrison II, a reform Democrat, for mayor; presumably for his efforts, he was later appointed to the motion picture censor board. In 1912 Carey supported Democrat Edward Dunne for governor, and in 1913 he got $25,000 from the state legislature for the fiftieth anniversary celebration of Emancipation. Carey's success, which caused Elijah John Fisher to complain that the Baptists had been ignored in the planning of the 1915 anniversary, also brought censure from Julius Taylor's *The Broad Ax*.[65]

Carey's forceful personality rankled others who were contending for leadership roles in the Black Belt. Criticisms of Carey were partly the result of the resistance of some voters to the clergy's involvement in politics. Without mentioning Carey by name, the *Chicago Defender* editorialized on June 6, 1914, "Chicago has a few divines who should either divorce themselves from church or politics before they are requested to do so."[66] The key to understanding this cavil lies in the strength of political forces in the Black Belt, symbolized in such personalities as Edward Wright and Oscar De Priest, that were not based on the church. Though they often came into conflict, De Priest and Wright were professional politicians who were attempting to build a political base that had room for the clergy only as auxiliary support. Carey was the one clerical figure who held his ground, chiefly by capitalizing on the failure of white politicians to recognize that a new political era was dawning.

As the demographics of the Second Ward changed in their favor, African Americans began to demand representation on the city council. Carey in 1914 refused to join the faction promoting an African American candidate, and Charles Griffen was defeated in a close election by the Republican incumbent. In 1915 Oscar De Priest, running as a regular Republican, defeated two black opponents in the primary; the black community then closed ranks, and De Priest won the ward's second aldermanic seat. Carey, who had initially allied himself with the insurgent Griffen-Wright forces against the regular Republicans, acknowledged De Priest's victory with telling ambivalence:

> Somebody spoke about the regular organization being responsible for the election of Oscar De Priest. The organization is not responsible;

that always steps on my corns. We Negroes would have voted for a Democrat if we had not been given a man and they knew it. I have said before and I say now, I am with the organization when the organization is with the black man. Oh there is no gainsaying it. If it had not been for Ed Wright and Charley Griffen, Oscar would not be alderman. Let us put laurels where they belong. One sows and another reaps. Ed Wright and Charley Griffen sowed, and Oscar reaped.[67]

De Priest's election marked the rise of a new set of community leaders in the Black Belt. As these politicians who benefited from the formation of a formidable bloc of voters gained influence because of the Great Migration, less and less room was left for the clergy to act as self-designated ambassadors from the South Side.[68]

In the short term, however, Carey used his considerable abilities as an orator and local church leader to gain access to Chicago's political inner circles. William Hale Thompson's election as mayor in 1915 gave Carey his first significant opportunity. The Thompson-Carey alliance had been forged in the aldermanic election of 1910 when Carey squired Thompson throughout the black neighborhoods on the South Side.[69] Mayor Thompson rewarded his black supporters by successfully putting a public playground, said to be the first in the country, in the Black Belt. Not surprisingly, it was located across the street from Quinn Chapel, Carey's church. Carey, with backing from Thompson, allied himself with the Republican faction headed by William J. Lorimer, the "blond boss" of the machine, whose major opponent was Charles Deneen, head of the reform Republicans, some of whom were Progressives loyal to Theodore Roosevelt. Because of his association with Thompson and Lorimer, Quinn's pastor wielded "considerable influence as a prominent Southside civic and religious leader." Branham notes, however, that Carey lacked the power of white politicians who controlled the South Side before the Great Migration. The fact that he was "by 1910, the most influential black Republican in Chicago is less a reflection of his own exalted stature than the general political impoverishment of the city's black leadership."[70]

Carey's willingness to align himself with the white political faction, Republican or Democrat, that appeared to offer him or, as he argued, Chicago's African American population the most rankled others. Carey was criticized by the *Chicago Tribune* for supporting Lorimer, the political boss of the West Side who was elected to the U.S. Senate in 1909 and then unseated amid bribery charges three years later. Carey gave a lengthy rebuttal to those who thought him opportunistic in his support of a Democratic candidate for mayor in 1911 and of Edward Dunne, the state's Democratic governor:

> I may have been represented to you as a "political preacher." I do not deny that I have been very deeply interested in the civic and political affairs of this city, state and nation. . . . When I came to Chicago six-teen years ago I learned from those in position to know that there were certain white men in this city who were disposed to give the Negro fair play. Among them were Martin B. Madden, Frank O. Lowden, Marcus Kavanaugh, Elbridge Hanecy, William Lorimer et al. (Re-publican); Edward F. Dunne, Carter H. Harrison, Edward O. Brown et al. (Democrats). At first I could see no good in any Democrat because of my southern traditions and my southern training. When, however, I had watched the course of the Democrats, as well as Re-publicans named above, and saw that they were true to humanity, whether clothed in black skins or white, I became an ardent supporter, regardless of their political party creeds. . . . Is it a crime for a Negro minister, who loves his people and is interested in their securing their just and equal rights, to advocate the claims of men whom he believes will deal fairly with the people of his race?[71]

When the Democrats were defeated in 1915 by William ("Big Bill") Thompson, Carey abandoned his temporary alliance with them. Carey eulogized Thompson in September 1915 at the Half Century Anniversary Exposition as "the biggest man in all Chicago, the biggest man in all Illi-nois, and the best mayor Chicago ever had."[72] Thompson won again in 1919, did not run in 1923, and returned as mayor in 1927. Republicans held the mayor's office until the election of Anton J. Cermak, a Democrat, in 1931.[73]

Carey's decision to link up with Thompson was sagacious, for Thomp-son's strength in the Black Belt was more than doubled by the Great Mi-gration. Thompson's victory in 1915 was masterminded by Fred Lundin, a former Lorimer associate. Lundin, according to Joseph Logsdon, "pro-vided the master strategy which made minority groups and especially Negroes the foundation of their [the Republicans'] coalition."[74] Carey used his pulpit to portray Thompson as a second Lincoln.[75] Eighty percent of the vote in the Second Ward went to Thompson, thus enabling him to defeat his Republican rival in the primary. Thompson's victory in the general election was overwhelming, and he quickly acknowledged his debt to Carey, though Edward Wright and others did the tedious but necessary work of grassroots organization in the precincts of the Second Ward, which was 60 to 70 percent African American in 1915. From the pulpit at Quinn, Thompson declared, "When Dr. Carey calls for me, it matters not where I am or when it is made, I will come. You supported me loyally and I believe in reciprocity. The Colored people will have the greatest representation you have ever had."[76] Carey was appointed librarian in the office of the corporation counsel. Joseph Logsdon maintains that "until Wright became ward committeeman of the Second Ward in 1920, Carey probably held the most authority in the Negro community over the distribution of patronage."[77]

Oscar De Priest, leader of the other political faction in the Second Ward, had not allied himself with Thompson, and thus he drew opposition from Carey and Wright. Elected to the city council in 1915, De Priest was indicted in 1917 for conspiracy to protect gambling and prostitution on the South Side. When De Priest attempted a political comeback in 1918 as an independent, Carey and Wright campaigned for Major Robert R. Jackson. The *Defender* called the De Priest-Jackson contest "one of the most bitter fights that has ever been waged in the Second Ward." A *Defender* reporter interviewed Wright and Carey and was told that Thompson "was not with the Von Hindenburg of the Second Ward" and that the mayor "owed no allegiance to De Priest because those who helped the mayor carry the mayoralty nomination as the nominee of the Republican party three years ago were Wright, Carey, and Anderson. . . ."[78] The *Defender*'s list of Jackson's partisans included the Baptist Ministers and Deacons Alliance of Chicago, the Baptist Woman's Congress, and the Salem Baptist, Walters' AME Zion, Quinn, Bethel, Ebenezer Baptist, Olivet Baptist, St. John's, and Institutional churches. In a later issue the *Defender* commented further on Jackson's defeat of De Priest: "The church people played a significant part in the election. Most of the pastors spoke for Jackson and the Republican party. The following preachers are entitled to special mention for their services: Dr. Cook of Bethel; Dr. Anderson of Quinn; Dr. Blackwell of Walters A.M.E. [Zion] church; Dr. Williams of Olivet Baptist church; Dr. McCracken, presiding elder; Rev. Haywood; Dr. Gibson; Dr. Crackett, besides Dr. A. J. Carey."[79] Obviously, Carey was no longer the only player in the Chicago game of cultivating churches for political allies, but he was the most publicly visible.

Carey was heavily involved in Chicago politics, yet he thwarted the efforts of friends who wanted him to run in 1918 as the representative of Illinois' third senatorial district. Though the election of an African American candidate seemed likely, Carey responded,

> I sometimes fear the holding of any political position might be construed into a desire to push my own personal interest, and by reason of that I am almost persuaded that the greatest service [that] can be rendered by me can be done by devoting all of my energies to the interest of the church and the Christian ministry. And I refused to enter into any personal political contest for office, if such entrance means to impair the fundamental services I hope to render to my Race and my church. I find the ministry of the AME church such a splendid field for usefulness, both for God and the Race, that I find it very difficult to enter into any other activity that might interfere with the success of the work of the church.[80]

Had Carey been more candid, he might have explained that he had been campaigning aggressively for the office of bishop in the AME Church for several years. He believed that the midwestern districts of his denomination deserved greater respect from the traditional centers of power, which were the Northeast before the Civil War and, increasingly since Emancipation, the southern wing. With the growth of African American populations in cities such as Chicago and Detroit during the Great Migration, Carey saw an opportunity to press the claims of the western regions.

Armed with endorsements from his white political allies in Chicago, Carey went to the centennial convention of the AME held at Philadelphia in 1916 fully expecting to win. Campaign literature distributed at the general conference included a testimonial from Mayor Thompson: "To my mind Dr. Carey is pre-eminently qualified from every point of view to make an acceptable, useful, and aggressive Bishop of your church. He will not only serve and help your church, but he will help and serve your race. He'll do for you what but few other men can do."[81] Ida B. Wells-Barnett sent a letter to Philadelphia which, according to Le Roy C. Bundy, Carey's campaign manager, "turned the trick" and dashed Carey's hopes. In her autobiography Wells relates that she revealed "that white politicians had raised money to send a committee to the general conference with money in its pocket with which to buy votes just as if were a political organization, and that it was enough to make Richard Allen turn over in his grave." As a result of her intervention, Carey "shooed his committee, composed of Oscar De Priest, Louis Anderson, and Bob Jackson, over to New York, but it was too late."[82] Carey was not elected until the St. Louis General Conference of 1920, but he used the intervening period to increase his stature in denominational circles.

Carey continued to play a role in Chicago politics even after elevation to the bishopric in 1920. In 1927 Big Bill Thompson regained the office of mayor and appointed Carey as one of three members of the city's civil service commission.[83] Carey used his influence to obtain municipal jobs for blacks and monitored the treatment of the citizens of the Black Belt in Chicago industries. "In all my travels to and fro," commented AME bishop John Hurst, "I have not yet seen a man occupying a position where he can render so much real service in a material way to the people of our group as can Bishop Carey in his present position as Civil Service Commissioner of the City of Chicago."[84] Carey's appointment, however, may have been of more symbolic than material significance. Harold Gosnell argues that the civil service commission had no direct appointing powers and lacked the authority to stop discrimination by department heads. "Bishop Carey's position on this board," the noted political scientist concluded, "brought him little besides trouble."[85]

Whatever Carey's actual accomplishments, we can agree with Joseph Logsdon's observation that he "was truly one of the first Negro leaders to recognize the profit of participation in the political machines in Northern urban industrial areas."[86] This judgment must be qualified with the statement by Richard R. Wright, Jr., that Carey "did not care for politics for politics' sake. He was a 'race man' and the thing that lured him—perhaps too far—in politics was the thought of helping his race." Wright admitted that Carey "had more enemies than any man who ever occupied the bishopric—and possibly as many friends." He was, Wright asserted, "one of the few Negroes in America to prove the power of political organization." There was, however, "a general jealousy against the ministry in anything but the church, and men thought they could get popularity by striking Carey."[87] Carey was by all accounts the dominating clerical-political figure during the Great Migration era in Chicago. At his death in 1931, Wright testified that De Priest, who was often at odds with Carey, confessed that if it had not been for his rival, he would not have been elected to Congress.[88] Carey's preeminence, however, came with a price. He helped set the stage for De Priest, and in so doing he contributed to a new political order on the

South Side. Religious leaders such as Carey were cast into more marginal roles by the emergence of the professional politician who by virtue of the geographical concentration and weight of the African American vote could loft a career on the basis of the Black Belt's own version of ethnic politics.

Carey's ties to the Thompson machine precluded the rise of other clergy-politicians, for modified as the relationship was, it was still one of client and patron, and the machine preferred to deal with one client rather than many. Carey was a transitional figure. Like the clergy-politicians of the Reconstruction era such as Henry M. Turner in Georgia, Carey capitalized on his position as a religious leader to gain access to the political realm when African Americans were on the threshold of gaining political rights. The era's migration of thousands of southern blacks into the urban North was a political watershed as well as a religious one. The *Chicago Whip* observed, "Pioneers like Bishop Carey blazed the way to the polls for us, emphasized the importance of the ballot and preached to his people on the power of this constitutional guarantee. He awoke them to the sense of their duty and the importance of its performance.[89] Carey's legacy, important as it was, did not go unchallenged, for other voices wanted to be heard and other interests were anxious to demonstrate their political skills.

Community life in Chicago became more diversified during and after the Great Migration. Secular organizations such as the NAACP and the Urban League came into existence in response to the social and political crises surrounding World War I.[90] The black press played an increasingly influential role in shaping public opinion. Robert Abbot of the *Defender* did not shy away from criticizing the clergy when he felt that ministers had strayed too far from their principal role as religious leaders.

I have been unable to determine what circumstances triggered the following editorial in the *Defender* in 1916. It is, however, evidence that in the urban industrial North the black church was but one of a number of contenders for influencing the political views of those from the South:

There is absolutely no logical reason for the active participation of a minister in politics, because religion and politics do not, in any manner, harmonize, and it is difficult to understand how a man who aspires to be a good, honest and devout follower of the meek and lowly Christ, can also be a consistent political leader. On the other hand it shows bad taste on the part of any politician or set of politicians to accept the support of a minister of the gospel, make him promise to do certain duties, if success crowns the efforts, by and with the prelate's assistance, fall back behind the cowardly excuse that the minister had no right to be engaged in politics and how much more good he might be accomplishing in attending to the higher things in connection with his religious calling.

The *Defender* queried whether it was proper for ministers to force their political views on congregations composed of "different political faiths" and added, "Of course politicians find it greatly to their advantage to enlist the services of the influential minister, it is a great business stroke, and the few dollars they toss into the contribution box is well spent. The appointment, which is also a trump card, works like a charm. Of course if it never materializes that is all in the game. Our churches throughout the country have especially been victims of this political chicanery, and it is high time to take a firm stand and divorce politics from the church."[91]

How are we to understand the cynicism expressed by those who simultaneously called for greater involvement in civic affairs by African American churches and expressed varying degrees of ambivalence and skepticism over the clergy's role? Abbot's discontent may well have arisen from the failure of certain clergy to agree with him on specific political issues, but something more substantive may also be at stake.

Martin Kilson has suggested that the migrants whom the African American churches in Chicago were courting as the churches struggled to increase their membership were undergoing political modernization. Unlike their counterparts in the South, Chicago blacks had the right to vote. But the exercise of this right was limited by preexisting racial and political barriers in the city. Before the Great Migration of 1916–18 clientage politics allowed a few of the black middle class access to limited power by virtue of their personal ties to influential whites. Kilson offers the following critique of this pattern: "The black bourgeoisie ideologically portrayed clientage politics as 'race politics,' presumably beneficial to all blacks, though in reality it was of benefit more to the elites than to the urban Negro masses."[92]

This assertion is illustrated in Chicago by the failure of African American clergy to criticize the fundamental inequities in the economic order as well as by doubts about the long-term benefits to the African American community of Carey's alliance with the Thompson machine. Lacey Kirk Williams of Olivet and John F. Thomas of Ebenezer Baptist allowed labor organizers to speak in their churches, but, according to historian James Grossman, only James Henderson of Institutional AME actively assisted labor leaders. Carey opposed the Brotherhood of Sleeping Car Porters, received donations from white industrialists, and declared, "the interest of my people lies with the wealth of the nation and with the class of white people who control it."[93] Black clergy were known to recruit strikebreakers when labor unrest took place in the stockyards, and one South Side minister mustered 300 black women overnight to break a strike by hotel chambermaids in 1916.[94] The racism among the white, ethnic working class and the competition for jobs between blacks and whites must be accounted for. Nevertheless, few black clergy advocated radical solutions to the problems of an urban, industrial labor force. As late as 1930 the observation was made that "the Negro church, composed of laboring class people, is about as far from a labor program as the North Pole is from the South Pole."[95] Ralph J. Bunche argued in 1929 that despite the gains made by individual African Americans in Thompson's organization, "Negro political leaders have, by and large, been cogs in his well-oiled machine." Bunche found it "regrettable" that the black vote was widely associated "with a machine so nationally notorious for its rottenness" and contended that when Thompson was Chicago's mayor, patronage and favor were swapped for votes and vice was allowed to flourish in African American sectors.[96] A. L. Jackson of the Wabash Avenue YWCA told members of the City Club of Chicago in 1919, "If you can convince him [the black voter] that you are right on the 'question,' then there is hardly anything that you cannot do with him. This is the danger, and it is also an opportunity if the right leadership can be had."[97]

Clientage politics, the paradigm that existed in Chicago as the Great Migration got fully under way, eventually was challenged by another pattern, which Kilson calls "interest group articulation." With the growth and demographic transformation of the Black Belt, many different cliques and interest groups emerged. The church became only one of a number of contenders for influence.[98] The religious community on the South Side became increasingly diverse, lessening the chances for a single clergyman like Carey to be recognized as the Black Belt's broker in an exchange with city hall. Charles R. Branham argues that black politicians on the South Side remained in a stage of "political lieutenancy" between 1915 and 1920 because concrete political power was retained by Congressman Martin Madden and State Senator George Harding.[99] The emergence of the professional black politician provided both a challenge and an alternative to the leadership of the black church in community affairs. Robert Abbott's criticisms of the mixing of church and politics, while motivated by his own interests in being a "black Joshua" on the South Side during the Great Migration, are a reflection of the differentiation in black community life fostered by the Great Migration. In neoclientage machine politics, potential black leaders, who before 1915 used their fraternal, business, or church connections to parley themselves into prominence, now were better advised to apprentice themselves to the organization. "From building captain and precinct captain to alderman and ward committeeman," Branham argues, "the Madden-Harding machine became the school which forced a group of intensely ambitious and intrinsically individualistic men to subsume ambition and yield to an institutional hierarchy and leadership which was largely transmitted into black hands by 1920." [100]

These black hands generally belonged to the politicians, not the preachers. The twin forces of urbanization and secularization drew some migrants, particularly those who composed what later-day sociologists would call the "underclass," away from the church. As St. Clair Drake wrote in 1940, "It does not take long for a migrant Negro to learn the wielders of power in the city; who can get relief for him; who can get him out of jail; who can secure a job for him." Except for one or two influential ministers, Drake argued, this was usually the precinct captain or alderman. The migrant also learned that in the city one can be married or buried without church sanction and that one's children need not be christened. "Deprived of his power in this fashion," Drake wrote, "the [ordinary] minister is in a very precarious position, indeed." [101]

Here was the challenge and the dilemma for African American churches and clergy in the industrial North. The Great Migration stimulated a new awareness of the need to adapt the church to an urban environment with its multiple social problems. This necessitated, in Martin Kilson's words, "institutionalized interaction between the Negro urban community and the formal white power structure"—which, in Chicago, at least, took the form of "neoclientage machine politics." [102] In the Chicago version of neoclientage politics we can see vestiges of the way African American clergy had to operate in the South when racial apartheid separated blacks from whites and the white power structure dealt with African American communities through selected individuals. [103] But the boundaries of apartheid could not be as clearly defined or maintained in the northern city. Others took their place alongside the clergy as community leaders. Equally significant, the migrants eventually discovered "heavens of their own" that modified the institutional anchors of the pre-migration years or served as alternatives. In Chicago and elsewhere in the North the migrants provided their own cultural leaven in the reshaping of African American religious life.

7

A HEAVEN

ALL THEIR

OWN

The Great Migration brought about changes in the religious landscape of the urban North far beyond the expansion, proliferation, and relocation of existing churches and the efforts of national denominations and local congregations to respond to the new institutional demands placed on them. Uprooted but not without roots, the migrants brought cultural gifts, though an appreciation of this religious treasure was not always evident. By the end of the Great Migration era African American religious culture in northern cities was much more diverse and resistant to easy generalization than at the end of the nineteenth century.

The migrants resisted total assimilation into the cultural traditions of the Old Settlers and set up their own religious safe places in a hostile urban environment. The novelist Richard Wright wrote in *12 Million Black Voices*, "it is only when we are within the walls of our churches that we are wholly ourselves, that we keep alive a sense of our personalities in relation to the total world in which we live. . . . Our churches are where we dip our tired bodies in cool springs of hope, where we retain our wholeness and humanity despite the blows of death from the Bosses of the Buildings."[1] Wright's own encounter with the northern city came a generation after the Great Migration, but even then he could write, "After working all day in one civilization, we go home to our black belts and live, within the orbit of the surviving remnants of the culture of the South, our naive, casual, verbal, fluid folk life."[2]

Many witnesses commented on the new and often unconventional religious groups appearing in African American neighborhoods during and after World War I, and they were quick to blame the eruption of the exotic in their midst to the religious naïveté of the migrants from the South. In 1926 the African American sociologist Ira De A. Reid reported that black Harlem contained more than 140 churches. He expressed dismay at the diversity of religious options on display, the variety of structures housing them, and the activities of the self-styled religious leaders derisively called jackleg preachers. Reid felt that the "growth of the church esoteric in Harlem" was especially problematic. He pointed to the presence of the Commandment Keepers, Holy Church of the Living God; the Pillar and the Ground of the Truth; the Temple of the Gospel of the Kingdom; the Metaphysical Church of the Divine Investigation; Prophet Bess; Mt. Zion Pentecostal Church; St. Matthew's Church of the Divine Silence and Truth; Tabernacle of the Congregation of Beth B'Nai Abraham; Holy Temple of God in Christ; and the Church of the Temple of Love. According to Reid, these unorthodox groups practiced "various doctrines and creeds provocative of no good save the financial returns obtained by the leader." The profusion of voices calling for attention seemed too much like religious hucksterism, so Reid entitled his impressions, published in the Urban League's journal *Opportunity,* "Let Us Prey!"[3]

With less hostility than Reid displayed, Reverdy C. Ransom and James H. Robinson, editors of *The Year Book of Negro Churches,* called attention to new religious groups that existed in 1926 but were not listed in that year's federal religious census. Among these were the Pentecostal Faith of All Nations, the Peace Mission of Father Divine, the Commandment Keepers, and various self-styled Islamic groups.[4] Miles Mark Fisher, professor of church history at Shaw University in Raleigh, North Carolina, and pastor of White Rock Baptist Church in Durham, also took note of the new groups, "those led by Bishop Grace, Elder Michaux, Father Divine, et al.," that were having an impact on African American urban life. He predicted that the 1936 religious census would demonstrate that the "cults" profited from "considerable denominational losses during the last ten years."[5] In 1924 George E. Haynes authored an article on "Negro Migration" for *Opportunity* in which he discussed the effects of the Great Migration on family and community life in the North. To the question, "What has been the effect of migration on the Negro church, which we saw was the most influential institution in Negro life in the South?," Haynes responded, "It has increased greatly in membership, although many small mushroom storefront churches have sprung up and often become a hindrance to progress."[6]

The proliferation of storefront churches and the rise of nontraditional religious leaders has captured center stage in most portrayals of African American religion between the two world wars.[7] This focus has perpetuated the stereotype of the migrants as religiously unsophisticated ruralites who came to the city and fell victim to self-serving religious hucksters and hawkers of exotic and sometimes bizarre beliefs and practices. According to this line of argument, the cults and sects grew at the expense of the mainline churches that failed to recruit and welcome the migrants.

Before turning to some of the most important alternative religious groups, the so-called cults and sects that Reid and others observed, it is important to examine how the influx of hundreds of thousands of black southerners changed the climate in which the mainline northern churches operated. Joining one of the new religious communities deemed unorthodox or aberrant by traditional standards was not the only option exercised by migrants and their children as they sought "a heaven all their own." The cultural changes brought about by the Great Migration were not one-sided. African Americans who relocated "up North" brought religious folkways with them that they did not abandon overnight, despite efforts to acculturate them made by both national and local representatives of the large African American denominations. Sometimes disagreements over how best to assimilate migrants into existing congregations caused internal stress. Newcomers had their own habits of the heart.

Such was the case with historic Mother Bethel AME on Sixth Street, below Pine, in Philadelphia. Robert J. Williams was appointed Bethel's pastor in June 1916. Beset by financial problems and a dwindling membership, Bethel's lay leadership initially supported Williams in his effort to recruit migrants. An information bureau sent flyers to African Methodist churches in the South with the message that should migrants come to the City of Brotherly Love, they would find Mother Bethel to be "the home for the stranger, the pride of the connection, the center of attraction, the house of God."[8] The migrants responded, and Bethel's pews were soon occupied by scores of newcomers, mainly from South Carolina, Florida, and Georgia.

To attract and hold the southerners, Williams adopted a more evangelistic preaching style and introduced "snap and go" in church music. Contrary to denominational practice, he accepted new members who did not come with a letter of transfer from an African Methodist church in the South. Bethel's old guard grumbled at the many changes in their beloved church. "Williams's supporters," historian Robert Gregg tells us, "were mainly those members of Bethel who had recently arrived in Philadelphia; his opponents tended to be established Philadelphians who wished to maintain control of their church."[9] Williams lost the power struggle with conservative lay members who made up the Bethel Corporation, the congregation's governing board. Despite success in recruiting new members, he lost the pastorate of Mother Bethel in June 1920. The root cause of the conflict, Gregg suggests, lies between the desire of an ambitious pastor to gain influence over a lay-controlled church board and the prejudice of established members against the newcomers. However we interpret the tribulations of Williams's "heated term," it is clear that the influx of migrants added a new and highly combustible ingredient to preexisting church politics.

Bethel's troubles reflected divergent streams in African American religious life, one urban and northern, the other primarily southern and primarily rural. When the congregation's governing board adopted resolutions intended to foster order and decorum during worship, it hoped to maintain traditional standards in the face of the migrant influx. No one was allowed to pass beyond the ushers in the aisles during the sermon; all worshipers were requested to leave quietly after the benediction, and talking while the preacher was in the pulpit was frowned on. Loitering in the vestibule and near the doors after the service was discouraged.[10] To migrants accustomed to ritual informality and the intimacy of folk churches in the South, Mother Bethel's rules detracted from the kind of welcome that Williams knew was essential to increasing the membership. The troubles at Mother Bethel were symptomatic of the stress caused by the confluence of contrasting religious styles. Conflict between existing members and newcomers broke out at other churches in Philadelphia and elsewhere in the urban North.[11]

The Great Migration created a new source of potential members and thereby precipitated competition across the North among the existing churches. Preachers who successfully appealed to the migrants and simultaneously kept a core of supportive established members stood to reap their reward in the form of rapidly expanding congregations. Philadelphia, the site of Williams's tribulations, offers us an excellent example. Charles Albert Tindley's East Calvary Methodist Episcopal Church was often filled during the migration years. Noted as a pioneering composer of gospel hymns, Tindley conducted a street ministry and distributed free meals to the poor. He had a national reputation in Baptist circles as a spirited evangelist. His sermons were so popular that East Calvary's 5,000 members outgrew their building on Broad Street. Under the name of Union Baptist, the congregation took possession of a new and much larger sanctuary on May 17, 1916, just in time to capitalize on the exodus from the South.

Tindley demonstrated his interest in the welfare of the migrants by appealing to church members to take in lodgers, who were then invited to worship where they could hear the Tindley Gospel Singers. By 1919 Sunday morning attendance averaged 1,200, though East Calvary could seat only 1,000.[12] So successful was Tindley in attracting new members that by 1923, according to Ralph H. Jones, longtime church organist and Tindley associate, "active membership climbed above the 7,000 mark."[13] Tindley, like Williams, was from Berlin, Maryland, and he was familiar with how the migrants prayed and worshiped. But unlike Williams who was deposed during the Great Migration years, Tindley parlayed his preaching and administrative skills into becoming pastor of one of the largest congregations in Philadelphia. He became known as the "prince of preachers." Tindley Temple was hailed as "The Church that Welcomed 10,000 Strangers."[14]

As a consequence of the Great Migration, the major northern cities witnessed unprecedented growth in the number of their congregations. For one, the total number of African American churches in Detroit reportedly increased from six in 1910 to sixty in 1923. Most of the sixty, according to John Marshall Ragland of Detroit's Urban League, were "composed entirely of newcomers, including the ministers and official boards."[15] In Pittsburgh, African American churches also grew in number and size as migrants were lured to jobs in the steel plants. For example, Ebenezer Baptist went from 1,500 to 3,000 members between 1915 and 1926.[16] The statistical impact of the arrival of the migrants varied from city to city and congregation to congregation. Preachers rivaled one another in public declarations of the rapid increase in church membership. Even if we discount the exaggerations and acknowledge that churches experienced a great deal of turnover among their members, we must recognize that the Great Migration era was a boom time for African American churches in the North. Religious census materials make clear that when the dust of competition settled, Baptists had benefited the most. This is true of the number of churches as well as aggregate membership.

Chicago is a prime example of a city in which the Baptist growth curve ascends rapidly because of in-migration from the South. Before World War I Baptists ranked fifth in the number of congregations and members among the denominations, with Roman Catholics at the top. In 1927 Catholics still led the count, but Baptists now ranked in second place because of the tremendous growth of black Baptists. In 1927 fifty-five African American Baptist churches were active in the city with an estimated membership of nearly 66,000.[17]

Cleveland had a much smaller African American population than Chicago before the Great Migration. Fewer than 40 percent of the black residents of Cleveland were regular church members in 1884. Only five black churches were active before the 1890s; seventeen on the eve of the arrival of Cleveland's share of the refugees from the South. Two churches were considered elite, Mt. Zion Congregational and St. Andrew's Episcopal. But as a result of the Great Migration, Baptists and Methodists rapidly outstripped them in membership. In 1918 Cleveland boasted forty-four black churches; in 1921 the number had reached seventy-eight. Baptists made up the largest denomination with an estimated 14,000—64 percent—of Cleveland's 22,000 black church members.[18]

In city after city across the North, migrants voted with their feet and either established, joined, or transplanted Baptist churches in greater numbers than any other denomination. Seth M. Scheiner examined five selected northern cities and discovered that from 1916 until 1926 the number of Baptist churches increased 151 percent and Methodist churches only 85 percent.[19] African Methodist expansion during the nineteenth century had been impressive, but after the Great Migration it became clear that the twentieth century would belong to the Baptists. Why the African Methodists, particularly the AME Church, failed to capitalize on the growth possibilities inherent in the exodus from South as much as black Baptists did is difficult to answer. Perhaps the episcopal polity of the Methodist connections and their expectations that denominational expansion must take place in an orderly manner impeded the establishment of new congregations among migrants. Baptists operated more independently and set up new churches by spontaneous combustion. Given the statistical majority that Baptists enjoyed in the South, it is also highly likely that many more Baptists than Methodists participated in the exodus.

A great number of new churches in the Great Migration years were congregations transplanted from the South. But others were resulted from divisions, sometimes peaceful, sometimes acrimonious, of established northern churches that had multiplied in size at remarkable rates. Daughter congregations organized. In some cases they were pastored by clergymen who had acted as assistant ministers in the larger churches. Within the mother church these men attracted a following composed of migrants who preferred their style of preaching and pastoral care to the senior pastor's. When personal rivalries erupted, the assistant pastors withdrew to set up their own churches, taking many migrant members with them. In some instances the aspirations of migrant clergy to have their own churches were amicably fulfilled when the mother church sponsored a mission congregation where many migrants were taking up residence.

Ministers who migrated from the South found northern cities fertile soil for institutional experimentation. Enterprising pastors capitalized on the expanding religious market and created networks of congregations beholden to no one but themselves. In 1919 the Rev. R. C. Lawson began a street ministry in Harlem. Hailing from a family of revivalist preachers in Louisiana, he founded a new denomination called the Refuge Church of the Christ of the Apostolic Faith and installed himself as bishop. By 1927 the church claimed 600 members in New York City and had established branches elsewhere. Lawson favored self-help programs, restricted benefits to members only, and rarely joined fellow clergy in community projects. Historian William Welty writes, "Lawson was content that his church had transformed one of the worst blocks in Harlem to an environment dominated by the Refuge Church."[20]

Wherever the migrants settled, they made a difference in the number of new churches that were established. Many of these new congregations sought out alternative space. At the end of the religious boom of the 1920s the Greater New York Federation of Churches counted 160 Protestant churches in Harlem, only thirty-three of which owned their own property. Most were in residences, storefronts, halls, or borrowed premises. More than half of those enumerated were grouped as "other," since they bore no traditional denominational label. The survey probably underestimated both the number and size of storefront congregations.[21]

To help migrants offset their cultural shock and to keep them from falling into the hands of religious entrepreneurs like Lawson or from going over to the storefronts, large urban churches sponsored state clubs. Some clubs became churches within churches, though their ostensible purpose was to build a stronger bond between migrants and the new Christian fellowships that they joined. Alabama and South Carolina clubs existed within New York City's Abyssinian Baptist Church and were functioning many decades after the Great Migration. State-based affiliations fostered feelings of comradery and, in some cases, friendly competition when churches organized fund-raising campaigns pitting one state club or society against another. Mother Bethel in Philadelphia had state-based clubs composed of natives of South Carolina, Virginia, and Georgia.[22] Though more migrants from Florida and Georgia joined Mother Bethel during the Great Migration, the South Carolina club was so influential that Philadelphians labeled the congregation "the South Carolina church."[23] Northern church leaders recognized the importance of maintaining associational ties early in the campaign to assist migrants. In March 1917 Philadelphia's Interdenominational Ministers' Alliance sponsored a welcoming program for migrants at the Olympia Theater where newcomers from the same state were urged to sit together under their state banner in order to reunite them with friends and relatives.[24]

Allen B. Ballard's compelling and at times autobiographical account of the influence of church people from the cultural wellspring of the Greenville, South Carolina, region on Philadelphia confirms how tenaciously some migrants held onto their particular southern identities. In *One More Day's Journey* Ballard recalls discovering that many members of Mother Bethel had come from the Greenwood district, including a leading minister who left after the killing in 1916 of Anthony Crawford.[25] Many migrants from the Abbeville-Greenwood area settled in north Philadelphia. Five families who had been active in Morris Chapel Church in Greenwood started a prayer meeting in a private home, then rented a horse stable's second story for their first service in 1917. They named their congregation Morris Chapel and called a pastor from Edgefield County. By the mid-1920s migrants from other places in Georgia, from Virginia, and from other sections of Philadelphia joined Morris Chapel. This congregation, Ballard tells us, "gradually became an urban rather than a transplanted rural institution. But its roots and its music were still heavily Southern Black."[26]

The state-based societies within the large churches and the smaller congregations made up almost exclusively of migrants from a particular place provided migrants with intimate religious fellowships. Homecoming celebrations during the summer brought members of transplanted congregations and state societies back in touch with family and friends who had not journeyed to the Promised Land. After hearing of the opportunities up North from those who had gone before them, the undecided who had been resisting the Great Migration's pull often joined in. African American newspapers such as the *Chicago Defender* had southern informants who supplied those who settled in the North with reports on church events in their home congregations—late summer revivals, a pastor's anniversary. Letters written by migrants often inquired about church news from downhome. These mechanisms provided an essential cultural link with what novelist Richard Wright termed the "fluid folk life" of the South.

The proliferation of what have traditionally been called storefront churches has been considered one of the Great Migration's major religious consequences. A storefront church is thought of as a small congregation meeting in facilities not designed specifically for worship or other religious gatherings. Storefronts characteristically include independence from mainline denominations, institutional instability over time, the lack of formal theological training for clergy, the preponderance of women among members, and a proclivity for Pentecostal ritual and Holiness doctrine. Storefronts have been characterized as bizarre, doctrinally deviant religious groups with an appeal primarily to individuals who were both marginal to mainstream society and members of a city's lower economic strata.[27]

The characteristics associated with storefronts are neither limited to them nor determinative of a type of religious organization that rules out prayer groups meeting in homes or small churches organized before the migration by African American northerners. The nature of the structure, whether an abandoned storefront, an apartment, or a house in need of repair, tells little about the occupying religious organization. Many congregations, including those affiliated with mainline denominations, often met in commercial buildings until they were able to build or buy traditional churches. Clergy eager to establish ministries for themselves but with limited financial resources had no option but to find whatever shelters they could and open up religious shop.

Small congregations frequently began as house churches in the home of a migrant family and then, as their members increased, took up quarters in storefronts. Eventually the storefronts were abandoned for more traditional structures. Such happened with First Shiloh Baptist in Buffalo, which originated with twelve migrants who first worshiped in the home of Mrs. Hattie Causey at 25 Union Street. Forty-five members moved into a rented storefront on October 1, 1916, incorporated First Shiloh about a year later, and secured a pastor from Mississippi who began a fund-raising campaign that allowed them to purchase a small storefront in 1919. Additional migrants joined, and by 1920 Shiloh was able to purchase the old Cedar Street Baptist Church building from a predominantly white congregation. By 1939 Shiloh had 1,300 members and had become a fixture in Buffalo's African American community.[28]

Despite the difficulty of defining the type of religious organization customarily referred to as storefront churches, many such groups were given birth by the Great Migration. Storefronts were occupied by migrants trying to transplant and reorganize congregations composed of individuals and families who came from the same area of the South. Storefronts also arose when an enterprising preacher or perhaps a small group that had formed a prayer band decided to rent quarters and invite all comers. Southern preachers who witnessed their flocks drift away to the North followed to regather them in the storefronts. Clergy, even those whose theological education was northern-based, sought to identify with the migrants by operating from storefronts and stressing their own southern roots. For example, Emmanuel AME Church was established as a storefront on 119th Street in Harlem in 1926 by Decatur Ward Nichols. Though educated at Drew University, Nichols was able to attract many migrants from South Carolina because he had spent his first twenty years there. His father was a well-known AME minister in Charleston.[29]

Because storefronts often operated outside traditional denominational jurisdictions, statistics on their numbers in a particular city at any one time must be educated guesses. Historian Peter Gottlieb estimated that in Pittsburgh "most of the increase in these ten years [1916–26] was 'storefront' churches with comparatively few worshipers, no permanent meeting place, and poorly educated pastors."[30] In the early 1920s the Inter-Church-World-Movement sponsored a survey of 236 blocks of Harlem between 110th and 158th Streets and bordered by Eighth Avenue and the Harlem River. Drawing on this survey and his own forays into Harlem, Harold Cooke Phillips reported in 1922 that he found twenty-three mainline churches belonging to seven different denominations. To make the point that those who conducted religious censuses often overlooked the storefronts, he noted many small churches not accounted for in the survey; thus, the African American population of Harlem far exceeded the seating capacity of the identified mainline churches.[31]

Storefronts existed in cities wherever a sizable migrant population settled. Robert Austin Warner's study of African American life in New Haven, Connecticut, notes that in 1934 services were offered by nine small evangelistic churches, the oldest of which had been established as a storefront twenty-seven years earlier. The majority rented vacated business space. "The essential fittings," Warner wrote, "consisted of a pulpit; a Bible; some folding chairs, secondhand pews or benches; musical instruments such as a triangle, a tambourine, a pair of cymbals, or a battered piano; framed mottoes and a religious picture or two; and a dingy curtain shutting off a portion of the room behind the platform."[32] To offset the appeal of the storefronts, Methodists in New Haven brought the Rev. Alexander Willbanks to town for more than two weeks of revivals. Known as the "Black Billy Sunday," Willbanks made much of the fact that he had been "bred and born in the country districts of Mississippi."

Willbanks preached in a style familiar to many migrants. Though mainline Baptists and Methodists in the North, who considered the revivalists' techniques old-fashioned, might frown on shouting, they employed Willbanks's services and those of other revivalists to attempt to satisfy the portion of their membership who were uncomfortable with mainline decorum. The continual arrival of the southerners, Warner argues, helped "retain many of the older patterns, such as emotionalism in worship, an emphasis upon 'individual salvation as opposed to social reform,' and popular elements of show which have persisted in part to the present day in the rural South."[33]

Critics of the storefronts expressed reservations about their rapid increase. According to the conventional wisdom, storefronts weakened established congregations by drawing away potential members and financial support. Charges of overchurching were common. Characterized as jack-leg preachers, leaders of storefront congregations were, as William Welty notes, "derided for their lack of formal training and were subjected to accusations including defrauding their flock of money, being agents in the numbers racket, and of immoral sexual behavior."[34] Writing in 1926, Ira Reid placed the storefronts on the suspect margins of African American religious life in Harlem. "It is unfortunate that the efforts of sincere and well-established churches in Harlem, both small and large, have to be hampered by the manipulation of these groups—both orthodox and pagan —of the outer fringe. While the one steadily prods at social problems with instruments both spiritual and physical and methods religious and humanitarian, the others are saying, 'Let us prey.' And they do."[35]

Storefronts were criticized for stressing otherworldly religion at the expense of progressive social action. Reid's *In a Minor Key,* though published in 1940, contains a passage that reflects the tension between the progressive established churches and the nontraditional religious groups.

> There are indications that a new church is arising among Negroes, a militant church, one that is concerning itself with the problems of the masses. Sometimes it is the old-line Protestant church, sometimes a younger denomination, sometimes a Catholic congregation—and sometimes a community church. Its leaders organize and take part in aggressive social movements for the public and the race's weal. Led, in a few urban and rural centers, by outstanding men who are trained and practiced in religious thought as well as in economics, this church is vital. Yet it cannot be said that today even this church is an influential factor in the lives of the whole Negro working population. Extremely significant in Negro life, however, has been the inordinate rise of religious cults and sects. Even before the depression one noted this tendency . . . .[36]

If we take at face value the testimony of Reid and others who reported on religious changes during the interwar period, center stage is occupied by the many new or alternative religious organizations, some in storefronts, some not, which appeared in the wake of the Great Migration.

Yet for all the fascination with the otherness of the sects and cults, the majority of African American Christians in urban areas kept their affiliations with the traditional denominations. Not every storefront contained some new or exotic religion. Many housed congregations with memberships made up of migrants with Baptist or Methodist predilections who were seeking to create a cultural oasis in their environment.

Sociologist E. Franklin Frazier emphasized the churchly function of the storefronts in his classic *The Negro Church in America,* which captured something of the self-authenticating nature of migrant religious institutions. The storefront church, he wrote, represented "an attempt on the part of migrants, especially from the rural areas of the South, to re-establish a type of church in the urban environment to which they were accustomed.

They want a church, first of all, in which they are known as people."[37] Frazier contrasted the small, family churches of the South with the large, impersonal ones of the North. Of those who joined the storefronts, he wrote:

> Sometimes they complain with bitterness that the pastor of the large city church knows them only as the number on the envelope in which they place their dues. In wanting to be treated as human beings, they want status in the church which was the main or only organization in the South in which they had status. Some of the statements concerning their reason for leaving the big denominational churches was that "back home in the South" they had a seat in the church that everyone recognized as theirs and that if the seat were empty on Sunday the pastor came to their homes to find out the cause of their absence.[38]

Frazier's insight underscores the obvious. The migrants did not come North stripped of their religious institutions, nor did they develop the storefront type solely out of the raw materials of the urban experience. The explosion of storefronts after World War I is a prime example of the spatial extension of the religious culture of the African American South made possible through the Great Migration.

Baptist and Methodist denominations had dominated the southern black religious landscape. However, the larger cities of the North presented migrants with an unprecedented variety of religious options. Peter Gottlieb's description of the process by which migrants selected a church home in Pittsburgh could pertain to most cities with sizable African American populations. Gottlieb writes, "Through participation in churches, migrants could meet gatekeepers from their own level of the black community and join numerous voluntary organizations: missionary circles, choirs, and Sunday schools. Churches also offered ambitious migrants the possibility of gaining status in roles such as clerk, trustee, or deacon. In Pittsburgh the newcomers found many denominations and classes of black churches, each with its characteristic social composition, lay and clerical leadership, and style of worship."[39] Though scrutinized by the Old Settlers and sometimes ostracized because of their southern ways, the migrants were themselves examining what the city religious scene had to offer. Most of all, they wanted a church home where they felt welcome and at ease.

Their first impressions of the established churches were not always favorable. A female migrant to Pittsburgh told of her experience attending services at an AME church in the lower Hill District about 1919. Discovering that light-skinned members were seated separately from dark-skinned worshipers, she decided she "wanted none of that" and joined another church.[40] Migrants who had been significant figures in their home congregations demonstrated displeasure with the established churches by exercising the option of setting up new religious organizations or joining one of the groups characterized as a sect or cult. The pastor of a house church in Detroit, whom Benjamin E. Mays and Joseph W. Nicholson describe in *The Negro's Church* as "a leader in the rural South—pastor, moderator of conventions and associations, and a big man in his lodge," decided to organize his own congregation after he found it impossible to break the existing monopoly on church leadership. Mays and Nicholson report that this clergyman feared that migrants would "suffer moral and religious shipwreck" in the throes of adjusting to their new environments. This suggests that house churches and storefronts served as cultural halfway houses for migrants making the transition from rural to urban cultures. Mays and Nicholson then make the point more strongly: "Many members of storefront and house churches would forsake the church altogether if the big churches were the only reliance."[41]

When migrants finally found a congregation in which they felt at home, they expressed a new sense of ownership. A female migrant to Pittsburgh visited several churches before being invited to Second Baptist. There, the older female members embraced her and made her feel especially welcome. The pastor of Clark Memorial, one of the other churches she visited, encountered her on his way to services. Gottlieb recounts their exchange as follows. "Don't be late!" he told her. She replied, "I'm going to *my* church." He said, "*Your* church? What do you mean, 'your' church?" "Second Baptist," she said. "Those people down there were the most friendly and lovingest people I ever met."[42] Migrants steered other migrants to churches they thought would appeal to them. A steelworker from Mississippi urged a fellow work gang member to attend Homestead's Second Baptist Church. He liked what he found at Second Baptist, "The way they do, talk, and everything—so I joined."[43]

Migrants who were poor shied away from churches that they perceived as too high class. While not all storefront congregations were composed of the poorest of the poor, those that were poor tended to be Holiness or Pentecostal. The temptation to categorize these churches as inferior to the mainline denominations and the habit of lumping them together with the esoteric and exotic groups must be resisted. In his study of Pentecostal congregations in Boston belonging to the Mount Calvary Holy Church of America, Inc., sociologist Arthur Paris offers us very useful revisionist understanding of the storefront phenomenon:

> The rise of lower-class urban congregations within storefronts was the product of a historical process rooted in the rise of Holiness and Pentecostal churches as manifestations of reforming zeal within American and especially Southern Protestantism. The subsequent exhaustion of this impulse among the middle and upper classes led to the confining of this tendency to the lower classes, Black and White, where it continued to flourish. Blacks who moved north and west as part of the Great Migrations became carriers of this perfectionist impulse, along with their other religious traditions. As a large and impoverished population confined mainly to ghettos, these Black migrants placed enormous pressures upon available institutional resources; and their choices in the market for church edifices were and continue to be severely limited. These pressures, coupled with their history, led to the storefront phenomenon among urban Black (and Latin) populations.[44]

Some storefronts did indeed serve as the temporal abodes of unusual religious alternatives. Cleveland's only storefront with a predominantly lower-class membership was Lake City Spiritualist, founded in 1915 and located on Central Avenue near East 28th Street. "The church probably appealed mostly to recent arrivals from the South," Kenneth Kusmer speculates, "and because of its smaller size it offered its congregants a degree of emotional involvement and personal participation that the larger black churches could not match."[45] The establishment and growth of Spiritualist, Holiness, and Pentecostal churches in the North in the wake of the Great Migration is one of the more important developments of the interwar years, but as Arthur Paris has argued, "The point is that storefront churches do not constitute a substantive category. Storefronts are a physical characteristic that many groups share."[46]

Many storefronts proclaimed a religious identity new to the contest for members in northern cities. Church of God in Christ evangelists were particularly active in carrying the teachings of founder Charles H. Mason to the North. David Tucker tells us that Church of God evangelists traveled with migrants, "preaching holiness, telling the simple stories of the Bible, and offering religious joy and warmth not found in the established northern churches."⁴⁷ For example, Elder Fletcher planted the COGIC flag at 137th Street and Lenox Avenue in the heart of Harlem in 1925, and other branches located in Brooklyn, Pittsburgh, Philadelphia, St. Louis, Kansas City, and Detroit as early as 1917. The Rev. Rosewell Roles pastored the Church of God and Saints of Christ at 5102 State Street in Chicago in 1916.⁴⁸ Mother Lillian Coffey also carried Mason's message to Chicago. Her evangelistic work highlights the importance of women in the transfer of southern religious practices to the urban North, a subject that deserves more attention.⁴⁹

The migration experience fostered greater freedom for women to assume roles of religious leadership than northern black communities had been accustomed to. Discouraged or proscribed from holding the office of ordained minister in the mainline denominations, women exercised their spiritual gifts by establishing independent Holiness, Pentecostal, and Spiritualist churches, often of the storefront and house varieties. Women needed no male approval to set up as mediums, healers, and spiritual leaders of congregations of the dispossessed.

Elder Lucy Smith is an especially important example of a female religious entrepreneur who capitalized on the expanding religious market of the time. Born on a Georgia plantation in 1875, Smith came to Chicago in 1910. She initially attended Olivet Baptist and Ebenezer Baptist, but within a few years she was worshiping with white Pentecostals. In 1914 she felt the call to divine healing, and two years later she started a one-room prayer meeting in her house. Her healing services were so popular with the migrants that All Nations Pentecostal Church grew rapidly, and after several moves the members built a permanent home in 1926. Elder Smith was very proud that she was the only woman in Chicago to have erected a church and that her congregation "didn't buy no second-hand white church."⁵⁰

In *Black Milwaukee* Joseph Trotter attributes the competition that mainline denominations were given by Holiness preachers to the economic and cultural differences that emerged among the expanding African American populations of the northern cities. "Of all the new churches to emerge during the period," he asserts, "the storefront Holiness church depicted most clearly the profound changes in the Afro-American class structure." He notes that in Milwaukee by the mid-1920s Holiness "big summer camp meetings" were regularly conducted, and "working-class newcomers with the least economic means of subsistence" were drawn to the Pentecostal churches.[51] A Holiness or Pentecostal congregation often began informally through the initiative of a few individuals. For example, the parents of Idella Blakely, a Holiness minister's wife in Milwaukee, opened their home for the first Holiness-Pentecostal service in the city. Later, the congregation moved to space in a former fish market. Blakely described the birth and evolution of this urban Christian community:

> Pentecostalism started in my father's home. In the year 1924–25, a Rev. Anderson [Elder J. R. Anderson] came to the city and had no place to stay, and my father and mother took him in, and he began to preach the word of God. We as children were taken to our beds, put in bathrooms, under the beds, anyplace, so they had a place to stay, because he had a large family. The neighbors heard of this minister that was in town, and many came to our home and received salvation. In the early part of 1926, they moved to a fish market on . . . 6th and Vliet Street. . . . The odor of fish was so very strong, that we had to use all kind of soap and water and everything to get it out, but we insisted on having a place to serve . . . . My mother and father were so consistent in working and helping. My father was working in a foundry at the time, and he would come in the evenings, and work [late] at night to try and get this place ready. And many souls came to God thru it.[52]

In Cleveland, Holiness and Pentecostal storefront churches also multiplied as a result of the exodus from the South. These churches, along with the poorer Baptists, occupied makeshift edifices along lower Central and Scovil Avenues. Churches that had healings, tongue-speaking, and shouting reminded migrants of their southern roots.[53]

From the vantage point of the instrumentalists, a storefront church that limited its institutional goals to providing a refuge from the problems of the outside world, focusing on individual sin and salvation, and fostering emotional worship failed to meet the standards of a progressive, race-conscious, and "wide-awake" organization. Forrester B. Washington's survey of churches on behalf of the Detroit Bureau of Governmental Research exemplifies the critics' hostility. "There seems to be a general impression among them that shouting, dancing hither and thither, groaning, howling, crying, protracted prayers, frantic embracing, the waving of handkerchiefs, groveling on the floor, the throwing up of arms, and similar 'hysterical' outbursts are the sole means of expressing devotion to God."[54] Washington was unrestrained in his criticism. At one point he wrote, "It is impossible to find in the Christian religion any justification for such barbaric practices as go on in these so-called churches."[55]

The image of the storefronts was further tarnished by the tendency of their critics to group them with the cults or unorthodox religious groups, some with non-Christian theologies. These new religions took root side-by-side with the mainline churches in the urban North. Most leaders of the so-called cults and sects were migrants themselves, as is clear from the cohort that Arthur F. Fauset profiled in *Black Gods of the Metropolis,* the first scholarly examination of these groups.[56] Ida Robinson, founder of the Mt. Sinai Holy Church in Philadelphia, was born in Florida, grew up in Georgia, and came to Philadelphia in 1924. The United House of Prayer for all People was led by the flamboyant Charles Emmanuel Grace, widely known as "Daddy Grace." Though originally from the Cape Verde Islands, Grace had worked as a railway cook in the South. He began the United House of Prayer about 1921 in a storefront in New Bedford, Massachusetts, and soon planted churches in other eastern cities.[57] The leader of the black Jewish group that attracted attention in Philadelphia was Prophet F. S. Cherry. He founded the Church of the Living God, the Pillar Ground of Truth for All Nations, in 1886 in Chattanooga. After moving the group to Philadelphia, he sought some respectability for his congregation and disapproved of speaking in tongues and clamorous services.[58] The Moorish Science Temple of America was established in 1913. Timothy Drew, a native of North Carolina, called on the black Islamic group to seek recruits from among the migrants. George Baker, better known as Father Divine, was born in Maryland and preached in Georgia before coming North. Divine's Peace Mission Movement did not become formally organized until the eve of the Great Depression, but its founder was preaching his unique blend of "God in me, God in you" metaphysics in Harlem about 1922. Though not discussed by Fauset, Elijah Poole, better-known as Elijah Muhammad, was also a former southerner. He migrated to Detroit in the 1920s, and in 1930 he gravitated toward Islam as represented by the mysterious prophet known as Master Wali Fard Muhammad.[59]

The composition of the new or alternative religious groups cannot be determined with certitude. Local records, including membership rosters, are difficult to come by. The generalization that the cults and sects contained a disproportionately high percentage of migrants awaits further examination. But it is reasonable to assume that the most accessible clientele for the founders of the cults and sects were those individuals who felt overlooked by mainline churches in the North and who were receptive to the appeal of charismatic leaders who promised them a heaven of their own.

Arthur H. Fauset argued in *Black Gods of the Metropolis* that the increase in cult groups was "to be related in part to the psychological factors which are implied, first in a change from rural to urban life, and second in the adjustment of mental attitudes to new mores, especially with regard to the rights of men of different races, as these vary between the North and South."[60] The migrants were thrown into direct economic competition with whites and forced into a new and less predictable maze of class and caste behaviors. In their anxiety and confusion the refugees from the South sought salvation in unorthodox ways. "Hence one is led to believe," Fauset concluded, "that, for many of their members, certain religious cults in northern urban communities assist the transplanted southern worshiper, accustomed to the fixed racial mores and caste requirements of the South, to adjust his psychological and emotional reactions to conditions in the city, where all life and living are more fluid and intermingling of the races is inevitable."[61] The mainline African American churches in the North did lose a certain percentage of the migrants to the cults and sects, though the threat was exaggerated by the orthodox clergy.

The urban environment itself may have been equally important in drawing some migrants out of the circle of the church and into the company of those shunned by church elders. Some migrants discovered that the anonymity of large cities offered freedom to stay away from church and escape the censure of the more pious. Ira De A. Reid found that the majority of Pittsburgh blacks in the Hill District of the late 1920s did not attend church at all.[62] The less religiously devout migrants found their "heaven" on the streets, in secular and sometimes suspect entertainments, much to the consternation of the preachers. The Rev. James Walker Brown asserted that the greatest danger to Harlem was from "Sabbath desecration, neglect of church duties, Sunday games, gambling, immoral plays with improper dancing, and open pool halls."[63] Young males with leisure time were especially susceptible to the temptations of the city. Richard R. Wright, Jr., foresaw the dangers in extra leisure time to newcomers from the South before the Great Migration. He wrote in 1907:

> On the leisure side there is the amusement question. The dance halls and the pool rooms are far more popular than the Sunday school or the class meeting or Christian Endeavor, and the dance halls and pool

rooms are as a rule in the hands of bad men. The church concert, which is so popular in small towns, is not attractive when compared with the cheap theater; the saloons are open from twelve to eighteen hours a day, providing music, lunch, reading matter, tables, toilet, telephone, pen and ink and many conveniences to this homeless city lodger; but the church is closed tight, except for about one hour during the day— the pastor's office hour—and two to three hours at night.[64]

Wright called on the mainline churches to offset "the great social danger in the transition from small town and rural life to city life, which threatens the moral ruin of those making the change."[65]

Too much leisure time worried those who saw themselves as caregivers, if not custodians, of the migrants. In the summer of 1917 Forrester B. Washington, then director of the Urban League in Detroit, urged civic and church leaders to develop opportunities for wholesome recreation to keep migrants from the clutches of "the saloon keeper, the pool-room proprietor, the owner of gambling club and disorderly house." He doubted that the cultural offerings of the Old Settlers would be of interest to those for whom the city was a potential den of iniquity. "The hard-working laborer recently from a rural section of Alabama," Washington maintained, "cannot be attracted away from saloon or pool-room with art lectures or literary forums, or even the facilities of the average Y.M.C.A."[66] George E. Haynes observed in 1924 that monotony of life was a prevalent problem in the rural districts of the South, and except for an occasional hunt, picnic, or dance, opportunities "for wholesale recreation, intellectual or other culture are conspicuous by their absence."[67] In contrast, the cabarets and nightclubs in Harlem were replete with jazz bands and liquor. Theaters catered to African American audiences and offered both live entertainment and moving pictures and eagerly took a migrant's dollar. Dances such as the tango, turkey trot, and the Chicago were popular, though they drew the fire of African American clergymen such as Adam Clayton Powell, Sr., who complained, "The Negro race is dancing itself to death."[68]

The characterization of the city as infested with secular blandishments meant to entice migrants hailing from a land of virtue and piety away from the church is overdrawn, of course. As music historian Paul Oliver reminds us, African Americans attended dances in the rural South, and drinking and dancing parlors, called jukes, were open on Friday and Saturday nights. The evolution of the rural blues in the South predates the Great Migration.

Blues players and singers were already in ill-repute within church circles. "The old-time religion of the Southern churches," Oliver writes, "does not permit the singing of 'devil songs' and 'jumped-up' songs as the blues are commonly termed."[69] Nevertheless, the notion persisted that once the migrants set foot in Chicago or New York City or some other big city, they joined the battle between the church and "the Devil's music" more fully. That tension between the sacred and secular realms of African American culture is suggested by the practice of some blues singers not to perform on Sundays, though others functioned as jackleg preachers and evangelists on the streets.

Migrants who felt drawn to the new music but sought spiritual refreshment at the same time could join one of the many small Sanctified and Holiness churches. Housed most frequently in storefronts, the Sanctified churches offered a refuge from the environment of the city, yet they allowed for upbeat music as a means of praising the Lord.[70] These smaller congregations were havens in which the rural religious ethos was reinforced and migrants withdrew from the city's secularizing influences. The breaking up of African American rural folk culture begun by the migration to the city was temporarily offset in these churches, but the impact of urban environments could be seen nevertheless. Eventually, as Sterling Brown writes, "Jazzed-up gospel hymns provide a different sort of release from the old spirituals; the blues reflect the distortions of the new way of life."[71]

Case studies of specific congregations demonstrate the persistence of transplanted rural religious islands serving as refuges in urban environments. Zion Holiness Church (pseudonym) in Pittsburgh's Hill District, which anthropologist Melvin D. Williams describes in *Community in a Black Pentecostal Church,* is representative of the religious outposts of southern culture that migrants used as heavens of their own. Established about 1918 in the home of a woman known as Mother Beck, Zion belonged to the Church of the Holy Christ (pseudonym for the Church of God in Christ). Williams argues that Zion prospered as long as it did because its members resisted the city's pressures and enticements and turned inward. "In short," he writes, "Zion is an aggregation of Southern rural migrants who settled in Pittsburgh and attempted, by means of a religious community, to reestablish the nature of the life they had known in the rural South. They would live *in* the city but they would not be *of* the city. Or, as they would explain it, 'in the world but not of the world.' "[72] Urban black messiahs played on the insecurities of migrants such as those who found a haven in

Zion by offering them the familiar. A black Jewish leader in Harlem conducted worship services as if they were country camp meetings in the city.
"He handled his flock," Ruth Landes writes, "as though the setting were
still the rural South, and inadvertently profited from certain urban conditions, such as density of population."[73]

The descendants of the founders of Zion were not unlike those of the
Puritans of New England. As generation succeeded generation, commitment to maintaining the vision of Zion, to be a "City set Upon a Hill"
pure and separate, weakened. Declension set in. James Baldwin portrayed
just how powerful the sirens of the secular city were to younger members
of the Pentecostal urban islands in *Go Tell It on the Mountain,* a novel set
in a storefront church in Harlem. Baldwin's character, Roy Grimes, enjoys
the company he keeps among sinners in the outside world and is lost to
the Temple of the Fire Baptized. His brother John, the book's protagonist,
is torn between the narrow way leading to salvation as defined by his Pentecostal elders and the broad way that leads to perdition, symbolized by
New York City's Broadway with its movie houses and other temptations
that he can see from his favorite vantage point in Central Park.[74]

The African American sociologist Charles S. Johnson caught the essence
of what was happening to many migrants when he wrote in 1925, "The
city Negro is only now in evolution."[75] The contrast between rural and
urban environments was emphasized by Johnson's mentor, the noted sociologist Robert E. Park of the University of Chicago, whose point of
view influenced many other writers. Barbara Ballis Lal has summarized
Park's position: "Rural, Southern blacks constituted 'a folk' whose 'habitat' was 'fixed,' whose culture was 'local,' whose political influence was neg-
ligible, and whose intellectual horizon was circumscribed by 'the shadow
of the plantation,' outside of which 'the only centers of Negro life are the
rural churches and rural schools.'" In contrast, "blacks in Northern urban
ghettos were brought into close contact with each other and were presented with new opportunities for education, intellectual endeavor, business enterprise, religious organization, politics, a black press, and—in all
these areas—the emergence of black leadership."[76]

The impact of the twin forces of urbanization and secularization, which
tugged so insidiously on the pious, is seen in what Frederick Miller has
termed "an unusually comprehensive survey" by the Philadelphia Housing
Association in 1924 of more than 500 recently arrived migrants.[77] Of the
142 household heads surveyed, 83 responded that they had belonged to a

church in the South but had not joined one in Philadelphia, 22 said that they were not church members and had not been so in the South, and only 35, or one-quarter of those surveyed, indicated church membership in both regions. Church connections in Philadelphia were more likely to have been established by migrants from southern cities with populations above 50,000 than by those from small towns and rural areas. In addition, skilled workers were more inclined than unskilled laborers to take up church membership.[78]

Several factors may account for the surprisingly low percentage of migrants who established regular church ties in Philadelphia and elsewhere. Individuals and families, even after leaving the region, remained on the rosters of southern churches. The very process of relocation to the city loosened religious roots, especially among the young. Timothy Thomas Fortune wrote in the *Philadelphia Public Ledger* in 1917: "The old folks who came out of slavery stuck to the church and to church building with the pertinacity that the Pilgrim Fathers of New England did to theirs, and they strove diligently to bring up their children in the church habit and manners. But the young people began to break away from the parental faith and steadiness of character and purpose with the advent of the vaudeville and moving-picture shows and the ragtime dance halls, with saloon connections and the 'automobile craze'. . . ."[79] Fortune's jeremiad may border too closely on the land of nostalgia, but his concerns were shared by others in the city who feared a loss of faith.

While evidence of weakening church ties among some segments of the migrant population is clear, testimony also emphasizes the important impact that migrants were having on African American institutional life in the North. In 1927 Ethel McGhee, an African American worker for the Social Service Federation of Englewood, New Jersey, observed that in the decade or so since the onset of the Great Migration, many migrants had made their mark. She wrote, "Now in most Northern communities where there is an appreciable number of Negroes, their voices are heard on matters that are of interest to themselves and the community. They are building their own churches (far too many) and supporting them. They have their own banks, insurances, professional and business offices. They have made themselves conspicuous by their success, and they are recognized as a positive force in the community life."[80] Sadie T. Mossell (later Alexander) did a survey of the living standards of a hundred migrant families to Philadelphia in 1921. She reported that migrants were quickly establishing themselves as a force to be reckoned with in the African American community. In business, education, and the professions the migrants were beginning to "outstep the Northerner even in Philadelphia."[81] Mossell was particularly struck by how many Philadelphia churches were being pastored by former migrants. George E. Haynes observed in 1924 that the migrants were "taking part more and more in the civic and political affairs of the [northern] community," black newspapers were being read as never before, and "the headquarters of nearly every one of the Negro betterment organizations are now in Northern cities and many of the general officers of the Negro churches have moved North."[82]

After the economic depression that followed the Treaty of Versailles in 1919 when the rate of out-migration slowed from the South, some observers became more optimistic regarding the possibility of meeting the aspirations of African Americans in the Promised Land. The first issue of the National Urban League's journal *Opportunity* appeared in January 1923 under the editorship of Charles S. Johnson, director of the League's research and investigations department and formerly associate director of the Chicago Race Relations Commission that investigated the Chicago race riot of 1919. Johnson believed that new opportunities were imminent because employers were again casting anxious eyes southward.[83] The postwar movement was said to lack the hysteria of the earlier one, in part because the South no longer depended so much on black labor because of the mechanization and diversification of agriculture.[84] *Opportunity* declared that the second phase of the Great Migration contained a far greater percentage of "the more thrifty and responsible type" of black southerner than had the wartime exodus.[85]

In addition to the economic and social forces propelling the earlier exodus, observers noted that the second wave was motivated by the desire to participate in the cultural awakening of "the race." In 1919 the *Chicago Defender* termed this phenomenon "the New Consciousness" and called for the active participation of black churches and clergy: "With the new consciousness which has come to the Race in its desire for a fuller measure of civic and social justice, the voice of the pulpit [has the] most potential in inspiring and encouraging its efforts."[86] Though perhaps only a quarter of the 2 million migrants that Richard R. Wright, Jr., called for in 1916 left the South during the war years, this number was sufficient to bring about a heightened sense of "race" consciousness in northern cities.[87] No individual contributed more to the nationalism of the Black Renaissance of the 1920s in the urban North than the immigrant from Jamaica, Marcus Garvey. Garvey was not Moses leading the march to the Promised Land, but he offered hope to those disillusioned with life in the North.

Migrants anxious for a heaven of their own found it in the Universal Negro Improvement Association (1918–27) and Garveyism, a blend of black nationalism, charismatic messianism, and emotional commitment to the vision of return to Africa. Several organized religious groups were tied to the Garvey movement, notably the African Orthodox Church led by George Alexander McGuire, who was known as the honorary chaplain general of the Universal Negro Improvement Association. Local chapters had chaplains who used McGuire's *Universal Negro Ritual,* but Garvey was not a member of the African Orthodox Church, and McGuire, as Gavin White observes, did not want to provide the UNIA with a "mere pseudo-church, a buttress for Garvey's political movement."[88] McGuire was eclipsed by Garvey, for as Randall K. Burkett has argued, Garvey constructed a social movement imbued with symbols, rituals, and beliefs that constituted a civil religion. Burkett writes that the typical UNIA meeting "possessed many of the characteristics of a religious service," "the vocabulary of the UNIA was drawn from the religious realm," and the religious ethos of the Garvey movement was fostered by a "multitude of religiopolitical symbols of nationhood," none more popular than the passage from Psalms 68:31: "Princes shall come out of Egypt; Ethiopia shall soon stretch out her hands unto God."[89]

Garvey's cry "Up You Mighty Race, You Can Accomplish What You Will" caught fire after his arrival in the United States in 1916. Garvey's doctrine of racial pride, what he termed "a Universal Confraternity among the race," and black economic independence made him king of Harlem. Though convicted of mail fraud in 1923, imprisoned in 1925, and deported in 1927, Garvey's message continued to inspire those who were coping with the stress and disappointments of urban life.

Garvey's dream of "Africa for the Africans" was not realized in his lifetime. He himself never made it to Africa, his version of the Promised Land. He died in 1940 in London, largely forgotten and unsuccessful in his efforts to revive the UNIA. In 1935 he announced from London the inauguration of a "New Programme" that was to include an agricultural five-year plan "indulging in planting of bananas, citrus fruits, vegetables and dairying, with special attention to the sugar and rum industries" in various countries. He apparently hoped that the chaos spawned by war in Europe would provide the right historical moment for his black nationalist appeal. He acknowledged that the war of 1914–18 "with its after-conditions somewhat assisted in focusing the minds of some of our race upon the real object that inspired us . . . .[90]

Garvey's critics, notably W. E. B. Du Bois and others with ties to the NAACP, came into sharp conflict with the flamboyant messiah of the black masses. Du Bois characterized Garvey as "dictatorial, domineering, inordinately vain and very suspicious. . . . The great difficulty with him is that he has absolutely no business sense, no *flair* for real organization and his general objects are so shot through with bombast and exaggeration that it is difficult to pin them down for careful examination."[91] On occasion, Garvey's enthusiasts battled with leading local preachers. On August 22, 1920, Adam Clayton Powell, Sr., ran a gauntlet of verbal abuse and threats after Garveyites who could not get into Liberty Hall, Garvey's Harlem headquarters, drifted over to the tent revival that Abyssinian was sponsoring on the property it had purchased in Harlem. The Garveyites' discontent was sparked by Powell's guest preacher, Charles S. Morris of Norfolk. Morris, according to the *New York Age,* spoke disparagingly of Garvey and belittled his back-to-Africa plans. Several hundred Garveyites demonstrated against Morris and Powell, the police were called, and the revival ended in confusion.[92] Though other black clergy shared Du Bois's criticisms of Garvey's management of the UNIA, the major black denominations did not formerly condemn him, and some mainline ministers were active Garveyites.[93]

Garvey's deportation and the dissolution of the UNIA left a spiritual vacuum that groups filled in part with non-Christian teachings and practices. These have drawn popular and scholarly attention far out of proportion to their numbers in comparison to the mainline Protestant denominations, or, for that matter, to the newer Pentecostal and Holiness churches. It is impossible to determine what percentage of those who were attracted to the various black Jewish and black Muslim organizations came from the South, yet it is equally difficult to conceive of either the black Jews or black Muslims having much success *except* in the urban post-Great Migration environment when religious life in African American communities was undergoing such a significant transformation.

The Church of God and Saints of Christ was the first black Jewish group to be recognized by the federal religious census report. Established by William S. Crowdy in Lawrence, Kansas, in 1896, this group moved to

Philadelphia in 1900 and grew from 1,823 members in 1906 to 37,084 in 1936. About 1919 Wentworth Arthur Matthew, a native of Lagos, Nigeria, who came to New York City in 1913 from St. Kitts in the West Indies, organized what became known as the Ethiopian Hebrew Commandment Keepers Congregation. Arnold Josiah Ford organized the Beth B'Nai Abraham congregation in Harlem in 1924, a year after being expelled by Garvey from the UNIA. A West Indian, as was Garvey, Ford believed that peoples of African descent were blood Hebrews.[94] Though the various black Jewish groups grew slowly and contained migrants from the West Indies as well as from the American South, their presence in northern cities added yet another ingredient to the cosmopolitan religious character that developed after the Great Migration. Religious variety spawned more religious variety. It was a combustible mix when migrants who were steeped in the imagery and stories of the Old Testament were thrown together with Orthodox Jews, themselves recent newcomers, in New York City and elsewhere. Elias Fanayaye Jones writes, "It was with the Great Migration that blacks from the South and the Caribbean were attracted by black Hebrewism and came into contact with Jews in New York. This contact would be of crucial import, for it was to mark the beginning of the transition from a black Hebrewism based solely on the literal interpretation of the Old Testament to one informed by oral law and Talmudic tradition."[95]

Ford's disagreement with Garvey stemmed in part form Garvey's refusal to proclaim Judaism the official religion of the UNIA. In 1922 a delegation of Muslims sought Garvey's endorsement of Islam and also failed, though some symbols of Islam were incorporated into the civil religion of the UNIA, and Garvey was compared to the Prophet Muhammad.[96] Interest in Islam centered on the Moorish Science Temple of America, which began in Newark, New Jersey, under the leadership of Noble Drew Ali. Ali moved to Chicago in 1923 when his organization had an estimated 30,000 members nationally. There, he established permanent headquarters in 1925 and appropriated many of the practices and symbols of Islam, though he knew little of orthodox teachings. The Moorish movement split into rival fragments and declined in influence after Drew Ali's death in 1929, shortly after he had been arrested and jailed on murder charges. The following year a new Muslim missionary known as W. D. Fard appeared in a section of Detroit called "Paradise Valley" peddling umbrellas and silk goods and claiming to be from the Holy City of Mecca. Like Drew Ali, he sought recruits among former Garveyites and among those whose dreams of the

Promised Land had been shattered. Fard vanished in 1934. As the Great Depression deepened, the Nation of Islam expanded under the leadership of Elijah Muhammad, formerly Elijah Poole, a migrant to Detroit from Georgia, who was at one time a corporal in the Chicago UNIA.[97]

After examining data from the 1926 Federal Census of Religious Bodies, Miles Mark Fisher stated, "Almost in every center, particularly urban, is some unorthodox religious group which makes a definite appeal to Negroes."[98] Major George Baker, better known as Father Divine, certainly was one of the most unorthodox of the urban messiahs who appealed to those who had become discontented with life in the Promised Land. Claude McKay, the Harlem Renaissance poet, said of Divine that he was the originator of religion "on the chain-store plan" because of the havens, called "heavens," he established up and down the East Coast. Divine's Peace Mission Movement received widespread notoriety during the Great Depression and was made possible by the many potential recruits brought to urban areas by the wartime flight from the South.

Divine lived and preached in Baltimore at the turn of the century, but around 1915 he set up shop in Harlem as a street preacher. In 1919, then known as "the Messenger," he purchased an eight-room house in Sayville, Long Island, where he started a small "kingdom" and became Father Divine to his followers. Because he blended both spiritual and material realms, offering social welfare as well as a new religious identity, Divine attracted recruits from among those who had not found salvation in either form since leaving the South. In the Peace Mission Movement, devotees had their own "heavens" and even their own divinity—Major J. Divine, alias God. Robert Weisbrot has said of the appeal of the Peace Mission to southern migrants, "Scorned by long-settled ghetto residents as unrefined and ignorant, they found solace and communion as followers of Father Divine. The fact that Divine himself was obviously of southern origin added measurably to their feeling of belonging."[99]

The cults and sects that appeared in urban centers after World War I were seen as a threat to the dominance of the mainline churches, but actual damages were never as serious as predicted. The nontraditional groups remained relatively small; members of the new groups did not necessarily desert their churches but maintained dual allegiances, as in the case of the UNIA. In the end, many of the groups that critics complained of withered away when their charismatic founders died. The Holiness and Pentecostal churches, formerly identified as on the fringe of the religious establishment in African American communities, proved to be the exception. They made the transition from sect to denomination largely because of growth in urban areas after World War I.

Despite the failure of the alternative groups to displace the mainline churches, the established congregations did not emerge from the Great Migration era unchanged. By taking migrants into their folds, northern churches underwent a gradual process of cultural southernizing that would not become fully apparent until years later. The evolution of religious music in the cities of the North is paradigmatic of the cultural contributions that former southerners made in the post-Great Migration decades. The influence of gospel music, like other examples we could use, is best seen retrospectively. Though the seeds of gospel music were planted much earlier, they did not come to full bloom until after the migrant flood had been stopped by the Great Depression.

Mahalia Jackson arrived in Chicago in 1928 and made Greater Salem Baptist Church her second home. The more middle-class Baptist churches were initially reluctant to embrace the musical styles that Jackson brought with her. Her music began to "take wing," she said, in the 1930s and found a ready audience among former migrants. Jackson explains, "It was the kind of music colored people had left behind them down South, and they liked it because it was just like a letter from home."[100] Jackson had been influenced by the sounds she heard at the Sanctified church next door to her home in New Orleans. With the planting of Sanctified and Holiness churches in the North in greater numbers by southern migrants, new musical styles could be heard in urban worship services where participants engaged in religious dance, accompanied by instruments shunned by the mainline churches. Urban gospel music had an infectious sound and appeal. An anonymous church elder said, "The devil should not be allowed to keep all this good rhythm."[101] Langston Hughes first heard the migrants' music around World War I and recalled, "I was entranced by their stepped-up rhythms, tambourines, hand clapping, and uninhibited dynamics, rivaled only by Ma Rainey singing the blues at the old Monogram Theater. . . . The music of these less formal Negro churches early took hold of me, moved me and thrilled me."[102]

Gospel music found a ready audience among those struggling to cope with urban life. Popular among city revivalists and tent preachers, the new urban sacred music was given impetus by Charles Albert Tindley, who published a collection called *New Songs of Paradise* in 1916. One of Tindley's songs, "I'll Overcome Someday," was widely heard during the civil rights movement of the 1950s and 1960s. Thomas A. Dorsey joined Pilgrim Baptist in Chicago in 1921 and became director of its gospel chorus in 1930. He drew on Tindley's gospel hymns and added elements of the blues, thereby giving birth to the "golden age of gospel" about 1930. Today gospel music is widely accepted in mainline black churches, though it is most closely associated with the Pentecostal and Holiness tradition. Arna Bontemps wrote that observers of the Chicago scene noticed about 1930 "that Negro churches, particularly the storefront congregations, the Sanctified groups and the shouting Baptists, were swaying and jumping as never before. Mighty rhythms rocked the churches. A wave of fresh rapture came over the people."[103] A recent survey of 2,150 black churches disclosed that 96.9 percent approved of gospel music.[104]

No matter what the song or how strongly the migrants tried to hold on to the ways they did things down South, the urban experience exacted a heavy toll. Race riots, economic recession, and the day-to-day struggle to obtain and hold on to a portion of the American dream turned hope into despair. When migrants discovered, as David J. Hellwig has written, that "the rules for success" were not written for them, that their place was on the bottom of the ethnic ladder in urban America, they sought to create an alternative city.[105] This new city of the mind certainly included nationalistic movements such as Marcus Garvey's UNIA and the rise of cults and sects. Yet the planting of thousands of new churches by the migrants, especially Holiness and Pentecostal churches, and the flowering of gospel music and other cultural forms favored by the migrants has been of greater significance in the long term.[106] But some migrants became so disenchanted with life in the North that they entertained thoughts of returning to the South, where the bulk of the nation's African American population remained on the land.

8

RETURN

TO

THE

SOUTH

When the Great Migration was at high tide, newspapers featured stories describing disillusioned migrants returning to the South. The *Atlanta Constitution* carried an article on the hardships encountered by migrants with the subtitle " 'We Want to Go Home,' Now the Cry of Hundreds Who Left South, Yielding to High Wage Lure."[1] On November 15, 1916, the *Macon News* informed its readership that those who had gone North "are already pining for the sighing of the longleaf pines and the simple but contented life that revolved around the cabins from which they were lured."[2] The January 24, 1917, edition of the *Macon Telegraph* claimed that of a party of twenty-five migrants who went to Pennsylvania, seven returned to report that the others had died from the severe cold and "when any of their race died the hearts were taken from the bodies and the corpse burned."[3]

This kind of propaganda had little effect on either the intensity or the duration of the exodus to the Promised Land during the days when migration fever was high.[4] The trickle of returnees, which whites in the South pointed to as evidence that visions of prosperity in the North were illusory, has become a steady stream only since the 1980s. The U.S. Census Bureau reported that during the eighties the percentage of all African Americans who lived in the South went from 52 percent to 56 percent, the first increase in the twentieth century.[5]

Nevertheless, the return of even a small percentage of migrants during the interwar period is symbolically important. Their number swelled the African American population base that did not participate in the exodus and for whom there was no foot of land but the ones that they had always known. Though the Great Migration and subsequent outflows from the South before the post-World War II exodus took place initiated a reorientation of consciousness from the open country to the city, it must be remembered that from 1916 through 1921, only about 5 percent of the total African American population left the South. The estimated 1.5 million who left between 1910 and 1940 accounted for but 10 to 15 percent of the region's total black population. In 1910 89 percent of the nation's black population was in the South. In 1940 this figure had dropped only to 77 percent. The proportion of blacks in cities rose from 27 to 48 percent (35 percent in the South, 88 percent in the North).[6] These figures, even if they had been available, probably would not have disabused whites who believed that a northern plot was afoot to steal their labor force and bring their region to ruin.

Symptomatic of the migration hysteria, white southerners worried that African American workers would desert them even after World War I ended and the demand for labor in the North slackened. An editorial in the *Houston Observer,* dated May 24, 1919, stated, "Now the farm needs the Negro—just as the Negro needs the farm—and if there is to be any improvement in the situation the thinking South must break down these conditions—not to speak of the lynchings and other worse forms of brutal treatment that are steadily driving the Negro entirely out of reach of the farm and Southland as well."[7] The *New York Age,* a cheerleader for the exodus, estimated that more than 50 percent of the country's African American population in 1919 was engaged in the production of staple crops in the South. "If the South wants the Negro to remain an economic asset," the *Age* asserted, "it must deal with him justly. . . . The Negro of the country districts requires the same justice that is required by the Negro in the cities."[8]

The postwar resumption of out-migration that peaked in 1924–25 meant that agencies engaged in assisting rural blacks now had to contend with unsettled conditions without the prospect of a return to normalcy. Christian groups attempting to organize congregations in the South expressed alarm over the resumption of the exodus. "Among the lamentations of the Josephite missionary the migratory propensities of the Colored people of the South stand forth prominently. No one can blame them for trying to better their earthly conditions," an editorialist for the Josephite missionaries wrote in the *Colored Harvest* in 1922. He added, "but it does come hard on the man engaged in the difficult task of building up a congregation. Hardly has a respectable number of converts been gathered together when that 'Take up thy bed and walk' disease gets a strangle-hold on the town. When the dust of the exodus fades in the distance the priest takes a census of the survivors and finds to his dismay that a goodly slice of his congregation has scattered to the four winds, but more especially to the North."[9]

Norfolk's *Journal and Guide* did not think that the renewal of the exodus after the brief economic depression following World War I was all that mysterious, given the resurgence of the Ku Klux Klan, lynchings, and the general campaign of terror with which blacks contended. The February 22, 1919, edition editorialized, "All the colored people who are going North and West are not fleeing from the boll weevil and the potato worm. When the masses go in large numbers their preachers, teachers and other leaders follow them, taking out of the community many actual and potential factors for good, economic and otherwise. There are enough problems that portend difficulties for the South in the new exodus to warrant the serious consideration of Southern people, white and black, and the South is missing a great opportunity by delaying tangible action."[10] During the war years southern audiences frequently heard that efforts to counteract the exodus must center on improving the lot of blacks in the South. The Rev. Richard Carroll told delegates to the Southern Sociological Congress in 1917, "Making social service evangelism is the basis of the greatest movement I know for the salvation of the South. Right religion makes a man bathe, clean his house and yard, care for his horse and his cow, and cast out disease. You white folks should get in touch with the Negro preachers in your town and teach them this."[11] The postwar campaign to shore up the lives and institutions of rural dwellers was motivated by a mix of disinterested benevolence and crass desire to preserve the economic and racial status quo. Many southern reformers, black and white, realized that regional stability depended on shortening the list of grievances cited by migrants as reasons for fleeing. Northern progressives expressed an interest in the plight of southern blacks parallel to what was being done on behalf of those who occupied the northern ghettoes, especially when it became apparent that whatever the ultimate size of the exodus, the majority of the country's African American population would remain in the South.

The demand for labor in the North stimulated by World War I was symptomatic of a changing economic order that eventually took a heavy toll on the rural South and the institutions with which rural blacks identified. Using data from the 1920 census, E. Franklin Frazier concluded that despite the Great Migration, almost half the working segment (over ten years of age, gainfully employed) of the country's African American population remained in agriculture. Frazier believed that the exodus to the city, whether northern or southern, had a negative impact on rural institutions, notably the African American family and the African American church. Writing in 1926, a decade after the beginning of the Great Migration, Frazier concluded that the church's usefulness as an agency of social control in rural areas, specifically its influence on family relations, had noticeably weakened.[12] This same conclusion was reached by others (see below).

The declining significance of the rural church was of particular concern to Benjamin F. Hubert, director of the Agricultural Extension Service, State Agricultural and Mechanical College, Orangeburg, South Carolina, who echoed what many reformers were saying in the wake of the Great Migration: "The churches [of the rural Negro] must be made to function in the interests of community life."[13] Hubert, who had served as agricultural director of Tuskegee Normal and Industrial Institute, was one of a handful of reformers who were attempting to improve rural conditions according to the philosophy and methods of the Country Life Movement. His analysis of the problems plaguing churches and his proposals for change drew inspiration from Kenyon L. Butterfield, president of the Massachusetts Agricultural College in Amherst and president of the American Country Life Association.[14] The U.S. entry into the European conflict diverted attention to industrial and urban questions, but after the armistice the Country Life Movement again gathered momentum.

Some members of the National Commission on Country Life appointed by President Theodore Roosevelt believed that too much emphasis on rural churches by a government-sponsored agency violated the principle of church-state separation. The constitutional question did not bother Butterfield and those who shared his philosophy. He was a proponent of an agrarian Social Gospel and an advocate of rural cooperation that was not only economically satisfying but spiritually redemptive. Butterfield used instrumentalist language in defining the function of the country church: "The country church (and its allies) is to maintain and enlarge both individual and community ideals, under the inspiration and guidance of religious motive, and to help rural people to incarnate these ideals in personal and family life, in industrial effort and political development, and in all social relationships."[15] Butterfield and the early disciples of redemptive Christian agrarianism ignored the plight of the hundreds of thousands of African Americans in the rural South who worked acreage belonging to others and who dreamed of escaping from grinding poverty and racial oppression. No particular attention was initially paid to the special needs of the rural black church, though the weaknesses that researchers identified in their examination of these churches after World War I were replicated in their analyses of white rural congregations.[16]

In 1920 Robert Moton, the successor to Booker T. Washington as principal of the Tuskegee Institute, journeyed to Springfield, Massachusetts, to speak at the third annual National Country Life Conference. Noting that more than 80 percent of the nation's 12 million African Americans lived in rural districts of the South, Moton called attention to the serious problems caused by the movement cityward of "all classes of our people." Anxious to cultivate the support of the white Country Lifers, Moton told them, "Personally, I am not alarmed at what has been called the 'exodus' of the negro from the South. There is very little danger of the shifting of negro population on a vast scale." Moton hailed the American Country Life Association as the "best brain and heart in the nation focused upon the problems of rural development," and he urged its members to convene a national assembly of white and black delegates from North and South. Moton's list of concerns, such as rural education and the need for more farm demonstrators, complemented those of his audience. But Moton stressed that "no program for improving country life among negroes will be complete without consideration of the country church." Strongly aware of the social changes that brought the American Country Life Association into existence, Moton added, "The negro church and the preacher occupy the same place in negro life today that was occupied by the church and the preacher in New England one hundred years ago."[17]

Moton preached a similar message to the readership of the *Southern Workman* in 1921. "We must do more to make our churches and schools real centers of thought that will give such instruction and inspiration as will touch more directly the daily lives of the people. This will need an intelligent, godly ministry with a knowledge of, and sympathy with, country conditions, and not one that is interested merely in what it can get out of the country people to take back to the city."[18] Rosa Young, a young African American schoolteacher in Alabama, used much stronger language in her description of exploitive city preachers who preyed on their rural flocks. Of the worst of their lot, she wrote, "On Saturdays they would go out to their country churches, do their kind of preaching, get all the money, chickens, eggs, etc., they could from the people and on Monday mornings board the train for the city with these gifts, joking about the people, calling them 'niggers,' and saying, 'I told them niggers so and so.' Instead of trying to enlighten the people, they were calling them fools."[19]

The Association for the Advancement of Negro Country Life did not come into existence until 1928, a decade after the formation of the white-dominated American Country Life Association. In 1929 Hubert, by now president of Georgia State Industrial College, defended the necessity of a separate organization of African Americans interested in the revitalization of rural life. He called attention to the injurious effects of the exodus stimulated by the demand for industrial labor in the North, arguing that a breakdown had occurred in community life. "Homes have been left empty and this has resulted in empty churches and poor and vacant school houses and inactivity of community life."[20] In 1929 the Association for the Advancement of Negro Country Life proposed building a conference and demonstration center "for Negro country life" in central Georgia. The onset of the Great Depression crippled efforts to successfully carry out plans for an effective regional center, though Hubert did set up a model farm at Log Cabin in Hancock County, Georgia. Given the economic problems and racial oppression that blacks in the open country had to contend with during the 1920s, it is not surprising that Hubert's vision of a mecca for a new black rural civilization did not materialize.[21]

Nevertheless, a flurry of activity at a subregional level during the 1920s signaled a renewed interest in the quality of life that African Americans experienced in the rural South. For example, the Colored Rural Life Conference of Virginia was organized in 1923. It drew representatives from the tobacco-growing counties and solicited the involvement of African American educators, clergy, county agents, and other professionals.[22] Though more or less localized, these rural life conferences were attempts to implement the agrarian reform modeled at Hampton and Tuskegee. During the Great Migration, proponents of Booker T. Washington's agrarianism had been accused of deflecting attention away from the fundamental inequities

experienced by southern blacks. When it became clear that no wholesale regional displacement of the "rural Negro" would occur, the agricultural and
community improvement programs pioneered at Hampton and Tuskegee
enjoyed renewed respect, though the impetus now was on exporting them
to enhance rural civilization throughout the South and on involving the
churches more directly. There was widespread agreement that the postwar
resumption of migration was siphoning off many of the more successful
black farmers and that, on the whole, a larger number of skilled laborers
and their families were deserting the South than in the earlier exodus. This
trend made the postwar crusade to improve the country church all the
more important.[23]

In late June 1926 Hampton Institute held its thirteenth annual ministers'
conference. Comprising 761 clergy, the conference included representatives from many different denominations and from twenty-one states. The
mix of speakers called to address the conferees, most of whom pastored
churches in places that the U.S. Census Bureau classified as rural, suggests the rebirth of interest that northerners were having in the southern
rural church; it also indicates an attempt to import instrumentalist ideas
and methods of church revitalization. Ralph Sockman of Madison Avenue
Methodist Episcopal Church in New York City gave advice on how ministers could better address the "social perplexities" of their congregations.
R. Nathaniel Dett, a graduate of Oberlin College, spoke on church music.
Charles H. Wesley of Howard University lectured on "Negro History," and
William Adams Brown of Union Theological Seminary, New York, after
presenting a theologian's systematic view of how to make the purpose and
manner of prayer clearer, reported on the progress of the ecumenical movement at a recent international meeting in Stockholm. Charles A. Tindley
of Philadelphia, whose urban congregation contained many former migrants, gave an inspirational sermon, and Major T. J. Howard, professor of
Rural Church Work at Gammon Theological Seminary in Atlanta, spoke
on practical methods for improving country churches. When the clergy
delegates were not in session hearing of how they were to redefine their
ministry in progressive, practical, and ecumenical ways, they browsed display materials ranging from Sunday school supplies to guides on rural life.
The exhibit bore a banner with the conference's theme: "Where There Is
No Vision, the People Perish." The annual farmers' conference that same
month featured a roundtable discussion on profitable hog-raising, ways
to counteract the ravages of the boll weevil, and, especially for women,

lessons in the use of dye materials and the care of children. Carl C. Taylor, dean of the Graduate School, North Carolina College of Agriculture, spoke on "The Human Factor on the Farm."[24]

Taylor's presence at the farmers' conference was not incidental, for his was an important voice advocating that clergy not fall behind farmers in the crusade to create a "modern rural civilization." Taylor envisioned a more abundant life and a better standard of living in every element—food, clothing, shelter, health, education, recreation, and friendships. "Rural people," Taylor told the readership of *Rural America,* "must no longer be led to think of religion and the church as restrictive of life."[25] Farmers were developing cooperative marketing organizations, learning new techniques for the management of livestock, soils, and crops, and organizing politically.[26] Taylor foresaw a time when these farmers would not be satisfied with an otherworldly religion and inefficient rural church organizations. Influenced by a detailed study made of rural churches in Ohio, he offered the Par-Standard for Country Churches plan of the Inter-Church World Movement as a model of the ideal country church. This seven-point plan demanded adequate modernized facilities, a full-time pastor (formally trained and sufficiently compensated), a sound business policy, efficient organizations, community outreach, practical religious education, and a challenging program to reach young and old, male and female.[27]

The Country Life Movement, which Merwin Swanson aptly terms "a rural version of the Social Gospel,"[28] was spearheaded by social progressives who had battled urban problems and believed that rural America's malaise derived from a lost sense of community. Since the prevailing view was that the church had historically been the dominant institution in African American life, it was only natural that reformers would target the church as the agency around which rural society should be revitalized. White conservatives, especially those who belatedly recognized how central black labor was to the regional economy, tolerated the emphasis on church renewal as the least of all possible threats. Had the progressives advocated political organization or economic development inimical to the interests of the southern white oligarchy, opposition would have prevented significant gains. The reformers encountered less hostility than might have been expected because they were essentially carrying out the mission that Booker T. Washington had endorsed, an enterprise that began with efforts to improve farming conditions.

Northern-based philanthropic agencies sponsored programs for the improvement of church life, though they primarily emphasized public school education. The Phelps-Stokes Fund, established in 1911, encouraged the training of rural clergy. Phelps Hall on the campus of Tuskegee Institute was the gift of Olivia Phelps Stokes and designed to house and educate young men training for the ministry. Because of the demand for a better-prepared ministry, James H. Dillard, chair of the southern publicity committee, urged that rural clergy who were farmers be given the opportunity to attend summer classes when work in the fields was slack. The Phelps-Stokes Fund also underwrote instruction at Hampton Institute and Bettis Academy.[29] Edward Waters College of the AME Church was the first black denominational school in the South to offer summer institutes for pastors. Located in Jacksonville, Florida, the college opened its dormitories to 260 preachers in the summer of 1923.[30]

The campaign to improve rural churches was modeled after an earlier effort to upgrade farms by imparting practical knowledge and stressing tangible results. Seaman A. Knapp, known as the "schoolmaster of American Agriculture" and founder of demonstration work, sought to unite forces with Washington's Tuskegee program. The federally sponsored Farmers' Cooperative Demonstration Work employed two African American agents in 1906 and a hundred in 1914. By 1920 there were 268 agents. Agents offered advice on such practical matters as dairy husbandry, and they held canning demonstrations for African American women at rural Baptist churches.[31] Because of the belief that no agenda for enhancing the farmer's welfare should ignore where he worshiped, a number of faculty at land-grant agricultural colleges in the South taught courses on improving rural life with emphasis on the rural church to the consternation of the strict state-church separatists. Professorships in rural church work were established in southern seminaries and theological schools, including several operated by the historic black denominations.[32]

The Negro Demonstration Service sent agents out across the South to show African American farmers how to achieve a higher standard of living. Benjamin E. Hubert called attention to one successful effort in an essay written for the *Messenger* in 1923. Under the guidance of E. A. Williams, state agent for the Negro Demonstration Service in Georgia, farmers had cooperatively marketed more than $10,000 worth of melons and other perishable crops.[33] The number of successful models of progressive church extension work in the rural South lagged behind those of the agricultural department because it was commonly assumed that by focusing on the rural minister one could deal successfully with the whole range of problems of the rural church. The older pattern, begun pre-World War I, continued. Bettis Academy Ministers' Institute in Trenton, South Carolina, is a noteworthy example of post-Great Migration efforts to revitalize rural churches by bringing clergy to centers where the gospel of church efficiency was taught according to instrumentalist standards.

Located in the sandhill country of western South Carolina about eight miles from Trenton, the academy was founded in 1881 by Alexander Bettis, a former slave, and supported by black Baptists.[34] Annual ministers' conferences began at Bettis Academy in 1919 when James Dillard, then president of the Jeanes and Slater educational and philanthropic foundations, initiated a plan designed to reach the rural clergy, whom the *Southern Workman* described as "unquestionably the most powerful leaders among their people." More than 175 rural ministers attended the first four-day institute for daily lessons on topics ranging from "How to Make a Sermon" to "Church Records and Finance." The *Workman* heartily endorsed Dillard's enterprise, arguing that however illiterate or poorly trained the rural black clergy were, "they exert over their congregations a far greater influence than any other community workers. They may become giants of righteousness or most dangerous reactionaries."[35] Dillard attended the second ministers' institute in 1920 and reportedly received a hearty welcome and testimonials by rural ministers to the power of education. Dillard, after reporting that nine of ten letters he received about public education in South Carolina came from black preachers, stated, "The basis of progress is the increase and the spread of knowledge. Men must learn how to do better work, think better, pray better, and live better lives. Religion must be an intelligent religion, if it is to be the kind of religion that Christ would have."[36]

At the 1923 institute South Carolina's superintendent of public instruction praised the clergy as "tireless workers for education" and promised better schools for the state's children "regardless of race."[37] His audience doubtless thought this rhetoric hollow. Some 80 percent of South Carolina's African American public school students were in the second grade or below, and the separate but unequal educational system left them with hand-me-down textbooks, inadequate facilities, and poorly paid teachers. The Chicago philanthropist Julius Rosenwald was said to be donating more money to erect schools for African American children in the state than the legislature was allocating for school buildings for whites as well as blacks. By 1925 the Rosenwald Fund had put up almost 3,000 school buildings for black children throughout the South.[38]

Organized efforts by northern progressives to expend money and expertise on behalf of black churches in the South never matched those of the educational philanthropists. The Federal Council of Churches could not overcome the denominational and regional tensions that had plagued American Protestantism since the battles over slavery and Reconstruction. The Board of Home Missions and Church Extension of the Methodist Episcopal Church did contribute to the improvement of church buildings and assumed some of the financial burden of segregated conferences in the central jurisdiction, but as W. A. C. Hughes told members of the annual Washington conference in 1922, the task was overwhelming. Rural black Methodist preachers were likely to be poorly paid, preaching in church buildings of the old "square soap box" type, undereducated, and accustomed to operate without an organized program. Large geographic circuits and absentee pastors compounded the rural church's problems.[39] The major black denominations lacked the resources to wage an organized campaign to revitalize their southern churches, suffered from internal debates over the merits of the Social Gospel approach (whether urban or rural), and were still preoccupied with institutional problems precipitated by the movement North of many of their members. Southern white Protestants had taken tentative steps toward participating in the public realm during World War I, but in the 1920s they were ensnared in the fundamentalist/modernist debate and with political battles over Prohibition.[40]

As a consequence, the task of altering the environment so that rural churches could prosper fell to a select few—concerned African American clergy and laity, perpetuators of Booker T. Washington's legacy, converts to the Country Life Movement, Protestant progressives among the more liberal denominations, and a handful of white southerners, such as Will Alexander, who chipped away at the fortress of apartheid with small but persistent blows. Alexander was the founder of the Commission on Interracial Cooperation, which was born in the aftermath of the racial violence in 1919 when African American soldiers returned home to the South to encounter a firestorm of white hostility. Historian Gilbert Osofsky has written that the interracial commission served as "a white Southern equivalent of the Negro National Urban League."[41]

In 1927 Alexander penned an essay for *Opportunity* on the theme of the changing South. His list of significant changes included the "coming into power" of the descendants of non-slaveholding whites, the diminishing cultural isolation of the region, interest on the part of southern business-men in what was economically good for the region independent of the old racial and political alliances, and the many discussions about the "race problem" on college campuses and among "thoughtful people, generally." Alexander could not point to the white churches of the South as offering much to the climate of change, though he acknowledged that "fairly lib-eral programs of education" had been introduced for young people in two denominations. Alexander was troubled by the persistence of two prob-lems with which the South had long been identified—mob violence and the "backward rural South," where many blacks were kept isolated from the nation's industrial life.[42]

A desire to do something to reduce interracial conflict after World War I also motivated efforts to assess the progress made by African American churches. The Interchurch World Movement asked George E. Haynes to conduct a survey of black churches in 1919. Haynes's book *The Trend of the Races* was published in 1922 under the auspices of the Council of Women for Home Missions and the Mission Education Movement and was de-signed to inform white Americans about the accomplishments and aspira-tions of African Americans.[43] Widely distributed, the book drew contrast-ing portraits of rural and urban black churches and measured rural churches according to urban church standards. "The average Negro country church," Haynes wrote, "comprises usually a rectangular frame structure, often un-painted outside and in, with plain benches, and a platform and pulpit for the preacher. Sometimes there are special enclosures for the choir and a reed organ. Services are held once or twice a month with Sunday-school as a seasonal activity controlled by the weather and condition of the roads. Financial support is inadequate for a resident pastor, and he usually lives in a near-by town or city and visits two or more churches on successive Sab-baths." Of black churches in urban areas, Haynes wrote, "City churches are better supplied, as a rule, in both building and other equipment. The structures quite frequently are brick or stone with modern improvements, musical instruments, and other aids to worship. They are served by full-time ministers. Sunday-schools and other auxiliary organizations are better organized and led than in country churches."[44]

Armed with their surveys and assuming that knowledge about a prob-lem was a major step toward its solution, the reformers attempted to gather information about African American institutional life in the South after the Great Migration. The Committee on Social and Religious Surveys, an independent agency organized in 1921 and sponsored in part by the Rockefeller Foundation, gathered data on rural churches under the guidance of Edmund de S. Brunner, an early and important rural sociologist and member of the Church of the Moravian Brethren. The results were published in 1923 as *Church Life in the Rural South: A Study of the Opportunity of Protestantism Based Upon Data From Seventy Counties.*[45] Chapter 9 is "The Negro Rural Church" and focuses on three counties: Harford County, Maryland; Orange County, North Carolina; and Colbert County, Alabama. This sample was admittedly small, for Brunner estimated that about 3 million black church members lived "in the open country," with about 30,000 churches, and 25,000 preachers. Slightly more than 14,000 African Americans lived in the three counties covered in the 1923 study. Harford County was said to represent "conditions approaching those of the North"[46] and was the subject of a separate study of the effects of industrialism on church life in adjacent rural areas done by H. N. Morse for the Committee on Social and Religious Surveys and published in 1922.[47] Orange County, North Carolina, represented the non-cotton-producing sector of the South, and Colbert County, Alabama, the Black Belt of the Deep South.

Brunner noted that recent migrations to the North had resulted in the loss of from one-third to one-half the members of some black churches, yet signs of stabilization and recovery could be detected. The church was still perceived as the most important agency in the community. Seventy-two of the seventy-eight black congregations in the three counties occupied wooden buildings, two-thirds of which were judged to be in good or excellent condition. More churches, "a surprising number" according to Brunner, were using modern methods of finance, and the number of inactive members was not out of line with what the researchers found in their examination of white rural churches. The churches enrolled 43.6 percent of the total African American population in the three counties, were engaged in extension work, contributed to missions in Africa, and conducted educational and cultural programs. "Social and recreational features," Brunner wrote, "enter into the program of fifteen churches, while ten are taking some interest in civic affairs." When it came to recommendations, Brunner had but two, a better-trained ministry and more interest on the part of the churches in "popular Negro education."[48] Morse found fourteen ministers serving twenty-one churches in Harford County. Four of the clergy were college graduates.[49] As to the question of absentee ministers and the need for more formal clergy training, the results of the investigations drawn on by the Committee on Social and Religious Surveys did not differ significantly from the portrait given of the health of rural churches in the white South.

Though debate continued on the impact of the exodus, regional partisans agreed that improving the training of the African American clergy was critical to the welfare of "the Negro church." The Institute of Social and Religious Research sponsored a survey of ministerial education in all-black schools that offered theological courses in 1923–24. Conducted by W. A. Daniel and Robert L. Kelly, the study was done in part because the status of African American clergy was thought to be diminishing as the educational level of the laity increased and other avenues of leadership and vocational opportunities opened. Fifty-two institutions offered theological study, but fifty of these schools did so only at the departmental level. Slightly more than a thousand students were receiving some form of theological training. But many came so academically underprepared that they actually were being given a general literary education in conjunction with a few Bible courses.

Thirty-four of the schools had been founded by African Americans. The majority of these were in the South and were affiliated, directly or indirectly, with the mainline black denominations. Pessimists predicted that these schools would languish or even disappear because of out-migration and the redirecting of resources. Daniel offered a countervailing opinion. "The rapid urbanization of the Negro," he asserted, "has accelerated the growth of race-consciousness." Even though African Americans were moving to urban areas, the historic black schools and colleges in the South were likely to stay in operation because of "the growth of race-consciousness." Many were small, underfunded, and inefficiently operated. They accepted students who lacked the skills and educational preparation to benefit from theological training. Daniel recommended raising standards of admission to theological departments and seminaries, requiring students to complete at least fifteen high school units, upgrading the curriculum, and improving internal administration. *The Education of Negro Ministers* did not recommend closing or consolidating specific schools.[50]

The 1923 Brunner study's generally positive portrait of black rural churches failed to be replicated seven years later in *The Negro Church in*

Rural Virginia by C. Horace Hamilton and John M. Ellison.[51] Hamilton was a rural sociologist at the Virginia Agricultural Experiment Station, and Ellison was a professor of sociology at Virginia State College for Negroes. These researchers reported that church membership was below 25 percent of the black rural population in sixteen counties, and below 35 percent in eleven others.[52] They highlighted a host of problems: low Sunday school membership rates; overchurching; church schisms; difficulty in raising adequate funds for church budgets; undeveloped lay leadership; underpaid, poorly trained, and often nonresident ministers; and the inability to interest and hold young people. "The migration of large numbers of young Negroes from farms," Hamilton and Ellison concluded, "has been one of the major causes for the backwardness of the Negro rural church."[53] The authors found that 75 percent of the families surveyed had sons and daughters living in the North, mainly in cities. In Brunswick County only one black family still had older children at home. Churches were composed primarily of the old and the very young. Hamilton and Ellison listed other perceived deficiencies of the rural church—services held but once a month, worship that included shouting, ecstatic dancing, and convulsions, and revivals described as "emotional orgies" that were driving young people away.

Competition from other rural organizations, Hamilton and Ellison believed, resulted from the failure of the rural churches to meet the social needs of their communities. Lodges, aid societies, school leagues, agricultural clubs, and farmers' organizations provided country people with forums other than the church for socialization and organized activity. Though the authors pointed to several promising trends, such as a decline in church divisions and in the extreme emphasis on emotionalism, they concluded, "We do not, however, hold a 'Pollyanna' attitude about the future of the Negro rural church. The progress which we have mentioned is all too slow to justify extravagant predictions. The future of the church depends on the future of rural life itself, and on the social ingenuity that is used in the solution of the problem."[54]

Arthur Raper's *Preface to Peasantry: A Tale of Two Black Counties* describes many of the same weaknesses of the black rural church in the 1920s and early 1930s. Published in 1936, the study was based in part on research that Raper began in the summer of 1927 in Greene and Macon counties, Georgia.[55] Will Alexander, director of the Commission on Interracial Cooperation, and T. J. Woofter, Jr., research professor at the University of

North Carolina, encouraged Raper to update his data, which he did in the summer of 1934, because of his colleagues' interest in assessing the impact of farm-to-city migration since 1920 in the Black Belt. Woofter already had studied the problem at a general level, but Raper's research made it possible to compare one county, Macon, where the black population had remained relatively stable, with another, Greene, which had suffered significant losses, especially in the 1920s during a severe agricultural depression.[56]

Raper discovered that the 130 black churches in Greene and Macon counties were concentrated in the smaller towns and open country. Over-churching was evident. "The inevitable weakness of the typical rural Negro church," Raper wrote, "is obvious when one realizes that on average each one-teacher school community has one Baptist Church and one of another denomination."[57] Greene County had experienced an exodus to the cities, such as Atlanta, and some churches had closed since 1922, while others were so depleted that they could not maintain Sunday school services or adequately support the preacher who came but once a month. Overall resident church membership in seventeen churches that Raper studied in detail decreased by 57.3 percent between 1920 and 1928. Rural congregations had difficulty maintaining the active participation and support of men. The better-trained clergy were reluctant to take country charges. Preaching focused on the terrors of hell and the rewards of heaven and rarely dealt with what Raper termed "present day community and social needs." White churches in the rural areas had little if any interest in or contact with black ones, and the churches of both races emphasized personal salvation over social action and avoided undercutting the caste system.

By the end of the 1920s evidence abounded that the rural black church in the South was in a state of institutional anomie, at least insofar as the instrumentalists were concerned. On September 14, 1930, the *New York Times Book Review* featured commentary on a study of the church among rural southern blacks that was more pessimistic than any previous survey. Haynes Trebor paired a review of Louise Venable Kennedy's recently published *The Negro Peasant Turns Cityward* with Carter G. Woodson's *The Rural Negro,* published that year by the Association for the Study of Negro Life and History.

Trebor appropriately began with this observation: "Although originating from different sources and doubtless with unrelated objectives, these two books are so complementary that they might have been written by the same author, or at least in collaboration."[58] Trebor advised readers to start with Woodson's book and then move to Kennedy's, because he felt Woodson faithfully captured the conditions that continued to drive blacks out of the rural South. He applauded Kennedy for offering answers to the question of what happened to the migrants once they settled in the North. Trebor found Woodson's and Kennedy's findings strikingly similar. For example, low pay and discrimination proved to be the fate of many migrants, just as it was the norm among those who had remained behind. Hopes of the good life evaporated. By the onset of the Great Depression the exodus from the South was spoken of in the past tense rather than as an ongoing event in the salvation history of an entire people.

Woodson's *The Rural Negro* contains a wealth of information concerning African Americans living in the South on open land or in towns and villages with no more than 2,500 inhabitants. In 1926 the Association for the Study of Negro Life and History, of which Woodson was executive secretary, undertook a three-year examination of the social and economic conditions of blacks since the Civil War, drawing on census materials but also, as Woodson writes in his introduction, on "actual observation, personal knowledge, and documentary evidence."[59] Two of twelve chapters of the published results concern religious matters. In "Things of the Spirit" Woodson asks, "What, then, is this rural Negro church?" His answer, "It is the simple Protestant faith, largely of Methodists and Baptists, who, with the exception of the difference of opinion on immersion are very much alike everywhere among Negroes."[60] Noting that the rural church was still dominated by the preacher, Woodson asked rhetorically, "Who, then, is this high priest in the rural community?" Woodson's answer reveals how strongly his analysis was controlled by instrumentalist presuppositions. "He is not the man required to direct the religious work of an urban center, but 'an inspired man' whom the fates have superimposed."[61] Woodson acknowledged that "as a rule" rural clergy had a better reputation for being "morally clean" than their urban counterparts, but his overall conclusion was that the rural church had not improved much since the Civil War.

Woodson had none of the romanticism for black folk religious culture that W. E. B. Du Bois expressed in such a powerful way in *The Souls of Black Folk* or Zora Neale Hurston wrote about in the early 1930s.[62] Nor was Woodson swept away by the Harlem School of writers like Jean Toomer, Claude McKay, and Langston Hughes, who perpetuated a nostalgic view of the southern rural past that has been termed the myth of primitivism. Woodson's hard-hitting analysis of the weaknesses of the rural church remind one more of the literary naturalism of the novelist Richard Wright and the Chicago School.[63] "The urban church has become a sort of uplift agency," Woodson asserted. "The rural church has become a mystic shrine. While the urban church is often trying to make this a better world in which to live, the rural church is engaged in immediate preparation for the 'beautiful land of by and by.' The rural church building may be used for social uplift purposes, but this is not the church thus in action. These things originate without the spiritual group. When the rural church assembles in the spirit it is more of a seance."[64]

In his chapter "Religious Work Without a Program" Woodson continued his attack on the fundamentalist, otherworldly religious culture of "the rural Negro," though he admitted that rural white religion also was based on fear and preoccupied with the fires of hell and the hope of heaven. Except for preaching services and weekly prayer meetings, most rural churches had no program. Religious education was being neglected, especially that directed to youth. As a consequence, young people were deserting the church. Rural churches were being challenged by rural schools as centers of community activity, ministers had large circuits and little pay, buildings needed basic repairs, and overchurching was a serious problem. Sectarian differences made the cooperation and consolidation that Woodson felt was necessary difficult and unlikely.[65] Migration to the cities by young people and the better-educated, an ever-shifting population in many rural districts, and the reluctance of older members to support institutional change mitigated against the reforms that he wanted. "The Negro rural church," he concluded, "seems to be helpless in having no program for meeting these exigencies. It must be approached from without."[66]

External analysis of southern black rural culture, which Woodson generally referred to as a peasant way of life, proliferated in the decade following the publication of *The Rural Negro.* Subsequent studies employed instrumentalist presuppositions and methodologies that had been applied to examinations of the "race question" in the North following the Great Migration. Several studies were inspired by the research on northern communities done by W. Lloyd Warner.[67] Other researchers explicitly appropriated the sociological theories of Robert Park of the Chicago School of Sociology, notably his views on the evolution and articulation of ethnic groups and his conviction that the black migrant was the New World equivalent of the European peasant.[68] While researchers still made use of surveys and examined census materials, as Woodson and others did during the 1920s, the newer studies ventured into the domains of the cultural anthropologist and the social psychologist and, in the main, used the case study model rather than attempting a broad analysis of the nation's black churches.

The Negro's Church by Benjamin E. Mays and Joseph William Nicholson is a significant exception to the case-study model and therefore is worthy of extended comment. Mays, a South Carolina native and Bates College graduate, was on the staff of the national YMCA in the summer of 1930 when the Rockefeller-funded Institute of Social and Religious Research asked him to direct a national study of black churches. He and Nicholson, a CME minister, spent fourteen months gathering data and ten months writing. Published in 1933, *The Negro's Church* profiles 609 urban and 185 rural churches in twelve cities and four county areas. The coauthors thought of their effort as "the first comprehensive contemporary study of the Negro church" and intended it to be "a base line for other studies of the Negro church," offering the disclaimer that their work was neither exhaustive nor final.

The migration question was clearly central to Mays, Nicholson, and their consultants such as Monroe N. Work, Charles S. Johnson, L. K. Williams, H. M. Kingsley, W. A. Daniel, Howard Thurman, and Forrester B. Washington. "In view of the recent extensive migrations of Negroes from country to city and from South to North, together with the extension of education and sophistication among the Negro population as a whole," the authors write in the preface, "it may be considered fortunate that this study was made while the older patterns of religious life were still to be found." Mays and Nicholson expressed the hope that their research would stimulate greater public interest, cause church leaders to improve "the Negro church," and provide social scientists and others with a greater appreciation of "the church as a dominant factor in Negro development."[69] Though the authors acknowledged that 76 percent of the nation's black churches were still in rural areas, where more than half the country's black population resided when their study was done, their data were weighted in favor of urban churches. Their interpretation sent the message that unless the crisis of the rural church was resolved, it no longer would serve as a significant factor "in Negro development." The authors defended the urban/rural imbalance of churches studied on the grounds that rural areas lacked the diversity of types found in cities and that the messages of rural clergy were "uniformly otherworldly."[70] They selected Peach County, Georgia, Orangeburg County, South Carolina, Montgomery County, Alabama, and Fort

Bend County, Texas, for data collection and personal visits. Mays seems to have spent the most time in the counties surveyed. He was the principal author of four of the book's five chapters that deal with rural churches.

Mays and Nicholson invariably compare the rural to the urban church to the rural church's disadvantage. Even when rural churches are credited with having more active supporters and higher average attendance by regulars, the authors offer the caveat that this regularity results from country people having fewer distractions than city dwellers. This disparity was likely to diminish as urban influences permeated the countryside. Informants told the investigators that the migratory movements from 1914 until 1918 and 1921 until 1925 had reduced memberships and financial support. In light of their examination of population figures Mays and Nicholson doubted that the exodus fever had damaged church life as much as they were led to believe by church officials. But the two authors acknowledged that "the people who move into the counties are not as loyal to the church as were the migrants; and the instability of rural membership is probably more marked now than it was in 1910 and 1920."[71]

The litany of rural church ills offered in *The Negro's Church* might have been expressed by Carter G. Woodson himself, though Mays and Nicholson exercised more self-restraint in their use of disparaging adjectives. Rural churches were too small and too numerous. They were pastored by poorly paid and poorly trained individuals, who were generally older than urban clergy and burdened with more than one "point served (church or congregation)." A higher ministerial turnover than in urban areas indicated a more general problem: "It has been asserted, and with much truth," Mays and Nicholson emphasized, "that Negro rural ministers are preachers and not pastors." Ironically, advances in transportation had made the situation worse. "Before the days of the automobile," the authors argued, "the pastor came at week-ends, by train or in a buggy, and lived around with the members. Now, he can leave the city or the town early Sunday morning and arrive in time for the eleven o'clock service, and leave for home immediately after the evening service (if there is one)."[72]

The Negro's Church reserves its most severe criticism for the quality of southern rural preaching, which is described as "more consistently otherworldly" than that of urban churches. Mays, director of the study and principal author of the chapter on the rural ministry, would later publish a more exhaustive analysis of the otherworldly theological content of black preaching, which he believed had increased after 1914, in a volume called

The Negro's God as Reflected in His Literature.[73] Though himself a product of the rural black church and sensitive to the hardships and proscriptions experienced by rural pastors, Mays could not excuse the overemphasis on individual salvation and damnation that dominated the eschatological orientation of rural black preaching. "The country preaching," he wrote, "runs along lines of the magical and other-worldliness with scarcely a dissenting voice." By contrast, one could find clergy in the cities who were attempting to show that "religion has also real practical value here in this world." "In the country," Mays concluded, "religion is more of an opiate and an escape from life."[74]

Mays and Nicholson admitted that readers would find "a rather dark picture" in their analysis, and they tried to compensate by speaking of "the genius of the Negro Church." They refer specifically to ways in which churches offered African Americans institutional independence, opportunities for leadership, freedom of self-expression, community support, democratic participation, and a forum in which preachers could address controversial topics. These positive features, however, were more likely to be found in urban churches. Unless rural churches consolidated and became more efficient, the "inevitable outcome" would be death by natural causes. Mays and Nicholson had little to offer as an alternative scenario—short of a reversal of the exodus to cities, multiplication of the number of independent black farmers, and, in general, "a rapid return of healthier days in the rural South."[75]

Later case studies of selected parts of the South did not offer much hope for generally revitalizing the region or more positive portraying the rural church. Charles S. Johnson's classic *Shadow of the Plantation* was published in 1934 under the sponsorship of the Rosenwald Fund.[76] Johnson had been director of research for the National Urban League in New York and, beginning in 1923, editor of *Opportunity: A Journal of Negro Life.* Begun in June 1931, *Shadow of the Plantation* examined rural black social life based on 612 families in Macon County, Alabama, where Tuskegee Institute was located. Johnson was then a professor of sociology; he later became president of Fisk University. Johnson, like Woodson, was primarily interested in the church as a community institution, not in individual religious experience. Noting that only seventeen of the 612 families surveyed were without a church connection—generally Baptist or Methodist—Johnson echoed the now familiar refrain of the rural church's centrality to black life. He described the black churches in Macon County as having a threefold function—as social centers, as agencies of social control, and as mediums of spiritual expression. As social centers, "there has been a pronounced development," Johnson wrote; as agencies of control, "the church is less effective than in other communities with a different organization of Negro life"; with respect to spiritual expression, "there is a widening gap between doctrine and behavior which leaves the traditional doctrine empty and unconvincing in relation to normal currents of life."[77]

To illustrate how difficult it was for clergy with progressive ideas to bring their congregations along with them, Johnson included the text of a sermon in which the pastor of Macedonia Baptist Church in Macon County preached about the importance of supporting good schools, reducing overchurching, and developing "race spirit." Johnson observed that "any attack on the traditional ways is hazardous," and he concluded his chapter on "Religion and the Church," by asserting that "it seems just as true of the religious experiences of this group as of other similarly naive Negro groups of which it has been observed that they were not converted to God, but converted God to themselves."[78] Not incidentally, the concept of African Americans in the rural South converting God rather than being converted—a point of view that religion functioned in a compensatory way rather than in an instrumentalist one—was employed by Paul Radin in his introduction to *God Struck Me Dead,* a collection of conversion narratives of aged ex-slaves compiled on the basis of oral interviews done in the 1920s.[79] As long as southern blacks had to live in the shadow of the plantation, Johnson believed, the force of tradition would prevail. "The community studied," he wrote, "reflects a static economics not unlike the Mexican *hacienda,* or the condition of the Polish peasant—a situation in which the members of a group are 'muffled with a vast apathy.'"[80]

Subsequent studies of the environmental constraints within which southern black churches had to function underscored Johnson's conclusions. The cultural anthropologist Hortense Powdermaker lived and examined conditions in Indianola, Mississippi, for twelve months during 1932–34. Of the black church in "Cottonville," she wrote, "in both its secular and its religious character, it serves as an antidote, a palliative, an escape. Not one of these functions is designed to deny or to change the facts; each makes them easier to bear. By helping the Negro to endure the *status quo,* this institution has been a conservative force, tending to relieve and counteract the discontents that make for rebellion." To offset this bleak picture, Powdermaker added, "At the same time the equally vital function of maintaining the self-respect of the Negro individual is by no means a conservative one."[81] Powdermaker had completed her manuscript by 1937 when John Dollard's *Caste and Class in a Southern Town* was published. It, too, was a case study of Indianola, which Dollard referred to as "Southern-town."

Dollard, a psychologist at the Institute of Human Relations at Yale University, was told by a local informant that white planters tolerated the construction of more churches than schools because "the church . . . helped to keep the *status quo* by offering an illusory consolation to the Negroes."[82] Dollard thought this view of religion as social control was too narrow, so he offered the counterthesis that religion functioned for African Americans in Southerntown "as a form of collective activity which gives pleasure and is a center of social solidarity for Negroes."[83] The same could be said of Garvey's use of religion in the UNIA or of Ransom's understanding of the purposes of the institutional church, but as two chapters that followed the one dealing with "Caste Patterning of Religion" in Dollard's book reveal, the analogy would have to be forced. In "Accommodation Attitudes of Negroes" and in "Aggression Within the Negro Group," Dollard dealt with the social-psychological price that African Americans had to pay—including those who had achieved middle-class status—to survive in the shadow of the southern white caste system.

Dollard inadvertently found himself drawn into the intricate web of accommodationist behavior that typified black-white relations in the South when a black preacher, contrary to the wishes of his congregation, proposed to put forward the time of a baptizing so Dollard could observe it. "The Northerner," Dollard confessed, "often finds it embarrassing to be the object of such special solicitude, since he is not accustomed to the notion that no amount of trouble for Negroes is too much to gratify one of his wishes."[84] Migrants to the North took special pleasure in the freedom that city life afforded from these old patterns of deference. But for those who remained under the shadow, little had changed. Studies published after the Great Depression, such as *Deep South* by Allison Davis, Burleigh Gardner, and Mary Gardner, did not detect much improvement in the state of health of the rural black church.[85]

In 1940 the nation's urban African American population finally exceeded the rural. The continued drift cityward of the young was a major concern to many observers, including the American Education Council. The AEC sponsored Charles S. Johnson's *Growing Up in the Black Belt*, which appeared in 1941. Johnson examined the attitudes toward the church of rural African American youth in eight counties. He discovered a chasm between the generations. While their parents and grandparents found the conservative ethos of the rural church useful, young people were torn between religious fundamentalism and the aspirations to break free of the old system. Johnson wrote, "The introduction by the school of new values stressing literacy, economic improvement, and urbanization has brought significant changes in the role of the rural Negro church in the community. The institution itself has changed but little, but in its function it has a different impact upon new generations of Negroes."[86]

As had so many before him, Johnson believed that improving the educational standards of the rural clergy was essential. Here was the one remedy that all could agree on. The education gap between the clergy and the laity was widening. Since the black minister was still viewed as the central figure around which the church revolved, enhancing his qualifications was seen as essential by those who perceived the rural church as a dysfunctional institution. Without better-trained ministers to lead the way, few other improvements could be achieved. This was certainly the major conclusion of Harry V. Richardson's doctoral dissertation "Dark Glory: A Picture of the Church Among Negroes in the Rural South," written in 1945 and published for the Home Missions Council of North America and the Phelps-Stokes Fund two years later.[87] "If the church is to assume responsibility for the many areas of life," Richardson wrote, "it must have a ministry capable of giving spiritual direction in the many areas of life."[88] Richardson had been chaplain and director of religious activities at Tuskegee Institute before beginning graduate study. In 1947 when *Dark Glory* appeared in book form he was executive secretary and field director of a program to train African American rural clergy in the South. A native of Jacksonville, Florida, Richardson graduated from Harvard Divinity School and earned the Ph.D. degree at Drew University, a Methodist institution. At Drew he came under the influence of Ralph A. Felton, who was perhaps the most important link between the Country Life Movement of the World War I era and later efforts to institutionalize a program for the revitalization of the black rural church through the vehicle of better trained clergy. Felton was professor of rural sociology and head of Drew's rural church department from 1930 until 1952.

Drew University had been offering summer courses for rural pastors since 1919. Felton came to his post at Drew after seven years as director of the extension program in rural social organization at Cornell University. He expanded the rural church emphasis by offering graduate training. This offering attracted Richardson, who came in 1943. With assistance from Felton, Richardson obtained a grant from the Rockefeller-funded General Education Board of New York City to examine the rural church "among the disadvantaged Negro masses in the agricultural South." "After hours of study," Richardson recalled in a memorial sketch of Felton, "we came to the conclusion that the key to the problem was a larger supply of better trained Negro rural ministers."[89] Felton initiated a training program at Drew in 1945 that in two years sent more than twenty individuals, most of them with masters' degrees, into rural church work. During the next seven years more than 9,000 African American clergy enrolled in summer courses at Drew or did extension work. Demonstration parishes not unlike the model used in agricultural extension work were set up in the South. Successful rural churches, such as the one pastored by J. E. Wright in rural Middlesex County, Virginia, were offered as models.[90]

A revitalized rural church for African Americans in the South was an essential component of Felton's version of the agrarian Social Gospel, a vision that Richardson endorses with enthusiasm at the conclusion of *Dark Glory:*

> The day is coming, we believe, when every hill and valley will re-echo the music of the church bell; when every field and farm will feel the touch of Christian husbandmen; when the farm markets will be peopled by men who do justice and love mercy; when every highway shall lead to a place of worship; when men's hearts will be full of love for their neighbors; when children will be taught righteousness by devoted and trained teachers; when the nation will recognize the value of the rural church to our national idealism; when ministers will be proud to serve rural parishes; when those who worship in city centers will seek the companionship of rural folk because of their real worth.[91]

This idealistic picture of what rural life ought to be, sketched by Felton in 1926 and underscored by Richardson in 1947, was even more anachronistic after the Great Depression because of agricultural mechanization and the subsequent decline of African American farmers in the South.[92] It was a cultural artifact of the early days of the Country Life Movement and the educational philosophies of Tuskegee and Hampton. In 1920 James Gregg, principal of Hampton Normal and Agricultural Institute, had invited Felton to teach sociology and rural economy at Hampton, with particular responsibility for the training of rural pastors.[93] The program for the rural clergy at Drew was a belated expression of that interest.

By the end of the 1940s the interdenominational program to train black rural pastors had cooperative relationships with fifteen black colleges and seminaries in nine southern states. Sponsored by the Home Missions Council of the Federal Council of Churches, with support from the Phelps-Stokes Fund, and directed by Richardson, who had become president of Gammon Theological Seminary, the training program was designed to recruit, credential, and provide continuing education for rural black ministers. At the request of the national Home Missions Council and its sponsors, Felton directed an investigation of 570 black churches in seventeen counties in the rural South in 1949; he enlisted the aid of instructors in rural church and religious extension work from black colleges and seminaries to serve as fieldworkers. Many were his former students at Drew. The survey was published in 1950 as *These My Brethren*. Seeking a no-fault solution, Felton introduced the survey results with this caveat: "In this study it will be noted that no blame is placed on any group. The viewpoint here is not 'Northern' nor 'Southern,' neither white nor colored."[94]

Based on visits to 454 rural pastors, the picture given in *These My Brethren* revealed that little progress had been made since Brunner's study of the black rural church in 1923 or Woodson's critique in 1930. Less than 4 percent of the clergy had achieved the level of education that was deemed necessary for ministers, more than half were over fifty years of age, and nearly 60 percent farmed as well as preached. Salaries were still meager, and only two of every ten clergy were resident ministers. Though some pastors were involved in community organizations "seeking justice," the principal organizational activities were women's societies, choirs, and usher boards. Yet a few positive signs were present. Felton noted that several of the major black denominations were developing an interest in the special needs of churches in small towns and in rural areas. U. Z. McKinnon, professor of Town and Country Church at Phillips School of Theology, Lane College in Jackson, Tennessee, was writing a weekly column for the *Christian Index,* which was circulated to an estimated 2,000 clergy of the CME Church. The Rev. V. A. Edwards was serving as director of rural work for the National Baptist Church, the first black denomination to establish such a position. The Rev. R. H. Boyd, founder of the National Baptist Publishing House and a prominent figure in the 1915 split of the National Baptist Convention, spoke at a rural life conference held under the auspices of Lane College of the CME Church. Described as "himself a practical farmer," Boyd spoke to other black farmers on the subject of "Cotton." Others addressed the crowd concerning such topics as "Better Prepared Preachers" and "How Best to Fight the Boll Weevil." Though seemingly diverse, these themes were encompassed within the philosophy of the rural church revitalization movement.[95]

Though well-intentioned, the clergy training program faced tremendous difficulties in being replicated in the South, not the least of which was the perpetuation of racial caste, a state of affairs that was not effectively challenged until the 1950s and the start of the civil rights era. Felton acknowledged as much in the final paragraph of *These My Brethren:* "The lack of inter-racial cooperation as shown in this study was an astonishing revelation. In the judgment of the writer it was the most lacking of any of the findings in the survey."[96] Felton expressed the hope that this state of affairs was not final, though he acknowledged that not much progress had been made in nullifying racial prejudice in the South. Much of the burden still fell on the self-improvement efforts of blacks themselves. The chances of success were limited. As Clark Foreman wrote during the Great Depression when thousands of uprooted black sharecroppers aimlessly wandered from place to place in the South, "Any one familiar with the facts will hardly deny that the rural Negro, deprived of effective political power and subjected to taxation and farm assessments by agents over whom he has no control or influence, can expect little relief from his own efforts so long as the local government is left in complete control of the situation."[97]

The Great Depression did not spare the industrial North. Some of those who had been opposed to the Great Migration saw the despair and economic chaos that gripped the nation after 1929 as confirmation of their warnings against a wholesale exodus. Kelly Miller, choosing to overlook the social and political realities that Foreman pointed to, was still writing of the farm as "the Negro's best chance" in 1935. "The migration of the Negro to the North during the past two decades," Miller declared, "brings into evidence the most important and imminent phase of the race problem. The World War produced a vacuum in the labor market of the North. Negroes from the South, for a brief moment, rushed in to fill this vacancy hoping that they would find a permanent place in Northern industry." The return of white soldiers from World War I, race prejudice in the labor unions and big industry, and economic depression threw the black worker out of a job before his or her white counterpart might be dismissed. Confirmed in his antiurban prejudice, Miller urged blacks to remain in the South and on the land. And what of the two-fifths of the country's African Americans living in the cities? "They are so effeminated in mind and body by urban influences," Miller complained, "that they do not possess the virility, the stubbornness of spirit, the hardihood of purpose to grapple with crude agricultural conditions. They would be of no service to the farm should they return." Miller estimated that half of the urban black population was on the relief rolls and "so weakened in initiative and enterprise" that they would not "be of any great service to city or country. The cities must grapple with this problem as best they can."[98]

As long as the debate about how best to assist black churches in the South was framed as a rural/urban conflict made all the more problematic by sectional rivalries and the race question, a united front was impossible. Few regional partisans could see beyond their loyalties to place or group. Northerners who encouraged the exodus by exaggerating the assets of urban living and the debits of the South were not willing to invest scarce resources in improving rural life. Southerners like Kelly Miller clung to an anachronistic ideal of rural living despite the depopulation of the countryside and the movement to cities in the South as well as in the North. The unholy trinity of white oppression, natural disasters, and economic hardship that motivated migrants during World War I persisted in the 1920s. Agricultural mechanization and the onset of the Great Depression made the plight of black farmers and farm workers even more difficult. Accounts filtering back to the South of hardships in the Promised Land put the lie to claims of the most zealous advocates of migration. Few contemporaries were able to see that the needs of the black city dweller and those of the rural poor in the South ought to be viewed through a single lens because they were joined together at racism's root. Monroe N. Work saw more clearly than others that cooperation was necessary between the advocates of urbanization and those of the agrarian gospel.

Work's acuity was sharpened by his exposure to evidence from across the country that he gathered as director of the department of research and records at Tuskegee. When Emmett J. Scott received a grant from the Carnegie Corporation in 1917 to study the mass exodus from the South, he selected Work to do the field research in Alabama, Georgia, and Florida. Work used his investigations and research to argue that the Great Migration resulted as much from oppressive conditions in the South as from opportunities in the North.[99] Yet he realized that most of the country's African American population would remain in the South, most likely in rural or small-town environments. He was equally concerned about the fate of blacks who moved from rural districts to larger towns and cities in the South, where they encountered economic and social problems similar to those of northern ghettos. The custom disturbed him of considering "Negro city problems as relating to the North and Negro rural problems as relating to the South."[100]

Work took the position that the transition from country to city entailed difficulties that transcended regional differences and called for cooperation between those interested in urban welfare and those devoted to rural well-being. "There is no group in our composite American population," he argued, "in which there is so close a relation between urban and rural elements as is true of the Negro."[101] He was convinced that the problems of America's urban and rural black citizens were intertwined and that programs which pitted the interests of one segment against the other were ruinous to both. In 1923 Work expressed his views in *Opportunity:* "We are at present working largely on the theory that after all it is a good thing for the Negro to get out of the country into the city, out of the south into the north. A broader and perhaps more correct view of the situation is to look at it from the standpoint of endeavoring to secure for the Negro in every part of the nation, north and south, in the city and in the country, the same advantages of education, of health, of sanitation, of protection from mob violence and other wrongs which the Negro in the most favored communities of the nation enjoys."[102] Work was to be disappointed, for a comprehensive national perspective and plan to address the needs of black churches, rural and urban, never developed.

Tangible results of the concern expressed by instrumentalists about the welfare of the rural black church were minimal. Cynics might conclude that the most significant product of the post-Great Migration public discussion of rural church problems was the discussion itself, the small flood of academic and philanthropic studies briefly surveyed here.[103] Reconstruction measures were lacking. The North sent no army of benefactors to the South as had been done after the Civil War. The white South, initially worried about losing more of the region's agricultural labor force, talked about improving the lot of the black farmer, but eventually tractors were discovered to be more efficient than mules and men. Because of the transition from the tenant plantation system to mechanized capitalist agribusiness

during the 1930s and 1940s, out-migration and depopulation from the region to urban centers in the South resumed on a scale that dwarfed the
Great Migration.[104]

Setting aside the question of race, a parallel to the transformation of
the South's rural landscape can be discerned in New England. Rural New
England went through a period of out-migration and depopulation in the
nineteenth century when thousands succumbed to the "Western craze."
Thousands more fled the region's farms and small towns for its manufacturing centers. Jeremiads followed which predicted that New England
would soon have an illiterate rural peasantry sliding down to the level of
the folk degeneration said to characterize mountain whites of the South
or the impoverished peasants of Europe.[105] Articles appeared lamenting
"The Passing of the Country Church," and a host of reformers rushed in,
Hal S. Barron writes in *Those Who Stayed Behind,* with "solutions based
on precepts of social efficiency and social-scientific analysis." Barron points
out that the majority of Country Life activists, while perhaps born in rural
communities, lived in urban areas and academic centers. These educators,
professors, and clergymen thought systematic surveys essential to effective
social reform, and, like their counterparts interested in city questions, they
believed that knowledge about a problem was half the solution. But as Barron discovered, New England farmers resented the implication that their
way of life was somehow inferior and that their problems were cultural
rather than economic. He reports that when Theodore Roosevelt established his Commission on Country Life in 1908, disgruntled members of
the Grange in New England suggested that a "Commission on City Life"
be set up to study social problems in urban areas. Barron's examination of
Chelsea, Vermont, suggests that those who stayed behind did not necessarily view themselves or their institutions as being in need of outside redemption. Rather than seeking salvation in bureaucratic organizations and
other translocal institutions so dear to the reformers' hearts, they valued
the intimacy of local life.[106]

Evidence is scant in studies done by instrumentalists about what those
left behind in the black rural South thought of the intrusion of reformers—
academic, ecclesiastical, or philanthropic. That rural church members did
not share the instrumentalist view that their religious fellowships were dysfunctional and anachronistic in modern industrial society keyed to urban
life was suggested by discussion here of the transplanting of the folk church
during the Great Migration era. The proliferation of storefronts and house

churches, the establishment of small Baptist, Methodist, Holiness, and Pentecostal churches composed of former southerners, may well have been a rational response to the urban condition, just as they were under the pall of oppression in the South.

It also should be remembered that when the day did come that black rural clergy and congregations were called on to enlist in the struggle for civil rights from 1954 to 1968, they did so with greater individual and institutional strength and courage than their critics during the interwar years would have predicted. C. Eric Lincoln and Lawrence H. Mamiya, authors of the most comprehensive analysis of America's rural and urban black churches since the publication of the Mays-Nicholson study in 1933, draw this conclusion in *The Black Church in the African American Experience* (1991). Noting that from 1962 through 1965 ninety-three mostly rural black churches in the South were bombed or burned, that rural churches encouraged voter registration, and that many were centers for political protest, Lincoln and Mamiya write, "Confounding the sociological prophecies of the decline of religion or black religion as the opiate of the masses, at the height of the conflict many *rural* [emphasis mine] and urban folk stood up in their churches to be counted." [107]

CONCLUSION

African American religion reached an institutional climacteric during the Great Migration era. Exodus from the South that was their Egypt promised change and liberation to individual migrants. Yet the journey to the Promised Land was more than an outflow of atomized individuals. Despite the absence of a Moses, the hegira was seen as a second Emancipation with significant institutional impact. This critical stage in the corporate religious life of African Americans caught the eye of Richard R. Wright, Jr. In 1917 he called attention to the epochal nature of the changes in religion occurring as a result of the Great Migration. He correctly perceived that these cultural and institutional transformations ought to receive as much analysis as those in the economic realm. "The Negro, from today on," Wright wrote in the *Christian Recorder,* "will view religion not as apart from the things of this life as though one must have either this world or Jesus, but as a part of this worldly life."[1]

Wright, as noted, was one of a small number of African American clergy who attempted to sow the seeds of the Social Gospel within African American ecclesiastical circles before the Great Migration's onset. At that time his efforts were frustrated. The majority of his colleagues did not yet understand that the city, not the rural hamlet or small town, would become the most critical arena in which the twentieth-century black church had to function. Because of the institutional crisis set in motion by the inter-regional movement of hundreds of thousands of southern blacks, many more black religious leaders gravitated toward an understanding of the church's mission that bridged the traditional dichotomy of spiritual and material. Joseph R. Washington, Jr., always a provocative commentator on black religion, wrote in 1972:

> By World War I independents [the mainstream Baptist and Methodist denominations] had waxed fat and stuffy. They had managed to iso-late themselves from whites, but more important, they had cut them-selves off from the great pool of blacks who were surging forth to urban centers in the South and the North from southern rural com-munities. These were the great unwashed, the blacks who were left to find religion for themselves in the period when whites were no longer directly converting blacks and independents felt no need to engage in aggressive proselytism.[2]

Joseph Washington's critique needs to be amended in light of the story told in this study. The Great Migration was the wakeup call that brought large sectors of the African American religious establishment into closer harmony with those who sought to capture the church's latent power for ends other than individual salvation. The religious worldview that limited the church's mission to soul-winning dominated the old order in the South from which the migrants came and, as the black Social Gospelers discov-ered, in many mainline churches in the North. The Great Migration was the catalyst for the revitalization of a church doctrine that stressed the im-portance of more fully understanding the social dimensions of the Chris-tian witness to the world.

This instrumentalist point of view dominates most pioneering studies of the black church that appeared in ever-increasing number after the Great Migration. Chief among the instrumentalists were such African American authors as W. E. B. Du Bois and Carter G. Woodson, who were not known for being personally involved with the internal affairs of any of the de-nominational churches or for being notably "religious" in the traditional sense. Woodson's harsh critique of the African rural church as "religious work without a program" was predicated on his assumption that the task of "saving and edifying souls" was insufficient, given the plight of black America.[3] From the vantage point of Du Bois, as Manning Marable has written, "The black church found 'greatness' only as it linked the spiritual strivings of the masses with a social commitment to challenge Jim Crow laws, political disfranchisement, and all forms of bigotry and economic deprivation."[4] It is ironic that critics like Woodson and Du Bois were charging the black church with institutional inadequacy during the interwar decades when, stimulated by the Great Migration, denominations and local congregations were expanding efforts to deal with the material needs of not only their members but of the community at large.

The instrumentalist lens became the prevailing focal point through which "progress" in African American institutional religion was assessed after the Great Migration. In 1939 Woodson was still writing critically of ministers who emphasized the "narcotics" of religion and the church's need to "pay less attention to creeds and more to social uplift."[5] In the same year Harold M. Kingsley of Good Shepherd Congregational Church in Chicago argued, "The real problem of the Negro church is our great need for a social and economic ministry. Theological pietism is played out. We have overemphasized other-worldliness too long."[6] The instrumentalists rather than the theological pietists, to adapt Kingsley's nomenclature, prevail in the interpretative record both as contemporary observers and as academics.

The expectations of the instrumentalists were exceedingly high. They put so large a burden—an inordinate one, I have argued—on the church because they began with the widely shared presupposition that the church was the single most important institution in African American communities, especially in the South. "No race will rise above its religion" was the operative axiom.[7] From this postulate another widely held belief followed: "An educated and consecrated Negro pastor is the hope of his race. The pew will not rise higher than the pulpit."[8] It is likely that this popular notion of the church's centrality and the clergy's dominance was a corollary of the belief that African Americans would remain in the segregated South where the church, by virtue of the iron law of racial caste, served as the core institution of African American life, especially in rural areas. Critics with a romanticized concept of this institutional centrality also expected the church to be the vehicle of salvation in the urban, industrial North.

When it became clear that migration to the Promised Land was not the equivalent of total emancipation, critics faulted the churches for not doing enough or for collective myopia with regard to the real issues at hand. The mainline African American denominations, the black equivalent to the white Protestant establishment, underwent a period of declension according to this popular and scholarly consensus. "In the course of the period 1890 to 1930," Seth M. Scheiner writes, "the church declined significantly as the focal point of Negro life because secular alternatives and internal weaknesses that impaired its ability to grapple with the ramifications of the urbanization process."[9] This interpretation assumes that a golden age existed when African American churches functioned effectively in both the spiritual and material realms, though we are never told when this time was. "Secular alternatives" did emerge in northern urban settings to assist migrants to adjust and to deal with the African Americans' manifold problems during the early decades of the twentieth century. However, we must guard against viewing the appearance of secular agencies as evidence of the decline of the black Protestant mainline denominations, as in a kind of institutional zero-sum game.

Though the church was certainly important to African American life and culture before the Great Migration, and the clergy were principals at the center of the center, those who yoked church and clergy so closely to the salvation of "the race" in the interwar years were bound to be disappointed. They failed to recognize not only how unprepared African American denominations were to deal with the migrants' material needs, but also how strongly the Great Migration affected preexisting institutional structures. Because the perception prevailed that large southern constituencies were on the move, and small northern ones lacked the resources to respond to the crisis, denominational leaders understandably gave first attention to their "wandering Zion." Believing that the exodus from the South would result in a major redistribution of the nation's African American population, church leaders were most concerned about retaining members and expanding among migrants in the North.

Achieving these goals included competing with one another in redrawing the religious map of northern black urban communities, much as had been done in the South among freed slaves after the first Emancipation. It is not surprising that no comity arrangements emerged that were meant to conserve scare resources, human and material, or were to move them to areas of greatest critical need. African American Baptists entered into the Great Migration period still bearing the scars of the grudge match at Chicago in 1915, and black Methodists had failed to bring about union of their three major denominations. Wright's "Ecumenical Council of Dark Skinned Christians" never materialized. White church leaders as well as the wielders of civic power in the industrial North were only too happy to hand black churches the task of assisting the migrants. This deferral to black benefactors became particularly true once the spatial demarcations of northern urban black communities were drawn as tightly as those that had created a system of racial apartheid in the South.

Denominational competition was replicated at the local level when individual congregations and ministers sought to gain prestige and influence during the Great Migration. With so many potential new members arriving daily, church growth and larger, more modern facilities became valuable prizes. The number of African American churches multiplied dramatically in every major industrial center to which migrants came. Already existing congregations grew, and many new churches were established. Enterprising pastors attempted to garner a bountiful harvest of new members by appealing to denominational loyalties among migrants. The strongest draw came from the churches that offered a multidimensional ministry to refugees from the South. In analyzing the appeal of Father Divine, Elder Michaux, Bishop Grace, and other leaders of so-called cults active in 1936, Miles Mark Fisher wrote, "Unlike the Negro churches, the cults seek to cure the souls and bodies of men. They view social work differently from Negro denominations that have no social technique while their community is needy, while their church buildings represent idle wealth, except periodically, and while their race has few social agencies."[10] Fisher's commentary, which probably reflects his observations during the Great Depression, stems from the instrumentalist critique rooted in the Great Migration era.

On the whole, African American churches in the North did extend a helping hand to migrants. At least four motivations contributed to a broadened definition of the church's mission. Clergy and laity recognized that migrants were more likely to join congregations that tangibly assisted them in making the transition from South to North. Aiding migrants to find housing and employment was seen as a racial duty. Helping migrants adjust to urban life as smoothly as possible was thought to lessen the risk that, by invidious comparison, established urbanites, the Old Settlers, would suffer a loss of status. Finally, aid rendered was viewed as a necessary extension of the traditional practice of Christian benevolence.

In the process of reaching out to the migrants, churches and clergy discovered the need to become more directly engaged with existing urban power structures, which were invariably in the hands of white elites. This involvement sometimes entailed the need to negotiate the dangerous rapids of urban ethnic politics. It also meant that churches had to cooperate with secular agencies rather than compete. The civic and church-based effort to render assistance was never sufficient to meet the need, but this shortfall should not be taken as indicating a failure of will or a lack of intent. To appeal to the newcomers, established northern churches emphasized their theological and ideological identities. This evangelistic effort, especially when local churches competed with one another, attracted some and re-pelled others.[11]

Because the migrants were themselves carriers of culture, tensions in-evitably arose when different styles of worship and understandings of the purposes of religious belonging came together in northern cities. The establishment of a wide variety of new churches, many housed in store-fronts or begun as prayer meetings in private homes, is one of the most significant results of the Great Migration. The importation of southern religious folkways, including styles of preaching and worship thought in-appropriate by some established northern churches, eventually weakened the urban and rural differences in African American religious culture. Mi-grants who set up "heavens of their own" were attempting to transplant the kinds of churches that they had known in the South into the urban cultural landscape. Many churchgoers felt more comfortable in small con-gregations where they were known by name and where ritual styles were familiar. This extension of southern culture into the urban North initially functioned to protect participants from contamination by what they per-ceived to be a secular and sinful environment. Many of these small refuges eventually evolved into "regular" congregations, with black Baptists win-ning the numerical competition with black Methodists.

When the last federal census of religious bodies was taken in 1936, each major African American denomination was less rural than before the Great Migration (see Appendix). Though the percentage of the national black population classified as urban failed to equal that designated as rural until 1940, the city rather than the open country was now viewed as the critical battleground for the soul of African American religion. Except for indi-viduals such as Ralph Felton, the northern church establishment did not show much interest in revitalizing southern black rural churches after the Great Migration. The instrumentalists were preoccupied with urban prob-lems, and when they did survey religious conditions among the rural black peasantry of the South, they used assessment criteria derived from urban-based notions of what progressive churches ought to be.

Ironically, the instrumentalists' southern counterparts, the managers of the Tuskegee and Hampton programs, had their own instrumentalist pre-suppositions. Southern instrumentalists, despite their agrarian bias, also viewed the church in pragmatic terms. They sought to make the black church in the rural South coequal with the rural school as an agent for de-veloping a revitalized rural culture as depicted in the rhetoric of converts to the Country Life Movement. Neither the northern nor southern in-strumentalists had much interest in examining the self-understanding that members of the rural and small-town black congregations had of "church" —a conception of the utility of these social organizations that was trans-ferable to the urban, industrial North in the form of thousands of Zions. These transplanted churches were havens of rest in a world far less promis-ing than the migrants dreamed of.

The urbanization of African American Christianity was accelerated by the Great Migration to such a degree that it is now inconceivable to return to forms of ecclesiology dominated by the rural and small-town church model. This development has resulted in both a popular and a scholarly stereotype of black religion as essentially an urban cultural phenomenon. The dominant image of black churches is that they are houses of protest. Far less appreciation is shown them as houses of praise, for praise and protest often are seen as antithetical. It was not always so, and in more closely examining the impact of the Great Migration, both as an event and a process, we are witness to the historical confluence of praise and protest. The preaching, prayer, music, and shouting of today's urban black churches are shaped by influences born of that generation when hundreds of thousands of pilgrims came into the Promised Land in need of material assistance but also bearing spiritual gifts. The emphasis on the role of black churches in social action, a theme dominating the civil rights and Black Power generations, can also be found in the Great Migration era.

The contemporary Church of God in Christ exemplifies the fusion of the two purposes of African American Christianity, which were, in the main, kept distinct before the Great Migration. The male preachers and female missionaries who imported Pentecostal and Holiness religious cul-ture into the urban North, planted churches there, and watched them grow and proliferate could not have anticipated that their style of preaching, forms of prayer, musical preferences, and shouting traditions would be de-scribed many decades later as constituting "the core of urban black church culture."[12] These four "distinctive black conventions," to use Robert M. Franklin's phrase, were once disparaged by the cultural gatekeepers of northern African American communities. Yet now they are found within denominations once described as parts of the mainline black tradition. Indeed, the Pentecostal and Holiness style has been hailed by proponents and celebrants of a distinct African American religious culture as the most authentic because it is the least assimilated.

In the process of re-rooting themselves, the migrants underwent cultural transformations that again are best seen retrospectively. As coping skills with the urban environment improved, and one generation succeeded another, the churches that initially were havens to protect and isolate gradually became more open to the surrounding urban environment. The dramatic growth of the Church of God in Christ in northern cities was accompanied by a willingness to yoke traditional Pentecostal emphasis on a heaven-oriented ministry with an understanding of church that also stressed service to the community, a mission emphasized by northern churches of the Great Migration era. This remarkable synthesis is captured in Robert M. Franklin's description in 1989 of the contemporary Church of God in Christ. "While its language of soul-winning is similar to that of white fundamentalist churches, the Church of God in Christ weds evangelism to home mission work—attending to the total needs of those who are being proselytized. Often, home missionaries go into tenements and public housing projects to teach home economics skills, to care for children whose parents are sick or incarcerated, and to conduct street worship services challenging the hegemony of drug dealers and street gangs."[13] Such a combination of personal evangelism and social ministry would have drawn the enthusiastic approval of Richard R. Wright, Jr., who predicted in 1917 that the massive exodus of black southerners bound for the Promised Land would have a remarkable impact on African American Christianity.

In 1843 the fugitive slave and Presbyterian clergyman Henry Highland Garnet delivered a fiery address before an assembly of African Americans in Buffalo. Though allied with Liberty Party abolitionists and formerly certain of the usefulness of William Lloyd Garrison's philosophy of moral argument to bring about change, Garnet was now convinced that neither electoral politics nor moral suasion would free the slaves. He called for resistance from those yet in slavery's dark dungeon. His counsel was partly born out of his conviction that it was then impossible for African Americans to return to Africa because, as he proclaimed, there were "Pharaohs on both sides of the Blood-Red Waters."[14] There were Pharaohs on both sides of the Mason-Dixon Line preventing an African American exodus of significant magnitude until World War I. With the onset of the Great Migration, hope existed that by escaping the pharaohs of the South, thousands of African Americans might find the Promised Land in the North. Two African American church traditions—praise and protest—came together in the North to keep that hope alive. The fusion of these two understandings of the church's mission, born of the Great Migration years, is the opening chapter in modern African American religious history.

APPENDIX

Number of African American Members Reported in Specified Denominations
(compiled from U.S. Census of Religious Bodies, 1906 to 1936)

Table A. African American Denominations

Denomination	1906	1916	1926[e]	1936[d]
National Baptists	2,261,60794. 7% Southern[a]	2,938,579[b] 89.0% Southern	3,196,623 84.3% Southern 39% urban 61% rural	3,782,464 72.9% Southern 50% urban 50% rural
AME Church	494,777 85.9% Southern	548,355 81.2% Southern	545,814 75.2% Southern 50% urban 50% rural	493,357 65.6% Southern 58% urban 42% rural
AMEZ Church	184,542 88.6% Southern	257,169 84.6% Southern	456,813 82.1% Southern 42.5% urban 57.5% rural	414,244 65.6% Southern 52% urban 48% rural
CME Church	172,996 98.6% Southern	245,749 95.5% Southern	202,713 88.7% Southern 39.1% urban 60.9% rural	269,915 92.4% Southern 43% urban 57% rural
Church of God and Saints of Christ[e]	1,823 29.3% Southern	3,311 32.7% Southern	6,741 41.8% Southern 89.9% urban 10.2% rural	37,084 36% Southern 94% urban 6% rural
Church of God in Christ[f]	—	—	30,263 64.9% Southern 68.7% urban 31.3% rural	31,584 55.5% Southern 75% urban 25% rural
Church of Christ Holiness, U.S.A.[g]	—	—	4,919 70.9% Southern 61% urban 49% rural	7,379 79.7% Southern 48% urban 52% rural

Note: The U.S. Bureau of the Census conducted censuses of religious bodies in 1906, 1916, 1926, and 1936. A partial enumeration was taken in conjunction with the decennial census of population in 1890. Statistics given in the tables relate to the years indicated or to the church record year closest to the end of the specified year. After consultation with denominational officials, church schedules were sent to individual churches. Bureau agents visited churches that did not respond. No effort was made to tabulate African American members of primarily white local churches. The Censuses of Religious Bodies, which provided a check against ex-

Table B. Non–African American Denominations

Denomination	1906	1916	1926	1936
Methodist Episcopal	308,551	320,025	332,345 45% urban 55% rural	193,761 55% urban 45% rural
Roman Catholic	44,982	51,688	124,324 85.9% urban 14.1% rural	137,684 80% urban 20% rural
Baptists, Northern Convention	32,639	53,842	— [h]	45,821 99% urban 1% rural
Presbyterian Church in the United States	27,799	31,957	37,090 72.4% urban 10.3% rural	2,971 [i] 92% urban 8% rural
Episcopal	19,089	23,775	1,502 89.7% urban 10.3% rural	29,738 92% urban 8% rural

aggerated denominational claims, were generally well-received, especially by religious groups that lacked independent mechanisms for gathering statistical information at a national level and on a state-by-state basis. The 1926 enumeration is generally considered the most reliable; it is discussed at length in C. Luther Fry, *The U.S. Looks at Its Churches* (New York: Institute of Social and Religious Research, 1930). For a fuller discussion of statistics on religious affiliation gathered by the federal government, see Benson Y. Landis, "A Guide to the Literature on Statistics of Religious Affiliation with References to Related Social Studies," *Journal of the American Statistical Association* 54 (June 1959): 335–57.

a. The South as here defined includes Maryland, Virginia, West Virginia, North Carolina, South Carolina, Georgia, Florida, Missouri, Kentucky, Tennessee, Alabama, Mississippi, Louisiana, Arkansas, Texas, and the District of Columbia.

b. The U.S. Census Bureau mistakenly assumed that the schism of 1915 in the National Baptist Convention had been overcome and so reported no separate figures for the National Baptist Convention, Inc., the Boyd-Jones faction.

c. The 1926 census used "Negro Baptists" as a general category to include the National Baptist Convention, U.S.A., the National Baptist Convention, Inc., and African Americans who were members of the Northern Baptist Convention. The 1926 census, generally considered the most complete of the four, was the first to compile separate totals for rural and urban memberships. Members of churches in cities or other incorporated places with at least 2,500 inhabitants as of January 1, 1920, were classified as urban. About 75 percent of the African American churches reported in 1926 were located in places defined as rural.

d. The 1936 census used "Negro Baptists" to include both of the National Baptist Conventions. African Americans in the Northern Baptist Convention were reported separately. The Colored Primitive Baptists were credited with 43,897 members.

e. Founded by William S. Crowdy.

f. Led by C. P. Jones. Existing but not reported until 1926.

g. Led by Charles Mason. Existing but not reported until 1926.

h. Reported with the National Baptists in 1926.

i. The Colored Cumberland Presbyterian Church had 10,668 members in 1936, more African American members than the total number credited to white Presbyterian organizations, North and South, in 1936.

NOTES

INTRODUCTION

1 Henry Nash Smith, *Virgin Land: The American West as Symbol and Myth* (New York: Vintage Books, 1950). This classic account discusses the impact of Turner's essay, "The Significance of the Frontier in American History" (presented to American Historical Association, 1893) in chap. 22.

2 Bernard A. Weisberger, "The Immigrant Within," *American Heritage* 22 (December 1970): 32.

3 Spencer R. Crew, *Field to Factory: Afro-American Migration, 1915–1940* (Washington, D.C.: Smithsonian Institution Press, 1987). For a review of the exhibit, see James Borchert, "Field to Factory," *Journal of American History* 76 (June 1989): 224–28.

4 "'Field to Factory' to Alaska," *Ebony* 45 (September 1990): 90ff. The article notes that the exhibit evoked individual memories of leaving the "Lower 48." An estimated 15,000 African Americans lived in Alaska in 1990.

5 For a review of the literature up to the 1990s, see Joe William Trotter, Jr., "Black Migration in Historical Perspective," in *The Great Migration in Historical Perspective,* ed. Joe William Trotter, Jr. (Bloomington: Indiana University Press, 1991), pp. 1–21. Several of the essays in this collection attempt to offer new perspectives on the Great Migration by discussing gender questions and dealing more explicitly with the role of southern blacks in shaping their own movement. None of the authors gives adequate attention to the church.

6 No better barometer of the well-being and maturation of African American religious

studies exists than the back issues of the *Newsletter of the Afro-American Religious History Group.*

7   Allan Spear, *Black Chicago: The Making of a Negro Ghetto, 1890–1920* (Chicago: University of Chicago Press, 1967), pp. 174–75.

8   Anthropologists and sociologists, like historians, have used the methodological framework of "protest" and "accommodation" in their attempts at social-scientific description and classification of various African American religious groups. More so than some scholars, Hans A. Baer and Merrill Singer are sensitive to the dialectical tension between "accommodation" and "protest" in *African-American Religion in the Twentieth Century: Varieties of Protest and Accommodation* (Knoxville: University of Tennessee Press, 1992).

9   Joseph R. Washington, Jr., charges that Jackson primarily used his "political talents to maintain his position as head of his Baptist convention" and contributed to the otherworldliness of black folk religion by repressing those who wanted to engage in civil rights activism. See Joseph R. Washington, Jr., *Black Religion: The Negro and Christianity in the United States* (Boston: Beacon Press, 1964), pp. 67–69. See also Peter J. Paris, *Black Leaders in Conflict: Joseph H. Jackson, Martin Luther King, Jr., Malcolm X, Adam Clayton Powell, Jr.* (New York: Pilgrim Press, 1978). Anti-Jackson ministers, supported by Martin Luther King, Jr., and other civil rights activists, organized the Progressive National Baptist Convention in 1961.

10 Baer and Singer, *African-American Religion*, p. 147.

11 See table A in the Appendix, p. 252.

12 Somewhat in the vein of W. E. B. Du Bois's monumental *The Souls of Black Folk* (1903), black liberation theologians and cultural nationalists of more recent decades have looked for and celebrated the distinctive "genius" of African American religion. They found it by pointing to a cultural baseline in the "folk religion" of the black rural South. See James H. Cone, *The Spirituals and the Blues* (New York: Seabury Press, 1972).

13 Charles S. Johnson, "Illinois: Mecca of the Migrant Mob," *Messenger* 5 (December 1923): 928.

14 Randall K. Burkett and David W. Wills discuss the scholarly orthodoxy that posits a decline of black mainline denominations in the interwar period and the flourishing of the so-called sects and cults in an unpublished paper, "Afro-American Religious History, 1919–1939: A Resource Guide and Bibliographical Essay." Manuscript in my possession.

15 Carole Marks, *Farewell—We're Good and Gone: The Great Black Migration* (Bloomington: Indiana University Press, 1989), pp. 32–44. The question of whether participants in the Great Migration came directly off farms or had spent some time in a southern city may not be that significant in relation to my narrative and analysis. Even migrants with some urban experience in the South brought a religious culture into the Promised Land that differed from that which they encountered among the Old Settlers in Chicago and other northern industrial centers. More than 800,000 African Americans migrated to southern cities from 1900 through 1920. Many of these destinations, though defined as urban by the census takers, were small towns with rural cultures and outlooks.

16 Nicholas Lemann, *The Promised Land: The Great Black Migration and How It Changed America* (New York: Random House, 1991).

17 Tom Bethell, "Original Sin in the Promised Land," *American Spectator* 24 (June 1991): 9–11.

18 Baer and Singer, *African-American Religion,* p. 47.

I DOWN IN EGYPTLAND

1 "Anthony Crawford," *Crisis* 13 (December 1916): 67; *Crisis* 13 (January 1917): 120; Roy Nash, "The Lynching of Anthony Crawford," *Independent* 88 (December 11, 1916): 456–62; Allen B. Ballard, *One More Day's Journey: The Story of a Family and a People* (New York: McGraw-Hill, 1984), pp. 156–59.

2 C. Vann Woodward, *Origins of the New South, 1877–1913* (Baton Rouge: Louisiana State University Press, 1966), p. 352.

3 For statistics, see *Thirty Years of Lynching in the United States, 1889–1918* (New York: NAACP, 1919), p. 30; Southern Commission on the Study of Lynchings, *Lynchings and What They Mean* (Atlanta: Southern Commission on the Study of Lynchings, 1931), pp. 8–10; and Arthur F. Raper, *The Tragedy of Lynching* (Chapel Hill: University of North Carolina Press, 1933), pp. 480–83.

4 Edward E. Lewis, *The Mobility of the Negro* (1931; repr., New York: AMS Press, 1968), pp. 12–20. For a detailed discussion of African American migration from the South that employs the push-pull paradigm, see George A. Davis and O. Fred Donaldson, *Blacks in the United States: A Geographic Perspective* (Boston: Houghton Mifflin, 1975), pp. 53–93.

5 John Samuel Ezell, *The South Since 1865* (New York: Macmillan, 1963), p. 191. For a historiography of migration studies, see Joe William Trotter, Jr., "Black Migration in Historical Perspective," in *The Great Migration in Historical Perspective: New Dimensions of Race, Class, and Gender,* ed. Joe William Trotter, Jr. (Bloomington: Indiana University Press, 1991), pp. 1–21.

6 Cited in Loren Schweninger, *Black Property Owners in the South, 1790–1915* (Urbana: University of Illinois Press, 1990), p. 235.

7 August Meier, *Negro Thought in America, 1880–1915* (Ann Arbor: University of Michigan Press, 1963), p. 106.

8 *Atlanta Constitution,* December 10, 1916.

9 Cited in Waldo E. Martin, Jr., *The Mind of Frederick Douglass* (Chapel Hill: University of North Carolina Press), p. 72.

10 Cited in Leon F. Litwack, *Been in the Storm So Long: The Aftermath of Slavery* (New York: Random House, 1979), p. 218.

11 See Jay R. Mandle, *The Roots of Black Poverty: The Southern Plantation Economy After the Civil War* (Durham, N.C.: Duke University Press, 1978); James L. Roark, *Masters Without Slaves: Southern Planters in the Civil War and Reconstruction* (New York: W. W. Norton, 1977); Manning Marable, "The Land Question in Historical Perspective: The Economics of Poverty in the Blackbelt South, 1865–1920," in *The Black Rural Landowner—Endangered Species: Social, Political, and Economic Considerations,* ed. Leo McGee and Robert Bone (Westport, Conn.: Greenwood Press, 1979), pp. 165–206; and

Robert Higgs, *Competition and Coercion: Blacks in the American Economy, 1865–1914* (New York: Cambridge University Press, 1977).

12   Norman L. Crockett, *The Black Towns* (Lawrence: Regents Press of Kansas, 1979), pp. xii–xiii.

13   Nell Irvin Painter, *Exodusters: Black Migration to Kansas After Reconstruction* (New York: Alfred A. Knopf, 1977), pp. 175–83.

14   Cited in Martin, *Mind of Frederick Douglass*, pp. 76–77.

15   Painter, *Exodusters*, p. 260. See also Arvarh Strickland, "Toward the Promised Land: The Exodus to Kansas and Afterward," *Missouri Historical Review* 69 (July 1975): 376–412.

16   Carter G. Woodson characterized the largest number of these pre–World War I migrants as members of the "intelligent laboring class." See chap. 7 on "The Talented Tenth" in Carter G. Woodson, *A Century of Negro Migration* (Washington, D.C.: Association for the Study of Negro Life and History, 1918).

17   Allan H. Spear, *Black Chicago: The Making of a Negro Ghetto, 1890–1920* (Chicago: University of Chicago Press, 1967), pp. 39–40.

18   For more on Grady and southern white paternalism during the New South era, see George Fredrickson, *The Black Image in the White Mind* (New York: Harper and Row, 1971), chap. 7. See also Woodward, *Origins of the New South*, pp. 145–47, and Joel Williamson, *The Crucible of Race* (New York: Oxford University Press), pp. 100–104.

19   The Plessy case centered on the constitutionality of a Louisiana law that mandated "equal but separate accommodations for the white and colored races" on all passenger trains in the state. For a detailed examination of the case that attempts to explain why it evoked surprisingly little public attention at the time, see Charles A. Lofgren, *The Plessy Case: A Legal-Historical Interpretation* (New York: Oxford University Press, 1987), pp. 198–99.

20   Ray Stannard Baker, *Following the Color Line: American Negro Citizenship in the Progressive Era,* intro. Dewey W. Grantham, Jr. (1908; repr., New York: Harper and Row, 1964), p. 34. The classic study of the evolution and implementation of Jim Crow is C. Vann Woodward, *The Strange Career of Jim Crow* (New York: Oxford University Press, 1966). On the historical debate over Woodward's thesis of the origins of "Jim Crow," see Howard N. Rabinowitz, "More Than the Woodward Thesis: Assessing *The Strange Career of Jim Crow,*" *Journal of American History* 75 (December 1988): 842–56. Rabinowitz argues that it was normally the exclusion of blacks rather than integration that segregation replaced.

21   Cited in Woodward, *Origins of the New South*, p. 257.

22   The Populist leader Tom Watson's abandonment of southern blacks was typical of the political use of race. See C. Vann Woodward, *Tom Watson, Agrarian Rebel* (New York: Macmillan, 1938).

23   J. Morgan Kousser, *The Shaping of Southern Politics: Suffrage Restriction and the Establishment of the One-Party South, 1888–1910* (New Haven, Conn.: Yale University Press, 1974), pp. 104–30.

24   Cited in Woodward, *Strange Career of Jim Crow*, p. 96. Charles Chesnutt, *The Marrow of Tradition* (Boston: Houghton, Mifflin, 1901). On Chesnutt's ambivalent feelings about black life and culture in the South, see Williamson, *Crucible of Race,* pp. 61–66.

25 S. W. Layten, "A Northern Phase of a Southern Problem," *AME Church Review* 26 (March 1910): 315. For a brief but informative essay on the movement North of African American women, see Jacqueline Jones, *Labor of Love, Labor of Sorrow* (New York: Basic Books, 1985), chap. 5, "'To Get Out of This Land of Sufring': Black Women Migrants to the North, 1900–1930."

26 Quoted from Layten, "Northern Phase of a Southern Problem," p. 323.

27 Pete Daniel, *The Shadow of Slavery: Peonage in the South, 1901–1969* (Urbana: University of Illinois Press, 1972).

28 For a detailed analysis of the census of 1910, see Thomas Jesse Jones, "The Negroes of the Southern States and the U.S. Census of 1910," *Southern Workman* 41 (August 1912): 459–72. For discussion of the statistical high tide of blacks in both the rural United States and in the South, see T. Lynn Smith, "The Redistribution of the Negro Population of the United States, 1910–1960," *Journal of Negro History* 51 (July 1966): 155–73; and John Fraser Hart, "The Changing Distribution of the American Negro," *Annals of the Association of American Geographers* 50 (1960): 242–66. Also see U.S. Bureau of the Census, *Negro Population, 1790–1915* (1918; repr., New York: Arno Press, 1968), pp. 40–41.

29 T. J. Woofter, Jr., "The Negroes of Athens, Georgia," Phelps-Stokes Fellowship Studies, no. 1, *Bulletin of the University of Georgia* 14 (December 1913): 5.

30 Bernard Walter Hill, "Rural Survey of Clarke County, Georgia, with Special Reference to the Negroes," Phelps-Stokes Fellowship Studies, no. 2, *Bulletin of the University of Georgia* 15 (March 1915): 53. Hill notes that when blacks migrated into Clarke County from other parts of the South, they attended local churches but were "very loathe" to give up memberships in the churches from which they came.

31 Howard N. Rabinowitz, *Race Relations in the Urban South, 1865–1890* (New York: Oxford University Press, 1978); John Kellogg, "Negro Urban Clusters in the Postbellum South," *Geographical Review* 67 (July 1977): 310–21; John Cell, *The Highest Stage of White Supremacy: The Origins of Segregation in South Africa and the American South* (New York: Cambridge University Press, 1982).

32 See *Some Efforts of American Negroes for Their Own Social Betterment*, ed. W. E. B. Du Bois (Atlanta: Atlanta University Press, 1898), p. 51.

33 Roswell F. Jackson and Rosalyn M. Patterson, "A Brief History of Selected Black Churches in Atlanta, Georgia," *Journal of Negro History* 74 (1989): 37; Ralph E. Luker, "Missions, Institutional Churches, and Settlement Houses: The Black Experience, 1885–1910," *Journal of Negro History* 69 (Summer/Fall 1984): 106–7; John Dittmer, *Black Georgia in the Progressive Era, 1900–1920* (Urbana: University of Illinois Press, 1977), pp. 63–64. On the Atlanta riot, see Charles Crowe, "Racial Violence and Social Reform—Origins of the Atlanta Riot of 1906," *Journal of Negro History* 53 (July 1968): 234–56, and "Racial Massacre in Atlanta, Sep. 22, 1906," *Journal of Negro History* 54 (April 1969): 150–75.

34 James Samuel Stemons, "The Industrial Color Line in the North and the Remedy," *AME Church Review* 14 (January 1898): 346–48, 354–55.

35 Richard R. Wright, Jr., "The Negroes of Philadelphia," *AME Church Review* 23 (July 1907): 33. The essay is continued in the October 1907 issue where Wright notes that the majority of Philadelphia's working poor were southerners who left "as they say, 'to

better their condition.'" But for many migrants, "rosy pictures" of the North had already faded (p. 143). Wright also wrote a series of four articles on the subject, "The Economic Condition of Negroes in the North," for the *Southern Workman,* published in the March 1910, May 1911, December 1911, and January 1912 issues.

36 W. E. B. Du Bois, "The Problem of Work," *AME Church Review* 19 (October 1903): 163.

37 William Howard Taft, "The Spirit of Hampton," *Southern Workman* 43 (July 1914): 410. Hollis B. Frissell, head of Hampton Institute, wrote in 1915, "Men like Mr. Carnegie and Mr. Taft are impressed with the great advantage which the South has over other parts of the country in having a homogeneous body of laborers, all of them speaking the English language and most of them professing the Christian religion. They are also of a peaceable nature, which makes the strikes and labor uprisings of the North well nigh unknown in this part of the country." See Frissell, "Rural Segregation," *Southern Workman* 44 (March 1915): 137.

38 Robert R. Moton, "The Negro and the South's Industrial Life," *Southern Workman* 43 (July 1914): 413.

39 C. T. Shaffer, "Shall the Negro Leave the South?," *AME Church Review* 19 (October 1903): 144, 146. Shaffer eventually went to Liberia where he secured a hundred acres near Arthington and founded Shaffer Boys' High School.

40 E. C. Branson, "The Negro Working Out His Own Salvation," *Southern Workman* 43 (April 1914): 253.

41 *New York Age,* May 2, 1912.

42 George E. Haynes, *The Negro at Work in New York City: A Study in Economic Progress* (New York: Columbia University Press, 1912), chap. 1.

43 George E. Haynes, "The Movement of Negroes from the Country to the City," *Southern Workman* 42 (April 1913): 231. Haynes endorsed the Hampton and Tuskegee programs to improve rural conditions and called for cooperation in showing the disadvantages of "rushing to the city." But he also predicted that black urbanization would continue and asked for a new alliance between the agrarians and his National League on Urban Conditions to help migrants prepare for city life "while the movement is in its infancy."

44 Lilian Brandt, "The Make-Up of Negro City Groups," *Charities,* October 7, 1905, p. 7. Also see Booker T. Washington, "The Rural Negro and the South," in *Proceedings of the National Conference of Charities and Corrections* 41 (1914): 121–27.

45 Thomas Nelson Page, *The Negro: The Southerner's Problem* (New York: Charles Scribner's Sons, 1904), p. 286.

46 J. B. Gambrell, "The Race Question in the South," in *The Home Mission Task,* ed. Victor I. Masters (Atlanta: Home Mission Board of the Southern Baptist Convention, 1912), pp. 175, 177, 186.

47 Cited in Louis R. Harlan, *Booker T. Washington: The Making of a Black Leader, 1856–1901* (New York: Oxford University Press, 1972), p. 225.

48 W. E. B. Du Bois, *The Souls of Black Folk: Essays and Sketches* (Chicago: A. C. McClurg, 1903). On the Du Bois-Washington debate, see August Meier, *Negro Thought in America, 1880–1915: Racial Ideologies in the Age of Booker T. Washington* (Ann Arbor: University of Michigan Press, 1963), part 5.

49   Williamson, *Crucible of Race,* p. 75.

50   Cited in the *Springfield Republican,* c. 1916, TCF, Reel 5.

51   John H. Stanfield, *Philanthropy and Jim Crow in American Social Science* (Westport, Conn.: Greenwood Press, 1985), pp. 27–28.

52   For primary and secondary materials on the controversy over the film, see Fred Silva, comp., *Focus on* The Birth of a Nation (Englewood Cliffs, N.J.: Prentice-Hall, 1971). The integrationist response to *The Birth of a Nation* is discussed by Thomas Cripps, "Following the Paper Trail to the Birth of a Race (1918) and Its Times," *Film and History* 18 (1988): 50–62.

53   Williamson, *Crucible of Race,* p. 323.

54   Cited in Linda O. McMurry, *Recorder of the Black Experience: A Biography of Monroe Nathan Work* (Baton Rouge: Louisiana State University Press, 1985), p. 71. In an autobiographical sketch, written in 1940, Work stated, "When I came to Tuskegee, educators and others seeking to advance the interest of the Negro were confronted with such questions as: What has the Negro accomplished? What can he do? Does it pay to educate him? Morally and physically, is he not deteriorating? Has his emancipation been justified? The publication, by Hoffman in 1896 of 'Race Traits and Tendencies of the Negro,' presented a more or less hopeless view. To the indictment of this publication there was no effective answer. From 1908 on I was compiling a day by day record of what was taking place with reference to the Negro. Thus it became possible to answer in a factual manner questions relating to all matters concerning him." Quoted from a manuscript in the Monroe Nathan Work Papers, Tuskegee Institute Archives, by McMurry, *Recorder of the Black Experience,* p. 71.

55   Monroe Work, "Fifty Years of Negro Progress," *Southern Workman* 42 (January 1913): 9–15.

56   "The Exodus," *AME Church Review* 33 (January 1917): 149. Contemporary studies of the Great Migration gave primacy to the economic draw of the North and were influenced by wartime considerations. James H. Dillard, Emmett J. Scott, and George E. Haynes worked for the federal government. "By emphasizing economic motivations," James R. Grossman writes, "they reflected the Wilson administration's hope that the migration, with its unsettling effects on both Northern cities and the Southern labor market, would abate after the war boom." Grossman, *"Land of Hope": Chicago, Black Southerners, and the Great Migration* (Chicago: University of Chicago Press, 1989), p. 15.

57   June Sochen, *The Unbridgeable Gap: Blacks and Their Quest for the American Dream, 1900–1930* (Chicago: Rand McNally, 1972), p. 17.

58   John D. Anderson, *The Education of Blacks in the South, 1860–1935* (Chapel Hill: University of North Carolina Press, 1988), chaps. 2 and 7. Curricular changes in the late 1920s came about primarily because of student demands for a more academically challenging collegiate education. See Raymond Wolters, *The New Negro on Campus: Black College Rebellions of the 1920s* (Princeton, N.J.: Princeton University Press, 1975).

59   *Christian Recorder,* May 13, 1915.

60   Gilbert C. Fite, *Cotton Fields No More: Southern Agriculture, 1865–1980* (Lexington: University Press of Kentucky, 1984), pp. 93–95. See also C. T. Revere, "Effect of the War on Cotton," *North American Review* 200 (October 1914): 549–58.

61 Cited in Fite, *Cotton Fields No More,* p. 94. See also "Cotton's Magical Rise Enriching the Nation," *Literary Digest,* December 9, 1916, pp. 1517–22.

62 *Voice of the People,* February 5, 1916.

63 Lucius H. Holsey, "Race Segregation," in *The Possibilities of the Negro in Symposium,* ed. Willis B. Parks, as discussed in Clarence A. Bacote, "Negro Proscriptions, Protests, and Proposed Solutions in Georgia, 1880–1908," *Journal of Southern History* 25 (November 1959): 471–98.

64 Cited from the *Savannah Tribune,* January 18, 1902, by Bacote, "Negro Proscriptions," p. 179.

65 W. E. B. Du Bois, *Black Reconstruction in America: An Essay Toward a History of the Part Which Black Folk Played in the Attempt to Reconstruct Democracy in America, 1860–1880.* New York: Atheneum, 1977 (orig. pub. 1935), p. 124.

66 Cited in Leon Litwack, *Been in the Storm So Long* (New York: Vintage Books, 1979), p. 458.

67 Daniel A. Payne, *Recollections of Seventy Years* (Nashville: A.M.E. Sunday School Union, 1888), pp. 220–32.

68 William Wells Brown, *My Southern Home: or, The South and Its People* (Boston: A. G. Brown, 1880), pp. 90–97.

69 Lille B. Chace Wyman, "Colored Churches and Schools in the South," *New England Magazine* 3 (February 1891): 785–96. For a sympathetic critique of black church life by a white southern progressive, see W. D. Weatherford, *Negro Life in the South* (New York: Association Press, 1911), chapter 5.

70 W. E. B. Du Bois, ed., *The Negro Church* (Atlanta: Atlanta University Press, 1903). More than 200 pages and filled with tables, quotations from the surveys, and other valuable primary material, the Atlanta study deserves greater scholarly attention than it has received. On the significance of the Atlanta conferences within the Social Gospel movement, see Ralph E. Luker, *The Social Gospel in Black and White: American Racial Reform, 1885–1912* (Chapel Hill: University of North Carolina Press, 1991), pp. 183–84. Also see Clarence A. Bacote, *The Story of Atlanta University: A Century of Service, 1865–1965* (Atlanta: Atlanta University Press, 1969), pp. 132–39.

71 W. H. Holloway, "A Black Belt County, Georgia," in Du Bois, ed., *Negro Church,* pp. 57–64.

72 "A Southern City," in Du Bois, ed., *Negro Church,* pp. 69–79.

73 Du Bois, ed., *Negro Church,* p. 208.

74 Ibid., p. 161.

75 W. E. B. Du Bois, unsigned editorial, *Crisis* 4 (May 1912): 24–25. Du Bois's attitude toward the black church was often ambivalent. He bowed with respect before what the church had accomplished. Yet he was at odds with the conservative black clergy on the question of mixing religion and political protest. See Manning Marable, "The Black Faith of W. E. B. Du Bois: Sociocultural and Political Dimensions of Black Religion," *Southern Quarterly* 23 (Spring 1985): 15–33. See also Robert M. Franklin, "The Legacy of W. E. Burghardt Du Bois in Afro-American Religious Scholarship," *Criterion* 23 (Autumn 1984): 8–12.

76 W. E. B. Du Bois, unsigned editorial, *Crisis* 6 (October 1913): 290–91.

77 Du Bois, ed., *Negro Church,* p. 164.

78 Ibid., pp. 203–4.

79 Ibid., p. 204.

80 Ibid., p. 119.

81 J. E. Davis, "Tuskegee Institute and Its Conferences," *Southern Workman* 43 (March 1914): 158–62. For a fuller discussion of the role of the Tuskegee Negro Conference and the agrarian Social Gospel, see Allen W. Jones, "The Role of Tuskegee Institute in the Education of Black Farmers," *Journal of Negro History* 60 (April 1975): 252–67. Beginning in 1894, Washington added a second day, known as the workers' conference, for the benefit of teachers from black institutions of higher learning in the South. In 1906 Tuskegee began operating the "Jesup Agricultural Wagon" which went out into various communities to demonstrate improved farming methods. By 1910 the school had an extension department that helped to spread the results of the experiments of George Washington Carver, head of the school's division of agriculture.

82 *Negro Farmer,* February 14, 1914.

83 *Negro Farmer,* April 25, 1914.

84 *Negro Farmer,* February 27, 1915.

85 *Principal's Annual Report* (Tuskegee, Ala.: Tuskegee Normal and Industrial Institute, 1919), p. 14. For additional details on the Bible Training School, see Tuskegee Institute, *Tuskegee to Date* (Tuskegee, Ala.: Tuskegee Normal and Industrial Institute, 1915), p. 11.

86 *Negro Farmer,* December 4, 1915.

87 *Negro Farmer and Messenger,* June 17, 1916.

88 G. Lake Imes, "The Negro Minister and Country Life," *Religious Education* 7 (1912): 172–73, 175.

89 Cited in "Life Conditions in the City and in the Country," *New York Age,* May 2, 1912.

90 Luker, *Social Gospel in Black and White,* pp. 125–32.

91 William Anthony Aery, "The Hampton Farmers' Conference," *Southern Workman* 41 (1912): 234–35. By 1927 Hampton had hosted 857 different clergymen at the ministers' conferences. "The Ministers' Conference," *Southern Workman* 56 (August 1927): 354–55.

92 William Anthony Aery, "The Fifteenth Hampton Negro Conference, 1911," *Southern Workman* 40 (September 1911): 508.

93 W. E. B. Du Bois, "Religion in the South," chap. 4 of Booker T. Washington and W. E. B. Du Bois, *The Negro in the South,* intro. Herbert Aptheker (1907; repr., New York: Citadel Press, 1970), p. 126.

2 "NORTHBOUND THEIR CRY"

1 On the "shattering of hope" among the post-1890 generation of neoabolitionists, see James M. McPherson, *The Abolitionist Legacy: From Reconstruction to the NAACP* (Princeton, N.J.: Princeton University Press, 1975), chap. 16.

2 Carter G. Woodson, *A Century of Negro Migration* (1918; repr., New York: AMS Press, 1970), pref., and pp. 167, 183, 192.

3 Charles Wesley, "Book Review, *A Century of Negro Migration,*" *Journal of Negro History* 4 (July 1919): 341–42.

4 Some of the more important studies of the causes and effects of the Great Migration, written while it was in progress or shortly thereafter, include Emmett J. Scott, *Negro Migration During the War* (1920; repr., New York: Arno Press, 1969); U.S. Department of Labor, Division of Negro Economics, *Negro Migration in 1916–17*, intro. J. H. Dillard (Washington, D.C.: U.S. Government Printing Office, 1919); Abraham Epstein, *The Negro in Pittsburgh* (Pittsburgh: University of Pittsburgh Press, 1918); and Carter G. Woodson, *Century of Negro Migration*, chap. 9. A valuable tool for access to publications concerning the Great Migration is Frank A. Ross and Louise Veneable Kennedy, *A Bibliography of Negro Migration* (New York: Columbia University Press, 1934). For a useful collection of primary sources, see Robert B. Grant, ed., *The Black Man Comes to the City: A Documentary Account from the Great Migration to the Great Depression, 1915–1930* (Chicago: Nelson Hall, 1972). Of the many more recent secondary sources, special note should be given to Florette Henri's very readable *Black Migration: Movement North, 1900–1920* (Garden City, N.Y.: Anchor Books/Doubleday, 1976). For an evaluation of migration studies, see Joe William Trotter, Jr., "Black Migration in Historical Perspective," in Trotter, ed., *The Great Migration in Historical Perspective: New Dimensions of Race, Class, and Gender* (Bloomington: Indiana University Press, 1991), pp. 1–22.

5 Charles S. Johnson, "Substitution of Negro Labor for European Immigrant Labor," *Proceedings of the National Conference of Social Work* (1926), p. 320.

6 U.S. Department of Labor, *Negro Migration*, pp. 7–8. Haynes began his duties on May 1, 1918, with the title of director of Negro economics in the investigation and inspection service of the Department of Labor. For details on Haynes's activities, see Daniel Perlman, "Stirring the White Conscience: The Life of George Edmund Haynes" (Ph.D. diss., New York University, 1972), pp. 129–39. Also see James B. Stewart, "The Rise and Fall of Negro Economics: The Economic Thought of George Edmund Haynes," *American Economic Review* 81 (May 1991): 311–14; and Samuel K. Roberts, "George Edmund Haynes: Advocate for Interracial Cooperation," in *Black Apostles*, ed. Randall K. Burkett and Richard Newman (Boston: G. K. Hall, 1978), pp. 97–127.

7 Tipton Ray Snavely, "The Exodus of Negroes from the Southern States: Alabama and North Carolina," in U.S. Department of Labor, *Negro Migration*, p. 52.

8 Littell McClung, "'Our Labor Is Leaving—What Are We Going to Do?' Yes, What?," *Montgomery Advertiser,* September 24, 1916.

9 "Sees Great Negro Migration," c. 1916, TCF, Reel 5.

10 Jay R. Mandle, *The Roots of Black Poverty* (Durham, N.C.: Duke University Press, 1978), p. 74. On various estimates of the magnitude of the Great Migration, see Henderson H. Donald, "The Negro Migration of 1916–1918," *Journal of Negro History* 6 (October 1921): 403–4, and Henri, *Black Migration*, pp. 51, 70–72. The sources and quality of migration data are examined in Daniel M. Johnson and Rex R. Campbell, *Black Migration in America: A Social Demographic History* (Durham, N.C.: Duke University Press, 1981), pp. 71–89.

11 U.S. Bureau of the Census, *Negroes in the United States, 1920–32* (Washington, D.C.: U.S. Government Printing Office, 1935), p. 5; LaVerne Beles, "Negro Enumeration of 1920," *Scientific American* 14 (April 1922): 352–60; Kelly Miller, "Enumeration Errors

in Negro Population," *Scientific American* 14 (February 1922): 168–77; and V. D. Johnston, "Negro Migration and the Census of 1920," *Opportunity* 1 (June 1923): 235–38.

12 Scott, *Negro Migration,* p. 3. Scott drew on the research of Monroe Work and Charles S. Johnson. Work was director of Tuskegee's Division of Records and Research and edited the *Negro Year Book.* Johnson, then a graduate student of the University of Chicago, is perhaps best-known for his classic study *Shadow of the Plantation,* published in 1934. Work also gives credit to T. Thomas Fortune, the African American author and former editor of the well-regarded *New York Age,* though Fortune provided little assistance.

13 James W. Johnson to Charles S. Johnson, January 17, 1918, NAACP Papers, Library of Congress, Washington, D.C.

14 Scott, *Negro Migration,* p. 53.

15 Harold M. Baron offers this helpful summary of the magnitude of the Great Migration: "Migration out of the countryside started in 1915 and swept to a human tide by 1917. The major movement was to Northern cities, so that between 1910 and 1920 the black population increased in Chicago from 44,000 to 109,000; in New York from 92,000 to 152,000; in Detroit from 6,000 to 41,000; and in Philadelphia from 84,000 to 134,000. That decade there was a net increase of 322,000 in the number of Southern born blacks living in the North, exceeding the aggregate increase of the preceding 40 years. A secondary movement took place to Southern cities, especially those with ship-building and heavy industry." Harold M. Baron, "The Demand for Black Labor," in *Racial Conflict, Discrimination and Power: Historical and Contemporary Studies,* ed. William Barclay, Krishna Kumar, and Ruth P. Simms (New York: AMS Press, 1976), p. 105.

16 *National Baptist Union Review,* June 3, 1916.

17 Duckrey is a central figure in black Philadelphia's folklore of the Great Migration. See Charles Ashley Hardy III, "Race and Opportunity: Black Philadelphia During the Era of the Great Migration, 1916–1930" (Ph.D. diss., Temple University, 1989), pp. 75, 117 n. 11. Also see Ralph H. Jones, *Charles Albert Tindley: Prince of Preachers* (Nashville: Abingdon Press, 1982), p. 81.

18 Francis D. Tyson, "The Negro Migrant in the North," in U.S. Department of Labor, *Negro Migration,* p. 123.

19 Cited in Hardy, "Race and Opportunity," p. 385.

20 Scott, *Negro Migration,* p. 55.

21 *Philadelphia Record,* March 5, 1917. The Pennsylvania and Erie Railroad abandoned its policy of free transportation in September 1917.

22 Robert Gregg, *Sparks from the Anvil of Oppression* (Philadelphia: Temple University Press, 1993), p. 24.

23 From Sadie T. Mossell, "The Standard of Living among One Hundred Negro Migrant Families in Philadelphia," *Annals of the American Academy of Social and Political Science* 98 (November 1921): 174.

24 James R. Grossman, *"Land of Hope": Chicago, Black Southerners, and the Great Migration* (Chicago: University of Chicago Press, 1989), pp. 110–13.

25 As told to R. H. Leavell, "The Negro Migration from Mississippi with Special Reference to the Exodus to Northern Communities in 1916–17," in U.S. Department of

Labor, *Negro Migration*, p. 30. A variation of this colorful metaphor ("Negroes grab the *Defender* like a hungry mule grabs fodder.") was attributed by Charles S. Johnson to a black leader from Hattiesburg, Mississippi. See Charles Johnson, "Stimulation of the Movement," p. 2 in "Migration Study, Draft (Final) Chapters, 7–13" folder [1917], National Urban League Records, Series 6, Box 68, Library of Congress, Washington, D.C. I am indebted to James R. Grossman for this reference as well as for many of the details regarding Abbott, the influence of the *Chicago Defender,* and the migration to Chicago in general. See his *Land of Hope,* pp. 74–88.

26 *Chicago Defender,* February 10, 1917.

27 From letters collected by Emmett J. Scott, published as "Letters of Negro Migrants of 1916–1918," *Journal of Negro History* 4 (July 1919): 333–34.

28 James R. Grossman, "Blowing the Trumpet: The *Chicago Defender* and Black Migration During World War I," *Illinois Historical Journal* 78 (Summer 1985): 82–96.

29 Quoted by Scott, *Negro Migration,* p. 30.

30 *Macon Telegraph,* June 14, 1917.

31 *Danville* (Ga.) *Register,* October 16, 1920.

32 "Chicago a Mecca for Negroes from South," *Birmingham Age-Herald,* May 12, 1917.

33 *Columbus* (Ohio) *Dispatch,* May 8, 1918.

34 See "Will Round Up 50 Bogus Pastors Fleecing Negroes," *Philadelphia North American,* 1917, TCF, Reel 6.

35 Cited W. E. B. Du Bois, "The Migration of Negroes," *Crisis* 14 (June 1917): 66.

36 Robert Gregg makes the helpful suggestion that we should think of the composition of the Great Migration as continuum between the two ideal types of the rural refugee pushed out and the urban migrant pulled northward. Gregg, *Sparks from the Anvil of Oppression,* pp. 150–51.

37 Scott, comp., "Letters of Negro Migrants," pp. 291–92, 293, 297, 299, 304, 308, 319.

38 *Southwestern Christian Advocate,* July 3, 1919.

39 Henri, *Black Migration,* p. 54.

40 George E. Haynes, *The Negro at Work in New York City: A Study in Economic Progress* (New York: Columbia University Press, 1912), p. 27.

41 On employment expectations and realities, see Grossman, *Land of Hope,* chaps. 7 and 8; Gottlieb, *Making Their Own Way,* chaps. 4, 5, and 6; Carol Marks, *Farewell—We're Good and Gone,* chaps. 4 and 5; and James Grossman, "The White Man's Union: The Great Migration and the Resonance of Race and Class in Chicago, 1916–1922," in Trotter, ed., *The Great Migration,* pp. 83–105.

42 R. R. Downs, "How We Should Deal with Our People Who Are Migrating from the South," cited in Gregg, *Sparks from the Anvil of Oppression,* pp. 196–97.

43 Cited in *Atlanta Constitution,* January 2, 1917.

44 *New York Times,* July 2, 1917.

45 Cited in "Negro Exodus from South Laid to Oppression," *New York Tribune,* July 8, 1917.

46 Henry Blumenthal, "Woodrow Wilson and the Race Question," *Journal of Negro History* 48 (January 1963): 1–21; John Morton Blum, *Woodrow Wilson and the Politics of Morality* (Boston: Little, Brown, 1956), pp. 115–16.

47 Robert Moats Miller, "The Protestant Churches and Lynching, 1919–1930," *Journal of Negro History* 42 (April 1957): 118–31. Also see John Lee Eighmy, "Religious Liberalism in the South During the Progressive Era," *Church History* 38 (September 1969): 359–72.

48 *Daily Herald,* March 15, 1918.

49 *Montgomery Advertiser,* January 6, 1917; *Atlanta Constitution,* February 7, 1923.

50 *Minutes of the University Commission on Southern Race Questions,* appendix, pp. 45–48; *Jackson* (Miss.) *News,* November 11, 1917.

51 *New York Age,* June 21, 1917.

52 W. E. B. Du Bois, "The Passing of 'Jim Crow,'" *New York Independent,* July 14, 1917, pp. 53–54.

53 *Atlanta Independent,* December 25, 1916; "New Allies—Floods and the Boll Weevil," *Survey,* March 17, 1917, pp. 695–96.

54 Robert Higgs, "The Boll Weevil, the Cotton Economy, and Black Migration, 1910–1930," *Agricultural History* 50 (April 1976): 335–50; Arthur F. Raper, *Preface to Peasantry: A Tale of Two Black Belt Counties* (Chapel Hill: University of North Carolina Press, 1936), pp. 183–224; Jack Temple Kirby, *Rural Worlds Lost: The American South, 1920–1960* (Baton Rouge: Louisiana State University Press, 1987), pp. 53–55.

55 *Montgomery Advertiser,* September 10, 1916.

56 *Montgomery Advertiser,* September 24, 1916.

57 James W. Johnson, "The Importance of the Negro to the South," in Views and Reviews, *New York Age,* 1916, HCF.

58 *Georgia Baptist,* October 5, 1916.

59 Letter, *Atlanta Independent,* March 17, 1917.

60 [W. E. B. Du Bois], "Mr. B. Weevil," *Crisis* 23 (January 1924): 104.

61 Jesse O. Thomas, "A Social Program to Help the Migrant," *Opportunity* 2 (March 1924): 71.

62 *New York Times,* June 13, 1917.

63 *New York Evening Post,* January 17, 1917.

64 *New York Post,* January 17, 1918. Reports on additional meetings held to discourage the exodus can be found in the *Macon Telegraph,* June 12, 1917, and the *New York Age,* February 1, 1917.

65 *Atlanta Constitution,* August 25, 1918.

66 *Macon Telegraph,* September 4, 1917.

67 *Montgomery Advertiser,* November 1, 1916.

68 Letter to the editor, *Montgomery Advertiser,* January 12, 1917.

69 For an examination of several of the most significant extensions of the Tuskegee educational formula, including the Snow Hill Institute in Wilcox County, Alabama, see Arnold Cooper, *Between Struggle and Hope: Four Black Educators in the South, 1894–1915* (Ames: Iowa State University Press, 1989). Also see Arnold Cooper, "'We Rise Upon the Structure We Ourselves Have Builded': William H. Holtzclaw and Utica Institute, 1903–1915," *Journal of Mississippi History* 45 (1985): 15–33.

70 "Migration," *Crisis* 12 (October 1916): 270.

71 "The Tuskegee Resolutions," *Crisis* 13 (March 1917): 219.

72   G. Douglas Johnson, "The Hegira," *Crisis* 13 (March 1917): 225.

73   Robert R. Moton, in "After the War: A Symposium," *Southern Workman* 48 (March 1919): 135.

74   *Amsterdam News*, November 8, 1916.

75   "Conference on Negro Migration of White and Negro Church Leaders, February 23, 1923, Under Auspices of Commission on the Church and Race Relations, Federal Council of Churches," *AME Church Review* (July 1923), p. 32.

76   "The Negro Migration Conference," *Southern Workman* 46 (March 1917): 135; *New York Age*, March 24, 1923.

77   Cited from a report on the conference in the *New York Evening Post*, January 24, 1917.

78   For a detailed account of the conference, see *New York Age*, February 1, 1917.

79   Citations from Elwood Street, "Southern Social Problems," *Southern Workman* 46 (September 1917): 474–75.

80   Cited in Henri, *Black Migration*, p. 269.

81   See the analysis by Trotter, "Black Migration in Historical Perspective," pp. 4–10. Trotter argues that the "race relations" model waned by the mid-1930s, giving way, in part, to the emergence of another brand of scholarship. Succeeding studies employed the social anthropological caste-class model (based on interdisciplinary social-science research), but they too slighted the religious dimension of the Great Migration. Cultural interpretations of the Great Migration have yet to appear on the order of that done for African American folk thought from slavery to freedom by Lawrence W. Levine, *Black Culture and Black Consciousness* (New York: Oxford University Press 1977).

82   U.S. Department of Labor, *Negro Migration in 1916–17*, p. 12.

83   Cited in Henri, *Black Migration*, p. 56.

84   Peter Gottlieb, "Rethinking the Great Migration: A Perspective from Pittsburgh," in Trotter, ed., *The Great Migration*, p. 71.

3   THE SECOND EXODUS

1   "Tanner on the Second Exodus," *New York Age*, April 5, 1917. Tanner's book, which he promised would be a "plain unvarnished tale" in twelve chapters, apparently was never published. I have been unable to discover additional information regarding it.

2   Cited from *New York Age*, February 8, 1917.

3   *Georgia Baptist*, December 15, 1916.

4   *Philadelphia Record*, March 5, 1917.

5   Hunter Dickinson Farish, *The Circuit Rider Dismounts* (Richmond: Dietz Press, 1938), pp. 229–300.

6   *Southwestern Christian Advocate*, September 7, 1916.

7   *Macon Telegraph*, as cited by the *New York Current*, December 13, 1916.

8   *Atlanta Constitution*, December 15, 1916.

9   "Should Negroes Come North?" Mother Bethel Information Bureau, flyer supplied by Robert S. Gregg.

10   Emmett J. Scott, *Negro Migration During the War* (1920; repr., New York: Arno Press, 1969), p. 16.

11   *Detroit Times*, April 12, 1918.

12 *Christian Recorder,* February 1, 1917.

13 Monroe N. Work, *Negro Year Book, 1918–1919, An Annual Encyclopedia of the Negro* (Tuskegee, Ala.: Negro Year Book, 1919), p. 9.

14 *Chicago Whip,* December 23, 1922.

15 This story was reported by Monroe Work in his background study for Emmett Scott's *Negro Migration During the War,* pp. 45–46.

16 *Christian Recorder,* February 1, 1917.

17 *Chicago Defender,* August 12, 1916.

18 Cited in the Chicago Commission on Race Relations, *The Negro in Chicago: A Study of Race Relations and a Race Riot* (Chicago: University of Chicago Press, 1922), p. 89.

19 *Crisis* 14 (July 1917): 145. Arna Bontemps and Jack Conroy, *They Seek a City* (Garden City, N.Y.: Doubleday, Doran, 1945), p. 132.

20 Cited in Scott, *Negro Migration,* p. 41.

21 Ibid.

22 *New York Evening Post,* November 17, 1916.

23 W. T. B. Williams, "The Negro Exodus from the South," in U.S. Department of Labor, Division of Negro Economics, *Negro Migration in 1916–17* (Washington, D.C.: U.S. Government Printing Office, 1919), p. 101.

24 W. E. Dancer, "Farewell! We're Good An' Gone," 1917, TCF, Reel 8.

25 Lucy Ariel Williams, "Northboun'," *The Negro Caravan,* ed. Sterling A. Brown (New York: Citadel Press, 1941), p. 377.

26 George E. Haynes, "Migration of Negroes into Northern Cities," *Proceedings of the National Conference of Social Work* 44 (1917): 496.

27 Monroe N. Work, "The Negro Migration," *Southern Workman* 53 (May 1924): 203.

28 *Afro-American,* January 26, 1918.

29 Cited in Bontemps and Conroy, *They Seek a City,* pp. 139–40.

30 *Richmond Planet,* April 28, 1917.

31 Thomas T. Woofter, *Southern Race Progress: The Wavering Color Line* (Washington, D.C.: Public Affairs Press, 1957), p. 59.

32 Scott, *Negro Migration,* p. 40; Arvarh E. Strickland, "The Strange Affair of the Boll Weevil: The Pest as Liberator," *Agricultural History* 68 (Spring 1994): 157–68.

33 W. O. Saunders, "Why Jim Crow Is Flying North," *Collier's,* December 8, 1923, p. 15.

34 *Atlanta Constitution,* November 28, 1916.

35 *Macon Telegraph,* June 12, 1917.

36 *Norfolk Journal and Guide,* February 20, 1917.

37 *Norfolk Journal and Guide,* December 30, 1922.

38 *Chicago Defender,* January 26, 1916.

39 *Birmingham Age Herald,* September 25, 1916.

40 *Atlanta Constitution,* August 30, 1917.

41 *Atlanta Constitution,* January 11, 1917.

42 Ibid.

43 *Christian Index,* as cited in *Palatka* (Fla.) *Advocate,* March 10, 1917.

44 *Chicago Defender,* August 26, 1916.

45 Letter to the editor, *Chicago Defender,* March 10, 1917.

46   *Columbia* (S.C.) *State,* November 1, 1916; *Charleston News Courier,* December 17, 1916.

47   *Charleston News Courier,* December 17, 1916.

48   *Atlanta Constitution,* January 9, 1917.

49   Scott, *Negro Migration,* pp. 39–40.

50   *New York Age,* April 5, 1917.

51   *Buffalo Times,* December 5, 1922.

52   *Columbia* (Ga.) *Enquirer-Sun,* February ?, 1922, HCF.

53   Examples of the depletion of congregations can be found in Scott, *Negro Migration During the War,* as well as in the background studies in the NAACP files, Library of Congress, Washington, D.C.

54   W. T. B. Williams, "The Negro Exodus from the South," in U.S. Department of Labor, *Negro Migration,* p. 95.

55   *Montgomery Advertiser,* March 24, 1917.

56   *Montgomery Advertiser,* February 19, 1917.

57   *Atlanta Constitution,* July 16, 1917; Henry H. Proctor, *Between Black and White: Autobiographical Sketches* (Boston: Pilgrim Press, 1925).

58   *Montgomery Advertiser,* January 25, 1917.

59   Memphis, date illegible, TCF, Reel 5.

60   *American Presbyterian,* November 11, 1916.

61   *New Orleans Picayune,* July 24, 1918.

62   *Crisis,* May 1919. On African American participation in World War I and details regarding antiblack sentiment on the home front, as demonstrated in the riot in Houston in August 1917, see Emmett J. Scott, *Scott's Official History of the American Negro in the World War* (Chicago: Home Press, 1919); Arthur E. Barbeau and Florette Henri, *Unknown Soldiers: Black American Troops in World War I* (Philadelphia: Temple University Press, 1974); and John Hope Franklin and Alfred A. Moss, Jr., *From Slavery to Freedom,* 6th ed. (New York: Alfred A. Knopf, 1988), chaps. 16 and 17.

63   *Charlotte* (N.C.) *Observer,* September 2, 1917.

64   William Anthony Aery, "The Negro and the Present Crisis," *New York Tribune,* October 16, 1917.

65   *Norfolk Journal and Guide,* September 11, 1917.

66   *Atlanta Constitution,* March 2, 1918.

67   *Montgomery Advertiser,* April 28, 1917.

68   *Southern Standard,* October 20, 1916.

69   *Birmingham Age Herald,* April 21, 1917.

70   Cited in W. E. B. Du Bois, "The Hosts of Black Labor," *Nation,* May 9, 1923, p. 540.

71   *New York Times,* July 2, 1917; *New York Tribune,* July 2, 1917.

72   Cited in Bontemps and Conroy, *They Seek a City,* p. 139.

73   Letter from Pittsburgh, dated May 11, 1917, to "My dear Pastor and Wife," in Emmett J. Scott, comp., "Document: Additional Letters of Negro Migrants of 1916–1918," *Journal of Negro History* 4 (October 1919): 459–60.

74   Letter from Dayton, dated July 22, 1917, to "My dear Pastor and Wife," in Scott, "Additional Letters," p. 462.

75 Letter from Chicago, dated July 15, 1917, to "My dear Pastor," in Scott, comp., "Additional Letters," p. 463.

76 Cited in Bontemps and Conroy, *They Seek a City,* p. 146.

77 Ibid.

78 On visiting patterns, see Earl Lewis, "Afro-American Adaptive Strategies: The Visiting Habits of Kith and Kin Among Black Norfolkians During the First Great Migration," *Journal of Family History* 12 (1987): 407–20.

79 Letter from Dayton, dated October 17, 1917, to "Dear Pastor," in Scott, comp., "Additional Letters," pp. 463–64.

80 Letter from Akron, Ohio, dated May 21, 1917, to "Dear Friend," in Scott, comp., "Additional Letters," p. 465.

81 *The Afro-American,* January 26, 1918. The paper withheld the clergyman's name "for his own safety."

82 W. E. B. Du Bois, "The Migration of Negroes," *Crisis* 14 (June 1917): 66.

83 Ibid.

84 Cited by Russell Dyer Owen, "Lure of Higher Wages Not the Direct Cause, They Say, But a Nameless Dread Has Affected the People," *New York Post,* July 8, 1917. Also reported in the *New York Times,* July 2, 1917.

85 *Christian Recorder,* June 7, 1917.

86 Work, *Negro Year Book, 1918–1919,* p. 9.

87 *Cleveland Advocate,* April 28, 1917.

88 Quoted from the *Atlanta Constitution,* January 2, 1917.

89 *New York Age,* April 5, 1917.

90 *Southern Standard,* October 20, 1916.

91 Ruth Landes, "Negro Jews in Harlem," *Jewish Journal of Sociology* 9 (December 1967): 177–78. Landes wrote the original version of this essay in 1933.

92 E. Franklin Frazier, "The Garvey Movement," *Opportunity* 4 (November 1926): 346.

93 Letter to the editor, *Montgomery Advertiser,* January 2, 1917.

94 [Carter G. Woodson], "Suggestions for Improving the Negro Church," *Negro History Bulletin* 3 (October 1939): 9–10.

95 *Chicago Baptist Year Book, 1915* (Chicago: Chicago Baptist Association, 1915), p. 70.

96 *Christian Recorder,* March 15, 1917.

97 "Report of Miss Nannie H. Burroughs," *Journal of the Twentieth Annual Session of the Woman's Convention Auxiliary to the National Baptist Convention, Held with the Baptist Churches, Indianapolis, Indiana, September 8–15, 1920,* pp. 334–35.

98 Robert Gregg, *Sparks from the Anvil of Oppression* (Philadelphia: Temple University Press), p. 16.

99 Cited by Ira De A. Reid, "American Cities—Albany, N.Y.," *Opportunity* 7 (June 1929): 180.

100 Harold M. Kingsley, "The Negro in Chicago: A Spiritual Interpretation of an Economic Problem," p. 2, pamphlet found in Box 199 of the Federal Writers' Project, Illinois Records, Illinois State Historical Library, Springfield.

101 Letter, dated May 12, 1917, Augusta, Georgia, reproduced in Malaida Adero, ed., *Up-*

South: Stories, Studies and Letters of This Century's African-American Migrations (New York: New Press, 1993), p. 58.

4   "OUR WANDERING ZION"

1   W. E. B. Du Bois, ed., *The Negro Church* (Atlanta: Atlanta University Press, 1903), p. 123.

2   "Address of the Council of Bishops, A.M.E. Church," *Christian Recorder*, August 16, 1917. Also, "Bishops in Council Urge Action," *Christian Recorder*, March 8, 1917.

3   See for example, Milton C. Sernett, "A Question of Earnestness: American Lutheran Missions and Education in Alabama's 'Black Belt'," in *Essays and Reports: The Lutheran Historical Conference, 1980* 9 (1982): 80–117.

4   Wesley J. Gaines, *African Methodism in the South: or Twenty-Five Years of Freedom,* intro. W. S. Scarbourgh (Atlanta: Franklin Publishing House, 1890), p. x.

5   "Address of the Council of Bishops."

6   *Star of Zion,* March 9, 1911.

7   *New York Age,* February 9, 1911.

8   "A Great Meeting," *Star of Zion,* February 28, 1918. Also see "Negro Bishops See Migration Benefits," *Christian Science Monitor,* February 18, 1918, and "Joint Address of Colored Bishops to Membership," *Christian Recorder,* February 28, 1918.

9   "Articles of Agreement," *Star of Zion,* April 25, 1918. For more details regarding the negotiations, see Dennis C. Dickerson, "Black Ecumenicism: Efforts to Establish a United Methodist Episcopal Church, 1918–1932," *Church History* 52 (December 1983): 479–91; and Roy W. Trueblood, "Union Negotiations Between Black Methodists in America," *Methodist History* 8 (July 1970): 18–29. For documents relating to organic union, including the Birmingham Plan for "The United Methodist Episcopal Church," see Charles Spencer Smith, *A History of the African Methodist Episcopal Church* (Philadelphia: Book Concern of the A.M.E. Church, 1922), chap. 23.

10 Lewis Baldwin, *"Invisible" Strands in African Methodism: A History of the African Union Methodist Protestant and Union American Methodist Episcopal Churches, 1805–1980* (Metuchen, N.J.: Scarecrow Press, 1983), chap. 6. C. Eric Lincoln and Lawrence H. Mamiya, *The Black Church in the African American Experience* (Durham, N.C.: Duke University Press, 1990), pp. 48–49.

11 Larry G. Murphy, J. Gordon Melton, and Gary L. Ward, eds., *Encyclopedia of African American Religions* (New York: Garland, 1993), p. 642.

12 W. E. B. Du Bois, ed., *The Negro Church* (Atlanta: Atlanta University Press, 1903), publication no. 8 of *Atlanta University Publications,* vol. 2 (New York Octagon Books, 1968), p. 123. For a more complete profile of the AME Church, see Richard R. Wright, Jr., ed., *Centennial Encyclopedia of the African Methodist Episcopal Church, 1816–1916* (Philadelphia: n.p., 1916), and C. M. Tanner, *A Manual of the African Methodist Episcopal Church, Being a Course of Twelve Lectures for Probationers and Members* (Philadelphia: A.M.E. Publishing House, 1900).

13 William B. Gravely, "The Social, Political and Religious Significance of the Foundation of the Colored Methodist Episcopal Church (1870)," *Methodist History* 18 (October 1979): 3–25. Katherine L. Dvorak stresses the initiatives of the black members of the

Methodist Episcopal Church, South, in the process of self-definition and separation. See Katharine L. Dvorak, *An African-American Exodus: The Segregation of the Southern Churches* (Brooklyn, N.Y.: Carlson Publishing, 1991), pp. 160–68.

14 Clarence E. Walker, *A Rock in a Weary Land: The African Methodist Episcopal Church During the Civil War and Reconstruction* (Baton Rouge: Louisiana State University Press, 1982), pp. 103–6.

15 Charles E. Tatum and Lawrence M. Sommers, "The Spread of the Black Christian Methodist Episcopal Church in the United States, 1870–1970," *Journal of Geography* 74 (September 1975): 343–57. For more on the CME Church, see Othal H. Lakey, *The Rise of "Colored Methodism"* (Dallas: Crescendo, 1972); C. H. Phillips, *The History of the Colored Methodist Episcopal Church in America* (Jackson, Tenn.: C.M.E. Publishing House, 1900; and M. C. Pittigrew, *From Miles to Johnson* (Memphis: C.M.E. Publishing House, 1970).

16 For the text of the entire agreement, see *Christian Index,* July 15, 1915.

17 *New York Age,* June 15, 1911. Norwood's sentiments must be understood against the backdrop of the reunification negotiations of northern and southern Methodists. White Methodism had been split along sectional lines since the division over slavery in 1844. But after Reconstruction and the emergence of a generation not so scarred by Civil War memories, Methodists moved toward healing the old wounds. Black Methodists had been advocating the election of black bishops, and indeed two bishops were sent to Africa. But white southerners strenuously objected, and in 1916 the "Bishops for Races and Languages" proposal at the Philadelphia Methodist Episcopal conference was defeated. This vote was seen as advancing the possibility of reunion.

18 *New York World,* November 16, 1918. *Savannah News,* February 8, 1918.

19 *Montgomery Advertiser,* June 5, 1918.

20 *Savannah News,* February 8, 1918.

21 The churches of the Central Jurisdiction were not completely brought into the white conferences until 1972. For more on the story of African Americans in the Methodist Episcopal Church, see Harry V. Richardson, *Dark Salvation: The Story of Methodism as It Developed Among Blacks in America* (Garden City, N.Y.: Anchor Books/Doubleday, 1976), chap. 16, and Lawrence O. Kline, "The Negro in the Unification of American Methodism," *Drew Gateway* 34 (Spring 1964): 128–49.

22 See Randall M. Miller, "The Failed Mission: The Catholic Church and Black Catholics in the Old South," in *The Southern Common People: Studies in Nineteenth-Century Social History,* ed. Edward Magdol and Jon Wakelyn (Westport, Conn.: Greenwood Press, 1980), pp. 37–54. The rapid expansion of northern urban Roman Catholicism in the early twentieth century was not a result of an exchange of place by southern black Catholics. Nevertheless, urban parishes, dominated by ethnic Catholics from Europe, were affected by the influx of southern blacks. In 1889 the First Afro-American Catholic Congress was held in Washington, D.C. Never before had representatives of black parishes gathered at the national level to examine their status in both church and country. In a statement issued at the end of the assembly, black Catholics pointed to the problems of blacks living in the urban United States, such as exorbitant rents, poorly constructed tenements, and discrimination by real estate agents. The congress clearly expected that growth among black Catholics would take place in the cities.

23 Andrew Murray, *Presbyterians and the Negro: A History* (Philadelphia: Presbyterian Historical Society, 1966), p. 180. When John W. Lee, a graduate of Lincoln University, was appointed field missionary to African Americans by the board of freedmen of the Presbyterian Church in 1917, he reported that the denomination had 35,000 black communicants, 141 day schools, 490 teachers, 270 ministers, and 622 "workers" in its Negro department.

24 George F. Bragg, Jr., reported that of 260 black congregations in the Episcopal dioceses in 1917, nearly thirty were self-sustaining. He estimated that black clergy numbered between 150 and 160 and that the total number of black Episcopalians in "exclusively colored congregations" was more than 30,000. Thousands more were in white congregations in the North and West. See "Statistics on Negro Churches," *Living Church* (Milwaukee), July 14, 1917.

25 Richard Newman, "The Origins of the African Orthodox Church," introductory essay to *The Negro Churchman,* vols. 1–4, 1923–26 (Millwood, N.Y.: Kraus Reprint, 1977), iii–xxii.

26 For a portrait of C. H. Mason by his wife, see Elsie W. Mason, "Bishop C. H. Mason, Church of God in Christ," in Milton C. Sernett, ed., *Afro-American Religious History: A Documentary Witness* (Durham, N.C.: Duke University Press, 1985), pp. 285–95. See also Hans A. Baer, "The Socio-Religious Development of the Church of God in Christ," in *African Americans in the South: Issues of Race, Class, and Gender,* ed. Hans A. Baer and Yvonne Jones (Athens: University of Georgia Press, 1992), pp. 111–22. On Seymour, see James S. Tinney, "William J. Seymour: Father of Modern-Day Pentecostalism," in *Black Apostles,* ed. Randall K. Burkett and Richard Newman (Boston: G. K. Hall, 1978), pp. 213–25.

27 Joseph R. Washington, Jr., *Black Sects and Cults* (Garden City, N.Y.: Doubleday, 1972), pp. 80–81. Washington adds, "Long before ruralites reached urbanites, mobile Holiness and Pentecostal evangelicals had reached them. The urban man returned to the rural man a new form of the old religion."

28 Victor I. Masters, "Negro Baptist Statistics," *National Baptist Union Review,* July 29, 1916.

29 For an excellent account of the rise of black Baptist nationalism and the struggles leading to the formation of the National Baptist Convention, see James Melvin Washington, *Frustrated Fellowship: The Black Baptist Quest for Social Power* (Macon, Ga.: Mercer University Press, 1986), part 3. Also see Leroy Fitts, *A History of Black Baptists* (Nashville: Broadman Press, 1985), pp. 64–98. In 1896 discord between the nationalists and co-operationists resulted in the loss to the convention of clergy and laity located primarily in North Carolina and Virginia who desired to maintain ties with white Baptists who supported mission work in Africa. In 1905 the Lott Carey Baptist Foreign Mission Convention became a "district" of the larger body, but the debate over how black Baptists were to relate to their white counterparts, especially in the conduct of foreign missions and the governance of educational institutions for blacks, continued.

30 Fitts, *Black Baptists,* p. 82. Owen D. Pelt and Ralph Lee Smith, *The Story of the National Baptists* (New York: Vantage Press, 1960), pp. 102–4.

31 *Journal of the Thirty-Fourth Annual Session of the National Baptist Convention Held in Philadelphia, Pa., September 9–14, 1914,* p. 40.

32 *Chicago Daily News,* September 7 and 8, 1915.

33 *Journal of the Thirty-Sixth Annual Session of the National Baptist Convention (unincorporated) and the Sixteenth Annual Session of the Woman's Auxiliary Convention Held with the Baptist Church, Kansas City, Mo., September 6–11, 1916,* p. 20. For a more complete statement of positions held by the Jones-Boyd forces, see "An Address to the Baptists of the Country from the Executive Committee of the National Baptist Convention issued February 11, 1916," as published in the *Nashville Globe,* March 10, 1916. The unincorporated body created its own foreign mission, home mission, educational, youth, benefits, evangelism, and extension boards. The publishing board, center of the controversy, was given an advisory status.

34 *Journal of the Thirty-Sixth Session of the National Baptist Convention, Held with the Baptist Churches, Savannah, Ga., September 6th to 11th, 1916,* p. 31; *Savannah Tribune,* September 9, 1916.

35 U.S. Bureau of the Census, *Religious Bodies: 1916,* part 2 (Washington, D.C.: U.S. Government Printing Office, 1919), p. 98.

36 Masters, "Negro Baptist Statistics."

37 *Savannah Tribune,* September 9, 1916.

38 U.S. Bureau of the Census, *Religious Bodies: 1926,* part 2 (Washington, D.C.: U.S. Government Printing Office, 1930), p. 131. Several small black Baptist groups, such as the Colored Free Will Baptists and the Colored Primitive Baptists, with a predominantly southern membership, were not party to the dispute within the National Baptist Convention but should be mentioned to indicate the diversity among Baptists.

39 *Nashville Globe,* March 22, 1918.

40 [Richard R. Wright, Jr.], "Where Is the Federal Council of Negro Methodists," *Christian Recorder,* 1917, TCF, Reel 6.

41 Mary R. Sawyer, "Black Ecumenical Movements: Proponents of Social Change," *Review of Religious Research* 30 (December 1988): 151–61.

42 W. A. Blackwell, "The Uplifting of a Race," in *Christian Unity at Work,* ed. Charles S. Macfarland, 4th ed. (New York: Federal Council of the Churches of Christ in America, 1912), p. 225.

43 "Federal Council of Churches of Christ," *Christian Recorder,* December 14, 1916. Charles S. Macfarland, *The Progress of Church Federation* (New York: Fleming H. Revel, 1917), pp. 117–20. *Annual Reports of the Federal Council of the Churches of Christ in America for the Year 1919* (New York: Federal Council of the Churches of Christ in America, 1919), pp. 155–58.

44 R. C. Ransom, "A.M.E. Churchmen Tell of Conditions," *Christian Recorder,* December 14, 1916.

45 Ibid.

46 Samuel McCrea Cavert, ed., *The Churches Allied for Common Tasks: Report of the Third Quadrennium of the Federal Council of Churches of Christ in America, 1916–1920* (New York: Federal Council of the Churches of Christ in America, 1921), p. 143.

47 Ibid., p. 145. Haynes eventually became secretary of the commission on the church and race relations of the Federal Council of Churches. For a report of his research, see George E. Haynes, *Negro Migration and Its Implications North and South* (New York: American Missionary Association, 1923).

48 [Richard R. Wright, Jr.], "Should Negroes Come North," *Christian Recorder,* August 31, 1916.

49 Ibid.

50 Richard R. Wright, Jr., "Social Work and Influence of the Negro Church," *Annals of the American Academy of Political and Social Science* 30 (November 1907): 516–17. Wright's appeal for aid to the AME Church can be found in *Annual Reports of the Federal Council of the Churches of Christ in America* (New York: Federal Council of Churches of Christ in America, 1917), p. 156. For Wright's views on the challenges of urban America, see Wright, "Negro in Times of Industrial Unrest," *Charities,* October 7, 1905, pp. 69–73.

51 "Bishops in Council Urge Action," *Christian Recorder,* March 8, 1917. See also "Bishops in Council Discuss Negro Migration North," *Southern Christian Advocate,* March 1, 1917.

52 Coppin was editor of the *AME Church Review* from 1888 until 1896 and bishop from 1900 until 1920. Levi J. Coppin, "The Thorn in the Flesh . . . What's the Remedy," *AME Church Review* 26 (January 1910): 263–66. See also David W. Wills, "Aspects of Social Thought in the African Methodist Episcopal Church, 1884–1910" (Ph.D. diss., Harvard University, 1975), p. 233. For a profile of Coppin, see Robert Gregg, *Sparks from the Anvil of Oppression* (Philadelphia: Temple University Press, 1993), pp. 88–95.

53 "Negroes Are Advised to Stay in the South," *Montgomery Advertiser,* December 11, 1916.

54 Ibid.

55 *Philadelphia Public Ledger,* July 16, 1917.

56 "The Southerner's Cause of Exodus," *Chicago Defender,* January 26, 1916.

57 Letter to the editor, *Montgomery Advertiser,* March 24, 1917.

58 Carter's remarks are to be found in "Colored Pastors Lament the Spread of Negro Exodus," *Birmingham Herald,* April 21, 1917.

59 *Birmingham Age-Herald,* May 21, 1917.

60 Cited in James R. Grossman, *"Land of Hope": Chicago, Black Southerners, and the Great Migration* (Chicago: University of Chicago Press, 1989), p. 94.

61 *Charlotte Observer,* October 24, 1916.

62 G. E. Queen, "The Negro Exodus: A Problem for the Washington and Delaware Conferences," (New York) *Christian Advocate,* 1917, HCF.

63 Letter, Robert E. Jones to Robert E. Park, March 2, 1917, Carter G. Woodson Papers, Library of Congress, Washington, D.C.

64 R. R. Downs, "How We Should Deal with Our People Who Are Migrating from the South," *Voice of Missions,* June 1917, HCF.

65 "Hail Colored Methodism in Detroit," *Christian Index,* October 18, 1917. See also *Christian Index,* November 14, 1918.

66 "Randall Albert Carter," *Journal of Negro History* 39 (April 1954): 158–60.

67 *Christian Index,* July 19, 1917.

68 "An Appeal by the Bishops to the Ministers and Friends of the Colored Methodist Episcopal Church in America," *Christian Index,* November 14, 1918. See also "The Challenge

of the Migration Movement and the Need of a Great Centenary Missionary Rally in the c.m.e. Church," *Christian Index,* August 8, 1918.

69 Dennis C. Dickerson, "The Black Church in Industrializing Western Pennsylvania, *1870–1950,*" *Western Pennsylvania Historical Magazine* 64 (October 1981): 333, 337–38.

70 James Mason, "Zion in Council," *Star of Zion,* October 1, 1917.

71 "Colored Migration Brings Responsibilities to Church," *Syracuse Post-Standard,* October 4, 1917.

72 G. L. Blackwell, *Who Is Who in the Fifth Episcopal District in the African Methodist Episcopal Zion Church* (Philadelphia: n.p., 1920), p. 38.

73 Reginald F. Hildebrand, *The Times Were Strange and Stirring: Methodist Preachers and the Crisis of Emancipation* (Durham, N.C.: Duke Universitiy Press, 1995).

74 *Christian Advocate,* September 1, 1917.

75 Cited in W. H. Peck, "Proceedings of the Board of Church Extension," *Christian Recorder,* May 9, 1918. See also "Negro Migration Creates Difficult Industrial Problem," *Voice of Missions,* June 18, 1918.

76 James T. Campbell, *Songs of Zion: The African Methodist Episcopal Church in the United States and South Africa* (New York: Oxford University Press, 1995), p. 298.

77 J. W. Rankin, "The Active Mission Work," *Christian Recorder,* July 26, 1917.

78 *Christian Recorder,* May 3, 1917.

79 *Christian Recorder,* May 9, 1918.

80 John C. Dancy, "Report by Department of Church Extension and Home Missions," *Official Journal of the General Conference of the A.M.E. Zion Church, 25th Session and 26th Session, 1916–1920* (Charlotte, N.C.: a.m.e. Zion Publication House, 1920), p. 193.

81 *Journal of the Thirty-Fifth Annual Session of the National Baptist Convention Held with the Baptist Churches of Chicago, Ill., September 8–15, 1915,* pp. 28–29, contained in *Journal of the Thirty-Sixth Session of the National Baptist Convention, Held with the Baptist Churches, Savannah, Ga., September 6th to 11th, 1916.*

82 *Christian Banner,* February 23, 1917.

83 *Journal of the Thirty-Eighth Annual Session, National Baptist Convention, Held with the Baptist Churches, St. Louis, Mo., September 4–9, 1918,* p. 65.

84 *Journal of the Thirty-Ninth Annual Session of the National Baptist Convention, Held with the Baptist Churches, Newark, N.J., September 10–15, 1919,* pp. 44–47.

85 *Atlanta Independent,* September 15, 1917.

86 *Union Review,* March 30, 1918.

87 Ibid., p. 48.

88 *Journal of the Fortieth Annual Session of the National Baptist Convention, Held with the Baptist Churches, Indianapolis, Indiana, September 8–13, 1920,* pp. 118–20.

89 *Journal of the Forty-Fourth Annual Session of the National Baptist Convention, Held with the Baptist Churches, Nashville, Tenn., September 10–15, 1924,* p. 176.

90 *Journal of the Forty-first Annual Session of the National Baptist Convention, Held with the Baptist Churches, Chicago, Illinois, Sept. 7–12, 1921,* p. 103.

91 Ibid., pp. 104–5.

92 *Journal of the Twentieth Annual Session of the National Baptist Convention, Held in Richmond, Virginia, September 12–17, 1900,* pp. 195–96. Burroughs, whose home was in Louis-

ville, where she did clerical work, was only twenty-one when she challenged the male leadership of the National Baptist Convention to come to terms with the "righteous discontent" of black Baptist women. The Woman's Convention, while part of the National Baptist Convention, operated independently from the male-dominated convention with its own programs, finances, and leadership. S. Wille Layten, whose father was pastor of Shiloh Baptist Church in Philadelphia and who had been active in the club movement, was elected president of the Woman's Convention in 1900. Burroughs, who served as corresponding secretary from 1900 until her death in 1961, was the more influential leader and, as Evelyn Brooks Higginbotham has written, "more than anyone else, embodied the Baptist women's independent spirit." For additional information on the formation of the Woman's Convention, see Evelyn Brooks Higginbotham, *Righteous Discontent: The Women's Movement in the Black Baptist Church, 1880–1920* (Cambridge, Mass.: Harvard University Press, 1993), chap. 6.

93   *Journal of the Fourteenth Annual Assembly of the Woman's Convention Auxiliary to the National Baptist Convention, Held with the Holy Trinity Baptist Church, Philadelphia, Pa., Sept. 9 to 15, 1914*, p. 169.

94   *Annual Address of Mrs. S. W. Layten, President of Woman's Convention Auxiliary to National Baptist Convention, Savannah, Georgia, September 6–11, 1916*, in *Journal of National Baptist Convention, 1916*, p. 185.

95   "National Baptist Woman's Convention Is Auxiliary to National Baptist Convention," *Christian Banner*, March 2, 1917. Published in Philadelphia, the *Christian Banner* declared itself to be the "Official Organ of the National Baptist Convention." Brooks Higginbotham, *Righteous Discontent*, pp. 211–21.

96   Evelyn Brooks, "Religion, Politics, and Gender: The Leadership of Nannie Helen Burroughs," *Journal of Religious Thought* 44 (Winter–Spring 1988): 7–22.

97   For details on the struggle of Baptist women to maintain control of the training school, see the *Christian Banner*, July 7, 1916. Higginbotham, *Righteous Discontent*, pp. 171–80.

98   W. E. B. Du Bois, *Efforts for Social Betterment Among Negro Americans,* Atlanta University Publications, no. 14 (Atlanta: Atlanta University Press, 1909), p. 22.

99   Brooks, "Religion, Politics, and Gender," 12–13.

100   Allan H. Spear, *Black Chicago: The Making of a Negro Ghetto, 1890–1920* (Chicago: University of Chicago Press, 1967), pp. 96, 101.

101   Brooks Higginbotham, *Righteous Discontent*, p. 182.

102   Robert T. Handy, "The City and the Church: Historical Interlockings," in Kendig Brubaker Cully and F. Nile Harper, eds., *Will the Church Lose the City?* (New York: World, 1969), pp. 92–94. See also Paul S. Boyer, *Urban Masses and Moral Order in America, 1820–1920* (Cambridge, Mass.: Harvard University Press, 1978), pp. 213–14.

103   Luker, *Social Gospel in Black and White,* pp. 171–73.

104   Ibid., p. 174. See also David Wills, "Reverdy C. Ransom: The Making of an A.M.E. Bishop," in *Black Apostles,* ed. Randall K. Burkett and Richard Newman (Boston: G. K. Hall, 1978), pp. 181–212.

105   "To Help Negro Race," *Chicago Inter-Ocean,* July 29, 1900. For more on Ransom and his tenure at Institutional, see Reverdy C. Ransom, *The Pilgrimage of Harriet Ransom's Son* (Nashville: A.M.E. Sunday School Union, c. 1948), chap. 8; and Wills, "Reverdy C. Ran-

som," pp. 181–211. Ransom resurrected his model of urban ministry in New York City at Bethel A.M.E. Church and later at a mission church of his own, called the Church of Simon of the Cyrene, located in one of the city's poorest sections. Townsend's statement is cited by Richard R. Wright, Jr., *87 Years Behind the Black Curtain: An Autobiography* (Philadelphia: Rare Book, 1965), p. 148.

106 Ransom to Claude A. Barnett, May 14, 1945. Claude A. Barnett Papers, Chicago Historical Society.

107 Richard R. Wright, Jr., "Negro in Times of Industrial Unrest," *Charities*, October 7, 1905, pp. 69–73.

108 Robert Gregg, *Sparks from the Anvil of Oppression: Philadelphia African Methodists and the Great Migration, 1890–1930* (Philadelphia: Temple University Press, 1989), pp. 88–95.

109 Wright, *87 Years*, pp. 148–49. For more on Wright's conversion to the Social Gospel, see William H. Ferris, "Dr. R. R. Wright, Jr.," *AME Church Review* 44 (July 1927): 15–17, and Ralph E. Luker, *The Social Gospel in Black and White: American Racial Reform, 1885–1912* (Chapel Hill: University of North Carolina Press, 1991), p. 176.

110 *Chicago Inter-Ocean*, August 6, 1905; Richard R. Wright, Jr., "Social Work and Influence of the Negro Church," *Annals of the American Academy of Political and Social Science* 30 (November 1907): 509–21.

111 *Christian Recorder*, August 20, 1916.

112 See John Henry Lewis, "Social Service in Negro Churches" (M.A. thesis, Divinity School, University of Chicago, 1914).

113 Ethel E. Johnson, "Church Institutional Work," *Southern Workman* 46 (March 1917): 153–58. Johnson served as St. John's parish visitor and gives a very detailed account of DeBerry's multifaceted ministry. Additional accounts of the institutional work at St. John's are L. H. Hammond, *In the Vanguard of a Race* (New York: Council of Women for Home Missions and Missionary Education Movement of the United States and Canada, 1914), pp. 63–77, and Charles H. Williams, "The Negro Church and Recreation," *Opportunity* 55 (February 1926): 63–69.

114 Miles Mark Fisher, *The Master's Slave, Elijah John Fisher, a Biography* (Philadelphia: Judson Press, 1922), pp. 98–100. Olivet Baptist Church, *"Just A Decade in Olivet," 1916–1926* (Chicago: Olivet Baptist Church, 1926), pp. 4–5, 38–39.

115 The report is included in *From Ocean to Ocean, 1918–1919: A Record of the Work of the Women's American Baptist Home Mission Society,* ed. Alice T. Anderson, pp. 189–91. Copy in the Library of the American Baptist Historical Society, Rochester, N.Y.

116 Cited in Lillian B. Horace, "*'Crowned with Glory and Honor'*": The Life of Rev. Lacy Kirk Williams,* ed. Venchael Booth (Hicksville, N.Y.: Exposition Press, 1978), p. 148.

117 The pastors of a few of the larger city churches in the South also experimented with forms of ministry that went beyond praying, preaching, and teaching. The Reverend Richard H. Bowling, a Hampton graduate, established the first institutional church in the South—First Baptist Church, Norfolk. After his death in 1914, his son, Richard, Jr., continued the work. The institutional church model was also adopted in Atlanta, Harlem, Kansas City, Detroit, and other urban centers.

118 Miles Mark Fisher, "The Negro Church and the World-War," *Journal of Religion* 5 (September 1925): 483.

119 A[dam] Clayton Powell, Sr., *Upon This Rock* (New York: Abyssinian Baptist Church, 1949), pp. 7–12.

5 "INTO THE PROMISED LAND"

1 Ralph Borsodi, *Flight from the City: The Story of a New Way to Family Security* (New York: Harper and Brothers, 1933), pp. 1–3, 10–19, 129. Vivien E. Dreves, "The New Woman Goes Home: Myrtle Mae Borsodi Pits Home Production Against Industrialization, 1929–1940," *New York History* (July 1990), pp. 282–307.

2 On the transformation of city life during the years when the black populations of every major northern industrial region dramatically increased, see Hollis Lynch, ed., *The Black Urban Condition: A Documentary History, 1866–1971* (New York: Thomas Y. Crowell, 1973). Also George W. Groh, *The Black Migration: The Journey to Urban America* (New York: Weybright and Talley, 1972), chap. 3.

3 Quoted in Chicago Commission on Race Relations, *Negro in Chicago* (Chicago: University of Chicago Press, 1922), p. 88.

4 *Record Herald,* October 13, 1916.

5 Charles N. Glaab and A. Theodore Brown, *A History of Urban America* (New York: Macmillan, 1967), p. 133. Glaab and Brown are referring primarily to the North. The South lagged about fifty years behind the North in the trend toward urbanization.

6 Farah Jasmine Griffin, *"Who Set You Flowing'?": The African-American Migration Narrative* (New York: Oxford University Press, 1995), p. 51.

7 Richard Sherman, ed., *The Negro and the American City* (Englewood Cliffs, N.J.: Prentice-Hall, 1970), p. 2.

8 On the weakening of Progressivism after the flood tide of the reform movement in 1912, see Robert H. Wiebe, *The Search for Order, 1877–1920* (New York: Hill and Wang, 1967), chaps. 8 and 11.

9 *Youngstown* (Ohio) *Vindicator,* March 23, 1918.

10 "The Negro in Yankeeland," *Montgomery Advertiser,* November 5, 1916.

11 *Newark* (N.J.) *Evening Star,* November 24, 1918.

12 *Boston Traveler,* October 16, 1917.

13 *Christian Recorder,* August 16, 1917.

14 W. E. B. Du Bois, "The Hosts of Black Labor," *Nation,* May 9, 1923, pp. 540–41.

15 *New York Times,* September 9, 1916.

16 Ibid.

17 "Migration," *Crisis* 10 (October 1916): 270.

18 Eugene Kinkle Jones, "Address: Tenth Anniversary Conference of the National Association for the Advancement of Colored People," June 24, 1919, NAACP Papers, Library of Congress, Washington, D.C.

19 *Toledo* (Ohio) *Times,* October 27, 1916.

20 Richard R. Wright, Jr., "The Economic Conditions of Negroes in the North: Tendencies Downward." Second paper: Negro criminal statistics, *Southern Workman* 40 (May 5, 1911): 291.

21 *Advocate,* April 13, 1918.

22 *Star of Zion,* August 16, 1917.

23 "Freed Negroes Join Churches," 1916, TCF, Reel 5.

24 David J. Hellwig, "Strangers in Their Own Land: Patterns of Black Nativism, 1830–1930," *American Studies* 23 (Spring 1982): 94–95.

25 Elliott Rudwick's *Race Riot at East St. Louis, July 2, 1917* (Carbondale: Southern Illinois University Press, 1964) is the most exhaustive study of the riot and its aftermath. Nine whites and an estimated thirty-nine blacks were killed on July 2, 1917.

26 The best contemporary account is William M. Tuttle, Jr., *Race Riot: Chicago in the Red Summer of 1919* (New York: Atheneum, 1970).

27 Walter F. White, "Chicago and Its Eight Reasons," *Crisis* 17 (October 1919): 293–94.

28 Alan D. Grinshaw, "A Study in Social Violence" (Ph.D. diss., University of Pennsylvania, 1959), pp. 178–80, cited in Rudwick, *Race Riot,* p. 3.

29 *New York American,* July 29, 1917; *New York Age,* August 21, 1917.

30 *Philadelphia Public Ledger,* July 16, 1917.

31 *Columbus* (Ohio) *State Journal,* July 13, 1917.

32 "For Justice to the Negro: Appeal of the Federal Council of Churches," *Southern Workman* 48 (November 1919): 609.

33 Richard R. Wright, "The Negroes of Philadelphia," *AME Church Review* (October 1907), p. 137.

34 W. E. B. Du Bois, "Results of the Investigation," in *Some Efforts of American Negroes for Their Own Social Betterment* (Atlanta: Atlanta University Press, 1898), pp. 4–5.

35 *Chicago Defender,* October 18, 1919.

36 *Voice of Missions,* June 18, 1918.

37 *Charleston Messenger,* October 11, 1919.

38 *Norfolk Journal and Guide,* October 11, 1919.

39 Joel Williamson, *The Crucible of Race* (New York: Oxford University Press, 1984), p. 53.

40 Howard N. Rabinowitz, *Race Relations in the Urban South, 1865–1890* (New York: Oxford University Press, 1978), p. 223.

41 Mary McCleod Bethune, "The Problems of the City Dweller," *Opportunity* 3 (February 1925): 111–12.

42 *Pittsburgh Courier,* November 24, 1918.

43 W. E. B. Du Bois, *The Black North in 1901,* intro. E. Digby Baltzell (1901; repr., New York: Arno Press, 1969), p. 39.

44 W. E. B. Du Bois, *The Philadelphia Negro* (1899; repr., New York: Schocken Books, 1967), p. 202.

45 Ibid., p. 207.

46 Du Bois, ed. *Some Efforts of American Negroes for Their Own Social Betterment,* pp. 16–29.

47 Maude K. Griffin, "The Negro Church and Its Social Work—St. Mark's," *Charities,* October 7, 1905, p. 75. Griffin noted that St. Mark's Methodist Episcopal Church on West 53rd Street in New York City under the leadership of W. H. Brooks was an exception.

48 Du Bois, "The Negro Church," p. 85.

49 Thomas Lee Philpott, *The Slum and the Ghetto: Neighborhood Deterioration and Middle-Class Reform in Chicago, 1880–1930* (New York: Oxford University Press, 1978), p. 316.

50 Commission on Race Relations, *Negro in Chicago,* p. 143. Subsequent to the riots, the

Industrial Relations Department of the Inter-church World Movement commissioned a survey of conditions in Chicago for the purpose of remedial action. The preliminary report called for the development of community programs by Chicago's black and white churches. George E. Haynes introduced the report, stressing the theme that became a commonplace in the wake of the conflict in urban centers after World War I: Churches, black and white, should be devoted to the problems of "every day life." Howard R. Gold and Byron K. Armstrong, *A Preliminary Study of Inter-Racial Conditions in Chicago*, intro. George E. Haynes (New York: Home Missions Council, 1920.)

51   *New York Age,* June 24, 1909.

52   *New York Age,* May 17, 1917.

53   John William Kinney, "Adam Clayton Powell, Sr., and Adam Clayton Powell, Jr.: A Historical Exposition and Theological Analysis" (Ph.D. diss., Columbia University, 1979), pp. 80–86.

54   Ibid., p. 77.

55   *New York Age,* May 17, 1917. The League was particularly concerned about the fifty-six saloons in the district and the existence of street gangs.

56   *New York Age,* April 17, 1920.

57   "Abyssinian Baptist Church Shocked and Surprised When Rev. A. Clayton Powell Reads Resignation Sunday," *New York Age,* December 17, 1921; Adam Clayton Powell, Sr., *Upon This Rock* (New York: Abyssinian Baptist Church, 1949), p. 20.

58   A. Clayton Powell, Sr., "The Church in Social Work," *Opportunity* 1 (January 1923): 15.

59   Adam Clayton Powell, Sr., *Against the Tide* (New York: n.p., 1938), pp. 67–78; Powell, "How Did We Do It?," address at the mortgage burning, Schomberg Clipping File, Schomberg Library, New York City; William Welty, "Black Shepherds: A Study of the Leading Negro Clergymen in New York City, 1900–1940" (Ph.D. diss., New York University, 1969), pp. 122–25.

60   Welty, "Black Shepherds," pp. 129–32, 134–38.

61   Ibid., pp. 125–28.

62   Ibid., p. 155.

63   In 1924 George E. Haynes identified the following as institutional churches in New York City: Abyssinian Baptist, St. Philip's Protestant Episcopal, Williams Institutional CME, and Mother Zion AME. He also recognized St. John's Congregational in Springfield, Massachusetts, Mount Zion Congregational Church and St. John's AME Church in Cleveland, Sharpe Street ME Church in Baltimore, and Olivet Baptist Church and two unnamed community churches in Chicago. Haynes, "Negro Migration—Its Effect on Family and Community Life in the North," in *Proceedings of the National Conference of Social Work, Toronto, Ontario, June 25–July 2, 1924* (Chicago: University of Chicago Press, 1924), p. 72.

64   "'Cooperation' and 'Opportunity,'" *Opportunity* 1 (January 1923): 5.

65   Quoted in Seth M. Scheiner, *Negro Mecca: A History of the Negro in New York City, 1865–1920* (New York: New York University Press, 1965), p. 90.

66   Welty, "Black Shepherds," pp. 140–41.

67   W. E. B. Du Bois, "The New Negro Church," in *Against Racism: Unpublished Essays, Papers, and Addresses, 1887–1961* (Amherst: University of Massachusetts Press, 1985), p. 85.

68 Richard R. Wright, Jr., "Social Work and Influence of the Negro Church," *Annals of the American Academy of Political and Social Science* 30 (November 1907): 516–17.

69 Ibid., p. 520.

70 Richard R. Wright, Jr., "The Industrial Condition of Negroes in Chicago" (B.D. thesis, University of Chicago, 1901).

71 *Christian Recorder,* March 14, 1918.

72 *Cleveland Plain Dealer,* October 19, 1916; Felix James, "The Civic and Political Activities of George A. Myers," *Journal of Negro History* 58 (April 1973): 166–78.

73 Letter to the *Republican,* March 6, 1917, republished in *Atlanta Independent,* March 17, 1917.

74 *The Afro-American,* December 15, 1917.

75 "The Urban League Conference," *Southern Workman* 48 (November 1919): 583. For an overview of Urban League social service efforts during the Great Migration, see Nancy J. Weiss, *The National Urban League, 1910–1940* (New York: Oxford University Press, 1974), chaps. 7 and 8.

76 John T. Clark, "The Migrant in Pittsburgh," *Opportunity* 1 (October 1923): 303–7.

77 Lillian S. Williams, "Afro-Americans in Buffalo, 1900–1930: A Study in Community Formation," *Afro-Americans in New York Life and History* 8 (July 1984): 25–27.

78 *Cleveland Plain Dealer,* July 20, 1917.

79 *Cleveland Press,* July 11, 1917.

80 *Newark Evening Star,* November 14, 1916.

81 *Philadelphia Record,* September 17, 1916.

82 Letter to the *New York Times,* September 9, 1916.

83 *Freeman,* March 31, 1923.

84 *Atlanta Constitution,* December 15, 1916.

85 W. E. B. Du Bois, "Brothers, Come North," *Crisis* 19 (January 1920): 105.

86 Mary McCleod Bethune, "The Problems of the City Dweller," *Opportunity* 3 (February 1925): 55.

87 Cited by Robert Wernick, "Jacob Lawrence: Art as Seen through a People's History," *Smithsonian* 18 (June 1987): 62. Lawrence's series called "The Migration of the Negro" brought him national attention and captured the epochal character of the exodus.

88 *Christian Recorder,* November 16, 1916. John T. Emlen, "Negro Immigration in Philadelphia," *Southern Workman* 46 (October 1917): 555–57.

89 "Migration and Help," *Crisis* 13 (January 1917): 115.

90 Dennis Dickerson, "The Black Church in Industrializing Western Pennsylvania, 1870–1950," *Western Pennsylvania Historical Magazine* 64 (October 1981): 339–40.

91 Peter Gottlieb, *Making Their Own Way: Southern Blacks' Migration to Pittsburgh, 1916–1930* (Urbana: University of Illinois Press, 1987), pp. 47–52. Carole Marks suggests that we expand the concept of "chain migration" to other than primary relationships, such as family and friends. She discusses the importance of labor agents, service organizations such as the Urban League, and the ethnic press. See her "Lines of Communication, Recruitment Mechanisms, and the Great Migration of 1916–1918," *Social Problems* 31 (October 1983): 73–83.

92 Grossman, *Land of Hope,* pp. 66–67.

93 *Springfield News,* March 6, 1918.

94 L. H. Hammond, *In the Vanguard of a Race* (New York: Council of Women for Home Missions, 1914), pp. 73–77.

95 Everett Johnson, "A Study of the Negro Families in the Pinewood Avenue District of Toledo, Ohio," *Journal of Negro Life* 7 (August 1929): 243–45.

96 *Columbus Journal,* October 31, 1916.

97 Grossman, *Land of Hope,* pp. 129–30. The Chicago "colored YMCA" was erected using funds raised in the African American community and matched by the philanthropist Julius Rosenwald. Located on Wabash Avenue, the YMCA offered refugees from the South safe housing, assistance in finding employment, and free night classes. Nina Mjagkij, *Light in the Darkness: African Americans and the YMCA, 1852–1946* (Lexington: University Press of Kentucky, 1994), p. 83.

98 S. Mattie Fischer reports on her work in *From Ocean to Ocean, 1918–1919: A Record of the Work of the Women's American Baptist Home Mission Society,* ed. Alice T. Anderson (Chicago: n.p., 1919), pp. 189–90; E. B. Bohannon, "The History and Accomplishment of the Free Employment Bureau," in Olivet Baptist Church, *"Just A Decade in Olivet,"* pp. 29–30; Susie A. Houser, "A Community-Serving Church," *Opportunity* 54 (February 1920): 58–64.

99 For Agnew's letter and a sampling of others, see the Carter G. Woodson Papers, Library of Congress, Washington, D.C.

100 Kenneth L. Kusmer, *A Ghetto Takes Shape: Black Cleveland, 1870–1930* (Urbana: University of Illinois Press, 1976), p. 252.

101 Larry Cuban, "A Strategy for Racial Peace: Negro Leadership in Cleveland, 1900–1919," *Phylon* 28 (Fall 1967): 306. Cuban argues that the tradition of accommodation practiced by Cleveland's conservative African American leadership accounts for the lack of overt racial conflict during the Great Migration.

102 The statement was by George A. Myers, cited in Kusmer, *A Ghetto Takes Shape,* p. 187.

103 Ibid., pp. 95–96.

104 David Allen Levine, *Internal Combustion: The Races in Detroit, 1915–1926* (Westport, Conn.: Greenwood Press, 1976), pp. 7, 51, 54.

105 *Detroit Tribune,* July 15, 1917; Forrester B. Washington, *The Negro in Detroit: A Survey of the Conditions of a Negro Group in a Northern Industrial Center During the War Prosperity Period* (Detroit: Research Bureau, Associated Charities of Detroit, 1920).

106 *Historical Sketch Published on the Eighty-Sixth Anniversary of Bethel A.M.E. Church, Detroit, Michigan, 1841–1927* (Detroit: n.p., 1927), in Charles Spencer Smith Papers, Michigan Historical Collections, Bentley Historical Library, Ann Arbor. See also David M. Katzman, *Before the Ghetto: Black Detroit in the Nineteenth Century* (Urbana: University of Illinois Press, 1973), pp. 140–41.

107 "Work for Hundreds—Bethel A.M.E. Church Free Employment Bureau," *Voice of Missions* 31 (March 1923): 3.

108 *Christian Recorder,* June 7, 1917.

109 Cited in George Edmund Haynes, *Negro New-Comers in Detroit, Michigan* (New York: Home Missions Council, 1918), p. 30.

110 Ibid., pp. 30–31, 37–38.

111 Levine, *Internal Combustion,* p. 54.

112 Bureau of Governmental Research, "Religion," *The Negro in Detroit* (Detroit: Bureau of Governmental Research, 1926), pp. 10–11.

113 Charles Ashley Hardy III, "Race and Opportunity: Black Philadelphia During the Era of the Great Migration, 1916–1930" (Ph.D. diss., Temple University, 1989), p. 53.

114 John T. Emlen, "Negro Immigration in Philadelphia," *Southern Workman* 46 (October 1917): 555–57; Hardy, "Race and Opportunity," p. 90.

115 Frederick Miller, "The Black Migration to Philadelphia: A 1924 Profile," *Pennsylvania Magazine of History and Biography* 108 (July 1984): 346. Almost half of those surveyed had migrated to Philadelphia between the spring of 1922 and the autumn of 1923.

116 "Many Agencies Aiding Negroes from South," 1917, TCF, Reel 6.

117 *Chicago Tribune,* March 6, 1917.

118 "Resolutions," *Christian Recorder,* March 15, 1917.

119 Clark, "Migrant in Pittsburgh," p. 306.

120 *Detroit Tribune,* July 15, 1917.

121 *Newark News,* April 15 and June 29, 1917.

122 John Marshall Ragland, "The Negro in Detroit," *Southern Workman* 52 (November 1923): 536.

123 *Detroit Tribune,* July 15, 1917.

124 Levine, *Internal Combustion,* p. 98. See also August Meier and Elliott Rudwick, *Black Detroit and the Rise of the UAW* (New York: Oxford University Press, 1979), p. 9.

125 Meier and Rudwick, *Black Detroit,* p. 11.

126 Cited in ibid., p. 16. On the connection between religion and jobs, see Levine, *Internal Combustion,* pp. 97–98.

127 Cited in Grossman, *Land of Hope,* p. 230.

128 Dickerson, "The Black Church in Industrializing Western Pennsylvania," pp. 329–30, 333.

129 *Journal of the Twenty-Sixth Quadrennial Session of the General Conference of the African Methodist Episcopal Church, Held in St. Louis, Missouri, May 3rd to 18th, 1920* (Nashville: A.M.E. Sunday School Union, 1922), p. 205.

130 *Southwest Christian Advocate,* July 19, 1917.

131 *Chicago Whip,* December 29, 1920.

132 *Chicago Defender,* April 4, 1917.

133 *Chicago Whip,* October 20, 1920, December 25, 1920; *Christian Recorder,* March 15, 1917; *Chicago Searchlight,* October 16, 1920; *Detroit Tribune,* July 15, 1917.

134 *Chicago Searchlight,* October 16, 1920.

135 Emmett J. Scott, "The Migration: A Northern View," *Opportunity* 2 (June 1924): 184.

136 "1923," *Opportunity,* 1 (January 1923): 3.

137 "A New Negro Migration," *Survey* 45 (February 26, 1921); Abraham Epstein, *The Negro Migrant in Pittsburgh* (Pittsburgh: University of Pittsburgh Press, 1918), p. 67.

138 *New York Globe,* January 29, 1923.

139 Hardy, "Race and Opportunity," p. 157.

140   Sadie Tanner Mossell, "The Standard of Living Among One Hundred Negro Migrant Families in Philadelphia," *Annals of the American Academy of Political and Social Science* 98 (November 1921): 176.

141   Ibid., p. 216.

142   Ibid., p. 218.

143   "Conference on Negro Migration of White and Negro Church Leaders, February 23, 1923, Under Auspices of Commission on the Church and Race Relations, Federal Council of Churches," *AME Church Review* (July 1923), p. 34.

144   Miles Mark Fisher, "The Negro Church and the World-War," *Journal of Religion* 5 (September 1925): 483, 486–87.

145   This is also the conclusion of historian Robert Gregg after an intensive study of the response of African Methodists in Philadelphia. Gregg points out that the class structure among Philadelphia's African American residents, including differentiation among the churches, was not entirely the result of the exclusiveness of the black elite. He argues that northerners were "not always hostile" to the newcomers, attempted to help where they could, and that "the heterogeneous character of the migrant population" also influenced the multiplication of new church organizations. Gregg, *Sparks from the Anvil of Oppression: Philadelphia's African Methodists and Southern Migrants, 1890–1940* (Philadelphia: Temple University Press, 1993), pp. vii and 15.

6   WHEN CHICAGO WAS CANAAN

1   Charles S. Johnson, *The New Negro*, ed. Alain Locke (New York: Albert and Charles Boni, 1925), p. 278.

2   Quoted in James Richard Grossman, *"Land of Hope": Chicago, Black Southerners and the Great Migration* (Chicago: University of Chicago Press, 1989), p. 5. Grossman's excellent study, though somewhat narrower in scope, complements Allan H. Spear's *Black Chicago: The Making of a Negro Ghetto, 1890–1920* (Chicago: University of Chicago Press, 1967). *Black Metropolis*, by St. Clair Drake and Horace R. Cayton, is based on data gathered under the Works Progress Administration at the end of the 1930s, but it contains valuable information on Chicago during the Great Migration. See esp. chaps. 2 and 3, part 1, *Black Metropolis: A Study of Negro Life in a Northern City* (1945; repr., 2 vols., New York: Harper Torchbooks, 1962).

3   James R. Grossman, "Blowing the Trumpet: The *Chicago Defender* and Black Migration During World War I," *Illinois Historical Journal* 78 (Summer 1985): 82–96. Abbott is referred to as a "black Joshua" by Florette Henri, *Black Migration: Movement North, 1900–1920* (Garden City, N.Y.: Anchor Books/Doubleday, 1975), p. 79. Abbott's biographer is Roi Ottley, *The Lonely Warrior: The Life and Times of Robert S. Abbott* (Chicago: Henry Regnery, 1955). See also Metz T. P. Lochard, "The Negro Press in Illinois," *Journal of the Illinois State Historical Society* 56 (Autumn 1963): 570–91.

4   Chicago Commission on Race Relations, *The Negro in Chicago* (Chicago: University of Chicago Press, 1922), p. 107; Thomas Lee Philpott, *The Slum and the Ghetto: Neighborhood Deterioration and Middle-Class Reform, Chicago, 1880–1930* (New York: Oxford University Press, 1978), pp. 119–27; Grossman, *Land of Hope*, pp. 171–74; Spear, *Black Chi-*

cago, chap. 1; Paul Frederick Cressey, "Population Succession in Chicago: 1898–1930," *American Journal of Sociology* 44 (July 1938): 59–69.

5   Fannie Barrier Williams, "Social Bonds in the 'Black Belt' of Chicago," *Charities,* October 7, 1905, p. 41. Williams was a social worker assigned to the Frederick Douglass Center.

6   *Christian Recorder,* April 14, 1916; Josephine Copeland, "The History of St. Paul c.m.e. Church," typescript in Illinois Writers Project files, "The Negro in Illinois," Vivian G. Harsh Collection, Woodson Regional Library, Chicago. Subsequent references to the Writers Project files will be designated iwp. Miles Mark Fisher, "Negro Churches in Illinois: A Fragmentary History with Emphasis on Chicago," *Journal of the Illinois State Historical Society* 56 (Autumn 1963): 554, 559–60.

7   "African Methodists Meet in Convention," *Chicago Inter-Ocean,* November 10, 1911.

8   Copeland, "History of St. Paul's," typescript, iwp, p. 1.

9   *Chicago Daily News,* September 7 and 8, 1915.

10   Spear, *Black Chicago,* p. 174.

11   Cited in J. G. St. Clair Drake, "The Negro Church and Associations in Chicago," a research memorandum, book 2, June 1, 1940. Drake's memorandum was prepared as background material for the project that resulted in the publication of the Carnegie-Myrdal study *An American Dilemma.*

12   Miles Mark Fisher, "The History of the Olivet Baptist Church of Chicago" (M.A. thesis, University of Chicago, 1922), pp. 86, 104. A migrant from Alabama who went to Olivet during her first week in Chicago in 1922 reported, "We couldn't get in. We'd have to stand up. I don't care how early we'd go, you couldn't get in." Cited in Grossman, *Land of Hope,* p. 210.

13   Quoted in Perry J. Stackhouse, *Chicago and the Baptists: A Century of Progress* (Chicago: University of Chicago Press, 1933), pp. 206–7.

14   South Parkway was originally Grand Boulevard. It is now Dr. Martin Luther King, Jr., Drive.

15   "Olivet Congregation Acquires Fine Church on South Side," *Chicago Defender,* May 18, 1918; "Olivet Church Members March to New Home of Worship," *Chicago Defender,* October 5, 1918.

16   *Christian Century,* October 24, 1918; *Chicago Daily Tribune,* May 13, 1918.

17   *Southwestern Christian Advocate,* May 22, 1918.

18   *Chicago Defender,* April 13, 1918.

19   *Southwestern Christian Advocate,* March 18, 1920. Ida B. Wells recalled that she was "greatly disappointed to find that no specific attention was being paid to the Negro communicants of the [Methodist] church" when she came to Chicago in the 1890s. St. Mark's was worshiping in a storefront, and the white Methodist authorities were opposed to including her reading room and social center under the rubric of church work. Alfreda M. Duster, ed., *Crusade for Justice: The Autobiography of Ida B. Wells* (Chicago: University of Chicago Press, 1970), pp. 355–58.

20   *Southwestern Christian Advocate,* March 18, 1920.

21   *Chicago Defender,* February 12, 1916.

22   The full text of Mundelein's letter is in *Two Crowded Years: Being Selected Addresses, Pas-*

torals, and Letters Issued During the First Twenty-four Months of the Episcopate of the Most Rev. George William Mundelein, D.D. as Archbishop of Chicago (Chicago: Extension Press, 1918), pp. 291–300. For a fuller discussion of the Catholic story, see Marvin R. Schafer, "The Catholic Church in Chicago: Its Growth and Administration" (Ph.D. diss., University of Chicago, 1929).

23 *Chicago Defender,* April 14, 1917.

24 In 1933, according to Drake and Cayton, Chicago's black congregations were burdened with the second-highest per capita indebtedness among urban black churches in the United States. *Black Metropolis,* vol. 2, p. 415. For more on church indebtedness and the strain in racial relations caused by the conflicts over purchasing property from whites, see Benjamin E. Mays and Joseph William Nicholson, *The Negro's Church* (New York: Institute of Social and Religious Research, 1933), pp. 175–85.

25 Josephine Copeland, "The History of Liberty Baptist Church," typescript, IWP, p. 1.

26 "Bethesda," typescript, IWP, p. 1. See also Orange Winkfield, "Bethesda Baptist Church," typescript, March 3, 1937, Federal Writers' Project, Illinois Records, Illinois State Historical Library, Springfield. This archival collection contains eleven manuscript boxes on specific churches and religious sects in Chicago and will be designated FWP.

27 A. Williams and E. Jenkins, "Monumental Baptist," typescript, July 1938, IWP, pp. 1–2.

28 A. Williams and E. Jenkins, "Pilgrim Baptist Church," typescript, IWP, p. 1.

29 The historian of Chicago's Bethlehem Baptist Association welcomed the new arrivals who flocked to the existing churches and crowded their services. When the migrants set up for themselves in tenement places and storefronts, he worried about their impact on the culture of the pulpit. "In those days prior to the War, we had real standard preachers, but in 1913 [*sic*] the standard went down; they had to get and do the best they could. The demand was so great. It is going up now." Drake, "The Negro Church and Associations in Chicago," pp. 308–9.

30 Horton's shaving parlor on Rhodes Avenue was situated in a colony of more than 150 families from Hattiesburg. Grossman, *Land of Hope,* pp. 98–99, 209. The transplanting of rural churches to Chicago continued in the post-Great Migration years. For example, migrants from Wilkes County, Georgia, came to Chicago about 1926 and formed "The Drexel Club." When members encountered someone else from down home, they would invite them to join. The group members soon invited their former pastor to come to Chicago, persuaded him to stay, and organized a Missionary Baptist Church. See St. Clair Drake, "Churches and Voluntary Associations in the Chicago Negro Community" (Report of Official Project 465-54-3-386, Works Progress Administration, Chicago, December 1940), pp. 149–50.

31 Robert Sutherland counted 278 black churches within the city limits of Chicago. He found twenty-four storefronts and only one "regular" church building on State Street from 26th Street to 60th Street. Sutherland, "An Analysis of Negro Churches in Chicago" (Ph.D. diss., University of Chicago, 1930), pp. 54A, 57.

32 Drake, "Negro Church and Associations," pp. 308–9.

33 The Church of God and Saints of Christ and the Church of the Living God may have been represented in Chicago before 1900, but the identity of specific congregations remains elusive. See Drake, "Churches and Voluntary Associations," p. 122. All Nations

Pentecostal Church was founded in one room at 36th Street and Cottage Avenue by Lucy Smith in 1916. She held services during the summer months in a tent, and until locating at 3716 Langley Avenue in 1925 she used various rented quarters. Fenton Johnson, typescript, "All Nations Pentecostal Church," typescript, FWP. A Spiritualist congregation, the Church of Redemption of Souls, preceded the Great Migration. Spear, *Black Chicago*, pp. 96–97.

34 "Sanctified in Chicago," typescript, IWP, p. 27. Sutherland, "Negro Churches in Chicago," p. 56. In 1928 Holiness churches in Chicago were outnumbered only by Baptist ones. Chicago Commission on Race Relations, *Negro in Chicago*, p. 145.

35 Grossman, *Land of Hope*, p. 213.

36 David Wills and Randall Burkett have argued that writers who are preoccupied with the cults and sects during the interwar years at the expense of the mainline black denominations have distorted the historical picture. Typescript, "Afro-American Religious History, 1919–1939: A Resource Guide and Bibliographical Essay," esp. pp. 5–6 (in my possession).

37 Quoted in Grossman, *Land of Hope*, p. 211.

38 Ibid., p. 212.

39 Ibid. A black businessman located in an area with many storefronts told a researcher, "Many of the older people especially from the South like small churches, because they are homelike. . . . Then too, the people are poor, and some of them can't dress fancy enough to want to be seen in a big church. . . . Some want to lead the prayer meetings, teach Sunday school and the like who feel that their old backwoods prayers and their manner of speech won't fit into the larger churches." Cited by Drake, "Churches and Voluntary Associations," p. 299.

40 Interview on March 9, 1938, with Joseph Borgere by Robert H. Mays, typescript, IWP. On the ministerial career of J. C. Austin, see Randall K. Burkett, "The Black Church in the Years of Crisis: J. C. Austin and Pilgrim Baptist Church, 1926–1950," in *African-American Religion: Interpretive Essays in History and Culture*, ed. Timothy E. Fulop and Albert J. Raboteau (New York: Routledge, 1996), pp. 312–39.

41 On Austin's multidimensional ministry, see Burkett, "The Black Church in the Years of Crisis."

42 *Grand Rapids* (Mich.) *Press*, September 10, 1917.

43 *Chicago Defender*, April 21, 1917.

44 Ibid., September 10, 1921.

45 A. Williams and E. Jennings, "Migration Era Churches: Coppin A.M.E. Chapel and Carey A.M.E. Temple," typescript, IWP, p. 1.

46 Grossman, *Land of Hope*, pp. 183, 211. On the Chicago Urban League, see Chicago Urban League, *Two Decades of Service* (Chicago: William Mason Press, 1936), and Arvarh Strickland, *History of the Chicago Urban League* (Urbana: University of Illinois Press, 1966). The NAACP was beset with internal problems during its early years. See Christopher Robert Reed, "Organized Racial Reform in Chicago During the Progressive Era: The Chicago NAACP, 1910–1920," *Michigan Historical Review* 14 (Spring 1988): 75–99.

47 Cited in Carl Sandburg, "Chicago a Receiving Station for Negroes After Each Lynching in the South," *Daily Herald*, January 9, 1920.

48   Magnolia L. Butts, "Résumé of the Growth of the Metropolitan Community Church," in *South Side Business and Professional Review* (Chicago: Five Hundred Men's Club of the Metropolitan Community Church, 1936), pp. 5, 49; Josephine Copeland, "The History of the Metropolitan Community Church," typescript, IWP, p. 2.

49   A. Williams, "The Peoples Community Church of Christ," typescript, IWP, p. 1. Williams consulted a church-authorized pamphlet dated 1927. "Cook Severs Connection with A.M.E. Conference," *Chicago Defender,* October 9, 1920.

50   Harold M. Kingsley, "The Negro Goes to Church," *Opportunity* 7 (March 1929): 90. Sutherland asserts that Cook's withdrawal was "largely in protest to Bishop Carey's rule." See Sutherland, "Negro Churches in Chicago," p. 69.

51   "Metropolitan Center Buys Masonic Temple Home," *Chicago Defender,* November 5, 1921; Orange Winkfield, "Metropolitan Community Center, the People's Church," typescript, c. 1937, FWP.

52   Sutherland, "Negro Churches in Chicago," pp. 69–70; A. Williams and E. Jennings, "Cosmopolitan Independent Community Church," typescript, IWP, p. 1. Cosmopolitan had the distinction in 1932 of being the only "orthodox" Christian church in the Chicago area to be pastored by a woman, the Rev. Mary G. Evans. See Copeland, "History of St. Paul C.M.E. Church," typescript, IWP, p. 2.

53   *Chicago Defender,* October 9, 1920.

54   Lacy K. Williams, "The Urbanization of Negroes: The Effect on Their Religious Life," *Chicago Daily Tribune,* January 13, 1929.

55   Ibid. Williams's critique reveals a tension between wanting to address the "religious psychology" of the migrants by offering them an intimate fellowship as found in the rural churches of the South and a desire to provide them with the social services of a large, highly structured urban church. On Olivet's extensive educational and social ministry program that attracted many migrants, see Mattie S. Fisher, "Olivet as a Christian Center," *Missions* 10 (March 1919): 199–202.

56   Carl Sandburg, *The Chicago Race Riots, July, 1919* (New York: Harcourt, Brace and Howe, 1919), p. 5.

57   Quoted from Duster, ed., *Crusade for Justice,* pp. xxviii–xxix.

58   Among the most helpful specialized studies are Charles Russell Branham, "Black Chicago: Accommodationist Politics Before the Great Migration," in *The Ethnic Frontier,* ed. Melvin G. Holli and Peter d'A Jones (Grand Rapids, Mich.: William B. Eerdmans, 1977), pp. 211–62; Charles Russell Branham, "The Transformation of Black Political Leadership in Chicago, 1864–1942" (Ph.D. diss., University of Chicago, 1981); Harold F. Gosnell, *Negro Politicians: The Rise of Negro Politics in Chicago* (Chicago: University of Chicago Press, 1935); Joseph Logsdon, "The Reverend A. J. Carey and the Negro in Chicago Politics" (M.A. thesis, University of Chicago, 1961); Spear, *Black Chicago,* chaps. 6 and 10; and William M. Tuttle, Jr., *Race Riot: Chicago in the Red Summer of 1919* (New York: Atheneum, 1970), pp. 184–207.

59   John D. Buenker, "Dynamics of Chicago Ethnic Politics, 1900–1930," *Journal of the Illinois State Historical Society* 67 (April 1974): 190.

60   Branham, "Black Chicago," p. 260.

61 Fisher, *Master's Slave*, pp. 75, 145. Note the "appreciation" by Congressman Martin B. Madden at the beginning of this biography. Branham, "Black Chicago," p. 235.

62 Fisher, "Olivet Baptist Church," p. 79.

63 Lillian B. Horace, *"'Crowned with Glory and Honor',": The Life of Rev. Lacy Kirk Williams,* ed. Venchael Booth (Hicksville, N.Y.: Exposition Press, 1978), p. 144.

64 Fisher, "Olivet Baptist Church," p. 93.

65 *Broad Ax,* October 18, 1913, and July 11, 1914. Taylor, editor and publisher of this largely personal paper, constantly maintained an anticlerical posture. Though it is difficult to assess how widely his opinions were shared, he may have voiced the sentiments of a younger, more secularized element in the Black Belt.

66 *Chicago Defender,* June 6, 1914.

67 *Broad Ax,* May 15, 1916, cited in Logsdon, "Carey and the Negro in Chicago Politics," p. 32.

68 Logsdon, "Carey and the Negro in Chicago Politics," pp. 32–33. The concentration of African Americans in wards two and three, intensified by the Great Migration, made the election of race candidates possible. Migrants were steered to the black wards and quickly recruited by precinct captains eager to bolster the voting strength of these wards. Any movement to break down residential or political segregation was, therefore, viewed as counterproductive. Drake and Cayton cite a prominent newspaperman on this point: "It's okay to break it down in principle and get a few Negroes over the line. But we want the majority to stay here so they can vote in a bloc." *Black Metropolis,* p. 348; Gosnell, *Negro Politicians,* pp. 170–72.

69 George Schottenhamel, "How Big Bill Thompson Won Control of Chicago," *Journal of the Illinois State Historical Society* 45 (Spring 1952): 32–36; Logsdon, "Archibald J. Carey and the Negro in Chicago Politics," pp. 35–37.

70 Branham, "Black Political Leadership," p. 70.

71 *Chicago Defender,* June 26, 1914, p. 4. On Carey's friendship with Lorimar, see Gosnell, *Negro Politicians,* p. 39, n. 5.

72 *Chicago Defender,* September 18, 1915.

73 Schottenhamel, "Big Bill Thompson," p. 47.

74 Logsdon, "Carey and the Negro in Chicago Politics," p. 48.

75 Gosnell maintains that Carey did not think of himself "primarily as a political leader." *Negro Politicians,* p. 98. Given Carey's attempts to exercise political influence and obtain benefits from the machine for his people, we ought to expand the category of "politician" to include him.

76 *Broad Ax,* May 1, 1915, cited in Logsdon, "Carey and the Negro in Chicago Politics," p. 50.

77 Logsdon, "Carey and the Negro in Chicago Politics," p. 51.

78 *Chicago Defender,* March 2, 1918. In 1928 De Priest triumphed over his clerical critics when he was elected to the U.S. House of Representatives, becoming the first African American from a northern state to sit in the U.S. Congress.

79 *Chicago Defender,* April 16, 1918.

80 Ibid., June 29, 1918.

81 Letter reprinted in the *Broad Ax,* Jay 27, 1916, cited in Logsdon, "Carey and the Negro in Politics," p. 58.

82 Duster, ed., *Crusade for Justice,* p. 393. Wells had come into conflict with Carey earlier when she was attempting to obtain the Pekin Theater, formerly a saloon run by Robert T. Motts, for a benefit to support the Douglass Center. Carey, then pastor at Bethel, denounced the effort because of Motts's reputation as "the keeper of a low gambling dive." Both Carey and Elijah J. Fisher, whose church was directly across from the Pekin Theater and who also spoke against the benefit, had long been active in the antivice crusade in Chicago. See ibid., pp. 289–92.

83 James R. Haydon, "Son of Slave Given Civil Service Seat," *Chicago Daily Journal,* April 13, 1927. George F. Robinson, Jr., makes the interesting observation that "this position was asked for because its dignity, the financial remuneration, and its infrequent duties would allow the bishop to carry on his many other affairs. Then, too, the appointment required no confirmation by the City Council." See Robinson, "The Negro in Politics in Chicago," *Journal of Negro History* 17 (April 1932): 216.

84 Cited in "The Civil Service Commission of Chicago—Bishop A. J. Carey," *AME Church Review* 44 (July 1927): 43.

85 Gosnell, *Negro Politicians,* p. 98.

86 Logsdon, "Carey and the Negro in Politics," p. 80.

87 *Christian Recorder,* April 9, 1931.

88 Ibid.

89 *Chicago Whip,* March 10, 1928.

90 Howard Preston Smith II, "The Limitations of Racial Democracy: The Politics of the Chicago Urban League, 1916–1940" (Ph.D. diss., University of Massachusetts, 1990). See also Arvarh Strickland, *History of the Chicago Urban League* (Urbana: University of Illinois Press, 1966).

91 *Chicago Defender,* February 19, 1916. Similar criticisms of clerical involvement in politics can be found in the *Defender,* March 27, 1920, and November 21, 1924.

92 Martin Kilson, "Political Change in the Negro Ghetto, 1900–1940s," in *Key Issues in the Afro-American Experience,* ed. Nathan I. Huggins, Martin Kilson, and Daniel M. Fox (New York: Harcourt Brace Jovanovich, 1971), p. 171.

93 Quoted in Sterling Spero and Abram Harris, *The Black Worker* (New York: Columbia University Press, 1931), p. 135. Carey's position must be understood against the background of working-class fragmentation in Chicago. See James R. Barrett, "Unity and Fragmentation: Class, Race, and Ethnicity on Chicago's South Side, 1900–1922," *Journal of Social History* 18 (Fall 1984): 37–56.

94 Grossman, *Land of Hope,* pp. 319–22.

95 "Colored Chicago: A Study in Contrasts," FWP, Box 199, 1930. The author of this sentiment was probably Harold M. Kingsley, pastor of Chicago's Church of the Good Shepherd, which actively fed the unemployed during the depression.

96 Ralph J. Bunche, "The Thompson-Negro Alliance," *Opportunity* 7 (March 1929): 78–80.

97 A. L. Jackson, "Chicago's Negro Problem," *City Club Bulletin,* March 17, 1919, p. 76.

98 This remarkable historical transition was noted in 1945 in Drake and Cayton's study of

Chicago: "Forty years ago, church news was 'big news' in Negro newspapers. Today, churches and preachers seldom make the front page unless some sensational incident is involved. In total bulk, too, church news falls far behind club news. The church is not the *center* of community life as it was in Midwest Metropolis before the Great Migration or as it is today in the small towns of the South." *Black Metropolis*, p. 418.

99   Branham, "Black Political Leadership in Chicago," p. 147.

100   Ibid., pp. 148–49.

101   Drake, "Negro Church and Associations," p. 388. E. Franklin Frazier also yoked urbanization with secularization. He wrote: "The urbanization of Negroes on a large scale, beginning with the First World War, has brought about a transformation of the Negro church and changed the outlook of Negroes upon the world and their place in the world. There has been a secularization of outlook and Negro churches have not failed to reflect this change in outlook. The regularly established Negro churches placed less emphasis upon salvation after death and directed their activities increasingly to the economic, social, and political problems of Negroes in this world. The reorganization of the religious life of Negroes in the urban environment has been influenced largely by the new class structure of Negro communities, especially in the North, which is the result of the increasing occupational differentiation of the Negro population." Frazier, *The Negro Church in America* (New York: Schocken Books, 1964), p. 84.

102   Kilson, "Political Change in the Negro Ghetto," p. 185.

103   I have in mind Joel Williamson's discussion of one of the results of the feudalization of black life in the South after Reconstruction and the rise of what he calls the "black baron." See Williamson, *The Crucible of Race: Black-White Relations in the American South Since Emancipation* (New York: Oxford University Press, 1984), pp. 54–57.

7   A HEAVEN ALL THEIR OWN

1   Richard Wright, *12 Million Black Voices* (New York: Viking Press, 1941), p. 131.

2   Ibid., p. 127.

3   Ira De A. Reid, "Let Us Prey!", *Opportunity* 4 (September 1926): 276.

4   Reverdy C. Ransom and James H. Robinson, *Year Book of Negro Churches, 1939–40* (Philadelphia: A.M.E. Book Concern, 1940), p. 45.

5   Miles Mark Fisher, "Organized Religion and the Cults," *Crisis* 44 (January 1937): 8–10, 29–30. Also see Miles Mark Fisher, "Negroes Get Religion," *Opportunity* 14 (May 1936): 147–50.

6   George E. Haynes, "Negro Migration," *Opportunity* 2 (September 1924): 304.

7   For example, Sydney E. Ahlstrom, *A Religious History of the American People* (New Haven, Conn.: Yale University Press, 1972), and Winthrop Hudson, *Religion in America* (New York: Scribner, 1965).

8   Mother Bethel A.M.E. Church, *Information Bureau Leaflet* (n.p.), copy supplied to me by Robert S. Gregg. The definitive account of these years at Bethel is by Gregg, "The Earnest Pastor's Heated Term: Robert J. Williams's Pastorate at 'Mother' Bethel, 1916–1920," *Pennsylvania Magazine of History & Biography* 113 (January 1989): 67–88.

9   Ibid., pp. 76–77.

10 April 10, 1916, "Minutes of the Corporation, 1894–1950," Mother Bethel African Methodist Episcopal Church, Philadelphia, microfilm (Harvard University).

11 Gregg cites schisms in Pinn Memorial Baptist and Varick Temple AME Zion churches as parallels to what happened to Williams at Bethel. Gregg, "Earnest Pastor's Heated Term," p. 87.

12 *Philadelphia North American,* January 31, 1919.

13 Ralph H. Jones, *Charles Albert Tindley: Prince of Preachers* (Nashville: Abingdon Press, 1982), p. 102.

14 Charles A. Tindley, "The Church That Welcomed 10,000 Strangers," *World Outlook* 5 (October 1919): 5–6.

15 John Marshall Ragland, "The Negro in Detroit," *Southern Workman* 52 (November 1923): 538–39.

16 Dennis C. Dickerson, "The Black Church in Industrializing Western Pennsylvania, 1870–1950," *Western Pennsylvania Historical Magazine* 64 (October 1981): 338.

17 Arthur E. Holt, "Religion," *American Journal of Sociology* 34 (July 1928): 175.

18 Kenneth L. Kusmer, *A Ghetto Takes Shape* (Urbana: University of Illinois Press, 1976), pp. 93–94, 207.

19 Seth M. Scheiner, "The Negro Church and the Northern City, 1890–1930," in *Seven on Black,* ed. William G. Shade and Roy C. Herrenkohl (Philadelphia: J. B. Lippincott, 1969), p. 99.

20 Ibid., pp. 160–61.

21 Ibid., p. 157.

22 Allan B. Ballard, *One More Day's Journey: The Story of a Family and a People* (New York: McGraw-Hill, 1984), p. 176. State clubs still function. Harold Dean-Trulear writes of those in the Community Baptist Church in Paterson, New Jersey: "On 'South Carolina Sunday,' the South Carolina club will have an afternoon program, invite a preacher either from South Carolina or with roots in the Palmetto State, renew ties with South Carolinians from their church and others, and raise money for the church budget. Historically, some of these state clubs have become so powerful that they leave the church and form their own congregation; of course, they will then call a pastor from their home state." Harold Dean-Trulear, "The Role of the Church in Black Migration: Some Preliminary Observations," *Journal of the Afro-American Historical and Genealogical Society* 8 (Summer 1987): 55.

23 Robert Gregg, *Sparks from the Anvil of Oppression: Philadelphia African Methodists and the Great Migration, 1890–1930* (Philadelphia: Temple University Press, 1993), p. 232.

24 *Christian Recorder,* February 8, 1917.

25 For details on the Abbeville affair, see Loren Schweninger, *Black Property Owners in the South, 1790–1915* (Urbana: University of Illinois Press, 1990), pp. 233–35.

26 Ibid., p. 175.

27 The definition used by G. Norman Eddy, professor of human relations at Boston University in the mid-1950s, is representative of the traditional understanding of a storefront. "More formally, I mean by this term 'store-front religion' those groups found in the socially disorganized areas of large urban communities and generally housed in small secular buildings. These faiths are characterized by a more or less marked deviation from

that of any established religious body. They differ in many ways from the denominations and ecclesia; specifically, in the lower economic stratification of their congregations, in the bizarre nature of their theology, and in their unpretentious store-front meeting places. Marked contrasts with the more traditional religious bodies are apparent both in their ritual and in their social and psychological objectives. Store-front religions range all the way from ephemeral groups to those which have a history of two or more generations. Some of these groups are entirely independent, but a majority have at least a loose affiliation with other groups in an ecclesiastical organization. . . . All store-front groups, however, are characterized by the marginal, social, and economic status of their congregations." G. Norman Eddy, "Store-Front Religion," *Religion in Life* 28 (Winter 1958–59): 177–78.

28 ` Lennox Yearwood, "First Shiloh Baptist Church of Buffalo, New York: From Storefront to Major Religious Institution," *Afro-Americans in New York Life and History* 1 (January 1977): 81–92.

29 William M. Welty, "Black Shepherds: A Study of the Leading Negro Clergymen in New York City, 1900–1940" (Ph.D. diss., New York University, 1969), pp. 163–64.

30 Peter Gottlieb, *Making Their Own Way: Southern Blacks' Migration to Pittsburgh, 1916–30* (Urbana: University of Illinois Press, 1987), p. 198.

31 Harold Cooke Phillips, "The Social Significance of Negro Churches in Harlem" (M.A. thesis, Columbia University, 1922), p. 23. The "colored section" of Harlem defined by Phillips extended from 130th to 146th streets but was moving toward downtown Manhattan.

32 Robert Austin Warner, *New Haven Negroes* (New Haven, Conn.: Yale University Press, for the Institute of Human Relations, 1940), p. 214. For an earlier portrait of African Americans in New Haven, see William H. Ferris, "These 'Colored' United States: Connecticut: The Nutmeg State," *Messenger* 6 (January 1924): 24–25. Ferris enumerated seven "colored churches" but listed eight—one Congregational, one Episcopal, one Baptist, three Methodist, one Seventh Day Adventist, and one African Orthodox Church. He did not include any of the then existing storefronts.

33 Warner, *New Haven Negroes,* p. 213. Warner took this characterization of southern religion from Edwin McNeill Poteat, Jr., in *Culture in the South,* ed. W. T. Couch (Chapel Hill: University of North Carolina Press, 1934), p. 248.

34 Welty, "Black Shepherds," pp. 209–10.

35 Reid, "Let Us Prey!," p. 278.

36 Ira De A. Reid, *In a Minor Key: Negro Youth in Story and Fact* (Washington, D.C.: American Council on Education, 1940), pp. 84–85.

37 E. Franklin Frazier, *The Negro Church in America* (New York: Schocken Books, 1964), p. 53. Frazier had been sharply critical of the failure of the traditional black church to deal with the social problems confronting African Americans in the wake of the Great Migration. In 1924, he wrote that institutionalized religion was "primarily a conservative social force" and that religious leaders were "still more interested in getting Negroes into heaven than in getting them out of the hell they live in on earth." Cited in Anthony M. Platt, *E. Franklin Frazier Reconsidered* (New Brunswick, N.J.: Rutgers University Press, 1991), p. 74.

38   Frazier, *Negro Church,* pp. 53–54.

39   Gottlieb, *Making Their Own Way,* p. 197.

40   Ibid., pp. 202–3.

41   Benjamin E. Mays and Joseph W. Nicholson, *The Negro's Church* (New York: Institute of Social and Religious Research, 1933), p. 99.

42   Cited in Gottlieb, *Making Their Own Way,* p. 203.

43   Ibid.

44   Arthur E. Paris, *Black Pentecostalism: Southern Religion in an Urban World* (Amherst: University of Massachusetts Press, 1982), p. 27.

45   Kusmer, *A Ghetto Takes Shape,* p. 96.

46   Paris, *Black Pentecostalism,* p. 28.

47   David M. Tucker, *Black Pastors and Leaders: Memphis, 1819–1972* (Memphis: Memphis State University Press, 1975), p. 95.

48   Ford S. Black, comp., *Black's Blue Book* (Chicago: Ford S. Black, 1916), p. 47.

49   The AME Zion Church began the ordination of women in 1894. The AME and CME followed suit, respectively, in 1948 and 1954. Black Baptist denominations do not officially proscribe the ordination of women, but little encouragement is given to women who wish to be ordained and pastor churches. Opposition against women clergy is strong in many sectors. See C. Eric Lincoln and Lawrence H. Mamiya, *The Black Church in the African American Experience* (Durham, N.C.: Duke University Press, 1990), chap. 10.

50   Elder Lucy Smith maintained that All Nations was not "a colored church, but a church for all nations." Her Pentecostal and healing services did attract a wide variety of participants, but the core membership was African American. For a contemporary description of Elder Smith and her ministry, including the use of radio broadcasts, see Herbert Morrisohn Smith, "Three Negro Preachers in Chicago: A Study in Religious Leadership" (M.A. thesis, Divinity School, University of Chicago, 1935), pp. 10–14. See also Fenton Johnson, "All Nations Pentecostal Church," typescript, IWP.

51   Joe W. Trotter, *Black Milwaukee: The Making of an Industrial Proletariat, 1915–1945* (Urbana: University of Illinois Press, 1985), p. 130.

52   Cited in ibid., p. 130.

53   Kusmer, *A Ghetto Takes Shape,* p. 208.

54   To emphasize his point, Washington reported that basement churches also attracted what he termed "a number of emotional and unbalanced white people." In Bureau of Governmental Research, "The Negro in Detroit," mimeo. (Detroit: Detroit Bureau of Governmental Research, 1926), pp. 94–95.

55   Ibid.

56   Arthur H. Fauset, *Black Gods of the Metropolis* (Philadelphia: University of Pennsylvania Press, 1944).

57   Albert N. Whiting, "The United House of Prayer for All People: A Case Study of a Charismatic Sect" (Ph.D. diss., American University, Washington, D.C., 1952). For a typology of members, see Albert N. Whiting, "'From Saint to Shuttler,'—An Analysis of Sectarian Types," *Quarterly Review of Higher Education Among Negroes* 23 (October 1955): 133–40.

58   The southern roots of black Judaism are discussed by Merrill Singer, "The Southern

Origin of Black Judaism," in *African Americans in the South: Issues of Race, Class, and Gender,* ed. Hans A. Baer and Yvonne Jones (Athens: University of Georgia Press, 1992), pp. 124–38.

59 Erdmann Doane Benyon, "The Voodoo Cult Among Negro Migrants in Detroit," *American Journal of Sociology* 43 (May 1938): 894–907.

60 Fauset, *Black Gods of the Metropolis,* p. 80.

61 Ibid., p. 81.

62 Ira De A. Reid, *Social Conditions of the Negro in the Hill District of Pittsburgh* (Pittsburgh: General Committee on the Hill Survey, 1930).

63 Cited in Welty, "Black Shepherds," p. 138.

64 Richard R. Wright, Jr., "Social Work and Influence of the Negro Church," *Annals of the American Academy of Political and Social Science* 30 (November 1907): 91.

65 Ibid., p. 92.

66 *New York Post,* July 13, 1917. On the establishment and growth of YMCA branches for African Americans, see Nina Mjag Kij, "History of the Black YMCA in America" (Ph.D. diss., University of Cincinnati, 1990).

67 George E. Haynes, "Negro Migration: Its Effect on Family and Community Life in the North," *Opportunity* 2 (September 1924): 273.

68 Seth M. Scheiner, *Negro Mecca* (New York: New York University Press, 1965), pp. 96–101. Powell is quoted on p. 100. On the attractions of Harlem, see David Levering Lewis, *When Harlem Was in Vogue* (New York: Oxford University Press, 1981), chap. 2.

69 Paul Oliver, *Songsters & Saints: Vocal Traditions on Race Records* (New York: Cambridge University Press, 1984), pp. 5, 41–42. See also Paul Oliver, *Blues Fell This Morning: The Meaning of the Blues* (New York: Horizon Press, 1960), p. 132. The church-blues conflict is discussed in Albert Murray, *Stomping the Blues* (New York: Vintage Press, 1976).

70 On songs of the Sanctified churches, see Oliver, *Songsters & Saints,* chap. 6. Oliver discusses the impact of the Great Migration on African American religious music in his *Screening the Blues: Aspects of the Blues Tradition* (New York: Da Capo Press, 1989), pp. 44–89. See also Michael Harris, *The Rise of Gospel Blues: The Music of Thomas Andrew Dorsey in the Urban Church* (New York: Oxford University Press, 1992).

71 Sterling Brown, "Negro Folk Expression: Spirituals, Seculars, Ballads and Work Songs," *Phylon* 14 (January 1953): 60–61.

72 Melvin D. Williams, *Community in a Black Pentecostal Church* (Pittsburgh: University of Pittsburgh Pres, 1974), p. 47. When Williams did his fieldwork in the early 1970s, Zion still functioned, though original members were few in number. Williams argues that the "gradual disappearance of one of the original needs (an intimate association for Southern rural migrants)" along with competition from other subcultures in Pittsburgh's African American ghetto had "produced a recruitment crisis" (p. 172). A social-space analysis by Bobby M. Wilson of churches in the Bedford-Stuyvesant section of Brooklyn also underscores how strongly black in-migrants in an urban environment sought to replicate the communal nature of the rural church decades after the Great Migration. See Wilson, "Church Participation: A Social Space Analysis in a Community of Black In-Migrants," *Journal of Black Studies* 10 (December 1979): 198–217.

73 Ruth Landes, "Negro Jews in Harlem," *Jewish Journal of Sociology* 9 (December 1967): 179.

74   James Baldwin, *Go Tell It On the Mountain* (New York: Alfred A. Knopf, 1953). See Charles Scruggs, "The Tale of Two Cities in James Baldwin's *Go Tell It On the Mountain*," *American Literature* 52 (1980): 1–17.

75   Charles S. Johnson, "Black Workers and the City," *Survey*, March 1, 1925, p. 642.

76   Barbara Ballis Lal, "Black and Blue in Chicago: Robert E. Park's Perspective on Race Relations in Urban America, 1914–44," *British Journal of Sociology* 38 (1987): 550. See also Martin Bulmer, "The Chicago School of Sociology: What Made It a 'School'?," *History of Sociology* 5 (Spring 1985): 61–77.

77   Frederick Miller, "The Black Migration to Philadelphia: A 1924 Profile," *Pennsylvania Magazine of History and Biography* 108 (July 1984): 318.

78   Ibid., pp. 336–37.

79   Timothy Thomas Fortune, "New Negro Type of Person; His Traits and His Failings," *Philadelphia Public Ledger*, August 7, 1917.

80   McGhee's remarks are abstracted in "The Conference Note Book," *Opportunity* 5 (June 1927): 177–78.

81   Cited in *Philadelphia Tribune*, March 10, 1923. Mossell's study was published as "The Standard of Living Among 100 Negro Migrant Families in Philadelphia," *Annals of the American Academy of Political and Social Science* 98 (November 1921), 173–222.

82   George E. Haynes, "Negro Migration—Its Effect on Family and Community Life in the North," in *Proceedings of the National Conference of Social Work, Toronto, Ontario, June 25–July 2, 1924* (Chicago: University of Chicago Press, 1924), pp. 71–72.

83   "Editorial," *Opportunity* 1 (January 1923): 1. Exactly when the "new migration" began is subject to debate. *Survey* announced a "new Negro migration" in February 1921, but much of this movement involved unskilled labor thrown out of industrial jobs as a result of the downturn in the postwar economy. "A New Negro Migration," *Survey*, February 26, 1921.

84   "The Migration Continues," *Opportunity* 1 (February 1923): 28.

85   Editorial, "Negro Migration and the Immigration Quota," *Opportunity* 1 (April 1923): 18–20.

86   *Chicago Defender*, October 18, 1919.

87   Richard R. Wright, Jr., "Should Negroes Come North?," *Christian Recorder*, August 31, 1916.

88   Gavin White, "Patriarch McGuire and the Episcopal Church," in *Black Apostles*, ed. Randall K. Burkett and Richard Newman (Boston: G. K. Hall, 1978), p. 159.

89   Randall K. Burkett, "The Religious Ethos of the Universal Negro Improvement Association," in *African American Religious Studies: An Interdisciplinary Anthology*, ed. Gayraud Wilmore (Durham, N.C.: Duke University Press, 1989), pp. 60–81.

90   Marcus Garvey, "Our Lesson—Remember It," *The Black Man* 1 (August–September 1935): 11. This issue also contains details of "The New Programme."

91   *Crisis* 21 (1920–21): 58–60. See Elliott M. Rudwick, "Du Bois Versus Garvey: Race Propagandists at War," *Journal of Negro Education* 28 (Fall 1959): 421–29.

92   *New York Age*, August 28, 1920.

93   Randall K. Burkett, *Black Redemption: Churchmen Speak for the Garvey Movement* (Philadelphia: Temple University Press, 1978), p. 9.

94 Howard M. Brotz, *The Black Jews of Harlem* (New York: Schocken Books, 1964); Albert Ehrman, "The Commandment Keepers: A Negro 'Jewish' Cult in America Today," *Judaism* 8 (1959): 266–72; Ruth Landes, "Negro Jews in Harlem," pp. 175–90; Deanne Shapiro, "Factors in the Development of Black Judaism," in *The Black Experience in Religion,* ed. C. Eric Lincoln (Garden City, N.Y.: Doubleday, 1974), pp. 254–72. For a fascinating account of the discovery by B. Levitin of a group of black Jews calling themselves the Hebrew Settlement Society and located at 2367 Seventh Avenue in upper Manhattan, see the *Brooklyn Standard Union,* November 7, 1920.

95 Elias Fanayaye Jones, "Black Hebrews: The Quest for Authentic Identity," *Journal of Religious Thought* 44 (Winter–Spring 1988): 39–40.

96 Tony Martin, *Race First* (Westport, Conn.: Greenwood Press, 1976), p. 74.

97 Though the movement called the "Nation of Islam" did not begin until the early 1930s, it had its roots in the despair found among migrants from the South. The Black Muslim/migrant connection is discussed in an early account by E. D. Benyon, "The Voodoo Cult Among Negro-Migrants in Detroit," *American Journal of Sociology* 43 (May 1938): 898–907; and by C. Eric Lincoln in his classic *The Black Muslims in America* (Rev. ed.; Boston: Beacon Press, 1973), pp. xxiii–xiv.

98 Fisher, "Organized Religion and the Cults," p. 2.

99 Claude McKay, "There Goes God!": The Story of Father Divine and His Angels," *Nation,* February 6, 1935; Robert Weisbrot, *Father Divine and the Struggle for Racial Equality* (Urbana: University of Illinois Press, 1983), pp. 61–62. See also Kenneth E. Burnham, *God Comes to America: Father Divine and the Peace Mission Movement* (Boston: Lambeth Press, 1978).

100 Mahalia Jackson with Evan McLeod Wylie, *Movin' on Up* (New York: Hawthorn Books, 1966), p. 60.

101 Cited in Farah Jasmine Griffin, *"Who Set You Flowin'?": The African-American Migration Narrative* (New York: Oxford University Press, 1995), p. 61.

102 Cited in Lawrence W. Levine, *Black Culture and Black Consciousness* (New York: Oxford University Press, 1977), p. 180.

103 Arna Bontemps, "Rock, Church, Rock!," *Common Ground,* Autumn 1942, p. 75. Dorsey played the piano as "Georgia Tom" at the Monogram Theater in Chicago as early as 1925. He composed his first "gospel" song in 1921, but he did not dedicate himself to the genre until several years later. Horace C. Boyer, "Thomas A. Dorsey, Father of Gospel Music," *Black World* 23 (July 1974): 21–28. The most complete study of Dorsey and his influence is Michael Harris's *Rise of Gospel Blues: The Music of Thomas Andrew Dorsey in the Urban Church* (New York: Oxford University Press, 1992).

104 Lincoln and Mamiya, *The Black Church,* p. 378. The survey question did not distinguish between kinds of gospel music. Some contemporary forms, though commercially successful, are not thought appropriate for worship settings.

105 David J. Hellwig, "Strangers in Their Own Land: Patterns of Black Nativism, 1830–1930," *American Studies* 23 (Spring 1982): 94.

106 Wilson J. Moses, *The Golden Age of Black Nationalism, 1850–1925* (Hamden, Conn.: Archon Books, 1978); Levine, *Black Culture and Black Consciousness,* p. 269.

8 RETURN TO THE SOUTH

1 *Atlanta Constitution,* January 8, 1917.

2 *Macon News,* November 15, 1916.

3 *Macon Telegraph,* January 24, 1917.

4 Writing in 1921, Donald Hendersen noted that no systematic study had been made of re-turnees; however, he thought that 10 percent of the total number who had left the South was a reasonable estimate. H. Donald Hendersen, "The Negro Migration of 1916–18," *Journal of Negro History* 6 (October 1921): 468. For a discussion of why return migra-tion, other than periodic visits to see family and friends, was minimal, see Carole Marks, *Farewell—We're Good and Gone: The Great Migration* (Bloomington: Indiana University Press, 1989), pp. 158–62.

5 "An Exodus Turns Around," *Time,* January 22, 1990, p. 27. First noticed in the late 1970s, the reversal of the fifty-year trend of migration from the South accelerated during the 1980s. From 1985 through 1990, 355,000 more black Americans moved to the South than migrated out of the region. "You Can Go Home Again," *Time,* December 24, 1990, p. 72. Isaac Robinson, "Blacks Move Back to the South," *American Demographics* 8 (June 1986): 40–43. Kevin E. McHugh, "Black Migration Reversal in the United States," *Geo-graphical Review* 77 (April 1987): 171–82.

6 Richard L. Morrill and O. Fred Donaldson, "Geographical Perspectives on the History of Black America," *Economic Geography* 48 (January 1972): 14.

7 *Houston Observer,* May 24, 1919.

8 *New York Age,* November 29, 1919.

9 "Good Out of Evil," *Colored Harvest* (November–December 1922), HCF.

10 *Norfolk Journal and Guide,* February 22, 1919.

11 Cited in Elwood Street, "Southern Social Problems," *Southern Workman* 46 (September 1917): 476–77.

12 E. Franklin Frazier, "Three Scourges of the Negro Family," *Opportunity* 4 (July 1926): 210–12. On the loss of faith experienced by migrants who came north, see E. Franklin Frazier, *The Negro Family in Chicago* (Chicago: University of Chicago Press, 1932), pp. 75–76.

13 *Atlanta Independent,* February 13, 1919.

14 Kenyon L. Butterfield advocated that the rural church "be less of a social club and more of a community school of practical religion." Butterfield, *The Farmer and the New Day* (New York: Macmillan, 1919), p. 181. For a fuller expression of Butterfield's rural church program, see his *The Country Church and the Rural Problem* (Chicago: University of Chi-cago Press, 1911).

15 Butterfield, *Country Church,* p. 75. Butterfield's agrarianism contained a strong thread of romanticism intertwined with theological idealism: "Finally, it seems to me that in some ways it ought to be true that the farmer is the most religious of men. Every step he takes, every time he plows the field, every time he plants the seed, every time he har-vests a crop, he is dealing with God's world, with God's soil, with God's plants, with God's animals, day in and day out. That is his job, to find out what the laws of God

are and then to work with them. He is a worker with God." Butterfield, "A Satisfying Country Life," *Southern Workman* 50 (October 1921): 448.

16 Concerns about rural depletion and rural degeneracy in New England and the Midwest motivated many of the researchers. See, for example, G. Walter Fiske, *The Challenge of the Country* (New York: Association Press, 1919). Leaders of the Country Life Movement singled out the church and secondarily the school as the two most critical institutions to rural revitalization. Fiske wanted the church to be "the climax of the social, educational, philanthropic, health-restoring, peace-preserving forces of the community" (p. 182). A survey of Ohio located and mapped 1,058 abandoned rural churches in 1921. See C. E. Lively, "Some Rural Social Agencies in Ohio, 1922–23," *Ohio State University Agricultural Extension Service Bulletin* (1924), p. 17.

17 Robert R. Moton, "The American Negro in Agriculture," in *Rural Organization: Proceedings of the Third National Country Life Conference* (Chicago: University of Chicago Press, 1920), pp. 44, 48.

18 Robert R. Moton, "Negro Rural Life," *Southern Workman* 50 (July 1921): 324.

19 Rosa Young, *Light in the Dark Belt* (St. Louis: Concordia, 1930), p. 55. Born in 1890, Rosa Young's father was an African Methodist preacher. A graduate of Payne University in Selma, Alabama, she started a small school known as the Rosebud Literary and Industrial Institute in 1912. Following the advice of Booker T. Washington, she solicited aid from the German-speaking Evangelical Lutheran Synodical Conference, based in St. Louis, when the viability of her school was threatened because of the boll weevil infestation of the Black Belt.

20 Benjamin F. Hubert, "The Country Life Movement for Negroes," *Rural America* 7 (May 1929): 4.

21 "Negro Country Life Conference," *Southern Workman* 58 (March 1929): 108–10. Throughout the 1920s black farmers lagged behind their white counterparts in farm size, productivity, and income. The Great Depression aggravated the plight of the black farmer, and a rapid exodus from the land was again under way in the early 1930s. See Gilbert C. Fite, *Cotton Fields No More* (Lexington: University Press of Kentucky, 1984), pp. 99, 156. For a comprehensive analysis of the social and economic changes taking place in the South between World War I and the Great Depression, with special attention to the interrelationships of blacks and whites on the land, see Jack Temple Kirby, *Rural Worlds Lost* (Baton Rouge: Louisiana State University Press, 1987), chap. 7.

22 Thomas L. Dabney, "Colored Rural Life Conference," *Southern Workman* 55 (May 1926): 224–27.

23 Monroe N. Work, "The Negro Migration," *Southern Workman* 53 (May 1924): 209–11.

24 "Hampton's Farmers' Conference," *Southern Workman* 55 (August 1926): 343–47.

25 Carl C. Taylor, "The Task of the Rural Church," *Rural America* 3 (September 1925): 3–4. Also by Taylor, see "The Program of the Rural Church," *Rural America* 3 (October 1925): 7, 10. *Rural America* was the official publication of the American Country Life Association, and Taylor was a pioneer in the development of rural sociology. For a wider sample of his views, see the essays in Carl C. Taylor et al., *Rural Life in the United States* (New York: Alfred A. Knopf, 1949).

26   On black farmers' alliances, see Theodore Saloutos, *Farmer Movements in the South, 1865–1933* (Berkeley: University of California Press, 1960), pp. 94–95.

27   Taylor, "Program of the Rural Church," pp. 7–8. For more on the "Par-Standard," see Mark Rich, *The Rural Church Movement* (Columbia, Mo: Jupiter Knoll Press, 1957), pp. 102–3. On the Ohio survey, which includes information on African American churches in the state, see Charles O. Gill and Gifford Pinchot, *Six Thousand Country Churches* (New York: Macmillan, 1919).

28   Swanson, "Country Life Movement," p. 358.

29   Thomas Jesse Jones, *Educational Adaptations: Report of Ten Years' Work of the Phelps-Stokes Fund, 1910–1920* (New York: Phelps-Stokes Fund, 1921), pp. 65–66.

30   John C. Wright, "Teaching Preachers to be Human," *Southern Workman* 53 (January 1924): 13–15.

31   Joseph Cannon Bailey, *Seaman A. Knapp: Schoolmaster of American Agriculture* (New York: Columbia University Press, 1945), p. 228; Jackson Davis, "Seaman A. Knapp: Pioneer in Southern Agriculture," *Southern Workman* 57 (September 1929): 387–94; Clement Richardson, "Negro Farmers of Alabama: A Phase of Tuskegee's Extension Work," *Southern Workman* 46 (July 1917): 382–91.

32   Ralph A. Felton, "Ministerial Training for Negro Rural Churches," mimeo., Ralph A. Felton Papers, Drew University. See also Felton, *These My Brethren* (Madison, N.J.: Department of the Rural Church, Drew Theological Seminary, 1950), pp. 9–10.

33   Benjamin F. Hubert, "Marketing of the Negro Farmer," *Messenger* 5 (November 1923): 875, 903.

34   [Thomas Jesse Jones], *Negro Education*, 1916, Bulletin 39, vol. 2, U.S. Department of the Interior (Washington, D.C.: U.S. Government Printing Office, 1917), pp. 492–93.

35   "Bettis Academy Institute," *Southern Workman* 48 (October 1919): 471–73; "Bettis Academy Ministers' Conference," *Southern Workman* 51 (September 1922): 398–400; William Anthony Aery, "Bettis Academy and Racial Goodwill," *Southern Workman* 54 (September 1925): 394–98.

36   William Anthony Aery, "Better Education for Negro Rural Ministers," *Southern Workman* 49 (October 1920): 462. Dillard also assisted William M. Hubbard in starting another nondenominational ministers' institute at the county training school, Forsyth, Georgia.

37   "Rural Preachers at Bettis," *Southern Workman* 52 (September 1923): 424.

38   William Anthony Aery, "Negro Teachers and Ministers Co-operate in South Carolina," *Southern Workman* 50 (November 1921): 503–10; W. T. B. Williams, "The South's Changing Attitude Toward Negro Education," *Southern Workman* 50 (November 1921): 398; Francis W. Shepardson, "Rosenwald Rural Schools," *Opportunity* 4 (November 1923): 324–30.

39   *Clarksburg* (W.Va.) *Telegram,* March 26, 1922.

40   Kenneth K. Bailey, *Southern White Protestantism in the Twentieth Century* (New York: Harper and Row, 1965), chap. 3.

41   See Wilma Dykeman and James Stokely, *Seeds of Southern Change: The Life of Will Alexander* (New York: W. W. Norton, 1976), for more information regarding Alexander and activities of the Commission on Interracial Cooperation. Gilbert Osofsky, preface to

Arthur F. Raper, *Preface to Peasantry: A Tale of Two Black Belt Counties* (1936; repr., New York: Atheneum, 1968), p. vii.

42 Will W. Alexander, "The Changing South," *Opportunity* 5 (October 1927): 294–96.

43 George Edmund Haynes, *The Trend of the Races,* intro. James H. Dillard (New York: Council of Women for Home Missions and Missionary Education Movement of the United States and Canada, 1922); Daniel Perlman, "Stirring the White Conscience: The Life of Edmund Haynes" (Ph.D. diss., New York University, New York, 1972), pp. 151–53.

44 Haynes, *Trend of the Races,* pp. 57–58.

45 Edmund de S. Brunner, *Church Life in the Rural South* (New York: George H. Doran, 1923). Based in New York City, the committee declared that its aim was "to combine the scientific method with religious motive. It cooperates with other social and religious agencies, but is itself an independent organization." This survey of the rural church drew on some data gathered in earlier studies done by the Town and Country Survey Department of the Interchurch World Movement, which Brunner also directed. Though the federal census bureau still used 2,500 as the maximum population figure for a rural community, Brunner used 5,000. Brunner was secretary of the Department of Town and Country Church, National Council of Churches, from 1919 until 1925.

46 Ibid., p. 81.

47 H. N. Morse, *The Country Church in Industrial Zones* (New York: George H. Doran, 1922), pp. 77–80.

48 Ibid., pp. 88–91.

49 Ibid., p. 80.

50 W. A. Daniel, *The Education of Negro Ministers* (New York: George H. Doran, 1925), pp. 14–15, 30–32, 107–9. Daniel specifically cites R. E. Park, "Racial Assimilation in Secondary Groups," *Publications of the American Sociological Society* 8 (1913): 77.

51 C. Horace Hamilton and John M. Ellison, *The Negro Church in Rural Virginia,* Bulletin 273 (Blacksburg: Virginia Agricultural Experiment Station, 1930). Case studies were made of nine Virginia counties, and data were drawn from the 1926 U.S. census of religious bodies. H. J. McGuinn, professor of sociology, Virginia Union University, did some of the fieldwork, and W. E. Garnett, rural sociologist of the Virginia Agricultural Experiment Station, directed the study.

52 Ibid., p. 5. The authors noted that according to the 1926 census of religious bodies 56 percent of the rural black population of Virginia were church members. This compared to 38 percent for urban blacks, 42 percent for rural whites, and 57 percent for urban whites (p. 4).

53 Ibid., p. 21.

54 Ibid., p. 38.

55 Raper, *Preface to Peasantry.*

56 More than two-fifths of Greene County's African American population left between 1920 and 1930; nearly half of this number emigrated in 1923, 1924, and 1925. Raper argues that these migrants were "virtual refugees. They were *fleeing from* something rather than being *attracted* to something. They were fleeing from hunger and exposure, they were going to . . . they didn't know what." Raper, *Preface to Peasantry,* p. 191.

57 Ibid., p. 360.

58 *New York Times,* September 14, 1930. Kennedy's dissertation was done in political science at Columbia University and appeared in 1930 in the Columbia University monograph series Studies in History, Economics, and Public Law.

59 Carter G. Woodson, *The Rural Negro* (Washington, D.C.: Association for the Study of Negro Life and History, 1930), p. xvi. A striking similarity is apparent between Woodson's portrait of southern black religion and that drawn before the Great Migration by W. D. Weatherford, the white southern progressive. See Weatherford, *Negro Life in the South* (New York: Association Press, 1911), chap. 5. For an account of Woodson's founding of the Association for the Study of Negro Life and History on the eve of the Great Migration and his subsequent career, see August Meier and Elliott Rudwick, *Black History and the Historical Profession, 1915–1980* (Urbana: University of Illinois Press, 1986), chap. 1.

60 Woodson, *Rural Negro,* p. 152.

61 Ibid., p. 156.

62 Though a self-described agnostic and frequent critic of conservative black church dogma, Du Bois felt a powerful attraction to the folk religiosity he discovered while teaching in rural Tennessee in the summers of 1886 and 1887. He wrote poetically of his experience in *Souls of Black Folk,* published in 1903. See the discussion of Du Bois's often paradoxical attitudes toward religion in Manning Marable, "The Black Faith of W. E. B. Du Bois: Sociocultural and Political Dimensions of Black Religion," *Southern Quarterly* 23 (Spring 1965): 15–33. Also see Zora Neale Hurston, "Hoodoo in America," *Journal of American Folk-Lore* 44 (October–December 1931): 317–417.

63 See Robert Bone, "Richard Wright and the Chicago Renaissance," *Callaloo* 9 (Summer 1986): 446–68.

64 Woodson, *Rural Negro,* pp. 159–60.

65 Ibid., p. 178.

66 Ibid., pp. 178–79. Woodson's model of the ideal church was that of the institutional churches with their multifaceted "social uplift" programs and educated clergy. This exemplar can be seen in his critique of the ministry in *The Negro Professional Man and the Community* (Washington, D.C.: Association for the Study of Negro Life and History, 1934), chap. 5, "Preachers and Their Competitors."

67 W. Lloyd Warner, *Yankee City* (New Haven, Conn.: Yale University Press, 1963). On Warner's influence, see Mildred Reed Hall, *W. Lloyd Warner: Social Anthropologist* (New York: Publishing Center for Cultural Resources, 1987).

68 Park believed that spatial isolation and separate development of cultural institutions facilitated the movement of minority groups into the American mainstream. Robert E. Park, "Racial Assimilation in Secondary Groups with Particular Reference to the Negro," in *American Sociological Society: Papers and Proceedings* 8 (December 1913): 66–83. On Park's "ethnicity paradox," see Barbara Ballis Lal, "Black and Blue in Chicago: Robert E. Park's Perspective on Race Relations in Urban America, 1914–44," *British Journal of Sociology* 38 (1987): 546–66.

69 Benjamin E. Mays and Joseph William Nicholson, *The Negro's Church* (New York: Institute of Social and Religious Research, 1933), pp. v–vi.

70   Ibid., p. 230.

71   Ibid., p. 236.

72   Ibid., p. 251.

73   Benjamin E. Mays, *The Negro's God as Reflected in His Literature* (1938; repr., New York: Atheneum, 1968), pp. 248–49.

74   Ibid., p. 249.

75   Ibid., p. 277.

76   For a detailed discussion of Johnson's connection to the Julius Rosenwald Fund and his "social conditioning" interpretation of rural black society, see John H. Stanfield, *Philanthropy and Jim Crow in American Social Science* (Westport, Conn.: Greenwood Press, 1985), chap. 6.

77   Charles S. Johnson, *Shadow of the Plantation*, intro. Robert E. Park (Chicago: University of Chicago Press, 1934), pp. 150–51. Johnson's mentor was Park at the University of Chicago. Manning Marable has argued that Johnson, along with Du Bois and Frazier, established "the modern foundations of the Afro-American sociology." Manning Marable, "Race, Class and Conflict: Intellectual Debates on Race Relations Research in the United States Since 1960, A Social Science Bibliographical Essay," in *Paradigms in Black Studies: Intellectual History, Cultural Meaning and Political Ideology*, ed. Abdul Alkalimat (Chicago: Twenty-First Century Books, 1990), pp. 166–67.

78   Marable, "Race, Class and Conflict," p. 179.

79   Clifton H. Johnson, ed., *Religious Conversion Experiences and Autobiographies of Ex-Slaves*, foreword Paul Radin (Philadelphia: Pilgrim Press, 1969), pp. vii–xiii.

80   Ibid., p. 208.

81   Hortense Powdermaker, *After Freedom: A Cultural Study of the Deep South* (1939, repr., New York: Atheneum, 1969), p. 285.

82   John Dollard, *Caste and Class in a Southern Town* (3rd ed., Garden City, N.Y.: Doubleday, 1957), p. 248.

83   Ibid., p. 249.

84   Ibid., pp. 261–62.

85   The application of methodology from anthropology, including an adaptation of "free associative" interviewing, as opposed to older survey techniques was innovative in the production of *Deep South*. Allison Davis, Burleigh B. Gardner, and Mary R. Gardner examined Natchez, Mississippi, and environs in Adams and Wilkinson counties. St. Clair Drake was asked in 1935 by Davis to examine "the bottom" of the social structure. He came to the conclusion that class norms sometimes overpowered racial ones. Drake provided this insight in a scholarly reminiscence of his association with the production of *Deep South:* "At the very bottom of the social pyramid, in some of the Holiness Churches, Blacks and whites were rolling together on the floor, singing and shouting together, and eating together. . . . Thus at the lower-lower-class level there was a great deal of interaction between the two races. It was the upwardly mobile lower-class white crowd that was the most rabidly anti-black." St. Clair Drake, "In the Mirror of Black Scholarship: W. Allison Davis and *Deep South*," *Harvard Educational Review*, monograph 2, 1974: 50. *Deep South* provides a portrait of African American life in the rural South during the late 1930s on the eve of what can be called the Second Great Migration. See Ronald

Bailey, "'Deep South' Revisited: An Assessment of a Classical Text," *The CAAS News-letter,* UCLA Center for Afro-American Studies 11 (1988): 10–14.

86 Charles S. Johnson, *Growing Up in the Black Belt* (Washington, D.C.: American Council on Education, 1941), p. 136. The study was prepared for the American Youth Commission, established in 1935 by the American Council on Education.

87 Harry V. Richardson, *Dark Glory: A Picture of the Church Among Negroes in the Rural South* (New York: Friendship Press, 1947). An earlier but much more limited study is William Kappen Fox, "Experiments in Southern Rural Religious Development Among Negroes" (B.D. diss., University of Chicago Divinity School, 1943). See also Harry W. Roberts, "The Rural Negro Minister: His Work and Salary," *Rural Sociology* 12 (September 1947): 284–97.

88 Ibid., p. 192.

89 Harry V. Richardson, "A Teacher and a Prophet," *Drew Gateway* 22 (Summer 1952): 133.

90 Ralph A. Felton, *One Foot on the Land* (Madison, N.J.: Rural Church Department, Drew University, 1947), pp. 23–28. See also Felton, *Go Down, Moses: A Study of 21 Successful Negro Rural Pastors* (Madison, N.J.: Drew Theological Seminary, 1952).

91 Richardson, *Dark Glory,* p. 193.

92 In 1920 one out of every seven farmers in the United States was African American. This number dropped to one in every sixty-seven by 1982. The U.S. Commission on Civil Rights predicted in 1982 that almost no blacks would be operating farms by the end of the century. In an effort to forestall the demise of the black farmer, the National Council of Churches and several of its member denominations began a program to assist black farmers. See David Barlett, "Black Farm Loss at Critical Level," *Vanguard* 31 (December 1984): 1.

93 Letter, James Gregg to Ralph Felton, July 26, 1920, Felton Papers, Drew University, Madison, N.J.

94 Felton, *These My Brethren,* p. 10.

95 *Nashville Globe,* February 23, 1917.

96 Ibid., p. 102.

97 Clark Foreman, "What Hope for the Rural Negro?," *Opportunity* 12 (April 1934): 105.

98 Kelly Miller, "The Farm—The Negro's Best Chance," *Opportunity* 13 (January 1935): 23–24. Miller wanted a "special dispensation" from the New Deal to enable black farmers to buy and cultivate land.

99 Monroe N. Work, "Negro Migration in 1916–1917," *Southern Workman* 47 (November 1919): 614–15; Monroe N. Work, "Conditions and Problems After the War," *National Economic League Quarterly* 2 (November 1916): 141; Linda O. McMurry, *Recorder of the Black Experience* (Baton Rouge: Louisiana State University Press, 1985), pp. 80–84.

100 Monroe N. Work, "Problems of Negro Urban Welfare," *Southern Workman* 51 (January 1922): 10–16.

101 Monroe N. Work, "Research with Respect to Cooperation Between Urban and Rural Communities," *Opportunity* 1 (February 1923): 7.

102 Ibid., p. 9.

103 One attempt to survey the literature is Thomas Richard Frazier, "An Analysis of Social Scientific Writing on American Negro Religion" (Ph.D. diss., Columbia University,

New York, 1967). Frazier is primarily concerned with the methodological and theoretical presuppositions of the authors he examines.

104 Neil Fligstein, *Going North: Migration of Blacks and Whites from the South, 1900–1950* (New York: Academic Press, 1981), pp. 162–66. On the continuing loss of land ownership, see David Dybiec, ed., *Slippin' Away: The Loss of Black Owned Farms* (Atlanta: Glenmary Research Center, 1988).

105 See Henry D. Shapiro, *Appalachia on Our Mind: The Southern Mountains and Mountaineers in the American Consciousness, 1870–1920* (Chapel Hill: University of North Carolina Press, 1977).

106 Hal S. Barron, *Those Who Stayed Behind: Rural Society in Nineteenth-Century New England* (Cambridge: Cambridge University Press, 1984), pp. 31, 37–39, 49–50, 135–36.

107 C. Eric Lincoln and Lawrence H. Mamiya, *The Black Church in the African American Experience* (Durham, N.C.: Duke University Press, 1991), p. 97.

CONCLUSION

1 [Richard R. Wright, Jr.], "Where Is the Federal Council of Negro Methodists?," *Christian Recorder,* 1917, TCF, Reel 6.

2 Joseph R. Washington, Jr., *Black Sects and Cults* (Garden City, N.Y.: Doubleday, 1972), p. 58.

3 Carter G. Woodson, *The Rural Negro* (Washington, D.C.: Association for the Study of Negro Life and History, 1930), p. 167.

4 Manning Marable, "The Black Faith of W. E. B. Du Bois: Sociocultural and Political Dimensions of Black Religion," *Southern Quarterly* 23 (Spring 1985): 27.

5 [Carter G. Woodson], "Suggestions for Improving the Negro Church," *Negro History Bulletin* 3 (October 1939): 9.

6 Cited in "The Good Shepherd Congregational Church in Chicago," *Negro History Bulletin* 3 (October 1939): 12.

7 Cited in J. E. Moorland, "Some Defects of the Church and Recommendation of Plans for Improvement," in *Proceedings of the Hampton Negro Conference,* no. 7 (Hampton, Va.: Hampton Institute Press, 1903), p. 59.

8 G. R. Waller, "The Relation of the Pastor to the Community," *Proceedings of the Hampton Negro Conference,* no. 5 (Hampton, Va.: Hampton Institute Press, 1901), p. 55.

9 Seth M. Scheiner, "The Negro Church and the Northern City, 1890–1930," in *Seven on Black: Reflections on the Negro Experience in America,* ed. William G. Shade and Roy C. Herrenkohl (Philadelphia: J. B. Lippincott, 1969), p. 98.

10 Miles Mark Fisher, "Negroes Get Religion," *Opportunity* 14 (May 1936): 150.

11 Robert Gregg's assessment is worth quoting in full: "In the process of becoming evangelical, however, churches accentuated what was unique about their theological and ideological identities. Consequently, while they solidified the commitment of people who already shared their outlooks and appealed to others who were persuaded by the fresh presentation of these ideas, they repelled larger numbers who had not shared the same heritage. In other words, evangelism brought to the fore particular religious, class, and gender attitudes that would be attractive to people for whom those ideas had some

relevance. Meanwhile, other people were likely to be alienated." Gregg, *Sparks from the Anvil of Oppression* (Philadelphia: Temple University Press, 1993), p. 66.

12 Robert Michael Franklin, "Church and City: Black Christianity's Ministry," *Christian Ministry* 20 (March–April 1989): 18.

13 Ibid., p. 19.

14 Henry Highland Garnet, "An Address to the Slaves of the United States of America," in *Walker's Appeal, with a Brief Sketch of His Life. Also Garnet's Address to the Slaves of America* (New York: S. H. Tobbitt, 1848), pp. 94–95.

BIBLIOGRAPHY

References to newspapers in the footnotes pertain, for the most part, to the Tuskegee Institute News Clipping File or the Hampton University Newspaper Clipping File, listed under manuscript and archival material. These collections are invaluable. They contain clippings from many newspapers of the period under consideration. The Hampton file is now available on microfiche, though I examined the original scrapbooks at Virginia's Hampton University. The Tuskegee file is available on microfilm. Both collections were extremely useful, particularly so because they contain a wealth of material from African American newspapers, including many Southern ones, that are long defunct and extremely rare or impossible to find elsewhere. The custodians of the collections generally wrote the date and source on the clippings, but in some instances the information is missing or the handwritten note is illegible. In these cases, I have cited the newspaper by name and indicated the microfilm reel where the clipping is located in the Tuskegee file. The Tuskegee Institute News Clipping File is referenced as TCF in the notes. The Hampton Clipping File is abbreviated as HCF.

Articles and essays cited from the following periodicals are not independently listed in the bibliography: the *Crisis* (National Association for the Advancement of Colored People); *Opportunity* (National Urban League); the *Southern Workman* (Hampton Institute); the *Negro Farmer* (Tuskegee Institute), and *Rural America* (American Country Life Association). Denominational journals and newspapers, such as the African Methodist Episcopal Church's *Church Review* (cited as *AME Church Review*) and the *Christian Recorder,* or the *National Baptist Union Review* of the National Baptist Convention, appear frequently in the footnotes but are not listed in the bibliography. References to denominational minutes and conference appear only in the chapter notes.

MANUSCRIPT AND ARCHIVAL MATERIAL

Chicago
  Chicago Historical Society
    Claude A. Barnett Papers
    Archibald J. Carey, Sr., Papers
  Carter Woodson Regional Library
    Vivian Harsh Collection
    Illinois Writers Project "The Negro in Illinois" (IWP)
Hampton, Virginia
  Hampton University
    The Hampton University Newspaper Clipping File (HCF)
Madison, New Jersey
  Drew University
    United Methodist Archives Center
    Ralph Felton Papers
Nashville, Tennessee
  Historical Commission of the Southern Baptist Convention
    Black Baptist Materials
New York
  Schomburg Center for Research in Black Culture
    Schomburg Clipping File
Rochester, New York
  American Baptist-Samuel Colgate Historical Library
    Black Baptist Collection
Tuskegee, Alabama
  Tuskegee Institute
    Tuskegee Institute News Clipping File (TCF)
Springfield, Illinois
  Illinois State Historical Library
    Illinois Federal Writers' Project Materials (FWP)
Washington, D.C.
  Library of Congress, Manuscripts Division
    Carter G. Woodson Collection
    National Association for the Advancement of Colored People. Records
      (NAACP Records).
    National Urban League. Records.

GOVERNMENT DOCUMENTS AND REPORTS

U.S. Bureau of the Census. *Negro Population in the United States, 1790–1915*. Washington, D.C.: U.S. Government Printing Office, 1918. Reprint. New York: Arno Press and the New York Times, 1968.

U.S. Bureau of the Census. *Negroes in the United States: 1920–1932*. Washington, D.C.: U.S. Government Printing Office, 1935.

U.S. Bureau of the Census. *Religious Bodies: 1906.* Part I, Summary and General Tables. Part II, Separate Denominations. Washington, D.C.: U.S. Government Printing Office, 1910.

U.S. Bureau of the Census. *Religious Bodies: 1916.* Part I, Summary and General Tables. Part II, Separate Denominations. Washington, D.C.: U. S. Government Printing Office, 1919.

U.S. Bureau of the Census. *Religious Bodies: 1926.* Vol. I, Summary and Detailed Tables. Vol. II, Separate Denominations. Washington, D.C.: U.S. Government Printing Office, 1930.

U.S. Bureau of the Census. *Religious Bodies: 1936.* Vol. I, Summary and Detailed Tables. Vol. II, Separate Denominations. Washington, D.C.: U.S. Government Printing Office, 1941.

U.S. Department of the Interior. *Negro Education.* Bulletin, 1916, No. 39, Vol. II. Washington, D.C.: U. S. Government Printing Office, 1917.

U.S. Department of Labor, Division of Negro Economics. *Negro Migration in 1916–17.* Intro. by J. H. Dillard. Washington, D.C.: U.S. Government Printing Office, 1919.

BOOKS AND PAMPHLETS

Abell, Aaron I. *The Urban Impact on American Protestantism, 1865–1900.* Cambridge, Mass.: Harvard University Press, 1943.

Adero, Malaika, ed. *UpSouth: Stories, Studies and Letters of This Century's African-American Migrations.* New York: New Press, 1993.

Anderson, James D. *The Education of Blacks in the South, 1860–1935.* Chapel Hill: University of North Carolina Press, 1988.

Angell, Stephan Ward. *Bishop Henry McNeal Turner and African-American Religion in the South.* Knoxville: University of Tennessee Press, 1992.

Baer, Hans A. *The Black Spiritual Movement: A Religious Response to Racism.* Knoxville: University of Tennessee Press, 1984.

Baer, Hans A., and Yvonne Jones, eds. *African Americans in the South: Issues of Race, Class, and Gender.* Athens: University of Georgia Press, 1992.

Baer, Hans A., and Merrill Singer. *African American Religion in the Twentieth Century: Varieties of Protest and Accommodation.* Knoxville: University of Tennessee Press, 1992.

Bailey, Joseph Cannon. *Seaman A. Knapp: Schoolmaster of American Agriculture.* New York: Columbia University Press, 1945.

Bailey, Kenneth K. *Southern White Protestantism in the Twentieth Century.* New York: Harper and Row, 1965.

Bailey, Liberty H. *The Country-Life Movement in the United States.* New York: Macmillan, 1915.

Baker, Ray Stannard. *Following the Color Line: American Negro Citizenship in the Progressive Era.* Intro. by Dewey W. Grantham, Jr. New York: Harper and Row, 1964 (orig. pub. 1908).

Ballard, Allen B. *One More Day's Journey: The Story of a Family and a People.* New York: McGraw-Hill, 1984.

Bardolph, Richard. *The Negro Vanguard.* New York: Random House, 1959.

Beck, Carolyn Stickney. *Our Own Vine and Fig Tree: The Persistence of the Mother Bethel Family.* New York: AMS, 1989.

Black, Ford S. *Black's Blue Book, Business and Professional Directory.* Chicago: Ford S. Black, 1916.

————. *Black's Blue Book, Business and Professional Directory.* Chicago: [Ford S. Black], 1917.

————, comp. *Black's Blue Book: Directory of Chicago's Active Colored People and Guide to Their Activities.* Chicago: Ford S. Black, 1921.

Blackwell, G. L. *Who Is Who in the Fifth Episcopal District in the African Methodist Episcopal Zion Church, With a Supplement of General Information about the Church* (Philadelphia: n.p., 1920.

Blum, John Morton. *Woodrow Wilson and the Politics of Morality.* Boston: Little, Brown, 1956.

Bodnar, John, Roger Simon, and Michael P. Webber. *Lives of Their Own: Blacks, Italians and Poles in Pittsburgh, 1900–1960.* Urbana: University of Illinois Press, 1982.

Bontemps, Arna. *100 Years of Negro Freedom.* New York: Dodd, Mead, 1961.

————, ed. *The Harlem Renaissance Remembered.* New York: Dodd, Mead, 1972.

Bontemps, Arna, and Jack Conroy. *They Seek a City.* Garden City, N.Y.: Doubleday, Doran, 1945.

Borchert, James. *Alley Life in Washington, 1850–1970.* Urbana: University of Illinois Press, 1980.

Bowen, Louise DeKovan. *The Colored People of Chicago: An Investigation Made for the Juvenile Protective Association.* Chicago: Rogers and Hall, 1913.

Bowers, William L. *The Country Life Movement in America, 1900–1920.* Port Washington, N.Y.: Kennikat Press, 1974.

Boyer, Paul S. *Urban Masses and Moral Order in America, 1820–1920.* Cambridge, Mass.: Harvard University Press, 1978.

Bracey, John H., August Meier, and Elliott Rudwick, eds. *The Black Sociologists: The First Half Century.* Belmont, Calif: Wadsworth, 1971.

Bradley, David H. *A History of the A.M.E. Zion Church.* 2 vols. Nashville: Parthenon Press, 1956, 1970.

Brotz, Howard M. *The Black Jews of Harlem.* New York: Schocken Books, 1970.

Brown, William Wells. *My Southern Home: or, The South and Its People.* Boston: A. G. Brown, 1880.

Brunner, Edmund de S. *Church Life in the Rural South: A Study of the Opportunity of Protestantism Based Upon Data from Seventy Counties.* New York: George H. Doran, 1923.

Burkett, Randall K. *Black Redemption: Churchmen Speak for the Garvey Movement.* Philadelphia: Temple University Press, 1978.

————. *Garveyism as a Religious Movement: The Institutionalization of a Black Civil Religion.* Metuchen, N.J.: Scarecrow Press, 1978.

Burkett, Randall K., and Richard Newman, eds. *Black Apostles: Afro-American Clergy Confront the Twentieth Century.* Boston: G. K. Hall, 1978.

Burnham, Kenneth E. *God Comes to America: Father Divine and the Peace Mission Movement.* Boston: Lambeth Press, 1979.

Butterfield, Kenyon. *The Country Church and the Rural Problem.* Chicago: University of Chicago Press, 1911.

————. *The Farmer and the New Day.* New York: Macmillan, 1919.

Campbell, Daniel M., and Rex R. Johnson. *Black Migration in America: A Social Demographic History.* Durham, N.C.: Duke University Press, 1981.

Campbell, James T. *Songs of Zion: The African Methodist Episcopal Church in the United States and South Africa.* New York: Oxford University Press, 1995.

Carter, Paul. *The Decline and Revival of Social Gospel: Social and Political Liberalism in American Protestant Churches, 1920–1940*. Ithaca, N.Y.: Cornell University Press, 1954.

Cavert, Samuel McCrea, ed. *The Churches Allied for Common Tasks: Report of the Third Quadrennium of the Federal Council of Churches of Christ in America, 1916–1920*. New York: Federal Council of the Churches of Christ in America, 1921.

Chicago Baptist Year Book, 1915. Chicago: Chicago Baptist Association, 1915.

Chicago Commission on Race Relations. *The Negro in Chicago: A Study of Race Relations and a Race Riot*. Prepared by Charles S. Johnson. Chicago: University of Chicago Press, 1922.

Chicago Urban League. *Two Decades of Service*. Chicago: William Mason Press, 1936.

Cooper, John Milton, Jr. *Pivotal Decades: The United States 1900–1920*. New York: W. W. Norton, 1990.

Cooper, Michael L. *Bound for the Promised Land*. New York: Dutton, 1995.

Crew, Spencer. *Field to Factory: Afro-American Migration, 1915–1940*. Washington, D.C.: Smithsonian Institution, 1987.

Cronon, David. *Black Moses: The Story of Marcus Garvey*. Second edition. Madison: University of Wisconsin Press, 1974.

Cross, R. D., ed. *The Church and the City: 1865–1910*. Indianapolis: Bobbs-Merrill, 1967.

Cully, Kendig Brubaker, and F. Nile Harper, eds. *Will the Church Lose the City?* New York: World, 1969.

Curry, Leonard P. *The Free Black in Urban America, 1800–1950*. Chicago: University of Chicago Press, 1981.

Dabney, Wendall P. *Cincinnati's Colored Citizens*. Cincinnati: Dabney, 1926.

Daniel, Pete. *The Shadow of Slavery: Peonage in the South, 1901–1969*. Urbana: University of Illinois Press, 1972.

Daniel, W[illiam] A. *The Education of Negro Ministers*. New York: George H. Doran, 1925.

Davis, Allison, Burleigh B. Gardner, and Mary R. Gardner. *Deep South: A Social Anthropological Study of Caste and Class*. Chicago: University of Chicago Press, 1941.

Davis, Lenwood G., comp. *Daddy Grace: an Annotated Bibliography*. New York: Greenwood Press, 1992.

Detroit Bureau of Governmental Research. *The Negro in Detroit*. Detroit: Bureau of Governmental Research, 1926.

Dittmer, John. *Black Georgia in the Progressive, 1900–1920*. Urbana: University of Illinois Press, 1977.

Dollard, John. *Caste and Class in a Southern Town*. Garden City, N.Y.: Doubleday, 1957.

Dowd, Jerome. *The Negro in American Life*. New York: Century, 1926.

Drake, St. Clair. "Churches and Voluntary Associations in the Chicago Negro Community." Report of Official Project 465-54-3-386, Work Projects Administration. Chicago, December 1940.

———. "The Negro Church and Associations in Chicago." A Research Memorandum Prepared for the Carnegie-Myrdal Study of the Negro in America. New York, June 1, 1940.

Drake, St. Clair, and Horace R. Cayton. *Black Metropolis: A Study of Negro Life in a Northern City*. New York: Harcourt, Brace, 1945. Revised edition. 2 vols. New York: Harper and Row, 1962.

Du Bois, W. E. B. *Against Racism: Unpublished Essays, Papers, and Addressees, 1897–1961.* Edited by Herbert Aptheker. Amherst: University of Massachusetts Press, 1985.

———. *The Black North in 1901.* New York: Arno Press and the New York Times, 1969 (orig. pub. 1901).

———. *Efforts for Social Betterment Among Negro Americans.* Atlanta University Publications, No. 14. Atlanta: Atlanta University Press, 1909.

———, ed. *The Negro Church.* Atlanta University Publications, No. 8. Atlanta: Atlanta University Press, 1903.

———. *The Philadelphia Negro.* Intro. by E. Digby Baltzell. New York: Schocken Books, 1967 (orig. pub. 1899).

———, ed. *Some Efforts of American Negroes for Their Own Social Betterment.* Atlanta: Atlanta University Press, 1898.

———. *The Souls of Black Folk: Essays and Sketches.* Chicago: A. C. McClurg, 1903.

Dvorak, Katharine L. *An African-American Exodus: The Segregation of the Southern Churches.* Preface by Jerald C. Brauer. Brooklyn, N.Y.: Carlson, 1991.

Dybiec, David., ed. *Slipping Away: The Loss of Black Owned Farms.* Atlanta: Glenmary Research Center, 1988.

Epstein, Abraham. *The Negro Migrant in Pittsburgh.* Pittsburgh: University of Pittsburgh Press, 1918.

Farish, Hunter Dickinson. *The Circuit Rider Dismounts: A Social History of Southern Methodism, 1865–1900.* Richmond, Va.: Dietz Press, 1938.

Fauset, Arthur H. *Black Gods of the Metropolis: Negro Religious Cults in the Urban North.* Intro. by John Szwed. Philadelphia: University of Pennsylvania Press, 1971 (orig. pub. 1944).

Felton, Ralph A. *Go Down, Moses: A Study of 21 Successful Negro Pastors.* Madison, N.J.: Rural Church Department, Drew University, 1951.

———. *The Ministry of the Central Jurisdiction of the Methodist Church.* Atlanta: Gammon Theological Seminary, 1953.

———. *One Foot on the Land.* Madison, N.J.: Drew Theological Seminary, 1952.

———. *These My Brethren: A Study of 570 Negro Churches.* Madison, N.J.: Rural Church Department, Drew University, 1950.

Fisher, Miles Mark. *The Master's Slave: Elijah John Fisher, a Biography.* Philadelphia: Judson Press, 1922.

Fiske, G. Walter. *The Challenge of the Country.* New York: Association Press, 1919.

Fite, Gilbert C. *Cotton Fields No More: Southern Agriculture, 1865–1980.* Lexington: University Press of Kentucky, 1984.

Fligstein, Neil. *Going North: Migration of Blacks and Whites from the South, 1900–1950.* New York: Academic Press, 1981.

Foner, Philip S., and Ronald L. Lewis, eds. *The Black Worker from 1900–1919.* Vol. V of *The Black Worker from 1900 to 1919.* Philadelphia: Temple University Press, 1980.

Frazier, E. Franklin. *Black Bourgeoisie.* New York: Collier Books, 1962.

———. *The Negro Church in America.* New York: Schocken Books, 1964.

———. *The Negro Family in Chicago.* Chicago: University of Chicago Press, 1932.

———. *The Negro Family in the United States.* Revised and abridged edition. New York: Dryden Press, 1951.

Fry, C. Luther. *The U. S. Looks at Its Churches.* New York: Institute of Social and Religious Research, 1930.

Fulop, Timothy E., and Albert I. Raboteau, eds. *African-American Religion: Interpretive Essays in History and Culture.* New York: Routledge, 1996.

Gaines, Wesley J. *African Methodism in the South; or Twenty-Five Years of Freedom.* Intro. by W. S. Scarbourgh. Atlanta: Franklin Publishing House, 1890.

Gavins, Raymond. *The Perils and Prospects of Southern Black Leadership: Gordon Blaine Hancock, 1884–1970.* Durham, N.C.: Duke University Press, 1977.

Gayle, Addison. *Richard Wright: Ordeal of a Native Son.* Garden City, N.Y.: Anchor Books/ Doubleday, 1980.

Gill, Charles O., and Gifford Pinchot. *Six Thousand Country Churches.* New York: Macmillan, 1919.

Gillard, John T. *The Catholic Church and the American Negro.* Baltimore: St. Joseph's Society Press, 1929.

Glaab, Charles N., and A. Theodore Brown, *A History of Urban America.* New York: Macmillan, 1967.

Gold, Howard R., and Byron K. Armstrong. *A Preliminary Study of Inter-Racial Conditions in Chicago.* Intro. by George E. Haynes. New York: Home Missions Council, 1920.

Goldsmith, Peter D. *When I Rise Cryin' Holy: African-American Denominationalism on the Georgia Coast.* New York: AMS Press, 1989.

Goggin, Jacqueline. *Carter G. Woodson: A Life in Black History.* Baton Rouge: Louisiana State University Press, 1993.

Gorrell, Donald K. *The Age of Social Responsibility: The Social Gospel in the Progressive Era, 1900–1920.* Macon, Ga.: Mercer University Press, 1988.

Gosnell, Harold F. *Negro Politicians: The Rise of Negro Politics in Chicago.* Chicago: University of Chicago Press, 1935.

Gottlieb, Peter. *Making Their Own Way: Southern Blacks' Migration to Pittsburgh, 1916–30.* Urbana: University of Illinois Press, 1987.

Grant, Robert B., ed. *The Black Man Comes to the City: A Documentary Account from the Great Migration to the Great Depression, 1915–1930.* Chicago: Nelson-Hall, 1972.

Griffin, Farah Jasmine. *"Who Set You Flowing'?" The African-American Migration Narrative.* New York: Oxford University Press, 1995.

Gregg, Howard D. *History of the A.M.E. Church: The Black Church in Action.* Nashville: A.M.E. Sunday School Union, 1980.

Gregg, Robert. *Sparks from the Anvil of Oppression: Philadelphia's African Methodists and Southern Migrants, 1890–1940.* Philadelphia: Temple University Press, 1993.

Groh, George W. *The Black Migration: The Journey to Urban America.* New York: Weybright and Talley, 1972.

Grossman, James R. *"Land of Hope": Chicago, Black Southerners, and the Great Migration.* Chicago: University of Chicago Press, 1989.

Gutman, Herbert G. *The Black Family in Slavery and Freedom, 1750–1925.* New York: Vintage Books, 1976.

Hall, Robert L., and Carol B. Stack, eds. *Holding on to the Land and the Lord: Kinship,*

Ritual, Land Tenure, and Social Policy in the Rural South. Athens: University of Georgia Press, 1982.

Hamilton, C. Horace, and John M. Ellison. *The Negro Church in Rural Virginia.* Bulletin 273. Blacksburg: Virginia Agricultural Experiment Station, 1929.

Hammond, L. H. *In the Vanguard of a Race.* New York: Council of Women for Home Missions, 1914.

Harlan, Louis R. *Booker T. Washington: The Making of a Black Leader, 1856–1901.* New York: Oxford University Press, 1972.

———. *Booker T. Washington: The Wizard of Tuskegee, 1901–1915.* New York: Oxford University Press, 1983.

Harris, Michael W. *The Rise of Gospel Blues: The Music of Thomas Andrew Dorsey in the Urban Church.* New York: Oxford University Press, 1992.

Harrison, Alferdeen, ed. *Black Exodus: The Great Migration from the American South.* Jackson: University Press of Mississippi, 1991.

Harrison, Ira E. *A Selected Annotated Bibliography on Store-Front Churches and Other Religious Writings.* Syracuse, N.Y.: Syracuse University Development Center, 1962.

Haskell, Thomas L. *The Emergence of Professional Social Science: The American Social Science Association and the Nineteenth-Century Crisis of Authority.* Urbana: University of Illinois Press, 1977.

Haynes, George E. *The Negro at Work in New York City: A Study in Economic Progress.* New York: Columbia University Press, 1912.

———. *Negro Migration and Its Implications North and South.* New York: American Missionary Association, 1923.

———. *Negro New-Comers in Detroit, Michigan.* New York: Home Missions Council, 1918.

———. *The Trend of the Races.* Intro. by John H. Dillard. New York: Council of Women for Home Missions and Missionary Education Movement of the United States and Canada, 1922.

Heilbut, Tony. *The Gospel Sound.* Garden City, N.Y.: Anchor Books/Doubleday, 1975.

Henri, Florette. *Black Migration: Movement North, 1900–1920.* Garden City, N.Y.: Anchor Books/Doubleday, 1976.

Higginbotham, Evelyn Brooks. *Righteous Discontent: The Women's Movement in the Black Baptist Church, 1880–1920.* Cambridge, Mass.: Harvard University Press, 1993.

Hill, Bernard Walter. *Rural Survey of Clarke County, Georgia, with Special Reference to the Negroes.* Phelps-Stokes Fellowship Studies, No. 2, *Bulletin of the University of Georgia* 15 (March 1916).

Hogan, David J. *Class and Reform: School and Society in Chicago, 1880–1930.* Philadelphia: University of Pennsylvania Press, 1985.

Holli, Melvin, and Peter d'A. Jones, eds. *The Ethnic Frontier: Essays in the History of Group Survival in Chicago and the Midwest.* Grand Rapids, Mich.: William B. Eerdmans, 1977.

Hopkins, C. Howard. *The Rise of the Social Gospel in American Protestantism, 1865–1915.* New Haven, Conn.: Yale University Press, 1940.

Horace, Lillian B. *"'Crowned with Glory and Honor'": The Life of Rev. Lacy Kirk Williams.* Edited by Venchael Booth. Hicksville, N.Y.: Exposition Press, 1978.

Huggins, Nathan Irvin. *Harlem Renaissance.* New York: Oxford University Press, 1971.

Hughes, Langston. *The Big Sea: An Autobiography.* New York: Hill and Wang, 1940.

Jackson, Mahalia, and Evan M. Wylie. *Movin' On Up.* New York: Hawthorn Books, 1966.

Johnson, Charles S. *Growing Up in the Black Belt: Negro Youth in the Rural South.* Washington, D.C.: American Council on Education, 1941.

———. *Shadow of the Plantation.* Intro. by Robert E. Park. Chicago: University of Chicago Press, 1934 (Phoenix edition, 1966).

Johnson, Clifton H., ed. *God Struck Me Dead: Religious Conversion Experiences and Autobiographies of Ex-Slaves.* Foreword by Paul Radin. Philadelphia: Pilgrim Press, 1969.

Johnson, James Weldon. *Black Manhattan.* Preface by Allan H. Spear. New York: Atheneum, 1969 (orig. pub. 1930).

Jones, Jacqueline. *Labor of Love, Labor of Sorrow: Black Women, Work and the Family from Slavery to the Present.* New York: Basic Books, 1985.

Jones, Ralph H. *Charles Albert Tindley: Prince of Preachers.* Nashville: Abingdon Press, 1982.

Jones, Thomas Jesse. *Educational Adaptations: Report of Ten Years' Work of the Phelps-Stokes Fund, 1910–1920.* New York: Phelps-Stokes Fund, 1921.

Jones-Jackson, Patricia. *When Roots Die: Endangered Traditions on the Sea Islands.* Athens: University of Georgia Press, 1987.

Jordan, Lewis G. *Negro Baptist History, U.S.A., 1750–1930.* Nashville: Sunday School Publishing Board, 1930.

Katzman, David M. *Before the Ghetto: Black Detroit in the Nineteenth Century.* Urbana: University of Illinois Press, 1973.

Katznelson, Ira. *Black Men, White Cities: Race, Politics, and the Migration in the United States, 1900–1930, and Britain, 1948–1968.* London: Published for the Institute of Race Relations by Oxford University Press, 1973.

Keil, Charles. *Urban Blues.* Chicago: University of Chicago Press, 1966.

Kellogg, Charles F. *NAACP: A History of the National Association for the Advancement of Colored People, 1909–1920.* Baltimore: Johns Hopkins University Press, 1967.

Kennedy, Louise Venable. *The Negro Peasant Turns Cityward: Effects of Recent Migrations to Northern Centers.* New York: Columbia University Press, 1930.

Kerlin, Robert T. *The Voice of the Negro, 1919.* New York: E. P. Dutton, 1920.

Kirby, Jack Temple. *Rural Worlds Lost: The American South, 1920–1960.* Baton Rouge: Louisiana State University Press, 1987.

Kirscher, Don S. *City and Country: Rural Responses to Urbanization in the 1920s.* Westport, Conn.: Greenwood Press, 1920.

Kiser, Clyde Vernon. *Sea Island to City: A Study of St. Helena Islanders in Harlem and Other Urban Centers.* New York: Columbia University Press, 1932.

Kornweibel, Jr., Theodore. *No Crystal Stair: Black Life and the* Messenger, *1917–1928.* Westport, Conn.: Greenwood Press, 1975.

Kusmer, Kenneth L. *A Ghetto Takes Shape: Black Cleveland, 1870–1930.* Urbana: University of Illinois Press, 1976.

Lakey, Othal H. *The Rise of "Colored Methodism".* Dallas: Crescendo, 1972.

Lamon, Lester C. *Black Tennesseans, 1900–1930.* Knoxville: University of Tennessee Press, 1977.

Lane, Roger. *William Dorsey's Philadelphia and Ours: On the Past and Future of the Black City in America.* New York: Oxford University Press, 1991.

Lasch-Quinn, Elizabeth. *Black Neighbors: Race and the Limits of Reform in the American Settlement House Movement, 1890–1945.* Chapel Hill: University of North Carolina Press, 1993.

Lee, Robert, ed. *Cities and Churches: Readings on the Urban Church.* Philadelphia: Westminster Press, 1962.

Lemann, Nicholas. *The Promised Land: The Great Black Migration and How It Changed America.* New York: Random House, 1991.

Levine, David Allan. *Internal Combustion: The Races in Detroit, 1915–1926.* Westport, Conn.: Greenwood Press, 1976.

Levine, Lawrence W. *Black Culture and Black Consciousness: Afro-American Thought from Slavery to Freedom.* New York: Oxford University Press, 1977.

Lewis, Edward E. *The Mobility of the Negro: A Study in the American Labor Supply.* New York: Columbia University Press, 1931.

Lieberson, Stanley. *A Piece of the Pie: Blacks and White Immigrants since 1880.* Berkeley: University of California Press, 1980.

Lincoln, C. Eric., and Lawrence H. Mamiya. *The Black Church in the African American Experience.* Durham, N.C.: Duke University Press, 1990.

Link, Arthur S. *Woodrow Wilson and the Progressive Era, 1910–1917.* New York: Harper Torchbooks, 1963.

Litwack, Leon. *Been in the Storm So Long: The Aftermath of Slavery.* New York: Vintage Books, 1979.

Locke, Alain, ed. *The New Negro: An Interpretation.* New York: Albert and Charles Boni, 1925.

Luker, Ralph E. *The Social Gospel in Black and White: American Racial Reform, 1885–1912.* Chapel Hill: University of North Carolina Press, 1991.

Lyman, Stanford. *The Black American in Sociological Thought: A Failure of Perspective.* New York: Putnam, 1973.

Lynch, Hollis, ed. *The Black Urban Condition: A Documentary History, 1866–1971.* New York: Thomas Y. Crowell, 1973.

Macfarland, Charles S., ed. *Christian Unity at Work.* 4th edition. New York: Federal Council of the Churches of Christ in America, 1912.

———. *The Progress of Church Federation.* New York: Fleming H. Revel, 1917.

McGee, Leo, and Robert Boone, eds. *The Black Rural Landowner-Endangered Species: Social, Political, and Economic Implications.* Westport, Conn.: Greenwood Press, 1979.

McKay, Claude. *Harlem: Negro Metropolis.* New York: E. P. Dutton, 1940.

McMurry, Linda O. *Recorder of the Black Experience: A Biography of Monroe Nathan Work.* Baton Rouge: Louisiana State University Press, 1985.

McPherson, James M., Laurence B. Holland, James M. Banner, Jr., Nancy J. Weiss, and Michael D. Bell, eds. *Blacks in America: Bibliographical Essays.* Garden City, N.Y.: Doubleday, 1972.

Mandle, Jay R. *Not Slave, Not Free.* Durham, N.C.: Duke University Press, 1992.

Marks, Carole. *Farewell—We're Good and Gone.* Bloomington: Indiana University Press, 1989.

Martin, Tony. *Race First: The Ideological and Organizational Struggles of Marcus Garvey and the Universal Negro Improvement Association.* Westport, Conn.: Greenwood Press, 1976.

Marty, Martin E. *Modern American Religion.* Volume I: *The Irony of It All, 1893–1919.* Chicago: University of Chicago Press, 1989.

———. *Modern American Religion.* Volume II: *The Noise of Conflict, 1919–1941.* Chicago: University of Chicago Press, 1991.

Masters, Victor I., ed. *The Home Mission Task.* Atlanta: Home Mission Board of the Southern Baptist Convention, 1912.

Matthews, Fred. *Quest for an American Sociology: Robert E. Park and the Chicago School.* Montreal and London: McGill-Queen's University Press, 1977.

May, Henry F. *Protestant Churches and Industrial America.* New York: Harper and Row, 1949.

Mays, Benjamin E. *Born to Rebel: An Autobiography.* New York: Scribners, 1971.

———. *The Negro's God as Reflected in His Literature.* New York: Atheneum, 1968 (orig. pub. 1938).

Mays, Benjamin E., and Joseph William Nicholson. *The Negro's Church.* New York: Institute of Social and Religious Research, 1933.

Meier, August. *Negro Thought in America, 1880–1915: Racial Ideologies in the Age of Booker T. Washington.* Ann Arbor: University of Michigan Press, 1963.

Meier, August, and Elliott Rudwick. *Black Detroit and the Rise of the UAW.* New York: Oxford University Press, 1979.

———, eds. *Black History and the Historical Profession, 1915–1980.* Urbana: University of Illinois Press, 1986.

Miller, Kelly. *Out of the House of Bondage.* New York: Neale, 1914. Repr. with an intro. by G. Franklin Edwards. New York: Schocken Books, 1971.

Mjagkij, Nina. *Light in the Darkness: African Americans and the YMCA, 1852–1946.* Lexington: University Press of Kentucky, 1994.

Moore, Jesse Thomas, Jr. *A Search for Equality: The National Urban League, 1910–1961.* University Park: Pennsylvania State University Press, 1981.

Morris, Calvin S. *Reverdy C. Ransom: Black Advocate of the Social Gospel.* New York: Lantham, 1990.

Morse, H. N. *The Country Church in Industrial Zones.* New York: George H. Doran, 1922.

Moses, Wilson J. *The Golden Age of Black Nationalism, 1850–1925.* New Haven, Conn.: Yale University Press, 1978.

Mukenge, Ida Rosseau. *The Black Church in Urban America: A Case Study in Political Economy.* Latham, Md.: University Press of America, 1983.

Murray, Albert. *Stomping the Blues.* New York: Vintage Press, 1976.

Murray, Andrew. *Presbyterians and the Negro—A History.* Philadelphia: Presbyterian Historical Society, 1966.

Myrdal, Gunnar. *An American Dilemma: The Negro Problem and Modern Democracy.* New York: Harper, 1944. Harper Torchbook edition. 2 vols. New York: Harper and Row, 1969.

Nieman, Donald G., ed. *Church and Community Among Black Southerners, 1865–1900.* Vol. 9 of *African American Life in the Post-Emancipation South, 1861–1900.* 12 vols. Edited by Donald G. Nieman. New York: Garland, 1994.

Newby, I. A. *Jim Crow's Defense: Anti-Negro Thought in America, 1900–1930.* Baton Rouge: Louisiana State University Press, 1965.

Nielson, David Gordon. *Black Ethos: Northern Urban Negro Life and Thought, 1890–1930.* Westport, Conn.: Greenwood Press, 1977.

Oakley, Giles. *The Devil's Music: A History of the Blues.* New York: Taplinger, 1976.

Odum, Howard W. *An American Epoch: Southern Portraiture in the National Picture.* New York: Henry Holt, 1930.

Oliver, Paul. *Blues Fell This Morning: The Meaning of the Blues.* New York: Horizon Press, 1960.

————. *Screening the Blues: Aspects of the Blues Tradition.* London: Cassell, 1968.

————. *Songsters & Saints: Vocal Traditions on Race Records.* New York: Cambridge University Press, 1984.

Olivet Baptist Church. *"Just A Decade" in Olivet, 1916–1926.* Chicago: Olivet Baptist Church, 1926.

Osofsky, Gilbert. *Harlem: The Making of a Ghetto.* New York: Harper and Row, 1968.

Ottley, Roi. *The Lonely Warrior: The Life and Times of Robert S. Abbott.* Chicago: Henry Regnery, 1955.

————. *"New World A-Coming": Inside Black America.* 1943. Repr., New York: Arno Press and the New York Times, 1969.

Ottley, Roi, and William J. Weatherby, eds. *The Negro in New York: An Informal Social History.* New York: New York Public Library and Oceana Publications, 1967.

Page, Thomas Nelson. *The Negro: The Southerner's Problem.* New York: Charles Scribner's Sons, 1904.

Painter, Nell Irvin. *Exodusters: Black Migration to Kansas After Reconstruction.* New York: Alfred A. Knopf, 1977.

Paris, Arthur E. *Black Pentecostalism: Southern Religion in an Urban World.* Amherst: University of Massachusetts Press, 1982.

Parris, Guichard, and Lester Brooks. *Blacks in the City: A History of the National Urban League.* Boston: Little, Brown, 1971.

Patterson, J. O., German R. Ross, and Julia Atkinson, eds. *History and Formative Years of the Church of God in Christ with Excerpts from the Life and Works of Its Founder—Bishop C. H. Mason.* Memphis: Church of God in Christ Publishing House, 1969.

Pelt, Owen D., and Ralph Lee Smith. *The Story of the National Baptists.* New York: Vantage Press, 1960.

Pettigrew, M. C. *From Miles to Johnson.* Memphis: C.M.E. Publishing House, 1970.

Phillips, Charles H. *The History of the Colored Methodist Episcopal Church in America.* Jackson, Tenn.: C.M.E. Publishing House, 1900.

Philpott, Thomas L. *The Slum and the Ghetto: Neighborhood Deterioration and Middle-Class Reform, Chicago, 1880–1930.* New York: Oxford University Press, 1978.

Platt, Anthony M. *E. Franklin Frazier Reconsidered.* New Brunswick, N.J.: Rutgers University Press, 1991.

Powdermaker, Hortense. *After Freedom: A Cultural Study in the Deep South.* New York: Atheneum, 1969 (orig. pub. 1939).

Powell, Adam Clayton, Sr. *Against the Tide.* New York: n. p., 1938.

————. *Upon This Rock.* New York: Abyssinian Baptist Church, 1949.

Proctor, Henry Hugh. *Between Black and White: Autobiographical Sketches.* Boston: Pilgrim Press, 1925.

Rabinowitz, Howard N. *Race Relations in the Urban South, 1865–1890.* New York: Oxford University Press, 1978.

Ransom, Reverdy C. *The Pilgrimage of Harriet Ransom's Son*. Nashville: A.M.E. Sunday School Union, c. 1950.

——, comp. *Year Book of Negro Churches, 1935–36*. Wilberforce, Ohio.: Bishops of the A.M.E. Church, 1936.

Raper, Arthur F. *Preface to Peasantry: A Tale of Two Black Belt Counties*. Preface by Gilbert Osofsky. New York: Atheneum, 1968 (orig. pub. 1936).

Raushenbush, Winifred. *Robert E. Park: Biography of a Sociologist*. Durham, N.C.: Duke University Press, 1979.

Redkey, Edwin S. *Black Exodus: Black Nationalist and Back-to-Africa Movements, 1890–1910*. New Haven, Conn.: Yale University Press, 1969.

Reid, Ira De A. *In a Minor Key: Negro Youth in Story and Fact*. Washington, D.C.: American Council on Education, 1940.

——. *The Negro Immigrant: His Background, Characteristics and Social Adjustment, 1899–1937*. New York: Columbia University Press, 1939.

——. *Social Conditions of the Negro in the Hill District of Pittsburgh*. Pittsburgh: General Committee on the Hill Survey, 1930.

Richardson, Harry V. *Dark Glory: A Picture of the Church Among Negroes in the Rural South*. New York: Published for Home Missions Council of North America and Phelps-Stokes Fund by Friendship Press, 1947.

——. *Dark Salvation: The Story of Methodism as It Developed Among Blacks in America*. Garden City, N.Y.: Anchor Press/Doubleday, 1976.

Richardson, James C., Jr. *With Water and Spirit: A History of the Black Apostolic Denominations in the United States*. Washington, D.C.: Spirit Press, 1980.

Ross, Frank A., and Louise Venable Kennedy. *A Bibliography of Negro Migration*. New York: Columbia University Press, 1934.

Royce, Edward. *The Origins of Southern Sharecropping*. Philadelphia: Temple University Press, 1993.

Rudwick, Elliott M. *Race Riot at East St. Louis, July 2, 1917*. Carbondale: Southern Illinois University Press, 1964.

Saloutos, Theodore. *Farmer Movements in the South, 1865–1933*. Berkeley: University of California Press, 1960.

Sandburg, Carl. *The Chicago Race Riots, July 1919*. New York: Harcourt, Brace and Howe, 1919.

Sawyer, Mary R. *Black Ecumenism: Implementing the Demands of Justice*. Valley Forge, Pa.: Trinity Press, 1994.

Scally, Sister Anthony. *Carter G. Woodson: A Bio-Bibliography*. Westport, Conn.: Greenwood Press, 1985.

Schall, Keith L., ed. *Stony the Road: Chapters in the History of Hampton Institute*. Charlottesville: University Press of Virginia, 1977.

Scheiner, Seth M. *Negro Mecca: A History of the Negro in New York City, 1865–1920*. New York: New York University Press, 1965.

Schweninger, Loren. *Black Property Owners in the South, 1790–1915*. Urbana: University of Illinois Press, 1990.

Scott, Emmett J. *Negro Migration During the War*. New York: Oxford University Press, 1920. Repr. New York: Arno Press and the New York Times, 1969.

Sernett, Milton C., ed. *Afro-American Religious History: A Documentary Witness.* Durham, N.C.: Duke University Press, 1985.

Sherman, Richard B., ed. *The Negro and the American City.* Englewood Cliffs, N.J.: Prentice-Hall, 1970.

Silva, Fred, comp. *Focus on* The Birth of a Nation. Englewood Cliffs, N.J.: Prentice-Hall, 1971.

Singleton, George A. *The Romance of African Methodism.* New York: Exposition Press, 1952.

Smith, Charles Spencer. *A History of the African Methodist Episcopal Church.* Philadelphia: Book Concern of the A.M.E. Church, 1922.

Sochen, June. *The Unbridgeable Gap: Blacks and Their Quest for the American Dream, 1900–1930.* Chicago: Rand McNally, 1972.

Spear, Allan H. *Black Chicago: The Making of a Negro Ghetto.* Chicago: University of Chicago Press, 1967.

Spero, Sterling D., and Abram L. Harris. *The Black Worker: The Negro and the Labor Movement.* New York: Columbia University Press, 1931.

Stackhouse, Perry J. *Chicago and the Baptists: A Century of Progress.* Chicago: University of Chicago Press, 1933.

Stanfield, John H. *Philanthropy and Jim Crow in American Social Science.* Westport, Conn.: Greenwood Press, 1985.

Strickland, Arvarh. *History of the Chicago Urban League.* Urbana: University of Illinois Press, 1966.

Taeuber, Karl E., and Alma F. Taeuber. *Negroes in Cities.* Chicago: Aldine, 1965.

Tanner, C. M. *A Manual of the African Methodist Episcopal Church, Being a Course of Twelve Lectures for Probationers and Members.* Philadelphia: A.M.E. Publishing House, 1900.

Tassal, David D. Van, and John J. Grabowski, eds. *The Encyclopedia of Cleveland History.* Bloomington: Indiana University Press, 1987.

Taylor, Carl C., and others. *Rural Life in the United States.* New York: Alfred A. Knopf, 1949.

Taylor, Clarence. *The Black Churches of Brooklyn.* New York: Columbia University Press, 1995.

Thrasher, Max Bennett. *Tuskegee: Its Story and Its Work.* Intro. by Booker T. Washington. Boston: Small, Maynard, 1901. Repr., New York: Negro Universities Press, 1969.

Three Catholic Afro-American Congresses. Cincinnati: American Catholic Tribune, 1893.

Tindall, George B. *The Emergence of the New South, 1913–1945.* Baton Rouge: Louisiana State University Press, 1967.

Titon, Jeff Todd. *Early Downhome Blues: A Musical and Cultural Analysis.* Urbana: University of Illinois Press, 1977.

Toll, William. *The Resurgence of Race: Black Social Theory from Reconstruction to the Pan-African Conferences.* Philadelphia: Temple University Press, 1979.

Trotter, Joe William, Jr. *Black Milwaukee: The Making of an Industrial Proletariat, 1915–1945.* Urbana: University of Illinois Press, 1985.

———, ed. *The Great Migration in Historical Perspective: New Dimensions of Race, Class, and Gender.* Bloomington: Indiana University Press, 1991.

Tucker, David M. *Black Pastors and Leaders: Memphis, 1819–1972.* Memphis: Memphis State University Press, 1975.

Tuskegee Institute. *Tuskegee to Date.* Tuskegee, Ala.: Tuskegee Institute, 1915.

Tuttle, William M., Jr. *Race Riot: Chicago in the Red Summer of 1919.* New York: Atheneum, 1970.

Vance, Rupert B. *Human Factors in Cotton Culture: A Study in the Social Geography of the American South.* Chapel Hill: University of North Carolina Press, 1929.

Walker, Clarence E. *A Rock in a Weary Land: The African Methodist Episcopal Church During the Civil War and Reconstruction.* Baton Rouge: Louisiana State University Press, 1982.

Walls, William J. *The African Methodist Episcopal Zion Church: Reality of the Black Church.* Charlotte: A.M.E. Zion Publishing House, 1974.

Ward, David. *Poverty, Ethnicity and the American City, 1840–1925: Changing Conceptions of the Slum and the Ghetto.* New York: Cambridge University Press, 1989.

Warner, Robert Austin. *New Haven Negroes: A Social History.* New Haven, Conn.: Yale University Press for the Institute of Human Relations, 1940.

Washington, Booker T., and W. E. B. Du Bois. *The Negro in the South.* Intro. by Herbert Aptheker. New York: Citadel Press, 1970 (orig. pub. 1907).

Washington, Forrester B. *The Negro in Detroit: A Survey of the Conditions of a Negro Group in a Northern Industrial Center During the War Prosperity Period.* Detroit: Research Bureau, Associated Charities of Detroit, 1920.

Washington, James M. *Frustrated Fellowship: The Black Baptist Quest for Social Power.* Macon, Ga.: Mercer University Press, 1986.

Washington, Joseph R. *Black Religion: The Negro and Christianity in the United States.* Boston: Beacon Press, 1965.

———. *Black Sects and Cults.* New York: Doubleday/Anchor, 1972.

Weatherford, W[illis] D. *Negro Life in the South: Present Conditions and Needs.* Revised edition. New York: Association Press, 1911.

Webb, Lillian Ashcraft. *About My Father's Business; The Life of Elder Michaux.* Westport, Conn.: Greenwood Press, 1981.

Weisbort, Robert. *Father Divine and the Struggle for Racial Equality.* Urbana: University of Illinois Press, 1983.

Weiss, Nancy. *The National Urban League: 1910–1940.* New York: Oxford University Press, 1974.

Wells, Ida B. *Crusade for Justice: The Autobiography of Ida B. Wells.* Edited by Alfreda M. Duster. Chicago: University of Chicago Press, 1970.

Wharton, Vernon L. *The Negro in Mississippi, 1865–1890.* Chapel Hill: University of North Carolina Press, 1947.

Wheeler, Edward C. *Uplifting the Race: The Black Minister in the New South, 1865–1902.* New York: University Press of America, 1986.

Wiebe, Robert H. *The Search for Order, 1877–1920.* New York: Hill and Wang, 1967.

Williams, Melvin D. *Community in a Black Pentecostal Church: An Anthropological Study.* Pittsburgh: University of Pittsburgh Press, 1974.

Williamson, Joel. *The Crucible of Race: Black-White Relations in the American South Since Emancipation.* New York: Oxford University Press, 1984.

Wilmore, Gayraud S. *Black Religion and Black Radicalism: An Interpretation of the Religious History of Afro-American People.* Second Edition. Maryknoll, N.Y.: Orbis Books, 1983.

Wood, Junius B. *The Negro in Chicago*. Chicago: Chicago Daily News, 1916.

Woodson, Carter G. *A Century of Negro Migration*. Washington, D.C.: Association for the Study of Negro Life and History, 1918.

———. *The History of the Negro Church*. Second Edition. Washington, D.C.: Associated Publishers, 1945.

———. *The Negro Professional Man and the Community*. Washington, D.C.: Association for the Study of Negro Life and History, 1934.

———. *The Rural Negro*. Washington, D.C.: Association for the Study of Negro Life and History, 1930.

Woofter, Thomas J., Jr. *The Negroes of Athens, Georgia*. Phelps Stokes Fellowship Studies, No. 1. *Bulletin of the University of Georgia* 14 (December 1913).

———. *Negro Migration: Changes in Rural Organization and Population of the Cotton Belt*. New York: W. D. Gray, 1920.

———. *Southern Race Progress: The Wavering Color Line*. Washington, D.C.: Public Affairs Press, 1957.

Woofter, Thomas J., et al. *Negro Problems in Cities*. Garden City, N.Y.: Doubleday, Doran, 1928.

Work, Monroe N. *Negro Year Book: 1918–1919, An Annual Encyclopedia of the Negro*. Tuskegee, Ala.: Negro Year Book, 1919.

———. *Negro Year Book: 1921–1922, An Annual Encyclopedia of the Negro*. Tuskegee, Ala.: Negro Year Book, 1922.

Wright, Richard. *American Hunger*. New York: Harper and Row, 1977.

Wright, Richard R., Jr. *The Bishops of the African Methodist Episcopal Church*. Nashville: A.M.E. Sunday School Union Press, 1963.

———, ed. *Centennial Encyclopaedia of the African Methodist Episcopal Church*. Philadelphia: A.M.E. Book Concern, 1916.

———. *87 Years Behind the Black Curtain: An Autobiography*. Philadelphia: Rare Book, 1965.

Wynia, Elly M. *The Church of God and Saints of Christ: The Rise of the Black Jews*. New York: Garland, 1994.

Young, Rosa. *Light in the Dark Belt*. St. Louis: Concordia, 1930.

Zunz, Oliver. *The Changing Face of Inequality: Urbanization, Industrial Development and Immigrants in Detroit, 1880–1920*. Chicago: University of Chicago Press, 1982.

ARTICLES AND ESSAYS

Bagnall, Robert W. "Michigan—the Land of Many Waters." *Messenger* 8 (April 1926): 101–2, 123.

Bailey, Ronald. "'Deep South' Revisited: An Assessment of a Classical Text." *The CAAS Newsletter* (UCLA Center for Afro-American Studies) 11 (1988): 10–14.

Baker, Ray Stannard. "The Negro Goes North: The Great Southern Migration to the Mirage-Land of War-Born High Wages, and Some Saddening as Well as Hopeful Sidelights on the Problem Thus Created." *World's Work* 34 (July 1917): 314–19.

Barrett, James R. "Unity and Fragmentation: Class, Race, and Ethnicity on Chicago's South Side, 1900–1922." *Journal of Social History* 18 (Fall 1984): 37–56.

Barton, John W. "Negro Migration." *Methodist Quarterly Review* 108 (January 1925): 84–101.

Beles, LaVerne. "Negro Enumeration of 1920." *Scientific American* 14 (April 1922): 352–60.

Benyon, Erdmann D. "The Voodoo Cult Among Negro Migrants in Detroit." *American Journal of Sociology* 43 (May 1938): 894–907.

Bethell, Tom. "Original Sin in the Promised Land." *American Spectator* 24 (June 1991): 9–11.

Blumenthal, Henry. "Woodrow Wilson and the Race Question." *Journal of Negro History* 48 (January 1963): 1–21.

Bone, Robert. "Richard Wright and the Chicago Renaissance." *Callaloo* 9 (Summer 1986): 446–68.

Borchert, James. "Field to Factory." *Journal of American History* 76 (June 1989): 224–28.

Boyer, Horace C. "Thomas A. Dorsey." *Black World* 23 (July 1974): 21–28.

Branham, Charles Russell. "Black Chicago: Accommodationist Politics Before the Great Migration." In *The Ethnic Frontier,* pp. 211–62. Edited by Melvin G. Holli and Peter d'A Jones. Grand Rapids, Mich.: William B. Eerdmans, 1977.

Brooks, Evelyn. "Religion, Politics, and Gender: The Leadership of Nannie Helen Burroughs." *Journal of Religious Thought* 44 (Winter/Spring 1988): 7–22.

Brown, Sterling. "Negro Folk Expression: Spirituals, Seculars, Ballads and Work Songs." *Phylon* 14 (January 1953): 45–61.

Buenker, John D. "Dynamics of Chicago Ethnic Politics, 1900–1930." *Journal of the Illinois State Historical Society* 67 (April 1974): 175–99.

Bulmer, Martin. "The Chicago School of Sociology: What Made It a 'School'?" *History of Sociology* 5 (Spring 1985): 61–77.

Bunche, Ralph J. "The Thompson-Negro Alliance." *Commentary* 7 (March 1929): 78–80.

Cohen, William. "Negro Involuntary Servitude in the South, 1865–1940: A Preliminary Analysis." *Journal of Southern History* 42 (February 1976): 31–60.

Cooper, Arnold. "Booker T. Washington and William J. Edward of Snow Hill Institute, 1893–1915." *Alabama Review* 40 (April 1987): 111–32.

———. "The Tuskegee Machine in Action: Booker T. Washington's Influence on Utica Institute, 1903–1915." *Journal of Mississippi History* 48 (1986): 283–95.

———. " 'We Rise Upon the Structure We Ourselves Have Builded': William H. Holtzclaw and Utica Institute, 1903–1915." *Journal of Mississippi History* 45 (1985): 15–33.

Cressey, Paul Frederick. "Population Succession in Chicago: 1898–1930." *American Journal of Sociology* 44 (July 1938): 59–69.

Cripps, Thomas R. "The Reaction of the Negro to the Motion Picture *Birth of a Nation.*" *Historian* 26 (1963): 344–62.

Cuban, Larry. "A Strategy for Racial Peace: Negro Leadership in Cleveland, 1900–1919." *Phylon* 28 (Fall 1967): 299–311.

Daniel, Vattel Elbert. "Ritual and Stratification in Chicago Negro Churches." *American Sociological Review* 7 (June 1942): 352–61.

Darden, Joe T. "The Effect of World War I on Black Occupational and Residential Segregation: The Case of Pittsburgh." *Journal of Black Studies* 18 (March 1988): 297–312.

Dean-Trulear, Harold. "The Role of the Church in Black Migration: Some Preliminary Observations." *Journal of the Afro-American Historical and Genealogical Society* 8 (Summer 1987): 51–56.

Dickerson, Dennis C. "The Black Church in Industrializing Western Pennsylvania, 1870–1950." *Western Pennsylvania Historical Magazine* 64 (October 1981): 329–44.

———. "Black Ecumenicism: Efforts to Establish a United Methodist Episcopal Church, 1918–1932." *Church History* 52 (December 1983): 479–91.

Diner, Steven J. "Chicago Social Workers and Blacks in the Progressive Era." *Social Service Review* 44 (December 1970): 393–410.

Donald, Hendersen H. "The Negro Migration of 1916–18." *Journal of Negro History* 6 (October 1921): 388–498.

Drake, St. Clair. "In the Mirror of Black Scholarship: W. Allison Davis and *Deep South*." *Harvard Educational Review*, Monograph no. 2 (1974): 42–54.

———. "The Tuskegee Connection: Booker T. Washington and Robert E. Park." *Society* 20 (May/June 1983): 82–92.

Du Bois, W. E. B. "The Hosts of Black Labor." *Nation*, May 9, 1923, pp. 540–41.

Eddy, C. Norman. "Store-Front Religion." *Religion in Life* 28 (Winter 1958–59): 68–85.

Ehrman, Albert. "The Commandment Keepers: A Negro Jewish Cult in America Today." *Judaism* 8 (1959): 266–72.

Eighmy, John Lee. "Religious Liberalism in the South During the Progressive Era." *Church History* 38 (September 1961): 359–72.

Ellis, Mark. "America's Black Press, 1914–18." *History Today* 41: 20–27.

Ellsworth, Clayton. "Theodore Roosevelt's Country Life Commission." *Agricultural History* 34 (1960): 155–72.

Farley, Reynolds. "The Urbanization of Negroes in the United States." *Journal of Social History* 1 (Spring 1968): 240–58.

Ferris, William H. "Connecticut: The Nutmeg State." *The Messenger* 6 (January 1924): 11, 24–25.

Fish, John D. "Southern Methodism and Accommodation of the Negro, 1902–1915." *Journal of Negro History* 55 (July 1970): 200–214.

Fisher, Miles Mark. "The Negro Church and the World War." *Journal of Religion* 5 (September 1925): 483–99.

———. "Negro Churches in Illinois: A Fragmentary History with Emphasis on Chicago." *Journal of the Illinois State Historical Society* 56 (Autumn 1963): 552–69.

Fisher, S. Mattie. "Olivet as a Christian Center." *Missions* 10 (March 1919): 199–202.

Franklin, Robert M. "The Legacy of W. E. Burghardt Du Bois in Afro-American Religious Scholarship." *Criterion* 23 (Autumn 1984): 8–12.

———. "Church and City: Black Christianity's Ministry." *Christian Ministry* 20 (March–April 1989): 17–19.

Frazier, Thomas R. "Changing Perspectives in the Study of Afro-American Religion." *Journal of the Interdenominational Theological Center* 6 (Fall 1978): 51–68.

Frey, Fred C. "Factors Conditioning the Incidence of Migration Among Louisiana Negroes." *Southwestern Social Science Quarterly* 15 (December 1934): 210–17.

Gravely, William B. "The Social, Political and Religious Significance of the Foundation of the Colored Methodist Episcopal Church (1870)." *Methodist History* 18 (October 1979): 3–25.

Gregg, Robert S. "The Earnest Pastor's Heated Term: Robert J. Williams' Pastorate at

'Mother' Bethel, 1916–1920." *Pennsylvania Magazine of History and Biography* 113 (January 1989): 67–88.

Griffin, Maude K. "The Negro Church and Its Social Work—St. Mark's." *Charities,* October 7, 1905, pp. 75–76.

Grossman, James R. "Blowing the Trumpet: The *Chicago Defender* and Black Migration During World War I." *Illinois Historical Journal* 78 (Summer 1985): 82–96.

———. "Migration, Race, and Class." *Journal of Urban History* 15 (1989): 224–32.

Hart, John Fraser. "The Changing Distribution of the American Negro." *Annals of the Association of American Geographers* 50 (1960): 242–66.

Haynes, George E. "Church and Negro Progress." *Annals* 140 (November 1928): 264–71.

———. "The Church and the Negro Spirit." *Survey* 53 (March 1925): 695–97.

———. "Conditions Among Negroes in the Cities." *Annals* 49 (September 1913): 105–19.

———. "Effect of War Conditions on Negro Labor." *Academy of Political Science Proceedings* 8 (February 1919): 299–312.

———. "Migration of Negroes into Northern Cities." *Proceedings of the National Conference of Social Work* 44 (1917): 494–97.

———. "Movement of Negroes from the Country to the City." *Southern Workman* 42 (April 1913): 230–36.

———. "Negroes Move North, I." *Survey,* May 4, 1918, pp. 115–22.

———. "Negroes Move North, II." *Survey,* January 4, 1919, pp. 455–61.

Hellwig, David J. "Strangers in Their Own Land: Patterns of Black Nativism, 1830–1930." *American Studies* 23 (Spring 1982): 85–98.

Higgs, Robert. "The Boll Weevil, the Cotton Economy, and Black Migration, 1910–1930." *Agricultural History* 50 (April 1976): 335–50.

Hill, T. Arnold. "Why Southern Negroes Don't Go South." *Survey,* November 29, 1919, pp. 183–95.

Holt, Arthur E. "Religion." *American Journal of Sociology* 34 (July 1928): 172–76.

Holt, John B. "Holiness Religion: Cultural Shock and Social Reorganization." *American Sociological Review* 5 (October 1940): 740–47.

Houser, Susie A. "Olivet—A Community-Serving Church in Chicago." *Messenger* 6 (September 1924): 282–87.

Hurston, Zora Neale. "Hoodoo in America." *Journal of American Folk-Lore* 44 (October–December 1931): 317–417.

Imes, G. Lake. "The Negro Minister and Country Life." *Religious Education* 7 (June 1912): 169–75.

———. "A Service of the Country Church in Helping the Negro." In *The New Voice in Race Adjustments,* pp. 145–53. Edited by Arcadius S. Trawick. New York: Student Volunteer Movement, 1914.

Jackson, Roswell F., and Rosalyn M. Patterson. "A Brief History of Selected Black Churches in Atlanta, Georgia." *Journal of Negro History* 74 (1989): 31–52.

James, Felix. "The Civic and Political Activities of George A. Myers." *Journal of Negro History* 58 (April 1973): 166–78.

Johnson, Charles S. "Illinois: Mecca to the Migrant Mob." *Messenger* 5 (December 1923): 926–28, 933.

———. "Substitution of Negro Labor for European Immigrant Labor." *Proceedings of the National Conference of Social Work* 53 (1926): 317–27.

Johnson, Everett. "A Study of the Negro Families in the Pinewood Avenue District of Toledo, Ohio." *Opportunity* 7 (August 1929): 243–45.

Jones, Allen W. "The Role of Tuskegee Institute in the Education of Black Farmers." *Journal of Negro History* 60 (April 1975): 252–67.

———. "The South's First Black Farm Agents." *Agricultural History* 50 (October 1976): 636–44.

Jones, Elias Fanayaye. "Black Hebrews: The Quest for Authentic Identity." *Journal of Religious Thought* 44 (Winter–Spring 1988): 35–49.

Jordan, William. " 'The Damnable Dilemma': African-American Accommodation and Protest during World War I." *Journal of American History* 81 (March 1995): 1562–83.

Kellogg, John. "Negro Urban Clusters in the Postbellum South." *Geographical Review* 67 (July 1977): 310–21.

Kilson, Martin. "Political Change in the Negro Ghetto, 1900–1940s." In *Key Issues in the Afro-American Experience,* vol. 2, pp. 167–92. Edited by Nathan I. Huggins, Martin Kilson, and Daniel Fox. New York: Harcourt, Brace, Jovanovich, 1971.

Kirby, Jack T. "The Southern Exodus, 1910–1960: A Primer for Historians." *Journal of Southern History* 49 (November 1983): 585–600.

Kline, Lawrence O. "The Negro in the Unification of American Methodism." *Drew Gateway* 34 (Spring 1964): 128–49.

Kusmer, Kenneth L. "The Black Urban Experience in American History." In *The State of Afro-American History,* pp. 91–122. Edited by Darlene Clark Hine. Baton Rouge: Louisiana State University Press, 1986.

Lal, Barbara Ballis. "Black and Blue in Chicago: Robert E. Park's Perspective on Race Relations in Urban America, 1914–44." *British Journal of Sociology* 38 (1987): 546–66.

Landes, Ruth. "Negro Jews in Harlem." *Jewish Journal of Sociology* 9 (December 1967): 175–89.

Lewis, Earl. "Afro-American Adaptive Strategies: The Visiting Habits of Kith and Kin among Black Norfolkians During the First Great Migration." *Journal of Family History* 12 (October 1987): 407–20.

———. "The Beginnings of a Renaissance: Black Migration, the Industrial Order, and the Search for Power." *Journal of Urban History* 17 (1991): 296–302.

Lochard, Metz T. P. "The Negro Press in Illinois." *Journal of the Illinois State Historical Society* 56 (Autumn 1963): 570–91.

Lucas, George W. "Negro Baptists Sail a Stormy Sea." *Foundations* 4 (July 1961): 207–15.

Luker, Ralph E. "Missions, Institutional Churches, and Settlement Houses: The Black Experience, 1885–1910." *Journal of Negro History* 69 (Summer/Fall 1984): 101–13.

McHugh, Kevin E. "Black Migration Reversal in the United States." *Geographical Review* 77 (April 1987): 171–82.

Marable, Manning. "The Black Faith of W. E. B. Du Bois: Sociocultural and Political Dimensions of Black Religion." *Southern Quarterly* 23 (Spring 1985): 15–33.

———. "The Land Question in Historical Perspective: The Economics of Poverty in the Blackbelt South, 1865–1920." In *The Black Rural Landowner—Endangered Species: Social,*

Political, and Economic Implications, pp. 165–206. Edited by Leo McGee and Robert Bone. Westport, Conn.: Greenwood Press, 1979.

————. "Race, Class, and Conflict: Intellectual Debates on Race Relations Research in the United States Since 1960, A Social Science Bibliographical Essay." In *Paradigms in Black Studies: Intellectual History, Cultural Meaning and Political Ideology,* pp. 165–206. Edited by Abdul Alkalimat. Chicago: Twenty-First Century, 1990.

Marks, Carole. "Lines of Communication, Recruitment Mechanisms, and the Great Migration of 1916–1918." *Social Problems* 31 (October 1983): 73–83.

Martin, Sandy D. "The American Baptist Home Mission Society and Black Higher Education in the South." *Foundations* 24 (October–December 1981): 310–27.

————. "The Debate Over Interracial Cooperation Among Black Baptists in the African Mission Movement, 1895–1905." *Journal of the Interdenominational Theological Center* 13 (Spring 1986): 291–303.

Meier, August. "The Racial and Educational Thought of Kelly Miller, 1895–1915." *Journal of Negro Education* 29 (Spring 1960): 121–27.

Miller, Frederick. "The Black Migration to Philadelphia: A 1924 Profile." *Pennsylvania Magazine of History and Biography* 108 (July 1984): 315–50.

Miller, Kelly. "Enumeration Errors in Negro Population." *Scientific Monthly* 14 (February 1922): 168–77.

————. "The Farm the Negro's Best Chance." *Manufacturers Record,* August 5, 1926, pp. 96–97.

Miller, Randall M. "Catholics in a Protestant World: The Old South Example." In *Varieties of Southern Religious Experience,* pp. 115–34. Edited by Samuel S. Hill. Baton Rouge: Louisiana State University Press, 1988.

————. "The Failed Mission: The Catholic Church and Black Catholics in the Old South." In *The Southern Common People: Studies in Nineteenth-Century Social History,* pp. 37–54. Edited by Edward Magdol and Jon Wakelyn. Westport, Conn.: Greenwood Press, 1980.

Miller, Robert Moats. "The Attitude of American Protestants Toward the Negro, 1919–39." *Journal of Negro History* 41 (1956): 185–214.

————. "The Protestant Churches and Lynching, 1919–1939." *Journal of Negro History* 42 (April 1957): 118–31.

Morrill, Richard L., and O. Fred Donaldson, "Geographical Perspectives on the History of Black America." *Economic Geography* 48 (January 1972): 1–23.

Mossell, Sadie Tanner. "The Standard of Living Among One Hundred Negro Migrant Families in Philadelphia." Reprint. *Annals of the American Academy of Social and Political Science* 98 (November 1921): 171–222.

Nelsen, Hart M., Raytha L. Yokley, and Thomas W. Madron. "Rural-Urban Differences in Religiosity." *Rural Sociology* 36 (September 1971): 389–96.

Newman, Richard. "The Origins of the African Orthodox Church." Introductory essay to *The Negro Churchman,* vols. 1–4, 1923–26. Milwood, N.Y.: Kraus, 1977, pp. iii–xxii.

Palmer, Dewey H. "Moving North: Migration of Negroes During World War I." *Phylon* 28 (Spring 1967): 52–62.

Park, Robert E. "Racial Assimilation in Secondary Groups." *American Sociological Society, Papers and Proceedings* 8 (December 1913): 66–83.

Raboteau, Albert J., and David W. Wills, with Randall K, Burkett, Will B. Gravely, and James Melvin Washington. "Retelling Carter Woodson's Story: Archival Sources for Afro-American Church History." *Journal of American History* 77 (June 1990): 183–99.

Reed, Christopher Robert. "Organized Racial Reform in Chicago During the Progressive Era: The Chicago NAACP, 1910–1920." *Michigan Historical Review* 14 (Spring 1988): 75–99.

Richardson, Harry V. "A Teacher and a Prophet." *Drew Gateway* 22 (Summer 1952): 131–35.

Roberts, Harry W. "The Rural Negro Minister: His Work and Salary." *Rural Sociology* 12 (September 1947): 284–97.

Robinson, George F. "The Negro in Politics in Chicago." *Journal of Negro History* 17 (April 1932): 180–229.

Robinson, Isaac. "Blacks Move Back to the South." *American Demographics* 8 (June 1986): 40–43.

Rudwick, Elliott M. "DuBois Versus Garvey: Race Propagandists at War." *Journal of Negro Education* 28 (Fall 1959): 421–29.

Sawyer, Mary R. "Black Ecumenical Movements: Proponents of Social Change." *Review of Religious Research* 30 (December 1988): 151–61.

Scheiner, Seth M. "The Negro Church and the Northern City, 1890–1930." In *Seven on Black*, pp. 93–117. Edited by William G. Shade and Roy C. Herrenkohl. Philadelphia: J. B. Lippincott, 1969.

Schottenhamel, George. "How Big Bill Thompson Won Control of Chicago." *Journal of the Illinois State Historical Society* 45 (Spring 1952): 30–49.

Scott, Emmett, J., comp. "Additional Letters of Negro Migrants of 1916–1918." *Journal of Negro History* 4 (October 1919): 412–75.

———. "Document: Letters of Negro Migrants of 1916–1918." *Journal of Negro History* 4 (July 1919): 290–340.

Scruggs, Charles. "The Tale of Two Cities in James Baldwin's *Go Tell It on the Mountain*." *American Literature* 52 (1980): 1–17.

Sernett, Milton C. "A Question of Earnestness: American Lutheran Missions and Education in Alabama's 'Black Belt.'" *Essays and Reports: The Lutheran Historical Conference, 1980* 9 (1982): 80–117.

Spencer, Jon Michael. "The Black Church and the Harlem Renaissance." *African American Review* 30 (Fall 1996): 453–60.

Smith, T. Lynn. "The Redistribution of the Negro Population of the United States, 1910–1960." *Journal of Negro History* 51 (July 1966): 155–73.

Stewart, James B. "The Rise and Fall of Negro Economics: The Economic Thought of George Edmund Haynes." *American Economic Review* 81 (May 1991): 311–14.

Strickland, Arvarh E. "The Strange Affair of the Boll Weevil: The Pest as Liberator." *Agricultural History* 68 (Spring 1994): 157–68.

———. "Toward the Promised Land: The Exodus to Kansas and Afterward." *Missouri Historical Review* 69 (July 1975): 376–412.

Swanson, Merwin. "The 'Country Life Movement' and the American Churches." *Church History* 46 (September 1977): 358–73.

Tatum, Charles E., and Lawrence M. Sommers. "The Spread of the Black Christian Methodist

Episcopal Church in the United States, 1870–1970." *Journal of Geography* 74 (September 1975): 343–57.

Tindley, Charles A. "The Church that Welcomed 10,000 Strangers." *World Outlook* 5 (October 1919): 5–6.

Trueblood, Roy W. "Union Negotiations Between Black Methodists in America." *Methodist History* 13 (July 1970): 18–29.

Tucker, Mark. " 'You Can't Argue with Facts': Monroe Nathan Work as Information Officer, Editor, and Bibliographer." *Libraries & Culture* 26 (1991): 151–68.

Washington, Booker T. "The Religious Life of the Negro." *North American Review* 181 (July 1905): 20–23.

———. "The Rural Negro and the South." *Proceedings of the National Conference of Charities and Corrections* 41 (1914): 121–27.

Washington, Forrester B. "A Program of Work for the Assimilation of Negro Immigrants in Northern Cities." *Proceedings of the National Conference of Social Work* 44 (1917): 497–503.

———, and O. Leonard. "Welcoming Southern Negroes—A Contrast." *Survey,* July 14, 1917, pp. 331–35.

Weisberger, Bernard A. "The Immigrant Within." *American Heritage* 22 (December 1970): 32–39, 104.

Wernick, Robert. "Jacob Lawrence: Art as Seen Through a People's History." *Smithsonian* 18 (June 1987): 56–64.

Whiting, Albert N. " 'From Saint to Shuttler,'—An Analysis of Sectarian Types." *Quarterly Review of Higher Education Among Negroes* 23 (October 1955): 133–40.

Williams, Fannie Barrier. "Social Bonds in the 'Black Belt' of Chicago." *Charities,* October 7, 1905, 40–44.

Williams, Lillian S. "Afro-Americans in Buffalo, 1900–1930: A Study in Community Formation." *Afro-Americans in New York Life and History* 8 (July 1984): 7–35.

Williams, Vernon J., Jr. 'Eny Kinde of Worke': A Review Essay on African-American Migrations." *Journal of American Ethnic History* 11 (1991): 86–89.

Wilson, Bobby M. "Church Participation: A Social Space Analysis in a Community of Black In-Migrants." *Journal of Black Studies* 10 (December 1979): 198–217.

[Woodson, Carter G.]. "Suggestions for Improving the Negro Church." *Negro History Bulletin* 3 (October 1939): 9–10.

Wolcott, Victoria W. " 'Bible, Bath, and Broom': Nannie Helen Burroughs, the National Training School, and the Uplift of the Race." *Journal of Women's History* (Winter 1997): forthcoming.

———. "Mediums, Messages, and Lucky Numbers: African-American Female Spiritualists and Numbers Runners in Inter-War Detroit." In *The Geography of Identity.* Edited by Patricia Yeager. Ann Arbor: University of Michigan, 1996, pp. 273–305.

Wright, Richard R., Jr. "Negro in Times of Industrial Unrest." *Charities,* October 7, 1905, pp. 69–73.

———. "Social Work and Influence of the Negro Church." *Annals of the American Academy of Political and Social Science* 30 (November 1907): 509–21.

Wyman, Lille B. Chace. "Colored Churches and Schools in the South." *New England Magazine* 3 (February 1891): 785–96.

Yearwood, Lennox. "First Shiloh Baptist Church of Buffalo, New York: From Storefront to Major Religious Institution." *Afro-Americans in New York Life and History* 1 (January 1977): 81–92.

DISSERTATIONS AND THESES

Branham, Charles R. "The Transformation of Black Political Leadership in Chicago, 1864–1942." Ph.D. diss., University of Chicago, 1981.

Carlson, Glen R. "The Negro in the Industries of Detroit." Ph.D. diss., University of Michigan, 1929.

Daniel, Vattel E. "Ritual in Chicago's South Side Churches for Negroes." Ph.D. diss., University of Chicago, 1940.

Fisher, Miles Mark. "The History of the Olivet Baptist Church of Chicago." M.A. thesis, University of Chicago, 1922.

Fox, William Kappen. "Experiments in Southern Rural Religious Development Among Negroes." B.D. diss., University of Chicago Divinity School, 1943.

Frazier, Thomas Richard. "An Analysis of Social Scientific Writing on American Negro Religion." Ph.D. diss., Columbia University, 1967.

Hardy, Charles Ashley III. "Race and Opportunity: Black Philadelphia During the Era of the Great Migration, 1916–1930." Ph.D. diss., Temple University, 1989.

Hornsby, Alton, Jr. "Southern Negroes, 1877–1929: The Outsider's View." Ph.D. diss., University of Texas at Austin, 1969.

Kinney, John William. "Adam Clayton Powell, Sr., and Adam Clayton Powell, Jr.: A Historical Exposition and Theological Analysis." Ph.D. diss., Columbia University, 1979.

Lewis, John Henry. "Social Service in Negro Churches." M.A. thesis, Divinity School, University of Chicago, 1914.

Logsdon, Joseph A. "The Rev. Archibald J. Carey and the Negro in Chicago Politics." M.A. thesis, University of Chicago, 1961.

McCarthy, Joseph J. "History of Black Catholic Education in Chicago, 1871–1971." Ph.D. diss., Loyola University, 1973.

McGreevy, John T. "American Catholics and the African-American Migration, 1919–1970." Ph.D. diss., Stanford University, 1992.

Montgomery, William Edward. "Negro Churches in the South, 1865–1915." Ph.D. diss., University of Texas, 1975.

Morris, Calvin S. "Reverdy C. Ransom: A Pioneer Black Social Gospeler." Ph.D. diss., Boston University, 1982.

Nelson, Douglas J. "For Such a Time as This: The Story of Bishop William J. Seymour and the Azuza Street Revival." Ph.D. diss., University of Birmingham, England, 1981.

Perlman, Daniel T. "Stirring the White Conscience: The Life of George Edmund Haynes." Ph.D. diss., New York University, 1972.

Phillips, Harold Cooke. "The Social Significance of Negro Churches in Harlem." M.A. thesis, Columbia University, 1922.

Piper, John Franklin, Jr. "The Social Policy of the Federal Council of the Churches of Christ in America During World War I." Ph.D. diss., Duke University, 1964.

Russell, Daniel. "The Negro Church in Relation to Migration." M.A. thesis, University of Chicago, 1923.

Schafer, Marvin R. "The Catholic Church in Chicago, Its Growth and Administration." Ph.D. diss., University of Chicago, 1929.

Smith, Herbert Morrisohn. "Three Negro Preachers in Chicago: A Study in Religious Leadership." M.A. thesis, University of Chicago Divinity School, 1935.

Smith, Howard Preston II. "The Limitations of Racial Democracy: The Politics of the Chicago Urban League, 1916–1940." Ph.D. diss., University of Massachusetts, 1990.

Somerville, Wendell Clary. "A Study of 311 Rural Negro Baptist Churches of 15 Counties in North Carolina, with a View to Suggesting Some Improvements." M.A. thesis, Oberlin College, 1939.

Sutherland, Robert. "An Analysis of Negro Churches in Chicago." Ph.D. diss., University of Chicago, 1930.

Tyler, Mary Ann Lancaster. "The Music of Charles Henry Pace and Its Relationship to the Afro-American Church Experience." Ph.D. diss., University of Pittsburgh, 1980.

Welty, William M. "Black Shepherds: A Study of the Leading Negro Clergymen in New York City, 1900–1940." Ph.D. diss., New York University, 1969.

White, Ronald Cedric, J. "Social Christianity and the Negro in the Progressive Era, 1890–1920." Ph.D. diss., Princeton University, 1972.

Whiting, Albert N. "The United House of Prayer for All People: A Case Study of a Charismatic Sect." Ph.D. diss., American University, 1952.

Williams, Chancellor. "The Socio-Economic Significance of the Store-Front Church Movement in the United States Since 1920." Ph.D. diss., American University, 1949.

Wills, David W. "Aspects of Social Thought in the African Methodist Episcopal Church, 1884–1910." Ph.D. diss., Harvard University, 1975.

Wright, Richard R., Jr. "The Industrial Condition of Negroes in Chicago." B.D. thesis, University of Chicago Divinity School, 1901.

INDEX

Milton C. Sernett is Professor of African American Studies and Adjunct Professor of Religion at Syracuse University. He is the author of *Black Religion and American Evangelicalism: White Protestants, Plantation Missions, and the Flowering of Negro Christianity, 1787–1865* (1975), editor of *Afro-American Religious History: A Documentary Witness* (1985), and author of *Abolition's Axe: Beriah Green, Oneida Institute and the Black Freedom Struggle* (1986).

Library of Congress Cataloging-in-Publication Data
Sernett, Milton C., 1942–
Bound for the promised land : African American religion and the great migration / Milton C. Sernett.
p.   cm. — (C. Eric Lincoln series on the Black experience)
Includes bibliographical references and index.
ISBN 0-8223-1984-5 (cloth : alk. paper). — ISBN 0-8223-1993-4 (paper : alk. paper)
1. Afro-Americans—Religion. 2. United States—Church history—20th century. 3. Afro-Americans—Migrations—History—20th century. 4. Migration, Internal—United States—History—20th century. 5. Rural-urban migration—United States—History—20th century. 6. Afro-Americans—History—1877–1964. I. Title. II. Series.
BR563.N4S474   1997
277.3'0821'08996073—dc21   97-6537 CIP